VIKING

THE PENGUIN SRI AUROBINDO READER

Aravinda Ackroyd Ghose, later known as Sri Aurobindo, was born in Calcutta on 15 August 1872. Sent to England when he was seven, he was educated at St Paul's School, London, and King's College, Cambridge. On his return to India in 1893, he joined the Baroda State Service, finishing his thirteen-year stint there as the Vice-Principal of Baroda College. From 1906 to 1910, he was a leader of the extremist faction of the Indian freedom movement and was thrice accused—and acquitted—of sedition and treason.

While an undertrial prisoner in the Alipore Jail in 1908–09, he underwent profound spiritual experiences culminating in the realization of cosmic consciousness. After his acquittal, he moved to Pondicherry in 1910 to devote himself to the pursuit of Yoga. In 1914 Sri Aurobindo started the philosophical monthly, *Arya,* in which many of his major works were first published serially. In 1920, Mirra Alfassa, later known as the Mother, joined Sri Aurobindo in Pondicherry, and eventually took over the management of the ashram, or spiritual community, which had sprung up around him.

After 24 November 1926, also known as the day of *siddhi* or realization, Sri Aurobindo withdrew into complete solitude to concentrate on his spiritual work. His aim was to transform earth-nature itself by effecting a descent of a higher consciousness. In 1938, after an accident in which his thigh bone was fractured, Sri Aurobindo's Yoga entered a new phase. Following the outbreak of World War II in 1939, he actively supported the Allies against the forces of darkness led by Hitler. On 15 August 1947, his seventy-fifth birthday, India became free. Sri Aurobindo passed away on 5 December 1950.

*

Makarand R. Paranjape has been Professor of English at Jawaharlal Nehru University, New Delhi, for over twenty-two years. He served as the Director, Indian Institute of Advanced Study, Shimla. The author/editor of over 50 books and hundreds of academic papers, he is also a poet, novelist, columnist, and public intellectual. His latest books include *JNU: Nationalism and India's Uncivil War* (2022), *Identity's Last Secret* (2022), and *Swami Vivekananda: Hinduism and India's Road to Modernity* (2020). He has been in touch with the works of Sri Aurobindo and modern India's spiritual masters for over forty years.

THE PENGUIN
SRI AUROBINDO
READER

MAKARAND R. PARANJAPE

PENGUIN
VIKING

An imprint of Penguin Random House

VIKING

USA | Canada | UK | Ireland | Australia
New Zealand | India | South Africa | China | Singapore

Viking is part of the Penguin Random House group of companies
whose addresses can be found at global.penguinrandomhouse.com

Published by Penguin Random House India Pvt. Ltd
4th Floor, Capital Tower 1, MG Road,
Gurugram 122 002, Haryana, India

First published by Penguin Books India 1999
This edition published in Viking by Penguin Random House India 2023

ISBN 9780670097180

This edition is for sale only in the Indian Subcontinent only

Typeset in Minion Pro by Manipal Technologies Limited, Manipal
Printed at Replika Press Pvt. Ltd, India

www.penguin.co.in

This is a legitimate digitally printed version of the book and therefore might not
have certain extra finishing on the cover.

Invocation

Be wide in me, O Varuna; be mighty in me, O Indra; O Sun, be very bright and luminous; O Moon, be full of charm and sweetness. Be fierce and terrible, O Rudra; be impetuous and swift, O Maruts; be strong and bold, O Aryaman; be voluptuous and pleasurable, O Bhaga; be tender and kind and loving and passionate, O Mitra. Be bright and revealing, O Dawn; O Night, be solemn and pregnant. O Life, be full, ready and buoyant; O Death, lead my steps from mansion to mansion. Harmonise all these, O Brahmanaspati. Let me not be subject to these gods, O Kali.

—Sri Aurobindo

This book is dedicated to Yogi Ramsuratkumar and Devaki Ma, Tiruvannamalai

Contents

The Supramental Transformation

The Seer-Poet

Pioneers of the Future

Thoughts and Aphorisms   409

Preface to the Third Edition

This revised and augmented third edition of *The Penguin Sri Aurobindo Reader* is offered as a heartfelt tribute to Sri Aurobindo on his sesquicentennial birth anniversary. By a special and unique conjuncture, Sri Aurobindo's 150th birthday also coincides with the 75th anniversary of India's independence, being celebrated nationwide as Azadi ka Amrit Mahotsav. I have revised and updated the Introduction, adding a special section on Sri Aurobindo's idea of the nation, which I thought would be appropriate for this special concurrence. Besides this, the third edition also includes a new section of selections from Sri Aurobindo's philosophical magnum opus, *The Life Divine*.

I am grateful to Jawaharlal Nehru University, especially to my colleagues and students, for a working environment in which I have managed academically and intellectually to survive, even thrive, these last twenty-two years. To the extended and expanding circle of the ashramites, devotees, followers, and admirers of Sri Aurobindo and the Mother I am thankful for their continued friendship and fellowship in my long journey into the heart of Sri Aurobindo's writings, philosophy, teaching, and sadhana. I would like to appreciate the continued support for this project that my publishers, Penguin India, have rendered despite all the changes that they have undergone over the last twenty-five years. My wife, Gayatri, and my mother, who is soon to enter the ninetieth year of her life, have been a constant source of strength and support.

They are also the first readers of whatever I write. My daughter, Malini, who is too little to read, will, I trust, one day find this book of interest. I hope the wider reading public will be inspired, if not awestruck, by the incredibly wide-ranging, protean, and prodigiously original genius that Sri Aurobindo was, which this one-volume anthology of his writings affords an initiation to.

1 December 2022

Preface to the Second Edition

It is gratifying that *The Penguin Sri Aurobindo Reader* has gone into a second edition. That the general reading public should show enough interest in Sri Aurobindo disproves the notion that his writings are either too esoteric or difficult for all except a chosen few to understand. On the contrary, all around we are witnessing a new interest in, and enthusiasm for, Sri Aurobindo's visionary ideas not just in India, but the world over. This is evidenced in a number of new movements, initiatives, and institutions inspired by his life and thought.

The first edition, published in 1999, had a number of errors which we have endeavoured to correct. I have also revised the last two sections of the Introduction. Apart from this, the contents are unaltered. Though I have received much help from friends both within and outside the ashram community, I must clarify that not only am I solely responsible for the interpretations and views in the Introduction, but, needless to say, also for whatever errors of fact or judgement that may have crept in.

Makarand R. Paranjape
21 February 2003

Preface

Those who are familiar with the vast oeuvre of Sri Aurobindo, not to speak of an even larger body of secondary and interpretative material on him, will at once sympathize, if not pity, the person who dares to anthologize him. And yet the task is imperative. Sri Aurobindo's own works extend into thirty-seven volumes; besides these original sources, there is a considerable amount of correspondence, records of talks and other unpublished material that continues to surface. It cannot be expected of any but the most serious, dedicated or devout of students to read, let alone absorb, this massive archive. The general reader may rightfully expect a briefer, one-volume omnibus which offers an authentic and satisfying selection of the master's works. This is precisely what I have tried to do in this anthology.

There is a widespread belief these days that we are at the verge of a new era in human consciousness. Sri Aurobindo and the Mother may be considered among the most consistent and systematic proponents of this idea. As Sri Aurobindo put it, 'It is a step for which the whole of evolution has been a preparation.' Or in the Mother's words: 'Humanity has been waiting for centuries for this moment. It has come.' In this new age, all the old religions are proving insufficient. Science and philosophy too are inadequate. That is why many believe that only a total transformation in human consciousness will do. The vision of Sri Aurobindo and the Mother is the ropeway which can help us climb to this next peak of evolution.

From what I have said so far, it will be clear that I don't pretend to be a neutral or uninvolved anthologist with merely a professional attitude to the task at hand. And yet, I have steered clear of an attitude of unthinking devotion or unquestioning adulation. I have tried, instead, to present Sri Aurobindo's thought in a rational and contextualized manner so that it not only reflects his major concerns and preoccupations, but also appeals to the widest number of readers. In other words, this compilation is the work of a critical insider to the spiritual tradition of which Sri Aurobindo was the founder and leader.

In this volume, I have tried to include representative texts from nearly all the areas in which Sri Aurobindo wrote and published. What has been left out are his translations, plays and several long poems. I have, however, included an extract from *Savitri*, his great, modern, 'unfinished' epic of over 24,000 lines. I have also tried to include samples of his writing in various genres and styles. Whole essays, chapters or self-contained textual units have been preferred. While the contents have been arranged into nine sections subject-wise, mostly chronologically within each section, there is also a gradual progression in time from the first section to the eighth. The last section, which contains a selection of Sri Aurobindo's Thoughts and Aphorisms, can be read as a separate unit. In addition, I have provided a Chronology, a glossary of Sanskrit and Indian words used in the text, a list of the sources of the texts, and a Bibliography.

A work of this kind would have been impossible without the help of several persons and institutions. I am grateful to Penguin India and to my editor, Krishan Chopra, for initiating the project; to my friends, Parveen Chopra, editor of *Life Positive,* and to Sachi Mohanty, for their good wishes; to Manoj Dasgupta and the Trustees of Sri Aurobindo Ashram, Pondicherry, for permission to reproduce the texts; to the Late Jayantilal-da and the whole team at the archives for their unstinting help; to Tara Jauhar of

Sri Aurobindo Ashram-Delhi Branch for her continued kindness; to Ravindra Joshi of Sri Aurobindo Ashram-Delhi Branch for his constant support and cooperation; to Prashant Khanna, Sri Aurobindo Ashram-Delhi Branch, for his conversation and insights; to those who worked on the *Sri Aurobindo Birth Centenary Library (SABCL)* and the *Collected Works of Sri Aurobindo (CWSA)* for enabling further research and study of Sri Aurobindo's works; to Peter Heehs and Georges Van Vrekhem whose books have benefitted me much; above all, a very special thanks to my friend, Matthijs Cornelissen for all his help, patience and generous assistance in sending the texts on a floppy. Finally, I am grateful to my copy editors at Penguin India without whose painstaking and unsparing efforts this book would have been a far inferior product.

Introduction

Birth and childhood; onward to England: Vidyabhoomi, 1879-1893

Born in Calcutta (now Kolkata) on 15 August 1872, Aravinda Ackroyd Ghose[1] was the third son of Krishna Dhan Ghose, a medical practitioner, and Swarnalata Devi, the eldest daughter of Rajnarayan Bose. His father was an avowed Anglophile and 'a tremendous atheist'. Krishna Dhan wish was that Aurobindo become an ICS officer and join the ruling classes of India. To this end, he gave his three eldest sons a British education, first sending them to Loreto Convent, Darjeeling, and then in 1879, to England. From the age of seven to twelve, Aurobindo was in Manchester, under the care of Rev. William H. Drewett. Later, Aurobindo and his elder brother, Manmohan, went to London to study at St. Paul's School.

Aurobindo was a brilliant student who excelled in Classics, Literature, and History. In 1890, at the age of eighteen, he was

---

[1] This was the name chosen by his father. The middle name came from Annette Akroyd, an Englishwoman and a friend of his father's, who was probably present at the naming ceremony. The first record of the name is a school document of 1884 in English; there the name is spelt 'Ackroyd'. At St. Paul's and at Cambridge the name was registered as Aravinda Ackroyd Ghose. Until 1906, he signed his name in two or three different ways; the Bengali spelling was adopted when he moved to Bengal. After 1926, he became known as Sri Aurobindo, a practice that I have also followed in the biographical section. Elsewhere, I have used the full form, as is now customary. In the naming of the phases of Sri Aurobindo's life, I owe much to Dr Karan Singh.

admitted to King's College, Cambridge, with a senior classical scholarship worth 80 pounds per annum. There he performed exceptionally, clearing the Classical Tripos in the first division and winning prizes for Greek and Latin verses. He also knew French and was conversant with German and Italian. In 1890, he passed the Indian Civil Services examination in the open competition. However, he absented himself from the riding test, as a consequence of which he failed to qualify. In 1892, he obtained an appointment with the Gaekwar of Baroda and set sail for India in January 1893.

Return to India; Baroda: Tapobhoomi, 1893–1906

After fourteen years in England, Sri Aurobindo set foot on Indian soil on 6 February 1893. A 'vast calm' descended on him as he disembarked, which remained with him for months afterwards. He worked for the Baroda State from 1893 to 1906. During this period, in 1901, he married Mrinalini, who was then fourteen years of age. Mrinalini, it would appear, expected a more normal marriage than what was in store for her. There were, besides, considerable disparities of age, education and temperament between them. The marriage cannot be described as a great success.

During the Baroda period, Sri Aurobindo's multifaceted genius began to flower. After serving very ably in various departments of the Baroda state, he settled down to teach, eventually becoming the Vice Principal of Baroda College. He also began writing articles and pamphlets, meeting important political leaders like Lokmanya Tilak and Bipin Chandra Pal. Before the end of his stint with the Gaekwar, he had elected to take on an active role in Indian politics.

Aurobindo, along with the celebrated trinity 'Bal-Pal-Lal' (Bal Gangadhar Tilak, Bipin Chandra Pal, and Lala Lajpat Rai), belonged to the so-called 'garam dal,' or 'Extremist' section of the Congress. The Extremists wanted complete independence for India. They did not like the 'petition-prayer-protest' mode of supplication that the dominant Congress faction, the 'Moderates,' usually adopted.

From behind the scenes, it was Aurobindo who was instrumental in engineering the split between the Extremists and the Moderates at Surat Congress in 1907. Prior to that, he had begun to harbour designs of freeing India through revolutionary action. To this end, he authored a pamphlet called *Bhavani Mandir* in 1905, though his name did not appear on it. He was the inspiration behind a secret society formed for that purpose.

Though he had scored poorly in Sanskrit and Bengali in his ICS exams in London, he now made up for his deficiencies in Indian culture with a passionate intensity. He embarked upon an ambitious programme of self-education, learning Sanskrit and several Indian languages, besides mastering Indian philosophy, history and literature. It was during the Baroda period that he also began his preliminary experiments in yoga.

In January 1908, he met a Maharashtrian yogi called Vishnu Bhaskar Lele in Baroda. Following Lele's instructions, he achieved the total silencing of his mind: 'Sit down,' he was told, 'look, and you will see that your thoughts come into you from outside. Before they enter, fling them back' (*CWSA* 35: 244; 247)[2]. Aurobindo followed these instructions, with the result that in three days, or more accurately in one day itself, his mind was filled with an 'eternal silence'.

---

[2] All quotations from Sri Aurobindo, referred to in parenthesis by volume number and page, are from *The Complete Works of Sri Aurobindo (CWSA)*, a library of 37 Volumes published by the Sri Aurobindo Ashram, Pondicherry, from 1997 onwards. Except vol. 37, consisting of the index, glossary, editorial notes, supplementary texts, all other volumes have been published and are available at https://www.sriaurobindoashram.org/sriaurobindo/writings.php.

Bande Mataram; Calcutta: Karmabhoomi, *1906-1910*

From 1906 to 1908, when he moved to Calcutta as the Principal of the newly established National College and took over the editorship of two influential periodicals, *Bande Mataram* and *Karmayogin,* Aurobindo was at the forefront of the freedom struggle. He wrote extensively on political issues and was one of the earliest advocates of *purna* or complete Swaraj.

On 2 May 1908, he was arrested for terrorist activities and imprisoned at Alipore, Calcutta, a few days later. During his incarceration he underwent several spiritual experiences which would change the course of his life forever. Some of these have been described in the famous Uttarpara Speech: 'I looked at the jail that secluded me from men and it was no longer by its high walls that I was imprisoned; no, it was Vasudeva who surrounded me' (*CWSA* 8: 7).

After he was released in 1909, he turned his full attention to yoga. Obeying an inner imperative, he went into hiding at Chandernagore, a French territory, then departed incognito to Pondicherry on 1 April 1910. Mrinalini was left behind. In the years to come she would undergo loneliness and terrible psychological and emotional suffering. She died of influenza in 1918, just when she was preparing to join her husband in Pondicherry.

'Beyond Knowings'; Pondicherry: Yogabhoomi, 1910-1950

Aurobindo remained in Pondicherry from his concealed arrival on 4 April 1910 until he left his body on 5 December 1950. From 1910 to 1914, he practiced his yoga in seclusion, but also kept up his contacts with revolutionaries in Bengal. But gradually, through the cataclysmic changes that took place in the world through two world wars and the Independence and Partition of India, he devoted himself almost completely to yoga, to the transformation of human consciousness. His work acquired a much larger collective and institutional dimension with the formation of the Sri Aurobindo Ashram, its various departments and ancillary bodies, mostly in Pondicherry, but later all over India and the rest of the world.

In Aurobindo's transformation from a national leader, author, and yogi to a world-famous spiritual master, Mirra Alfassa, who later came to be known as the Mother, played the most important role. Aurobindo first met Mirra on 29 March 1914, when she was married to Paul Richard. The Richards were travelling to India in search for partners in their plans for world transformation and amelioration. Mirra had earlier seen Aurobindo's photograph without it making a huge impact on her. But their first meeting was momentous: 'As soon as I saw Sri Aurobindo I recognized in him the well-known being whom I used to call Krishna' *(Collected Works* 13: 39)[3]. The next day she wrote these prophetic lines: 'It matters little that there are thousands of beings plunged in the densest ignorance, He whom we saw yesterday is on Earth; His presence is enough to prove that a day will come when darkness shall be transformed into light, and Thy reign shall be indeed established upon Earth' *(Collected Works* 13: 3).

Mirra Blanche Rachel Alfassa was herself an extraordinary person. Born in Paris on 21 February 1878 into a rationalist, atheist, thoroughly modernized and secularized middle-class family of Turkish-Egyptian-Sephardic Jewish descent, she showed early signs of genius. At the age of sixteen, she began to befriend artists and to study painting. Soon she came to know most of the famous painters of her time, especially the post- and neo-impressionists.

---

[3] *The Collected Works of the Mother* were published in 17 volumes by the Sri Aurobindo Ashram, Pondicherry (2nd ed., 1978). Quotations from the Mother are from this edition and are referred to by volume and page number. They are also available online at https://www.sriaurobindoashram.org/mother/writings.php.

At nineteen, she married a painter called Henri Morisset. A son, André, was born to them.

The marriage however soon broke up. All her life, Mirra showed a highly refined and well-developed aesthetic sensibility, which extended not only to conventional arts and crafts like painting, music, singing, dance and poetry, but also to embroidery, story-telling, flower arrangement, interior design, architecture, couture, physical education, and sports. Mirra now turned to occultism, learning the secret arts from Max Théon and his wife, Alma. Both Max and Alma were adepts of a very high order. They wished to develop the powers latent in the human psyche through spiritualist practices. Mirra went to study under them at their retreat in Tlemcen in the Algerian mountains in Africa. The Theons had reportedly developed several *siddhis* or occult powers including clairvoyance, astral travel, materialization, and telekinetics. Many of these Mirra learnt. And yet she was not satisfied. After Alma's death, Theon's powers seemed to diminish. Mirra was looking for something bigger, more intense, more real and meaningful, grounded in a higher spiritual truth.

This she found in Aurobindo. Throughout her earlier life Mirra had had premonitions of great things to come. She felt she had been chosen for a special role. She had seen visions and had paranormal experiences. After her legal divorce in 1908 she met Paul Richard, whom she married in 1911. Together they travelled to Pondicherry, then a French territory, where Richard had earlier met Aurobindo in 1910. He had been so impressed with the latter that he considered him 'the greatest among . . . the divine men of Asia' and 'the leader, the hero of tomorrow' (81–82).

In 1914, along with Mirra and Paul Richard, Aurobindo founded the *Arya,* in which most of his books were first published serially as chapters or essays. The first issue of the journal came out on 15 August, Aurobindo's birthday, and contained the opening chapters of *The Life Divine, The Synthesis of Yoga, The*

Secret of the Veda, and *The Isha Upanishad.* Aurobindo ran the *Arya* single-handedly for nearly seven years, filling up almost all of its sixty-four pages with his own writings every month until it ceased publication in January 1921.

In 1920, Mirra came to live in Pondicherry permanently. Her meeting with Aurobindo on 24 March 1920 was decisive. Paul Richard left her behind, pursuing his own life in Europe, eventually in the United States. Mirra's divorce from Richard came later that decade but on 24 November 1920, she had already moved into the same house in which Aurobindo was residing. In January 1922, she took charge of the management of his household. After the Mother's permanent residence in Pondicherry, the first signs of an organized ashram began to appear. After a series of essays by Aurobindo published as *The Mother* in 1927, she came to be called that and revered on an almost equal footing with the former.

The dramatic turning point in Aurobindo's sadhana came in 1926. In *Sri Aurobindo: A Biography and a History*, K.R. Srinivasa Iyengar shows how there was a sense of great expectation among the twenty-four disciples who were present: 'An air of intensity began building up slowly, an air of expectancy; and the sadhaks had the feeling that they were on the threshold of new developments. After Aurobindo's birthday, the evening talks took on a new fervour and potency . . .' (529).

Ambalal Balkrishna or A. B. Purani has left an invaluable record of what happened on 24 November, which came to be known as Siddhi Day: 'There was a deep silence in the atmosphere after the disciples had gathered there. Many saw an oceanic flood of light rushing down from above. Everyone present felt a kind of pressure above his head. The whole atmosphere was surcharged with some electrical energy . . . Silence absolute, living silence—not merely living but overflowing with divinity' (*Life of Sri Aurobindo*, 125). A more sober affirmation may be found in Sri Aurobindo's own words, 'the Divine (Krishna or the Divine Presence or whatever you like) had come down into the material. It was also declared that I was retiring—obviously to work things out' (Nirodbaran, *Correspondence with Sri Aurobindo*, 293).

Henceforth, he who was known as Aurobindo Ghose or AG earlier, began to be known as Sri Aurobindo. Mirra was called the Mother and she assumed control not only of the day-to-day management of the ashram, but also of the *sadhana* of the disciples. Sri Aurobindo went into seclusion to be able to conduct his yoga more effectively.

Regarding the Mother, Sri Aurobindo himself declared, 'The Mother and I are one but in two bodies' (*CWSA* 32: 82) and the Mother corroborated, 'Sri Aurobindo and I are always one and the same consciousness, one and the same person' (*Mother's Agenda*, 1: 121-122). Actually, as far as their personalities were concerned, they were very different. The Mother, always practical, was an extraordinary manager and administrator. She built one of India's most impressive and dynamic ashrams, with several departments and manufacturing units. She was also an extrovert. She loved the open air and used to exercise and play tennis until well past her seventies. Sri Aurobindo was shy, retiring, rarely displayed much emotion, and stayed confined to his room for nearly twenty-five years.

Yet, what is remarkable is the extent to which each had surrendered to the other. The Mother's surrender was so total that Sri Aurobindo was moved to remark that he had witnessed nothing of that quality and magnitude before. What is less known or realized is that Sri Aurobindo too had surrendered to the Mother, considering her his regent and *shakti*. It is he who declared that she was the embodiment of Mahashakti, Mahasaraswati, Mahalakshmi and Mahakali—the Divine Mother herself. Thus, there can be no doubt that the Mother was not merely Sri Aurobindo's disciple, but his associate, partner, and the co-author of *Integral Yoga*.

Together they created a unique spiritual community which in fact became the nucleus of an extraordinary experiment. After the outbreak of World War II, this community grew rapidly. Families, with their children, joined in. The Mother opened a school for them which would be among the best and most progressive not just in India but in the world. There were incredible innovations going on in all directions—in painting, poetry, weaving, handicrafts, farming, printing, building, architecture and several other fields—all under the Mother's direct gaze and supervision.

The Mother was a benevolent dictator; all power and authority was centralized in her, but she ruled with love, not just with force. There are innumerable testimonies to her superhuman energy, competence, wisdom, foresight and managerial skills. While Sri Aurobindo was in seclusion, she kept a large group of very diverse individuals not just busy, but progressing spiritually. What is more, the ashram did not collapse after Sri Aurobindo's death, but gathered greater strength under her leadership.

'Sanatan Dharma, that is nationalism': Nation of Spirit

The unique conjuncture of Sri Aurobindo's 150th Birth Anniversary and the 75th year of India's independence affords us an exceptional opportunity to examine his contribution to nationalism, both to its theory and practice.

On 24 January 1908, almost two years before Mohandas Karamchand, later Mahatma, Gandhi wrote his seminal treatise *Hind Swaraj* on his way back from England to South Africa aboard S.S. Kildonan Castle, Sri Aurobindo made a speech in Nashik, Maharashtra. It is not one of his famous or well-known orations because it is not available in its original English. It was translated into Marathi and published the following morning in a Marathi paper, *Nasik Vritta*. We know of it because the Bombay Presidency

Police retranslated into English in their Intelligence Abstract. It was first published by *Archives and Research,* a biannual journal published by Sri Aurobindo Ashram, in the first number of its first volume (April 1977) and subsequently included as 'The Meaning of Swaraj' in *CWSA* 6-7: 833-836.

Sri Aurobindo elaborates on the meaning of swaraj in this speech: 'If we do not acquaint ourselves with the object in view, viz., Swaraj, I am afraid we, thirty crores of people, will become extinct.' He reminds his listeners that it is the people of Maharashtra that kept the torch of swaraj burning even during the darkest night. It is after this that Aurobindo's speech rises to a new level, not only of eloquence but of spiritual inspiration: 'Swaraj is life, it is nectar and salvation. Swaraj in a nation is the breath of life. Without breath of life a man is dead. So also without Swaraj a nation is dead. Swaraj being the life of a nation it is essential for it.'

But those who aspire for it must realise that swaraj is to be 'gained by our own exertions. If it is gained otherwise, which is impossible, it cannot last long, for want of strength in us.' Imploring the sovereign won't do because 'he won't give it'.

Then he considers a second way to attain swaraj: 'Another way of obtaining Swaraj is to seek aid from a neighbouring nation. But this means jumping from the frying-pan into the fire. No matter from whom we seek assistance, their own interests will first be considered.' Later, when Netaji Subhas Chandra Bose wanted the help, first of Germany, then of Japan to win India's independence, Sri Aurobindo opposed this method. Now, Sri Aurobindo comes to the third way, one which Gandhi also advocated: 'We should, therefore, acquire it by our own efforts.' No other way would work; we had to fight for our own swaraj.

But the question remained: 'How we should do it. We do not possess Swaraj nor have we the power to retain it. The answer is, we cannot master the art of swimming unless we struggle in the water. We should, therefore, be prepared to undergo hardships in the struggle for Swaraj, as there is no other alternative.'

Here, all ways seem to be open, whether non-violent, violent, or some combination of them. Sri Aurobindo does not spell this out in this speech, but this is what we can glean from his other writings. Here he speaks of faith in God; 'God created us independent' therefore 'we should be full of inspiration. With full faith in God we should preach independence through the length and breadth of the country and a beginning should be made to impart national education.'

The importance he places on 'national education' is unmistakable. If in addition to education, Indians can 'take into their own hands judicial and executive work ... we shall have more than half of Swaraj in our hands.' In the present state, he urges all to heed to the 'divine inspiration,' to the 'the commandment of God.' He wants Indians to unify 'from the Himalayas to Kanyakumari.' He concludes by proclaiming, 'If we, imbued with this idea, become united with a firm resolution to obey the commandment of God, I feel sure we shall gain our Swaraj in twenty years. It won't take centuries…'

This speech, given two years before the definitive Uttarpara peroration, may be said to contain the early ideas of Sri Aurobindo's spiritual nationalism. But the roots of Sri Aurobindo's experiments and ideas for freeing India go much farther back. In 1905, while still in Baroda, Sri Aurobindo had received an intriguing message from 'Sri Ramakrishna' in a séance, with his younger brother Barindara serving as a medium. It consisted of only two words in Bangla: *Mandir Gado!*—raise a temple!

Sri Aurobindo interpreted it as a commandment to propagate a new revolutionary creed based on the consecration of a temple to Mother India. This would not be a physical temple, so much as a nation-wide invocation of Mother India as Bharat Shakti. To elaborate this plan, Sri Aurobindo wrote a small, but extraordinary manifesto, *Bhawani Mandir,* to free India. Probably written in 1905, a copy of this pamphlet was submitted as evidence in the Alipur bomb case in 1908–1909, with Barindra's signature on the cover, and police markings all over (*CWSA* 6-7: 79-89)

Sri Aurobindo starts with a startling assertion, which is still quite true over 115 years later: 'WE IN INDIA FAIL IN ALL THINGS FOR WANT OF SHAKTI'. He elaborates: 'We have all things else, but we are empty of strength, void of energy. We have abandoned Shakti and are therefore abandoned by Shakti.' The consequences of such weaknesses are disastrous, as the heading of another section avers: 'OUR KNOWLEDGE IS A DEAD THING FOR WANT OF SHAKTI'.

Sri Aurobindo next asks, 'Is it knowledge that is wanting? We Indians born and bred in a country where Jnana has been stored and accumulated since the race began, bear about in us the inherited gains of many thousands of years.' Yet our knowledge is almost useless; it cannot save us. Why? Because, as Sri Aurobindo puts it, it lacks strength; it is therefore 'a dead knowledge, a burden under which we are bowed, a poison which is corroding us rather than as it should be, a staff to support our feet, and a weapon in our hands.' The reason is simple, 'Our knowledge then, weighed down with a heavy load of *tamas,* lies under the curse of impotence and inertia.'

If India has been a knowledge society for millennia, we are also not lacking in Bhakti or devotion. But again, 'OUR BHAKTI CANNOT LIVE AND WORK FOR WANT OF SHAKTI' (ibid 82). Without strength, even devotion is useless: 'In the absence of Shakti we cannot concentrate, we cannot direct, we cannot even preserve it.' As Sri Aurobindo declares, 'If we have strength, everything else will be added to us easily and naturally.' He believes that India must be reborn to manifest its strength and genius. He believes, moreover, that India can be reborn: 'No man or nation need be weak unless *he* chooses, no man or nation need perish unless *he* deliberately chooses extinction' (ibid 83).

The cultivation and exaltation of strength as the crying want of Indians is Sri Aurobindo's motto in *Bhawani Mandir,* an idea that hearkens back to Swami Vivekananda's injunction: 'Strength and manliness are virtue; weakness and cowardice are sin' or 'This is a great fact: strength is life; weakness is death. Strength is felicity, life eternal, immortal; weakness is constant strain and misery, weakness is death.'

In his Bengali writings in *Dharma* published in October 1909, Sri Aurobindo elaborated his idea of Swaraj or full political independence, rather than Dominion Status within the British empire:

> Aryan Rishis used to designate the practical and spiritual freedom and its fruit, the inviolable Ananda, as 'Swarajya', self-empire. Political freedom is but a limb of Swarajya, self-empire. It has two aspects—external freedom and internal freedom. Complete liberty from foreign domination is the external freedom, and democracy is the highest expression of the internal freedom ... As long as there is an alien government or ruler, no nation can be called a free nation possessing self-empire. As long as democracy is not established, no individual belonging to a nation can be deemed a free man. We want complete independence, free from the servitude to foreigners, complete authority of the individual in his own home. This is our political aim.
>
> ('The Problem of the Past,' *CWSA* Vol. 09,
> Writings in Bengali and Sanskrit).

Sri Aurobindo proclaims that freedom is the law of the soul: 'For all people, subjection is a messenger and servitor of death.

Only freedom can protect life and make any progress possible.'
The nation would die out of 'weakness and sterility' as long as the
foreigner was in occupation of our country. But 'if even in our
bondage we can protect or resurrect the self-law of our being,
then the chains of slavery will automatically fall away from us.
Therefore, if any nation loses its freedom by its own fault, an
untruncated and full independence should be its first aim and
political ideal.' He criticises the Congress for trying to propose the
idea of partial independence or 'colonial self-government.'

'The solution to the question whether we should be
independent outside the British Empire or within it does not
seem to interest the National Party. We want full independence.
If the British were to organise such a united empire that the
Indians, while remaining within it, could realise their full
independence, why should we have any objection to it? We are
struggling for independence, not out of spite against the British,
but in order to save our country. However, we are not prepared
to show our countrymen the wrong path of false politics, the
wrong way to protect the country by admitting an ideal other
than that of full independence.' Full independence within the
Empire if possible, but without the Empire if necessary—this
was Sri Aurobindo's declaration of political intent. Long before
the Congress adopted Purna Swaraj or full independence as its
stated policy in 1929.

While Sri Aurobindo was in the forefront of the national
struggle for only a brief period of five years, 1905–1910, his actual
contribution was much larger. This sense of historic destiny is
evident in his All India Radio Independence-eve broadcast:

August 15th is the birthday of free India. It marks for her
the end of an old era, the beginning of a new age. But it has a
significance not only for us, but for Asia and the whole world;
for it signifies the entry into the comity of nations of a new

power with untold potentialities which has a great part to play in determining the political, social, cultural and spiritual future of humanity. To me personally it must naturally be gratifying that this date which was notable only for me because it was my own birthday celebrated annually by those who have accepted my gospel of life, should have acquired this vast significance. As a mystic, I take this identification, not as a coincidence or fortuitous accident, but as a sanction and seal of the Divine Power which guides my steps on the work with which I began life. Indeed almost all the world movements which I hoped to see fulfilled in my lifetime, though at that time they looked like impossible dreams, I can observe on this day either approaching fruition or initiated and on the way to their achievement.

('Short Version,' *CWSA* 36: 478-480)

This self-confidence in shaping India's destiny is reflected in a realization he had much earlier, when he explained his 'three madnesses' to his young wife in a letter from 30 August 1905:

While others look upon their country as an inert piece of matter—a few meadows and fields, forests and hills and rivers—I look upon Her as the Mother. What would a son do if a demon sat on his mother's breast and started sucking her blood? Would he quietly sit down to his dinner, amuse himself with his wife and children, or would he rush out to deliver his mother? I know I have the strength to deliver this fallen race. It is not physical strength—I am not going to fight with sword or gun—but it is the strength of knowledge. This feeling is not new in me, it is not of today. I was born with it, it is in my very marrow. God sent me to earth to accomplish this great mission.

(*CWSA* 9: 88-89)

The first part of the passage, the duty of a son when a demon is drinking his mother's lifeblood, is also the theme of Sri Aurobindo's only Sanskrit poem, '*Bhavani Bharati*'. But what is striking is the unmistakable sense of special mission to 'deliver this fallen race' by the special knowledge that he has, authorized by the Divine: 'God sent me to earth to accomplish this great mission.'

During his incarceration in Alipore jail, the conviction of his special role in India's freedom struggle is renewed:

> Once more He spoke to me and said, 'Behold the people among whom I have sent you to do a little of my work. This is the nature of the nation I am raising up and the reason why I raise them.'

This is part of Sri Aurobindo's famous Uttarpara Speech of 30 May 1909 (*CWSA* 9:3-12), the first public address delivered on his acquittal and release earlier in the month on 6 May:

> When you go forth, speak to your nation always this word, that it is for the Sanatan Dharma that they arise, it is for the world and not for themselves that they arise. I am giving them freedom for the service of the world. When therefore it is said that India shall rise, it is the Sanatan Dharma that shall be great.

What is crucial about this passage is not just Sri Aurobindo's mission and purpose in raising the consciousness of a nation, but the kind of nation it is to be:

> When it is said that India shall expand and extend herself, it is the Sanatan Dharma that shall expand and extend itself over the world. It is for the Dharma and by the Dharma that India exists.

But what is Sanatan Dharma? The Divine, which is revealing the message to Sri Aurobindo in prison, explains in terms that are quite unambiguous:

> But what is the Hindu religion? What is this religion which we call Sanatan, eternal? It is the Hindu religion only because the Hindu nation has kept it, because in this Peninsula it grew up in the seclusion of the sea and the Himalayas, because in this sacred and ancient land it was given as a charge to the Aryan race[4] to preserve through the ages.
>
> But it is not circumscribed by the confines of a single country, it does not belong peculiarly and for ever to a bounded part of the world. That which we call the Hindu religion is really the eternal religion, because it is the universal religion which embraces all others. If a religion is not universal, it cannot be eternal. A narrow religion, a sectarian religion, an exclusive religion can live only for a limited time and a limited purpose. This is the one religion that can triumph over materialism by including and anticipating the discoveries of science and the speculations of philosophy.

Even if India has been its guardian and custodian, Hindu or Sanatan Dharma is not a narrow or sectarian creed. No such limited or exclusive religion can be either universal or eternal, let alone be compatible with the discoveries of science or the rationality of philosophy.

Before he ends, Sri Aurobindo offers this resounding summation of his theory of nationalism in the 'Uttarpara Speech':

---

[4] It must be noted that Sri Aurobindo wrote these words before the rise of Nazi Germany and had already clarified in several places what he meant by 'Aryan' or Arya, which is quite different from the negative connotations it came to acquire later.

> I say no longer that nationalism is a creed, a religion, a faith; I
> say that it is the Sanatan Dharma which for us is nationalism.
> This Hindu nation was born with the Sanatan Dharma, with
> it it moves and with it it grows. When the Sanatan Dharma
> declines, then the nation declines, and if the Sanatan Dharma
> were capable of perishing, with the Sanatan Dharma it would
> perish.

'The Sanatan Dharma that is nationalism'—this might sum
up Sri Aurobindo's credo of what we might term a spiritual
nationalism. Or still better, the nation of the spirit. Different from
ethnic or civic nationalism, or even cultural nationalism based on
language, region, religion, or ways of life and cultural practices, Sri
Aurobindo's nation of the spirit is about humankind's march to
higher consciousness. In this manifest evolutionary destiny of the
species, past and present forms of nationalism were fated to prove
inadequate.

Towards the Life Divine: In the Laboratory of Consciousness

From his seclusion in 1926 to his Mahasamadhi in 1950, Sri
Aurobindo continued to work for the descent of the higher
consciousness, which he thought was necessary before earthly
life could be transformed. 'No one can write about my life', said
Sri Aurobindo in a letter to a disciple, 'because it has not been on
the surface for man to see' (Purani, *The Life of Sri Aurobindo* ix);
similarly, to a biographer he wrote, 'neither you nor anyone else
knows anything at all of my life; it has not been on the surface for
man to see' (*CWSA*).

This statement applies especially to the last twenty-four
years of his life. On 8 February 1927, Sri Aurobindo and the
Mother moved into the house on Rue François Martin, which is
the present ashram block. Sri Aurobindo never left his suite of

rooms on these premises. As Purani notes in his *Evening Talks,* 'Then the curtain fell. Sri Aurobindo retired completely . . .' (*Second Series:* 12). Until 1938, barring two or three exceptions including Rabindranath Tagore, Sri Aurobindo saw no one; he lived in almost absolute solitude. However on 21 February (the Mother's birthday), 15 August (Sri Aurobindo's birthday) and 24 November (Siddhi Day), the three 'darshan days', the inmates of the ashram could see him.

After 1930, Sri Aurobindo began to reply to the letters which his disciples sent him, answering their queries about spiritual practice. This correspondence gradually became so extensive and massive that it came to occupy over 2000 printed pages. Sri Aurobindo often spent twelve hours a day or more in this activity. Most of this record has been published and presents one of the most fascinating archives of spiritual life available anywhere. The letters were much more than merely words; each of them embodied a certain force and power which acted directly on the physical, vital, mental and spiritual being of the addressees.

During this period, Sri Aurobindo also resumed writing poetry. Unlike his earlier romantic or heroic poems, his new work belonged to his mature phase. During the 1930s and 1940s, he wrote several short poems, many of which are innovative, including the seldom-practiced quantitative metres. In addition, he wrote a series of seventy-three sonnets, unique for their spiritual content. What is more, he composed and revised his epic *Savitri* which is one of the most unusual and ambitious poems of this century. Besides poetry, Sri Aurobindo also worked on revising his major prose works during these two decades. *The Life Divine, Hymns to the Mystic Fire, The Synthesis of Yoga, The Human Cycle and The Ideal of Human Unity* were all reissued.

On 24 November 1938, in the early hours of darshan day, Sri Aurobindo fractured his leg in an accident. This incident necessitated a modification in his total retirement, rendering him available to those, including doctors, who attended upon him. Because two darshan days had been missed, Sri Aurobindo gave a special darshan on 24 April, the day of the Mother's final arrival in Pondicherry; subsequently, this became the fourth darshan day in the ashram calendar. In 1939, World War II broke out.

Throughout the war Sri Aurobindo kept himself well-informed about the latest developments. Though at first he did not show any active concern, when it seemed Hitler would triumph, he declared publicly his support for the Allies: 'He saw that behind Hitler and Nazism were dark Asuric forces and that their success would mean the enslavement of mankind to the tyranny of evil, and a set-back to the course of evolution and especially to the spiritual evolution of mankind . . .' (*CWSA* 36: 65). During this period Sri Aurobindo went against the prevailing national opinion, which was divided, if not bitterly anti-British.

In 1942, Sri Aurobindo supported Sir Stafford Cripps' proposals offering Dominion Status to India in return for support in the war effort. Sri Aurobindo not only sent a personal message to Cripps, but tried to persuade the Congress to accept the offer. The victory of the Allies in 1945 was celebrated in the ashram. When India became free on 15 August 1947, Sri Aurobindo, in a message issued on his seventy-fifth birthday, considered the event as 'the end of an old era, the beginning of a new age' (*CWSA 36:* 474). He spoke of five dreams of his which had seemed very impractical, but which now were arriving at fruition. The independence of India, the resurgence of Asia, the formation of a world-union, the spiritual gift of India to the world and the next step in evolution were the world-movements which Sri Aurobindo had supported and he had the satisfaction of seeing them progressing towards fulfilment in his own lifetime.

On 5 December 1950, Sri Aurobindo passed away. He was suffering from uraemia and had a kidney infection. It is documented that his body was bathed in an unearthly glow and remained uncorrupted for over 111 hours. It would be an understatement to say that his passing shocked those in the ashram. In fact, they were desolate, not just with the grief of the passing of their Guru, but with the realization that the work of supramentalizing the earth would now be postponed. Bravely, Mirra Alfassa or the Mother took on the mantle of sustaining the cherished mission of Sri Aurobindo, declaring that Sri Aurobindo had given her an assurance that he 'would remain here and not leave the earth atmosphere until earth is transformed' (quoted in Purani, *The Life of Sri Aurobindo,* 240).

Vedic Evolutionism: Sri Aurobindo's Thought

The keynote of Sri Aurobindo's thought is evolution. As he put it in one of his aphorisms, 'When we have passed beyond humanity, then we shall be the Man. The Animal was the helper; the Animal is the bar' (*CWSA* 13:199). He said repeatedly, 'Man is a transitional being, he is not final' (*CWSA* 3: 157) or 'Man is a transitional being, he is not final. He is a middle term of the evolution, not its end, crown or consummating masterpiece' (*CWSA* 3: 221).

From his earliest writings in 1890–1892 when he was an undergraduate at King's College, Cambridge, the notion of evolution influenced the basic orientation of his ideas. A remarkable unfinished work from that period called *The Harmony of Virtue* which most commentators fail to mention, affords us interesting proof of this. In this Socratic dialogue between Keshav Ganesh Desai who clearly stands for Aurobindo himself and his English friends, Aurobindo proposes a new theory of virtue, beyond, and if necessary, contrary to what is conventionally considered moral and ethical. To realize what virtue really is, a descent into the nether regions of consciousness, such as is later portrayed at great length in *Savitri,* is necessary. But the key to virtue is evolution: 'human virtue lies in the evolution by the human being of the inborn qualities and powers native to his humanity' (*CWSA* 1: 59). Here we see glimpses of his ideas of both evolution and involution—that which is inborn and native to our humanity and a glimpse of the glorious future in which our total potentialities will be manifested.

It is no wonder that according to Sri Aurobindo, humanity as we know it is not the end-point of evolution. Man[5] as he is at present is but a transitional being, largely mental, therefore not yet evolved enough to transcend the dualities and false consciousness of our present existence. All the conflict, distortions, and problems which beset humanity may be traced to this flawed consciousness. When we look back at the whole drama of evolution, we see life emerging from matter at first, and then evolving to the stage of mental self-consciousness in man. This evolution is not merely biological, confined to a changing of forms, but is an evolution of consciousness.

Sri Aurobindo held that the Absolute, the self-sufficient, the one without a second, or the Satchidanada Parabrahman of the Vedas and Upanishads, was itself involved in what we experience as the universe. Therefore, hidden in the heart of matter is a divine impulse seeking to manifest more and more fully through evolution until it attains its own fullest splendour. This whole process has no 'reason' as such except *ananda* or the endless, boundless joy of existence. So, evolution is the law of life but what makes man special is that he can consciously participate in it. This is precisely what Sri Aurobindo and the Mother sought to do, by inviting the Divine into the mental, vital and finally into the physical planes.

Indeed, even without reference to Sri Aurobindo, when we ask the question, 'After man, what?' we find a variety of answers

---

[5] I use 'man' because that is the word that, with its variations, occurs most frequently in Sri Aurobindo's thought. It includes woman and should be read as such.

depending on where we look. Friedrich Nietzsche conceived of the Superman as a being with a mighty will and urge to power, who could dominate and control the rest of humanity. Arguably, it was a mistaken development from this ideal, corrupted with an aberrant version of social Darwinism which resulted in the monstrous experiments of Hitler to produce the master race.

The comic-book notion of Superman is fundamentally the same—he is just like any one of us, but with much greater powers. A being with a flawed, dualistic and imperfect mind, but with infinitely greater powers both to help and harm is ultimately an Asura or Titan, not a Deva or divine being. All such creatures, endowed with some superior power but scarcely with a higher consciousness, cannot embody our hopes for a higher species. Science fiction, similarly, has given us even more frightening and unnerving portraits of supermen. These are cyborgs, part-men-part-machines, ruthless and predatory, programmed to wreak untold destruction on others, sometimes ceasing to be human altogether by turning into robots and terminators.

Sri Aurobindo's Superman however is an entirely different being. Though born and embodied like normal human beings, he has a consciousness which is totally and radically different. The Superman is not egocentric but has a wider, higher consciousness. This makes him automatically avoid the errors, conflicts and divisiveness of human consciousness, which are the causes of war, inequality, environmental degradation, pollution and overpopulation. The Superman, then, is an intermediate being between man and the fully divine, Supramentalized entity of the future.

By this logic, eventually, because total perfection is the destiny of consciousness, an even higher being than the Superman will emerge. This will be effected when the Supramental consciousness achieves its fullest fruition upon earth. The Supramental being will be even more different from man than man is from an ape. He will be a Divine Being in a fully Divine body. Aurobindonians believe, following the Mother, that it is impossible for us with our present level of development to fully even conceive of such a being. All we can do is form some mental picture from the glimpses and illuminations which we may receive from the higher planes of consciousness.

One of the great strengths of Sri Aurobindo's later work is its clear, detailed and convincing portrayal of this evolutionary process. Now that there is an unprecedented interest in future (s), the insights offered by Sri Aurobindo are invaluable because in the entire history of this century, there is scarcely a thinker or philosopher more concerned with the future than he. As some say, the Metahuman is already upon us, what with the progress in Artificial Intelligence, robotics, and cybernetics. The problems of humanity cannot be solved by the present level of human consciousness. That is why the Metahuman has become a bio-spiritual necessity for the very survival of the species.

In Sri Aurobindo's conception of the world, there is a ladder of consciousness, reaching upwards from the very depths of matter and inconscience, through life and mind, to regions above the mind, the Overmind planes, finally to the full manifestation of Divine Perfection and glory in the Supramentalized being. The Supermind is just a degree below the Absolute, which the Vedas define as Satchitananda. The Supermind is perfection in manifestation, while the Absolute is perfection 'before' manifestation.

It is at the level of the Overmind that the first glimmers of ignorance in the form of difference and diversity are evident. Yet, in the Overmind, there is differentiation without conflict. But once the descent into mind takes place, ignorance, conflict, violence and dissension all become habitual and routine. Beneath the mind is life, with all its vital instincts, passions and impulses. Beneath even life is physical matter, with its rigid laws and restrictions. This, broadly speaking, is Sri Aurobindo's notion of the evolutionary scheme.

This conception is in consonance with the wisdom of the Upanishads and the Yoga philosophy of unfolding levels of consciousness. Every evolutionary leap is accomplished by the wedding of an aspiration from below and the descent of grace from above. Sri Aurobindo, synthesizing the various traditions of ancient spirituality, offered the instrument of *purna* or Integral Yoga to accomplish the grand destiny of humanity.

In this yoga, the material was not to be shunned nor worshipped as the ultimate truth. The aim was instead to transform matter itself, to Divinize and Spiritualize all our mundane acts and works to lead a divine life while on earth and ultimately, in a divine body. This yoga neither shuns nor embraces the world, but tries to transform it. Another special feature of this yoga is that though individuals perform it, it is collective in its action. The aim is not personal salvation but total and general amelioration of earthly life itself. Finally, in this yoga, surrender is most important. After surrender, the Divine within each individual does the yoga; the ego-bound false self which considers itself as the doer, is no more.

An Extraordinary Fellowship: Sri Aurobindo and His Followers

The followers of Sri Aurobindo and the Mother are, of course, concentrated in Pondicherry (now Puducherry). The sadhaks and practitioners, members of the Sri Aurobindo Ashram, consider themselves directly carrying on in the path of their masters. The Sri Aurobindo Society, formed by the Mother on 19 September 1960, nearly ten years after Sri Aurobindo's death, to promote his teachings, has a large number of followers spread across many centres in India and overseas.

Auroville, an international city founded by the Mother in 1968, is a resident community with members from many parts of the world. It is also dedicated to the vision of Aurobindo and the Mother. The Sri Aurobindo Ashram, Delhi Branch, was dedicated on 12 February 1956 and consecrated with Sri Aurobindo's relics from Pondicherry on 4 December 1957. In addition to these main bodies, there are hundreds of other organisations, institutions, and centres, not to mention thousands of schools, that professedly follow and promote the masters' teachings.

While each individual devotee has his or her own approach to Sri Aurobindo and the Mother, a certain commonality does emerge in the belief systems of those who adhere to this path. Many assert the Avatarhood or Divine Incarnation of Sri Aurobindo and the Mother and approach them with worship and devotion. Several miracles and special interventions in world events are attributed to them, many of which have a basis in the words of the Masters themselves, yet they call into question our ordinary way of thinking. For instance, many followers commonly believed that Sri Aurobindo with his occult force turned the tide of World War II in favour of the Allies. Similarly, they hold that had the Congress accepted the Cripps proposal at Sri Aurobindo's behest, the partition of India and the bloody carnage that followed could have been prevented.

Yet, a careful reading of the Masters should clarify that it was never their intention to claim an incontrovertible and transhistorical infallibility or to encourage the formation of a cult or a sect. The Mother said, 'Truth is not a dogma that one can learn once and for all and impose as a rule. Truth is as infinite as the supreme Lord himself and It manifests every instant for those who are sincere and attentive' (Mother's Agenda 8: 84). She warned her devotees several times to not constitute a new theology out of Sri Aurobindo's works: 'I repeat that in connection with Sri Aurobindo, it is impossible to talk of a teaching or even of a revelation; his is a direct Action by the Lord, and thereon no religion can be founded. Spiritual life can only exist in its purity when it is free of all forms of mental dogma.'

Perhaps she had already observed signs of such mental dogma even during her own lifetime. That may be why she said, 'One must at any price prevent this from becoming a new religion. For as soon as it would be formulated in an elegant, impressive and somewhat forceful way, it would be finished.' *(Mother's Agenda* 9: 336). One of the most important statements of the Mother in this regard is 'Do not take my words for a teaching. Always they are a force in action, uttered with a definite purpose, and they lose their true power when separated from that purpose.' *(Collected Works* 13: 1.)

This makes it abundantly clear that no rigid theory or philosophy or system of beliefs or set of rituals can be extrapolated from Sri Aurobindo's or the Mother's words. Their words were 'a force in action', which therefore cannot be separated from their contexts. Now that their original contexts are no longer available to us, we need to exercise the utmost circumspection in taking their statements literally. The more plausible, sensible and reasonable interpretation should be preferred to the fanciful, far-fetched and irrational one. In issuing these admonitions, the Mother was reinforcing what Sri Aurobindo himself had declared: 'I may say that it is far from my purpose to propagate any religion, new or old, for humanity in the future' (*CWSA* 28: 411).

Though both Sri Aurobindo and the Mother repeatedly warned against the creation of a cult around them, Sri Aurobindo did emphasize the divinity of the Mother and vice versa. How is this paradox to be explained? Not just, it seems to me, by asserting the divinity of the Gurus and our own mental inadequacies as devotees are wont to do, but by having the maturity to admit that such contradictions and difficulties are a part of the spiritual enterprise; we could call them the risks, as it were, which are attendant to any venture for profit, whether secular or religious.

It is not by deification or glorification alone that the role of the Guru can be understood, but by carefully examining their agency in the historical contexts in which they lived and acted. By separating what is still relevant from what was specific to a particular time and age we can avoid the pitfalls of disillusionment and self-deception. Such was the approach that Sri Aurobindo himself recommended to a classic text like the Gita. A full resolution of the paradox, however, can only come by direct personal experience.

Like the early Christians whose lives were lived in hope and anticipation of the Second Coming and the Day of Judgement, some disciples of Sri Aurobindo and the Mother also believed that the fulfilment of their highest aspirations was imminent. Both Sri Aurobindo and the Mother stressed that the supramental transformation was extremely difficult to achieve and that it could only come at the end of a long and arduous journey. But the obviously millenarian and utopian dimensions of their thought, in addition to several of their pronouncements, contributed to a sense of awe and expectation in the ashram community. The most dramatic of these statements was the Mother's announcement of the Supramental Manifestation on earth on 29 February 1956, heralding the possibility of a transformed humanity and a divine life on earth.

While the rationalist critic may complain that what was promised was not accomplished, it would be unfortunate if such an approach was used to suspect, if not reject, the larger vision underlying these pronouncements of Sri Aurobindo and the Mother. Though the Mother was often asked about the time span it would take before things would manifest openly on the outside, she never made definite promises about this. The result is that many, in tune with their own inner experience, choose to believe what they think right about some of these pronouncements.

The Ashram, as well as other Aurobindonian institutions such as Auroville, have weathered their share of crises, conflicts, dissensions, splits, purges, even court cases. The stakes are very high. The Ashram, for instance, owns prime real estate in Pondicherry's erstwhile 'White Town' or the French quarter adjacent to the promenade which is valued at thousands of crores of rupees. Who controls the narrative is thus not merely a theoretical or theological issue.

In addition, there are the usual power struggles and differences of opinion as to what the Aurobindonian project was, is, and should be in the future. Yet, the members of the Ashram and of devotees of Sri Aurobindo and the Mother have, for most part, shown a remarkable nobility and sincerity of purpose as the custodians of the magnificent legacy of the Masters. They have also, more than occasionally if not always, displayed the marks of individuals working together for the higher cause of the evolution of human consciousness, keeping their own egos and ambitions in check.

What is remarkable and beyond doubt is that a diverse community of sadhaks, drawn from all corners of the land and representative of almost every personality type, were inspired to exceed themselves and excel in ways that would be unimaginable under ordinary circumstances. Given this record of extraordinary facts and feats, the future, although uncertain, looks promising if not certain.

L'avenir: Looking Ahead

During Sri Aurobindo's 150th birth anniversary celebrations, a better or more fitting tribute to his life and thought can scarcely be paid than by a proper study of his works. The writings themselves can be studied objectively and dispassionately, quite independently of what we think about the devotional aspects of life in the ashram.

Once the validity of such an approach is recognized, it will be possible to recover their energy and initiative. Their study can be facilitated by the new edition of *The Complete Works of Sri Aurobindo* (*CWSA*), a 37-volume edition, published completely, except for the final volume containing the index.

Once again, we are confronted by the extraordinary breadth and depth of Aurobindo's thought. What I have touched on in this Introduction, or offered by way of a selection in this anthology, is only a fragment, but I hope a powerfully illustrative and representative one. There is a great deal that is enduring in Aurobindo's work, that reaches beyond the confines of his time and place. It is important to showcase this.

Sri Aurobindo was not only a revolutionary patriot, great poet, philosopher and system builder *par excellence*, but a great yogi, who devoted his life to the goal of transforming and perfecting the human condition itself. He achieved, as Romain Rolland puts it, 'The completest synthesis that has been realized to this day of the genius of Asia and the genius of Europe' (*SABCL*, 30, Glossary and Index, 304). Whether or not he was indeed 'an Avatar of the future' (ibid), as the Mother considered him to be, is up to each individual to discover. Yet there is no doubt that he hewed a new pathway to the Infinite, one which includes rather than eschews life in all its variety and complexity.

Denying nothing, including everything, yet transforming matter, life and mind, Aurobindo believed that humanity must press onwards to a more glorious future. Otherwise, this experiment of human life on earth would be meaningless. All religions and prophets have vouched for and predicted the perfectibility of the human condition; Sri Aurobindo actually assured us that the day is probably not far off when this Golden Age will dawn upon us.

He said this moreover in a manner fully consistent with logic and science, quite in tune with the current knowledge of ourselves and our world, in the same tradition of the exalted and esoteric gnosis of the Vedas and Upanishads, according a special place to India in this great adventure, yet including and blending the best of other civilizations so as to affirm the unity and oneness of all humankind in our evolutionary march—this is the legacy that Sri Aurobindo leaves us with.

Sri Aurobindo poses a great challenge to us, as human beings, to choose higher consciousness at this juncture of our existence, or to continue in our age-old, flawed, even self-destructive ways, which are driving our whole species to the brink of disaster, if not extinction. In this new century and the advancing millennium, future generations will surely find new meaning and fresh inspiration in his works.

Chronology

1872 15 August	Birth in Calcutta.
1872-1877	In Rangpur, East Bengal (now Bangladesh).
1877-1879	At Loreto Convent, Darjeeling.
1879	To England, along with his two brothers, placed under the charge of Rev. William Drewett in Manchester.
1879-1884	In Manchester, tutored by Mr. and Mrs. Drewett at home.
1884-1889	In London, as a scholarship student at St. Paul's School.
1889 December	Passes the London Matriculation.
1890 July	Admitted as a probationer to the Indian Civil Service.
11 October	Admitted on a scholarship to King's College, Cambridge.
1890-1892	At King's College, preparing for his Tripos.
1892 May	Passes Part I of the Classical Tripos in First Class.
August	Passes the ICS final examination.
November	Disqualified from the ICS for his failure to take the riding test.
December	Obtains employment in the service of the Maharaja of Baroda.

1893 12 January	Leaves England by the S.S. Carthage, traveling via Gibraltar, Port Said, and Aden.
6 February	Arrives in India, landing at the Apollo Bunder, Bombay.
1893-1906	In the Baroda State service, at first in various administrative departments, then professor of French and English in Baroda College, then private secretary of the Maharaja, finally Vice-Principal of the college.
1893-1894	Contributes a series of articles, 'New Lamps for Old', in *Indu Prakash*, Bombay.
1898	*Songs to Myrtilla*, a collection of poems, privately printed.
1901 30 April	Marries Mrinalini Bose in Calcutta.
1902 December	Meets Lokmanya Tilak at the Ahmedabad session of the Indian National Congress.
1902-1903	Organizes a secret, revolutionary society in Bengal and begins to contact nationalist leaders in western India.
1903 May-August	Accompanies the Gaekwar to Kashmir; experiences the 'vacant infinite' at Takht-e-Suleman.
1905	Begins to practise yoga.
October	Bengal is partitioned.
1906	Goes to Bengal and participates in the anti-partition movement.
August	Becomes Principal of the newly founded Bengal National College; begins to write for *Bande Mataram*.
December	Actively participates in the Calcutta session of the Congress.
1907 2 August	Resigns Principalship of the National College.

16 August	Arrested on the charge of sedition for the articles published in *Bande Mataram*; released on bail.
23 September	Acquitted; becomes the leader of the extremist Nationalist Party in Bengal.
December	One of the leaders of the Extremist faction of the Congress at Surat; engineers the split between the Moderates and the Extremists.
1908 January	Meets Vishnu Bhaskar Lele, a Maharashtrian yogi; establishes complete silence of the mind under Lele's instructions.
January-April	Delivers several speeches.
2 May	Arrested in the 'Alipore Bomb Case' connected with a revolutionary group lead by his brother, Barindra; put in the Lal Bazar lock-up, Calcutta.
5 May	Taken to Alipore jail in Calcutta.
5 May-6 May 1909	An undertrial at Alipore Jail; spends time in reading and meditation; has the Visvarupa Darshan or the experience of the Cosmic Vasudeva Consciousness.
1909 6 May	Acquitted, after a brilliant defence by Chittaranjan Das.
19 June	Starts the *Karmayogin,* a weekly political and cultural journal; writes most of its articles.
23 August	Starts *Dharma*, a Bengali journal; writes many of its articles.
1910 February	Leaves secretly for Chandranagore, a French enclave, north of Calcutta.
31 March	Departs Chandranagore for Pondicherry.
4 April	Arrives in Pondicherry; on the same day, a warrant is issued charging Sri Aurobindo with sedition for his article 'To My

	Countrymen' published in *Karmayogin* on 25 December 1909.
7 November	The article is not found seditious; Sri Aurobindo announces, via a letter to *The Hindu,* his presence in Pondicherry and his retirement from active politics.
1914 29 March	First meeting with Mirra Richard (later known as the Mother).
1 June	Decision to publish the *Arya,* 'a philosophical review'.
15 August	First issue of the *Arya.* Nearly all of Sri Aurobindo's major works were published in this journal in monthly instalments until its closure in January 1921.
1918 17 December	Death of Mrinalini in Calcutta.
1920 24 April	Mirra Richard settles in Pondicherry.
August	Sri Aurobindo offered the Presidency of the Nagpur session of the Congress; declines.
1926 24 November	Siddhi Day; after a decisive spiritual realization, Sri Aurobindo withdraws from direct contact with others; the Mother takes over the material and spiritual responsibility of the ashram and its inmates.
1930-1938	Sri Aurobindo enters into extensive correspondence with disciples.
1938 24 November	Fractures his thigh, resulting in the restricted contact.
1939-1940	Revision and publication of *The Life Divine.*
1940 September	Sri Aurobindo declares his support for the Allies in World War II.
1942 March	Sri Aurobindo supports Cripps' Proposals offering India self-government after the war.

1947 15 August	India wins her freedom on Sri Aurobindo's birthday.
1948	Publication of Part I of *The Synthesis of Yoga*.
1949	Publication of the revised version of *The Human Cycle*.
1950	Publication of Part One of *Savitri*. Publication of the revised version of *The Ideal of Human Unity*.
5 December	Mahasamadhi after a brief illness.

Towards Swaraj and the Regeneration of India

The Doctrine of Passive Resistance: Conclusions

To sum up the conclusions at which we have arrived. The object of all our political movements and therefore the sole object with which we advocate passive resistance is Swaraj[1] or national freedom. The latest and most venerable of the older politicians who have sat in the Presidential Chair of the Congress, pronounced from that seat of authority Swaraj as the one object of our political endeavour, Swaraj as the only remedy for all our ills, Swaraj as the one demand nothing short of which will satisfy the people of India. Complete self-government as it exists in the United Kingdom or the Colonies, such was his definition of Swaraj. The Congress has contented itself with demanding self-government as it exists in the Colonies. We of the new school would not pitch our ideal one inch lower than absolute Swaraj, self-government as it exists in the United Kingdom. We believe that no smaller ideal can inspire national revival or nerve the people of India for

---

[1] The last of a series of seven articles published in April 1907 in the daily *Bande Mataram*, an English newspaper published from Calcutta and edited by Sri Aurobindo.

Swaraj or self-government, on the lines of other British colonies, was officially adopted as the goal of the struggle of the Indian National Congress in its Calcutta session in December 1906, which was presided over by Dadabhai Naoroji (1825-1917). The Congress declared 'purna swaraj' or complete independence as its objective much later, on 26 January 1930, in Lahore.

the fierce, stubborn and formidable struggle by which alone they can again become a nation. We believe that this newly awakened people, when it has gathered its strength together, neither can nor ought to consent to any relations with England less than that of equals in a confederacy. To be content with the relations of master and dependent or superior and subordinate, would be a mean and pitiful aspiration unworthy of manhood; to strive for anything less than a strong and glorious freedom would be to insult the greatness of our past and the magnificent possibilities of our future.

To the ideal we have at heart there are three paths, possible or impossible. Petitioning, which we have so long followed, we reject as impossible, the dream of a timid inexperience, the teaching of false friends who hope to keep us in perpetual subjection, foolish to reason, false to experience. Self-development by self-help which we now purpose to follow, is a possible though uncertain path, never yet attempted under such difficulties, but one which must be attempted, if for nothing else yet to get free of the habit of dependence and helplessness, and re-awaken and exercise our half-atrophied powers of self-government. Parallel to this attempt and to be practised simultaneously, the policy of organised resistance to the present system of government forms the old traditional way of nations which we also must tread. It is a vain dream to suppose that what other nations have won by struggle and battle, by suffering and tears of blood, we shall be allowed to accomplish easily, without terrible sacrifices, merely by spending the ink of the journalist and petition-framer and the breath of the orator. Petitioning will not bring us one yard nearer to freedom; self-development will not easily be suffered to advance to its goal. For self-development spells the doom of the ruling bureaucratic despotism, which must therefore oppose our progress with all the art and force of which it is the master; without organised resistance we could not take more than a few faltering steps towards self-emancipation. But resistance may be of many kinds, armed revolt, or aggressive resistance short of armed revolt, or defensive resistance whether passive or active; the circumstances of the country and the nature of the despotism from which it seeks to escape must determine what form of resistance is best justified and most likely to be effective at the time or finally successful.

The Congress has not formally abandoned the petitioning policy; but it is beginning to fall into discredit and gradual disuse, and time will accelerate its inevitable death by atrophy; for it can no longer even carry the little weight it had, since it has no longer the support of an undivided public opinion at its back. The alternative policy of self-development has received a partial recognition; it has been made an integral part of our political activities, but not in its entirety and purity. Self-help has been accepted as supplementary to the help of the very bureaucracy which it is our declared object to undermine and supplant, self-development as supplementary to development of the nation by its foreign rulers. Passive resistance has not been accepted as a national policy, but in the form of Boycott[2] it has been declared legitimate under circumstances which apply to all India.

This is a compromise good enough for the moment but in which the new school does not mean to allow the country to rest permanently. We desire to put an end to petitioning until such a strength is created in the country that a petition will only be a courteous form of demand. We wish to kill utterly the pernicious delusion that a foreign and adverse interest can be trusted to develop us to its own detriment, and entirely to do away with the foolish and ignoble hankering after help from our natural adversaries. Our attitude to bureaucratic concession is that of Laocoon:[3] 'We fear the Greeks even when they bring us gifts.'

---

[2] In August 1905 a general boycott of British goods was announced in a popular protest against the British government's decision to partition Bengal.

[3] A Trojan prince in Greek legend. In Sri Aurobindo's play *Ilion*, he is a son of Priam and priest of Apollo.

Our policy is self-development and defensive resistance. But we would extend the policy of self-development to every department of national life; not only Swadeshi and National Education, but national defence, national arbitration courts, sanitation, insurance against famine or relief of famine, whatever our hands find to do or urgently needs doing, we must attempt ourselves and no longer look to the alien to do it for us. And we would universalise and extend the policy of defensive resistance until it ran parallel on every line with our self-development. We would not only buy our own goods, but boycott British goods; not only have our own schools, but boycott Government institutions; not only erect our own Arbitration Courts, but boycott bureaucratic justice; not only organise our league of defence, but have nothing to do with the bureaucratic Executive except when we cannot avoid it. At present even in Bengal where Boycott is universally accepted, it is confined to the boycott of British goods and is aimed at the British merchant and only indirectly at the British bureaucrat. We would aim it directly both at the British merchant and at the British bureaucrat who stands behind and makes possible exploitation by the merchant.

The double policy we propose has three objects before it: to develop ourselves into a self-governing nation; to protect ourselves against and repel attack and opposition during the work of development; and to press in upon and extrude the foreign agency in each field of activity and so ultimately supplant it. Our defensive resistance must therefore be mainly passive in the beginning, although with a perpetual readiness to supplement it with active resistance whenever compelled. It must be confined for the present to Boycott, and we must avoid giving battle on the crucial question of taxation for the sole reason that a No-Taxes campaign demands a perfect organisation and an ultimate preparedness from which we are yet far off. We will attack the resources of the bureaucracy whenever we can do so by simple abstention, as in the case of its immoral Abkari revenue; but we do not propose at present to follow European precedents and refuse the payment of taxes legally demanded from us. We desire to keep our resistance within the bounds of law, so long as law does not seek directly to interfere with us and render impossible our progress and the conscientious discharge of our duty to our fellow-countrymen. But if, at any time, laws should be passed with the object of summarily checking our self-development or unduly limiting our rights as men, we must be prepared to break the law and endure the penalty imposed for the breach with the object of making it unworkable as has been done in other countries. We must equally be ready to challenge by our action arbitrary executive coercion, if we do not wish to see our resistance snuffed out by very cheap official extinguishers. Nor must we shrink from boycotting persons as well as things; we must make full though discriminating use of the social boycott against those of our countrymen who seek to baffle the will of the nation in a matter vital to its emancipation, for this is a crime of *lèse-nation* which is far more heinous than the legal offence of *lèse-majesté* and deserves the severest penalty with which the nation can visit traitors.

We advocate, finally, the creation of a strong central authority to carry out the will of the nation, supported by a close and active organisation of village, town, district and province. We desire to build up this organisation from the constitution the necessity of which the Congress has recognised and for which it has provided a meagre and imperfect beginning; but if, owing to Moderate obstruction, this constitution cannot develop or is not allowed to perform its true functions, the organisation and the authority must be built up otherwise by the people itself and, if necessary, outside the Congress.

The double policy of self-development and defensive resistance is the common standing-ground of the new spirit all over India. Some may not wish to go beyond its limits, others may look outside it; but so far all are agreed. For ourselves we avow that we advocate passive resistance without wishing to make a dogma of it. In a subject nationality, to win liberty for one's country is the first duty of all, by whatever means, at whatever sacrifice; and this duty must override all other considerations. The work of national emancipation is a great and holy *yajña* of which Boycott, Swadeshi, National Education and every other activity, great and small, are only major or minor parts. Liberty is the fruit we seek from the sacrifice and the Motherland the goddess to whom we offer it; into the seven leaping tongues of the fire of the *yajña* we must offer all that we are and all that we have, feeding the fire even with our blood and lives and happiness of our nearest and dearest; for the Motherland is a goddess who loves not a maimed and imperfect sacrifice, and freedom was never won from the gods by a grudging giver. But every great *yajña* has its Rakshasas who strive to baffle the sacrifice, to bespatter it with their own dirt or by guile or violence put out the flame. Passive resistance is an attempt to meet such disturbances by peaceful and self-contained *brahmatejas*; but even the greatest Rishis of old could not, when the Rakshasas were fierce and determined, keep up the sacrifice without calling in the bow of the Kshatriya. We should have the bow of the Kshatriya ready for use, though in the background. Politics is especially the business of the Kshatriya, and without Kshatriya strength at its back, all political struggle is unavailing.

Vedantism accepts no distinction of true or false religions, but considers only what will lead more or less surely, more or less quickly to *mokṣa*, spiritual emancipation and the realisation of the Divinity within. Our attitude is a political Vedantism. India, free, one and indivisible, is the divine realisation to which we move, emancipation our aim; to that end each nation must practise the political creed which is the most suited to its temperament and circumstances; for that is the best for it which leads most surely and completely to national liberty and national self-realisation. But whatever leads only to continued subjection must be spewed out as mere vileness and impurity. Passive resistance may be the final method of salvation in our case or it may be only the preparation for the final *sādhanā*. In either case, the sooner we put it into full and perfect practice, the nearer we shall be to national liberty.

23 April 1907

The Morality of Boycott

Ages ago there was a priest of Baal[1] who thought himself commissioned by the god to kill all who did not bow the knee to him. All men, terrified by the power and ferocity of the priest, bowed down before the idol and pretended to be his servants; and the few who refused had to take refuge in hills and deserts. At last a deliverer came and slew the priest and the world had rest. The slayer was blamed by those who placed religion in quietude and put passivity forward as the ideal ethics, but the world looked on him as an incarnation of God.

A certain class of minds shrink from aggressiveness as if it were a sin. Their temperament forbids them to feel the delight of battle and they look on what they cannot understand as something monstrous and sinful. 'Heal hate by love, drive out injustice by justice, slay sin by righteousness' is their cry. Love is a sacred name, but it is easier to speak of love than to love. The love which drives out hate, is a divine quality of which only one man in a thousand is capable. A saint full of love for all mankind possesses it, a philanthropist consumed with the desire to heal the miseries of the race possesses it, but the mass of mankind do not and cannot rise to that height. Politics is concerned with masses of mankind

---

[1] Written for the *Bande Mataram* probably in 1907 but not published; it was produced as an exhibit in the Alipore Bomb Case (May 1908) in connection with which Sri Aurobindo was arrested and imprisoned. Baal was a Canaanite deity.

and not with individuals, to ask masses of mankind to act as saints, to rise to the height of divine love and practise it in relation to their adversaries or oppressors is to ignore human nature. It is to set a premium on injustice and violence by paralysing the hand of the deliverer when raised to strike. The Gita is the best answer to those who shrink from battle as a sin and aggression as a lowering of morality.

A poet of sweetness and love who has done much to awaken Bengal, has written deprecating the Boycott as an act of hate.[2] The saintliness of spirit which he would see brought into politics is the reflex of his own personality colouring the political ideals of a sattwic race. But in reality the Boycott is not an act of hate. It is an act of self-defence, of aggression for the sake of self-preservation. To call it an act of hate is to say that a man who is being slowly murdered, is not justified in striking out at his murderer. To tell that man that he must desist from using the first effective weapon that comes to his hand because the blow would be an act of hate, is precisely on a par with this deprecation of boycott. Doubtless the self-defender is not precisely actuated by feelings of holy sweetness towards his assailant, but to expect so much from human nature is impracticable. Certain religions demand it, but they have never been practised to the letter by their followers.

Hinduism recognizes human nature and makes no such impossible demand. It sets one ideal for the saint, another for the man of action, a third for the trader, a fourth for the serf. To prescribe the same ideal for all is to bring about *varnasankara,* the confusion of duties, and destroy society and the race. If we are content to be serfs, then indeed boycott is a sin for us, not because it is a violation of love, but because it is a violation of the Sudra's duty of obedience and contentment. Politics is the field of the Kshatriya and the morality of the Kshatriya ought to govern

---

[2] Rabindranath Tagore (1861-1941).

our political actions. To impose on politics the Brahmanical duty of saintly sufferance, is to preach *varṇasaṇkara*.

Love has a place in politics, but it is the love for one's country, for one's countrymen, for the glory, greatness and happiness of the race, the divine *ānanda* of self-immolation for one's fellows, the ecstasy of relieving their sufferings, the joy of seeing one's blood flow for country and freedom, the bliss of union in death with the fathers of the race. The feeling of almost physical delight in the touch of the mother soil, of the winds that blow from Indian seas, of the rivers that stream from Indian hills, in the sight of Indian surroundings, Indian men, Indian women, Indian children, in the hearing of Indian speech, music, poetry, in the familiar sights, sounds, habits, dress, manners of our Indian life, this is the physical root of that love. The pride in our past, the pain of our present, the passion for the future are its trunk and branches. Self-sacrifice, self-forgetfulness, great service and high endurance for the country are its fruit. And the sap which keeps it alive is the realisation of the Motherhood of God in the country, the vision of the Mother, the knowledge of the Mother, the perpetual contemplation, adoration and service of the Mother.

Other love than this is foreign to the motives of political action. Between nation and nation there is justice, partiality, chivalry, duty but not love. All love is either individual or for the self in the race or for the self in mankind. It may exist between individuals of different races, but the love of one race for another is a thing foreign to nature. When, therefore, the Boycott as declared by the Indian race against the British is stigmatised for want of love, the charge is bad psychology as well as bad morality. It is interest warring against interest, and hatred is directed not really against the race but against the adverse interest. If the British exploitation were to cease tomorrow, the hatred against the British race would disappear in a moment. A partial *adhyāropa* makes the ignorant for the moment see in the exploiters and not in the exploitation the receptacle of the hostile feeling. But like all Maya it is an unreal and fleeting sentiment and is not shared by those who think. Not hatred against foreigners, but antipathy to the evils of foreign exploitation is the true root of Boycott.

If hatred is demoralising, it is also stimulating. The web of life has been made a mingled strain of good and evil and God works His ends through the evil as well as through the good. Let us discharge our minds of hate, but let us not deprecate a great and necessary movement because, in the inevitable course of human nature, it has engendered feelings of hostility and hatred. If hatred came, it was necessary that it should come as a stimulus, as a means of awakening. When *tamas,* inertia, torpor have benumbed a nation, the strongest forms of *rajas* are necessary to break the spell, and there is no form of *rajas* so strong as hatred. Through *rajas* we rise to *sattva,* and for the Indian temperament, the transition does not take long. Already the element of hatred is giving place to the clear conception of love for the Mother as the spring of our political actions.

Another question is the use of violence in the furtherance of Boycott. This is, in our view, purely a matter of policy and expediency. An act of violence brings us into conflict with the law and such a conflict may be inexpedient for a race circumstanced like ours. But the moral question does not arise. The argument that to use violence is to interfere with personal liberty involves a singular misunderstanding of the very nature of politics. The whole of politics is an interference with personal liberty. Law is such an interference, Protection is such an interference, the rule which makes the will of the majority prevail is such an interference. The right to prevent such use of personal liberty as will injure the interests of the race, is the fundamental law of society. From this point of view the nation is only using its primary right when it restrains the individual from buying or selling foreign goods.

It may be argued that peaceful compulsion is one thing and violent compulsion another. Social boycott may be justifiable, but not the burning or drowning of British goods. The latter method, we reply, is illegal and therefore may be inexpedient, but it is not morally unjustifiable. The morality of the Kshatriya justifies violence in times of war, and Boycott is a war. Nobody blames the Americans for throwing British tea into Boston harbour, nor can anybody blame similar action in India on moral grounds. It is reprehensible from the point of view of law, of social peace and order, not of political morality. It has been eschewed by us because it is unwise and carries the battle on to a ground where we are comparatively weak, from a ground where we are strong. Under other circumstances we might have followed the American precedent, and if we had done so, historians and moralists would have applauded, not censured.

Justice and righteousness are the atmosphere of political morality, but the justice and righteousness of the fighter, not of the priest. Aggression is unjust only when unprovoked, violence unrighteous when used wantonly or for unrighteous ends. It is a barren philosophy which applies a mechanical rule to all actions, or takes a word and tries to fit all human life into it. The sword of the warrior is as necessary to the fulfilment of justice and righteousness as the holiness of the saint. Ramdas[3] is not complete without Shivaji. To maintain justice and prevent the strong from despoiling and the weak from being oppressed is the function for which the Kshatriya was created. Therefore, says Sri Krishna in the Mahabharat, God created battle and armour, the sword, the bow and the dagger.

---

[3] Samartha Ramdas (1608-1681), a saint poet of Maharashtra and the guru of Shivaji (1627-1680), the Maratha ruler who founded an independent kingdom in the Deccan.

Mankind is of a less terrestrial mould than some would have him to be. He has an element of the divine which the practical politician ignores. The practical politician looks to the position at the moment and imagines that he has taken everything into consideration. He has indeed studied the surface and the immediate surroundings, but he has missed what lies beyond material vision. He has left out of account the divine, the incalculable in man, that element which upsets the calculations of the schemer and disconcerts the wisdom of the diplomat.

Asiatic Democracy[1]

Asia is not Europe and never will be Europe. The political ideals of the West are not the mainspring of the political movements in the East, and those who do not realise this great truth, are mistaken; for they suppose that the history of Europe is a sure and certain guide to India in her political development. A great deal of the political history of Europe will be repeated in Asia, no doubt; democracy has travelled from the East to the West in the shape of Christianity, and after a long struggle with the feudal instincts of the Germanic races has returned to Asia transformed and in a new body. But when Asia takes back democracy into herself she will first transmute it in her own temperament and make it once more Asiatic. Christianity was an assertion of human equality in the spirit, a great assertion of the unity of the divine spirit in man, which did not seek to overthrow the established systems of government and society but to inform them with the spirit of human brotherhood and unity. It was greatly hampered in this work by the fact that the European races were in a state of transition from the old Aryan civilisation of Greece and Rome to one less advanced and enlightened. The German nations were wedded to a military civilisation which was wholly inconsistent with the ideals of Christianity, and the new religion in their hands became a thing quite unrecognisable to the Asiatic mind which had engendered it. When Mahomedanism

---

[1] Published in the *Bande Mataram,* 16 March 1908.

16

appeared, Christianity vanished out of Asia, because it had lost its meaning. Mahomed tried to re-establish the Asiatic gospel of human equality in the spirit. All men are equal in Islam—whatever their social position or political power—nor is any man debarred from the full development of his manhood by his birth or low original station in life. All men are brothers in Islam and the bond of religious unity overrides all other divisions and differences. But Islam also was limited and imperfect, because it confined the ideal of brotherhood and equality to the limits of a single creed, and was further deflected from its true path by the rude and undeveloped races which it drew into its embrace. Another revelation of the old truth is needed.

India from ancient times had received the gospel of Vedanta which sought to establish the divine unity of man in spirit; but in order to secure an ordered society in which she could develop her spiritual insight and perfect her civilisation, she had invented the system of caste which by corruptions and departures from caste ideals came to be an obstacle to the fulfilment in society of the Vedantic ideal. From the time of Buddha to that of the saints of Maharashtra every great religious awakening has sought to restore the ancient meaning of Hinduism and reduce caste to its original subordinate importance as a social convenience, to exorcise the spirit of caste-pride and restore that of brotherhood and the eternal principles of love and justice in society. But the feudal spirit had taken possession of India and the feudal spirit is wedded to inequality and the pride of caste.

When the feudal system was broken in Europe by the rise of the middle class, the ideals of Christianity began to emerge once more to light, but by this time the Christian Church had itself become feudalised, and the curious spectacle presents itself of Christian ideals struggling to establish themselves by the destruction of the very institution which had been created to preserve Christianity. When the ideals of liberty, equality and fraternity were declared at the time of the French Revolution and mankind demanded that society should recognise them as the foundation of its structure, they were associated with a fierce revolt against the relics of feudalism and against the travesty of the Christian religion which had become an integral part of that feudalism. This was the weakness of European democracy and the source of its failure. It took as its motive the rights of man and not the *dharma* of humanity; it appealed to the selfishness of the lower classes against the pride of the upper; it made hatred and internecine war the permanent allies of Christian ideals and wrought an inextricable confusion which is the modern malady of Europe. It was in vain that the genius of Mazzini rediscovered the heart of Christianity and sought to remodel European ideas; the French Revolution had become the starting-point of European democracy and coloured the European mind. Now that democracy has returned to Asia, its cradle and home, it will be purged of its foreign elements and restored to its original purity. The movements of the nineteenth century in India were European movements, they were coloured with the hues of the West. Instead of seeking for strength in the spirit, they adopted the machinery and motives of Europe, the appeal to the rights of humanity or the equality of social status and an impossible dead level which Nature has always refused to allow. Mingled with these false gospels was a strain of hatred and bitterness, which showed itself in the condemnation of Brahminical priestcraft, the hostility to Hinduism and the ignorant breaking away from the hallowed traditions of the past. What was true and eternal in that past was likened to what was false or transitory, and the nation was in danger of losing its soul by an insensate surrender to the aberrations of European materialism. Not in this spirit was India intended to receive the mighty opportunity which the impact of Europe gave to her. When the danger was greatest, a number of great spirits were sent to stem the tide flowing in from the West and recall her to her mission; for, if she had gone astray the world would have gone astray with her.

Her mission is to point back humanity to the true source of human liberty, human equality, human brotherhood. When man is free in spirit, all other freedom is at his command; for the Free is the Lord who cannot be bound. When he is liberated from delusion, he perceives the divine equality of the world which fulfils itself through love and justice, and this perception transfuses itself into the law of government and society. When he has perceived this divine equality, he is brother to the whole world, and in whatever position he is placed he serves all men as his brothers by the law of love, by the law of justice. When this perception becomes the basis of religion, of philosophy, of social speculation and political aspiration, then will liberty, equality and fraternity take their place in the structure of society and the *satyayuga* return. This is the Asiatic reading of democracy which India must rediscover for herself before she can give it to the world. It is the *dharma* of every man to be free in soul, bound to service not by compulsion but by love; to be equal in spirit, apportioned his place in society by his capacity to serve society, not by the interested selfishness of others; to be in harmonious relations with his brother men, linked to them by mutual love and service, not by shackles of servitude, or the relations of the exploiter and the exploited, the eater and the eaten. It has been said that democracy is based on the rights of man; it has been replied that it should rather take its stand on the duties of man; but both rights and duties are European ideas. *Dharma* is the Indian conception in which rights and duties lose the artificial antagonism created by a view of the world which makes selfishness the root of action, and regain their deep and eternal unity. *Dharma* is the basis of democracy which Asia must recognise, for in this lies the distinction between the soul of Asia and the soul of Europe. Through *Dharma* the Asiatic evolution fulfils itself; this is her secret.

Uttarpara Speech

When I was asked to speak to you at the annual meeting of your *sabhā,* it was my intention to say a few words about the subject chosen for today—the subject of the Hindu religion. I do not know now whether I shall fulfil that intention; for as I sat here, there came into my mind a word that I have to speak to you, a word that I have to speak to the whole of the Indian Nation. It was spoken first to myself in jail and I have come out of jail to speak it to my people. It was more than a year ago that I came here last. When I came I was not alone; one of the mightiest prophets of Nationalism sat by my side. It was he who then came out of the seclusion to which God had sent him, so that in the silence and solitude of his cell he might hear the word that He had to say. It was he that you came in your hundreds to welcome. Now he is far away, separated from us by thousands of miles. Others whom I was accustomed to find working beside me are absent. The storm that swept over the country has scattered them far and wide. It is I this time who have spent one year in seclusion, and now that I come out I find all changed.[1] One who always sat by my side and was associated in my work is a prisoner in Burma; another is in the north rotting

---

[1] This speech was delivered in Uttarpara, near Calcutta, Bengal, on 30 May 1909 at the invitation of the town's Dharma Rakshini Sabha.
    Sri Aurobindo was arrested on 2 May 1908 and released on 6 May 1909.

in detention.[2] I looked round when I came out, I looked round for those to whom I had been accustomed to look for counsel and inspiration. I did not find them. There was more than that. When I went to jail, the whole country was alive with the cry of Bande Mataram, alive with the hope of a nation, the hope of millions of men who had newly risen out of degradation. When I came out of jail I listened for that cry, but there was instead a silence. A hush had fallen on the country and men seemed bewildered; for instead of God's bright heaven full of the vision of the future that had been before us, there seemed to be overhead a leaden sky from which human thunders and lightnings rained. No man seemed to know which way to move, and from all sides came the question, 'What shall we do next? What is there that we can do?' I too did not know which way to move, I too did not know what was next to be done. But one thing I knew, that as it was the Almighty Power of God which had raised that cry, that hope, so it was the same power which had sent down that silence. He who was in the shouting and the movement was also in the pause and the hush. He has sent it upon us, so that the nation might draw back for a moment and look into itself and know His will. I have not been disheartened by that silence, because I had been made familiar with silence in my prison and because I knew it was in the pause and the hush that I had myself learned this lesson through the long year of my detention. When Bipin Chandra Pal[3] came out of jail, he came with a message, and it was an inspired message. I remember the speech he made here. It was a speech not so much political as religious in its bearing and intention. He spoke of his realisation in jail, of God within us all, of the Lord within the nation, and in

---

[2] Shyamsundar Chakravarti was imprisoned in Burma and Subodh Chandra Malik in Bareilly and Almora. They were among the nine political leaders of Bengal arrested and deported without trial in December 1908.

[3] Bipin Chandra Pal (1858-1932) the prominent national leader who belonged to the extremist wing of the Congress.

his subsequent speeches also he spoke of a greater than ordinary force in the movement and a greater than ordinary purpose before it. Now I also meet you again, I also come out of jail, and again it is you of Uttarpara who are the first to welcome me, not at a political meeting but at a meeting of a society for the protection of our religion. That message which Bipin Chandra Pal received in Buxar jail, God gave to me in Alipore. That knowledge He gave to me day after day during my twelve months of imprisonment and it is that which He has commanded me to speak to you now that I have come out.

I knew I would come out. The year of detention was meant only for a year of seclusion and of training. How could anyone hold me in jail longer than was necessary for God's purpose? He had given me a word to speak and a work to do, and until that word was spoken I knew that no human power could hush me, until that work was done no human power could stop God's instrument, however weak that instrument might be or however small. Now that I have come out, even in these few minutes, a word has been suggested to me which I had no wish to speak. The thing I had in my mind He has thrown from it and what I speak is under an impulse and a compulsion.

When I was arrested and hurried to the Lal Bazar *hājat* I was shaken in faith for a while, for I could not look into the heart of His intention. Therefore I faltered for a moment and cried out in my heart to Him, 'What is this that has happened to me? I believed that I had a mission to work for the people of my country and until that work was done, I should have Thy protection. Why then am I here and on such a charge?' A day passed and a second day and a third, when a voice came to me from within, 'Wait and see.' Then I grew calm and waited. I was taken from Lal Bazar to Alipore and was placed for one month in a solitary cell apart from men. There I waited day and night for the voice of God within me, to know what He had to say to me, to learn what I had to do. In this seclusion the earliest realisation, the first lesson came to me. I remembered then that a month or more before my arrest, a call had come to me to put aside all activity, to go into seclusion and to look into myself, so that I might enter into closer communion with Him. I was weak and could not accept the call. My work was very dear to me and in the pride of my heart I thought that unless I was there, it would suffer or even fail and cease; therefore I would not leave it. It seemed to me that He spoke to me again and said, 'The bonds you had not strength to break, I have broken for you, because it is not my will nor was it ever my intention that that should continue. I have another thing for you to do and it is for that I have brought you here, to teach you what you could not learn for yourself and to train you for my work.' Then He placed the Gita in my hands. His strength entered into me and I was able to do the sadhana of the Gita. I was not only to understand intellectually but to realise what Sri Krishna demanded of Arjuna and what He demands of those who aspire to do His work, to be free from repulsion and desire, to do work for Him without the demand for fruit, to renounce self-will and become a passive and faithful instrument in His hands, to have an equal heart for high and low, friend and opponent, success and failure, yet not to do His work negligently. I realised what the Hindu religion meant. We speak often of the Hindu religion, of the *Sanātana Dharma*, but few of us really know what that religion is. Other religions are preponderatingly religions of faith and profession, but the Sanatana Dharma is life itself; it is a thing that has not so much to be believed as lived. This is the *dharma* that for the salvation of humanity was cherished in the seclusion of this peninsula from of old. It is to give this religion that India is rising. She does not rise as other countries do, for self or when she is strong, to trample on the weak. She is rising to shed the eternal light entrusted to her over the world. India has always existed for humanity and not for herself and it is for humanity and not for herself that she must be great.

Therefore this was the next thing He pointed out to me, He made me realise the central truth of the Hindu religion. He turned the hearts of my jailers to me and they spoke to the Englishman in charge of the jail, 'He is suffering in his confinement; let him at least walk outside his cell for half an hour in the morning and in the evening.' So it was arranged, and it was while I was walking that His strength again entered into me. I looked at the jail that secluded me from men and it was no longer by its high walls that I was imprisoned; no, it was Vasudeva who surrounded me. I walked under the branches of the tree in front of my cell, but it was not the tree, I knew it was Vasudeva, it was Sri Krishna whom I saw standing there and holding over me His shade. I looked at the bars of my cell, the very grating that did duty for a door and again I saw Vasudeva. It was Narayana who was guarding and standing sentry over me. Or I lay on the coarse blankets that were given me for a couch and felt the arms of Sri Krishna around me, the arms of my Friend and Lover. This was the first use of the deeper vision He gave me. I looked at the prisoners in the jail, the thieves, the murderers, the swindlers, and as I looked at them I saw Vasudeva, it was Narayana whom I found in these darkened souls and misused bodies. Amongst these thieves and dacoits there were many who put me to shame by their sympathy, their kindness, the humanity triumphant over such adverse circumstances. One I saw among them especially who seemed to me a saint, a peasant of my nation who did not know how to read and write, an alleged dacoit sentenced to ten years' rigorous imprisonment, one of those whom we look down upon in our Pharisaical pride of class as *chhotalok*. Once more He spoke to me and said, 'Behold the people among whom I have sent you to do a little of my work. This is the nature of the nation I am raising up and the reason why I raise them.'

When the case opened in the lower court and we were brought before the Magistrate I was followed by the same insight. He said to me, 'When you were cast into jail, did not your heart fail and did you not cry, out to me, where is Thy protection? Look now at the Magistrate, look now at the Prosecuting Counsel.' I looked and it was not the Magistrate whom I saw, it was Vasudeva, it was Narayana who was sitting there on the bench. I looked at the Prosecuting Counsel and it was not the Counsel for the prosecution that I saw; it was Sri Krishna who sat there, it was my Lover and Friend who sat there and smiled. 'Now do you fear?' He said, 'I am in all men and I overrule their actions and their words. My protection is still with you and you shall not fear. This case which is brought against you, leave it in My hands. It is not for you. It was not for the trial that I brought you here but for something else. The case itself is only a means for my work and nothing more.' Afterwards when the trial opened in the Sessions Court, I began to write many instructions for my Counsel as to what was false in the evidence against me and on what points the witnesses might be cross-examined. Then something happened which I had not expected. The arrangements which had been made for my defence were suddenly changed and another Counsel stood there to defend me. He came unexpectedly, a friend of mine, but I did not know he was coming. You have all heard the name of the man who put away from him all other thoughts and abandoned all his practice, who sat up half the night day after day for months and broke his health to save me, Srijut Chittaranjan Das.[4] When I saw him, I was satisfied, but I still thought it necessary to write instructions. Then all that was put from me and I had the message from within, 'This is the man who will save you from the snares put around your feet. Put aside those papers. It is not you who will instruct him. I will instruct him.' From that time I did not of myself speak a word to my Counsel about the case or give a single instruction and if ever I was

---

[4] Popularly known as Deshbandhu Chittaranjan Das (1870-1925), later became the most prominent leader of his time in Bengal and was Sri Aurobindo's defence lawyer in the Alipore Case.

asked a question, I always found that my answer did not help the case. I had left it to him and he took it entirely into his hands, with what result you know. I knew all along what He meant for me, for I heard it again and again, always I listened to the voice within: 'I am guiding, therefore fear not. Turn to your own work for which I have brought you to jail and when you come out, remember never to fear, never to hesitate. Remember that it is I who am doing this, not you nor any other. Therefore whatever clouds may come, whatever dangers and sufferings, whatever difficulties, whatever impossibilities, there is nothing impossible, nothing difficult. I am in the nation and its uprising and I am Vasudeva, I am Narayana, and what I will, shall be, not what others will. What I choose to bring about, no human power can stay.'

Meanwhile He had brought me out of solitude and placed me among those who had been accused along with me. You have spoken much today of my self-sacrifice and devotion to my country. I have heard that kind of speech ever since I came out of jail, but I hear it with embarrassment, with something of pain. For I know my weakness, I am a prey to my own faults and backslidings. I was not blind to them before and when they all rose up against me in seclusion, I felt them utterly. I knew then that I the man was a mass of weakness, a faulty and imperfect instrument, strong only when a higher strength entered into me. Then I found myself among these young men and in many of them I discovered a mighty courage, a power of self-effacement in comparison with which I was simply nothing. I saw one or two who were not only superior to me in force and character—very many were that—but in the promise of that intellectual ability on which I prided myself. He said to me, This is the young generation, the new and mighty nation that is arising at my command. They are greater than yourself. What have you to fear? If you stood aside or slept, the work would still be done. If you were cast aside tomorrow, here are the young men who will take up your work and do it more mightily than you have ever done. You have only got some strength from me to speak a word to this nation which will help to raise it.' This was the next thing He told me.

Then a thing happened suddenly and in a moment I was hurried away to the seclusion of a solitary cell. What happened to me during that period I am not impelled to say, but only this that day after day, He showed me His wonders and made me realise the utter truth of the Hindu religion. I had had many doubts before. I was brought up in England amongst foreign ideas and an atmosphere entirely foreign. About many things in Hinduism I had once been inclined to believe that it was all imagination; that there was much of dream in it, much that was delusion and *maya*. But now day after day I realised in the mind, I realised in the heart, I realised in the body the truths of the Hindu religion. They became living experiences to me, and things were opened to me which no material science could explain. When I first approached Him, it was not entirely in the spirit of the Bhakta, it was not entirely in the spirit of the Jñañi. I came to Him long ago in Baroda some years before the Swadeshi [movement] began and I was drawn into the public field.

When I approached God at that time, I hardly had a living faith in Him. The agnostic was in me, the atheist was in me, the sceptic was in me and I was not absolutely sure that there was a God at all. I did not feel His presence. Yet something drew me to the truth of the Vedas, the truth of the Gita, the truth of the Hindu religion. I felt there must be a mighty truth somewhere in this Yoga, a mighty truth in this religion based on the Vedanta. So when I turned to the Yoga and resolved to practise it and find out if my idea was right, I did it in this spirit and with this prayer to Him, 'If Thou art, then Thou knowest my heart. Thou knowest that I do not ask for Mukti, I do not ask for anything which others ask for. I ask only for strength to uplift this nation, I ask only to be allowed to live and work for this people whom I love and to whom I pray that

I may devote my life.' I strove long for the realisation of Yoga and at last to some extent I had it, but in what I most desired, I was not satisfied. Then in the seclusion of the jail, of the solitary cell, I asked for it again. I said, 'Give me Thy *adesh*. I do not know what work to do or how to do it. Give me a message.' In the communion of Yoga two messages came. The first message said, 'I have given you a work and it is to help to uplift this nation. Before long the time will come when you will have to go out of jail; for it is not My will that this time either you should be convicted or that you should pass the time as others have to do, in suffering for their country. I have called you to work, and that is the adesh for which you have asked. I give you the adesh to go forth and do My work.' The second message came and it said, 'Something has been shown to you in this year of seclusion, something about which you had your doubts and it is the truth of the Hindu religion. It is this religion that I am raising up before the world, it is this that I have perfected and developed through the rishis, saints and avatars, and now it is going forth to do my work among the nations. I am raising up this nation to send forth my word. This is the Sanatana Dharma, this is the eternal religion which you did not really know before, but which I have now revealed to you. The agnostic and the sceptic in you have been answered, for I have given you proofs within and without you, physical and subjective, which have satisfied you. When you go forth, speak to your nation always this word that it is for the Sanatana Dharma that they arise, it is for the world and not for themselves that they arise. I am giving them freedom for the service of the world. When therefore it is said that India shall rise, it is the Sanatana Dharma that shall rise. When it is said that India shall be great, it is the Sanatana Dharma that shall be great. When it is said that India shall expand and extend herself, it is the Sanatana Dharma that shall expand and extend itself over the world. It is for the *dharma* and by the *dharma* that India exists. To magnify the religion means to magnify the country. I have shown you that I am everywhere and in all men and in all things, that I am in this movement and I am not only working in those who are striving for the country but I am working also in those who oppose them and stand in their path. I am working in everybody and whatever men may think or do they can do nothing but help in My purpose. They also are doing My work; they are not My enemies but My instruments. In all your actions you are moving forward without knowing which way you move. You mean to do one thing and you do another. You aim at a result and your efforts subserve one that is different or contrary. It is Shakti that has gone forth and entered into the people. Since long ago I have been preparing this uprising and now the time has come and it is I who will lead it to its fulfilment.'

This then is what I have to say to you. The name of your society is 'Society for the Protection of Religion'. Well, the protection of the religion, the protection and upraising before the world of the Hindu religion, that is the work before us. But what is the Hindu religion? What is this religion which we call *sanātana,* eternal? It is the Hindu religion only because the Hindu nation has kept it, because in this peninsula it grew up in the seclusion of the sea and the Himalayas, because in this sacred and ancient land it was given as a charge to the Aryan race to preserve through the ages. But it is not circumscribed by the confines of a single country, it does not belong peculiarly and for ever to a bounded part of the world. That which we call the Hindu religion is really the eternal religion, because it is the universal religion which embraces all others. If a religion is not universal, it cannot be eternal. A narrow religion, a sectarian religion, an exclusive religion can live only for a limited time and a limited purpose. This is the one religion that can triumph over materialism by including and anticipating the discoveries of science and the speculations of philosophy. It is the one religion which impresses on mankind the closeness of God to us and embraces in its compass all the possible means by which man can approach God. It is the one religion which insists every moment on the truth which all religions acknowledge, that He is in all men and all things and that in Him we move and have our being. It is the one religion which enables us not only to understand and believe this truth but to realise it with every part of our being. It is the one religion which shows the world what the world is, that it is the *lila* of Vasudeva. It is the one religion which shows us how we can best play our part in that *lila,* its subtlest laws and its noblest rules. It is the one religion which does not separate life in any smallest detail from religion, which knows what immortality is and has utterly removed from us the reality of death.

This is the word that has been put into my mouth to speak to you today. What I intended to speak has been put away from me, and beyond what is given to me I have nothing to say. It is only the word that is put into me that I can speak to you. That word is now finished. I spoke once before with this force in me and I said then that this movement is not a political movement and that nationalism is not politics but a religion, a creed, a faith. I say it again today, but I put it in another way. I say no longer that nationalism is a creed, a religion, a faith; I say that it is the Sanatana Dharma which for us is nationalism. This Hindu nation was born with the Sanatana Dharma, with it it moves and with it it grows. When the Sanatana Dharma declines, then the nation declines, and if the Sanatana Dharma were capable of perishing, with the Sanatana Dharma it would perish. The Sanatana Dhanna, that is nationalism. This is the message that I have to speak to you.

The Ideal of the Karmayogin[1]

A nation is building in India today before the eyes of the world so swifly, so palpably that all can watch the process and those who have sympathy and intuition distinguish the forces at work, the materials in use, the lines of the divine architecture. This nation is not a new race raw from the workshop of Nature or created by modern circumstances. One of the oldest races and greatest civilisations on this earth, the most indomitable in vitality, the most fecund in greatness, the deepest in life, the most wonderful in potentiality, after taking into itself numerous sources of strength from foreign strains of blood and other types of human civilisation, is now seeking to lift itself for good into an organised national unity. Formerly a congeries of kindred nations with a single life and a single culture, always by the law of this essential oneness tending to unity, always by its excess of fecundity engendering fresh diversities and divisions, it has never yet been able to overcome permanently the almost insuperable obstacles to the organisation of a continent. The time has now come when those obstacles can be overcome. The attempt which our race has been making throughout its long history, it will now make under entirely new circumstances. A keen observer would predict its success because the only important obstacles have been or are in

---

[1] Published on 19 June 1909 in the first issue of the *Karmayogin*, a weekly newspaper edited by Sri Aurobindo.

the process of being removed. But we go farther and believe that it is sure to succeed because the freedom, unity and greatness of India have now become necessary to the world. This is the faith in which the *Karmayogin* puts its hand to the work and will persist in it, refusing to be discouraged by difficulties however immense and apparently insuperable. We believe that God is with us and in that faith we shall conquer. We believe that humanity needs us and it is the love and service of humanity, of our country, of the race, of our religion that will purify our heart and inspire our action in the struggle.

The task we set before ourselves is not mechanical but moral and spiritual. We aim not at the alteration of a form of government but at the building up of a nation. Of that task politics is a part, but only a part. We shall devote ourselves not to politics alone, nor to social questions alone, nor to theology or philosophy or literature or science by themselves, but we include all these in one entity which we believe to be all-important, the *dharma,* the national religion which we also believe to be universal. There is a mighty law of life, a great principle of human evolution, a body of spiritual knowledge and experience of which India has always been destined to be guardian, exemplar and missionary. This is the Sanatana Dharma, the eternal religion. Under the stress of alien impacts she has largely lost hold not of the structure of that *dharma,* but of its living reality. For the religion of India is nothing if it is not lived. It has to be applied not only to life, but to the whole of life; its spirit has to enter into and mould our society, our politics, our literature, our science, our individual character, affections and aspirations. To understand the heart of this *dharma,* to experience it as a truth, to feel the high emotions to which it rises and to express and execute it in life is what we understand by Karmayoga. We believe that it is to make the yoga the ideal of human life that India rises today; by the yoga she will get the strength to realise her freedom, unity and greatness, by the yoga she will keep the strength to preserve it. It is a spiritual revolution we foresee and the material is only its shadow and reflex.

The European sets great store by machinery. He seeks to renovate humanity by schemes of society and systems of government; he hopes to bring about the millennium by an act of Parliament. Machinery is of great importance, but only as a working means for the spirit within, the force behind. The nineteenth century in India aspired to political emancipation, social renovation, religious vision and rebirth, but it failed because it adopted Western motives and methods, ignored the spirit, history and destiny of our race and thought that by taking over European education, European machinery, European organisation and equipment we should reproduce in ourselves European prosperity, energy and progress. We of the twentieth century reject the aims, ideals and methods of the Anglicised nineteenth precisely because we accept its experience. We refuse to make an idol of the present; we look before and after, backward to the mighty history of our race, forward to the grandiose destiny for which that history has prepared it.

We do not believe that our political salvation can be attained by enlargement of Councils, introduction of the elective principle, colonial self-government or any other formula of European politics. We do not deny the use of some of these things as instruments, as weapons in a political struggle, but we deny their sufficiency whether as instruments or ideals and look beyond to an end which they do not serve except in a trifling degree. They might be sufficient if it were our ultimate destiny to be an outlying province of the British Empire or a dependent adjunct of European civilisation. That is a future which we do not think it worth making any sacrifice to accomplish. We believe on the other hand that India is destined to work out her own independent life and civilisation, to stand in the forefront of the world and solve the political, social, economical and moral problems which Europe has failed to solve, yet the pursuit of whose solution and the feverish passage in that pursuit from experiment to experiment, from failure to failure she calls her progress. Our means must be as great as our ends and the strength to discover and use the means so as to attain the end can only be found by seeking the eternal source of strength in ourselves.

We do not believe that by changing the machinery so as to make our society the ape of Europe we shall effect social renovation. Widow-remarriage, substitution of class for caste, adult marriage, intermarriages, interdining and the other nostrums of the social reformer are mechanical changes which, whatever their merits or demerits, cannot by themselves save the soul of the nation alive or stay the course of degradation and decline. It is the spirit alone that saves, and only by becoming great and free in heart can we become socially and politically great and free.

We do not believe that by multiplying new sects limited within the narrower and inferior ideas of religion imported from the West or by creating organisations for the perpetuation of the mere dress and body of Hinduism we can recover our spiritual health, energy and greatness. The world moves through an indispensable interregnum of free thought and materialism to a new synthesis of religious thought and experience, a new religious world-life free from intolerance, yet full of faith and fervour, accepting all forms of religion because it has an unshakable faith in the One. The religion which embraces Science and faith, Theism, Christianity, Mahomedanism and Buddhism and yet is none of these, is that to which the World-Spirit moves. In our own, which is the most sceptical and the most believing of all, the most sceptical because it has questioned and experimented the most, the most believing because it has the deepest experience and the most varied and positive spiritual knowledge—that wider Hinduism which is not a dogma or combination of dogmas but a law of life, which is not a social framework but the spirit of a past and future social evolution, which rejects nothing but insists on testing and experiencing everything and when tested and experienced turning it to the soul's uses, in this Hinduism we find the basis of the future world-religion. This Sanatana Dharma has many scriptures, *Veda, Vedanta, Gita, Upanishad, Darshana, Purana,* Tantra, nor could it reject the Bible or the Koran; but its real, most authoritative scripture is in the heart in which the Eternal has His dwelling. It is in our inner spiritual experiences that we shall find the proof and source of the world's Scriptures, the law of knowledge, love and conduct, the basis and inspiration of Karmayoga.

Our aim will therefore be to help in building up India for the sake of humanity—this is the spirit of the Nationalism which we profess and follow. We say to humanity, 'The time has come when you must take the great step and rise out of a material existence into the higher, deeper and wider life towards which humanity moves. The problems which have troubled mankind can only be solved by conquering the kingdom within, not by harnessing the forces of Nature to the service of comfort and luxury, but by mastering the forces of the intellect and the spirit, by vindicating the freedom of man within as well as without and by conquering from within external Nature. For that work the resurgence of Asia is necessary, therefore Asia rises. For that work the freedom and greatness of India is essential, therefore she claims her destined freedom and greatness, and it is to the interest of all humanity, not excluding England, that she should wholly establish her claim.'

We say to the nation, 'It is God's will that we should be ourselves and not Europe. We have sought to regain life by following the law of another being than our own. We must return and seek the sources of life and strength within ourselves. We must know our past and recover it for the purposes of our future. Our business is to realise ourselves first and to mould everything to the law of India's eternal life and nature. It will therefore be the object of the *Karmayogin* to read the heart of our religion, our society, our philosophy, politics, literature, art, jurisprudence, science, thought, everything that was and is ours, so that we may be able to say to ourselves and our nation, "This is our *dharma.*" We shall review European civilisation entirely from the standpoint of Indian thought and knowledge and seek to throw off from us the dominating stamp of the Occident; what we have to take from the West we shall take as Indians. And the *dharma* once discovered, we shall strive our utmost not only to profess but to live, in our individual actions, in our social life, in our political endeavours.'

We say to the individual and especially to the young who are now arising to do India's work, the world's work, God's work, 'You cannot cherish these ideals, still less can you fulfil them if you subject your minds to European ideas or look at life from the material standpoint. Materially you are nothing, spiritually you are everything. It is only the Indian who can believe everything, dare everything, sacrifice everything. First therefore become Indians. Recover the patrimony of your forefathers. Recover the Aryan thought, the Aryan discipline, the Aryan character, the Aryan life. Recover the Vedanta, the Gita, the Yoga. Recover them not only in intellect or sentiment but in your lives. Live them and you will be great and strong, mighty, invincible and fearless. Neither life nor death will have any terrors for you. Difficulty and impossibility will vanish from your vocabularies. For it is in the spirit that strength is eternal and you must win back the kingdom of yourselves, the inner Swaraj, before you can win back your outer empire. There the Mother dwells and She waits for worship that She may give strength. Believe in Her, serve Her, lose your wills in Hers, your egoism in the greater ego of the country, your separate selfishness in the service of humanity. Recover the source of all strength in yourselves and all else will be added to you, social soundness, intellectual pre-eminence, political freedom, the mastery of human thought, the hegemony of the world.'

The Hindu Sabha

An indication of the immense changes which are coming over our country, is the sudden leaping into being of new movements and organisations which are, by their very existence, evidence of revolutions in public feeling and omens of the future. The dead bones live indeed and the long sleep of the ages is broken. The Moslem League was indicative of much, the Hindu Sabha is indicative of yet more.[1] The Nationalist party, while in entire disagreement with the immediate objects and spirit of the League, welcomed its birth as a sign of renovated political life in the Mahomedan community. But the Mahomedan community was always coherent, united and separately self-conscious. The strength of Islam lay in its unity and cohesion, the fruit of a long discipline in equality and brotherhood, the strength of the Hindu in flexibility, progressiveness, elasticity, a divination of necessary changes, broad ideas, growing aspirations, the fruit of a long discipline in intellectual and moral sensitiveness. The Moslem League meant that the Mahomedan was awakening to the need

---

[1] Published on 6 November 1909 in the *Karmayogin*.
The Hindu Sabha, later known as the Hindu Mahasabha, was founded in 1906 ostensibly to protect and safeguard the interests of the Hindus. The All-India Muslim League, an organization to protect the political interests of the Muslims, was also founded in 1906 at the instance of Nawab Salimullah of Dacca. Later, the League, under the leadership of M.A. Jinnah spearheaded the movement for the formation of Pakistan.

of change, the growth of aspiration in the world around him—not yet to the broad ideas modern life demanded. The Hindu Sabha means that the Hindu is awakening to the need of unity and cohesion.

Does it mean more? Does it indicate a larger statesmanship, quicker impulse to action, a greater capacity for the unity and cohesion it seeks? Is the Hindu Sabha a novel body, with the power in it to effect a great object never before accomplished, the effective union of all shades of Hindu opinion from the lax Anglicised Agnostic, Hindu in nothing but birth and blood, to the intense and narrow worshipper of the institutes of Raghunandan?[2] Or is it merely an ineffectual aspiration, like the old Congress, capable of creating a general sympathy and oneness of aim, but not of practical purpose and effective organisation? There are only two things strong enough to unite Hinduism, a new spiritual impulse based on Vedanta, the essential oneness of man, the transience and utilitarian character of institutions, the lofty ideals of brotherhood, freedom, equality, and a recognition of the great mission and mighty future of Hindu spiritual ideas and discipline and of the Indian race—or else a political impulse strong enough to unite Hindus together for the preservation and advancement of their community. The Hindu Sabha could not have come into being but for the great national movement which awakened the national spirit, the sense of past greatness, the divination of a mighty future, transforming the whole spirit and character of the educated community. But we fear that in its immediate inception and work it leans for its hope of success on a lower and less powerful motive—rivalry with Mahomedan pretensions and a desire to put the mass and force of a united Hinduism against

---

[2] Popularly known as Smartha Bhattacharya, a famous writer on the Dharmashastras, supposedly a contemporary of Sri Chaitanya (c. 16th century).

the intensity of a Mahomedan self-assertion supported by official patronage and Anglo-Indian favour. Alarm and resentment at the pro-Mahomedan policy underlying the Reform Scheme and dissatisfaction with the Bombay conventionists for their suicidal support of the Government policy entered largely into the universal support given by Punjab Hindus to the new body and its great initial success. Mortification at the success of Mahomedans in securing Anglo-Indian sympathy and favour and the exclusion of Hindus from those blissful privileges figured largely in the speech of Sir Pratul Chandra Chatterji[3] who was hailed as the natural leader of Punjab Hinduism. These are not good omens. It is not by rivalry for Anglo-Indian favour, it is not by quarrelling for the loaves and fishes of British administration that Hinduism can rise into a united and effective force. If the Hindu Sabha takes its anchor on these petty aspirations or if it founds any part of its strength on political emulation with the Mahomedans, it will be impossible for the Nationalist party to join in a movement which would otherwise have their full sympathy and eager support.

Lala Lajpat Rai[4] struck a higher note, that of Hindu nationalism as a necessary preliminary to a greater Indian Nationality. We distrust this ideal. Not that we are blind to facts, not that we do not recognise Hindu-Mahomedan rivalry as a legacy of the past enhanced and not diminished by British ascendancy, a thing that has to be faced and worked out either by mutual concession or by a struggle between nationalism and separatism. But we do not understand Hindu nationalism as a possibility under modern conditions. Hindu nationalism had a meaning in the times of Shivaji and Ramdas, when the object of national revival was to overthrow a Mahomedan domination which, once tending to

---

[3] A leader of Hindus in Punjab who presided over the convocation of the Hindu Sabha in 1909.

[4] Lala Lajpat Rai (1865-1928) was a prominent Nationalist leader from Punjab.

Indian unity and toleration, had become oppressive and disruptive. It was possible because India was then a world to itself and the existence of two geographical units entirely Hindu, Maharashtra and Rajputana, provided it with a basis. It was necessary because the misuse of their domination by the Mahomedan element was fatal to India's future and had to be punished and corrected by the resurgence and domination of the Hindu. And because it was possible and necessary, it came into being. But under modern conditions India can only exist as a whole. A nation depends for its existence on geographical separateness and geographical compactness, on having a distinct and separate country. The existence of this geographical separateness is sure in the end to bear down all differences of race, language, religion, history. It has done so in Great Britain, in Switzerland, in Germany. It will do so in India. But geographical compactness is also necessary. In other words, the *desa* or country must be so compact that mutual communication and the organisation of a central government becomes easy or, at least, not prohibitively difficult. The absence of such compactness is the reason why great Empires are sure in the end to fall to pieces; they cannot get the support of that immortal and indestructible national self which can alone ensure permanence. This difficulty stands in the way of British Imperial Federation and is so great that any temporary success of that specious aspiration will surely result in the speedy disruption of the Empire. In addition, there must be a uniting force strong enough to take advantage of the geographical compactness and separateness, either a wise and skilfully organised government with a persistent tradition of beneficence, impartiality and oneness with the nation, or else a living national sense insisting on its separate inviolability and self-realisation. The secret of Roman success was in the organisation of such a government; even so, it failed, for want of geographical compactness, to create a world-wide Roman nationality. The failure of the British rule to root itself lies in its inability to become one with the nation either by the effacement of our national individuality or by the renunciation of its own separate pride and self-interest. These things are therefore necessary to Indian nationality, geographical separateness, geographical compactness and a living national spirit. The first was always ours and made India a people apart from the earliest times. The second we have attained by British rule. The third has just sprung into existence.

But the country, the Swadesh, which must be the base and fundament of our nationality, is India, a country where Mahomedan and Hindu live intermingled and side by side. What geographical base can a Hindu nationality possess? Maharashtra and Rajasthan are no longer separate geographical units but merely provincial divisions of a single country. The very first requisite of a Hindu nationalism is wanting. The Mahomedans base their separateness and their refusal to regard themselves as Indians first and Mahomedans afterwards on the existence of great Mahomedan nations to which they feel themselves more akin, in spite of our common birth and blood, than to us. Hindus have no such resource. For good or evil, they are bound to the soil and to the soil alone. They cannot deny their Mother, neither can they mutilate her. Our ideal therefore is an Indian Nationalism, largely Hindu in its spirit and traditions, because the Hindu made the land and the people and persists, by the greatness of his past, his civilisation and his culture and his invincible virility, in holding it, but wide enough also to include the Moslem and his culture and traditions and absorb them into itself. It is possible that the Mahomedan may not recognise the inevitable future and may prefer to throw himself into the opposite scale. If so, the Hindu, with what little Mahomedan help he may get, must win Swaraj both for himself and the Mahomedan in spite of that resistance. There is a sufficient force and manhood in us to do a greater and more difficult task than that, but we lack unity, brotherhood, intensity of single action among ourselves. It is to the creation of that unity, brotherhood and intensity that the Hindu Sabha should direct its whole efforts. Otherwise we must reject it as a disruptive and not a creative agency.

National Education[1]

Message for National Education Week

National Education is, next to self-government and along with it, the deepest and most immediate need of the country, and it is a matter of rejoicing for one to whom an earlier effort in that direction gave the first opportunity for identifying himself with the larger life and hope of the Nation, to see the idea, for a time submerged, moving so soon towards self-fulfilment.

Home Rule and National Education are two inseparable ideals, and none who follows the one, can fail the other, unless he is entirely wanting either in sincerity or in vision. We want not only a free India, but a great India, India taking worthily her place among the Nations and giving to the life of humanity what she alone can give. The greatest knowledge and the greatest riches man can possess are hers by inheritance; she has that for which all mankind is waiting. But she can only give it if her hands are free, her soul free, full and exalted, and her life dignified in all its parts. Home Rule, bringing with it the power of self-determination, can give the free hands, space for the soul to grow, strength for the life to raise itself again from darkness and narrow scope into light and nobility. But the full soul rich with the inheritance of the past, the widening gains of the present, and the large potentiality of

---

[1] First published in *New India,* edited by Annie Besant, on 8 April 1818.

the future, can come only by a system of National Education. It cannot come by any extension or imitation of the system of the existing universities with its radically false principles, its vicious and mechanical methods, its dead-alive routine tradition and its narrow and sightless spirit. Only a new spirit and a new body born from the heart of the Nation and full of the light and hope of its resurgence can create it.

We have a right to expect that the Nation will rise to the level of its opportunity and stand behind the movement as it has stood behind the movement for Home Rule. It should not be difficult to secure its intellectual sanction or its voice for National Education, but much more than that is wanted. The support it gives must be free from all taint of lip-service, passivity and lethargic inaction, evil habits born of long political servitude and inertia, and of that which largely led to it, subjection of the life and soul to a blend of unseeing and mechanical custom. Moral sympathy is not enough; active support from every individual is needed. Workers for the cause, money and means for its sustenance, students for its schools and colleges, are what the movement needs that it may prosper. The first will surely not be wanting; the second should come, for the control of the movement has in its personnel both influence and energy, and the habit of giving as well as self-giving for a great public cause is growing more widespread in the country. If the third condition is not from the beginning sufficiently satisfied, it will be because, habituated individually always to the customary groove, we prefer the safe and prescribed path, even when it leads nowhere, to the great and effective way, and cannot see our own interest because it presents itself in a new and untried form. But this is a littleness of spirit which the Nation must shake off that it may have the courage of its destiny.

If material and prudential considerations stand in the way, then let it be seen that, even in the vocational sphere, the old system opens only the doors of a few offices and professions over-crowded with applicants, whence the majority must go back disappointed and with empty hands, or be satisfied with a dwarfed life and a sordid pittance; while the new education will open careers which will be at once ways of honourable sufficiency, dignity and affluence to the individual, and paths of service to the country. For the men who come out equipped in every way from its institutions will be those who will give that impetus to the economic life and effort of the country without which it cannot survive in the press of the world, much less attain its high legitimate position. Individual interest and National interest are the same and call in the same direction. Whether as citizen, as worker or as parent and guardian, the duty of every Indian in this matter is clear: it lies in the great and new road the pioneers have been hewing, and not in the old stumbling cart-ruts.

This is an hour in which, for India as for all the world, its future destiny and the turn of its steps for a century are being powerfully decided, and for no ordinary century, but one which is itself a great turning-point, an immense turn-over in the inner and outer history of mankind. As we act now, so shall the reward of our Karma be meted out to us, and each call of this kind at such an hour is at once an opportunity, a choice, and a test offered to the spirit of our people. Let it be said that it rose in each to the full height of its being and deserved the visible intervention of the Master of Destiny in its favour.

Indian Culture and External Influence[1]

In considering Indian civilisation and its renascence, I suggested that a powerful new creation in all fields was our great need, the meaning of the renascence and the one way of preserving the civilisation. Confronted with the huge rush of modern life and thought, invaded by another dominant civilisation almost her opposite or inspired at least with a very different spirit to her own, India can only survive by confronting this raw, new, aggressive, powerful world with fresh diviner creations of her own spirit, cast in the mould of her own spiritual ideals. She must meet it by solving its greater problems—which she cannot avoid, even if such avoidance could be thought desirable—in her own way, through solutions arising out of her own being and from her own deepest and largest knowledge. In that connection I spoke of the acceptance and assimilation from the West of whatever in its knowledge, ideas, powers was assimilable, compatible with her spirit, reconcilable with her ideals, valuable for a new statement of life. This question of external influence and new creation from within is of very considerable importance; it calls for more than a passing mention. Especially it is necessary to form some more precise idea of what we mean by acceptance and of the actual effect of assimilation; for this is a problem of pressing incidence in which

[1] Published in the *Arya*, March 1919, and later included in *The Foundations of Indian Culture* (1953).

we have to get our ideas clear and fix firmly and seeingly [sic] on our line of solution.

But it is possible to hold that while new creation—and not a motionless sticking to old forms—is our one way of life and salvation, no acceptance of anything Western is called for, we can find in ourselves all that we need; no considerable acceptance is possible without creating a breach which will bring pouring in the rest of the occidental deluge. That, if I have not misread it, is the sense of a comment on these articles in a Bengali literary periodical[2] which holds up the ideal of a new creation to arise from within entirely on national lines and in the national spirit. The writer takes his stand on a position which is common ground, that humanity is one, but different peoples are variant soul-forms of the common humanity. When we find the oneness, the principle of variation is not destroyed but finds rather its justification; it is not by abolishing ourselves, our own special temperament and power, that we can get at the living oneness, but by following it out and raising it to its highest possibilities of freedom and action. That is a truth which I have myself insisted on repeatedly, with regard to the modern idea and attempt at some kind of political unification of humanity, as a very important part of the psychological sense of social development, and again in this question of a particular people's life and culture in all its parts and manifestations. I have insisted that uniformity is not a real but a dead unity: uniformity kills life while real unity, if well founded, becomes vigorous and fruitful by a rich energy of variation. But the writer adds that the idea of taking over what is best in occidental civilisation, is a false notion without a living meaning; to leave the bad and take the good sounds very well, but this bad and this good are not separable in that way: they are the inextricably mingled growth of one being, not separate blocks of a child's toy house set side by side and easily

---

[2] *Narayan*, edited by Mr C R Das. [Sri Aurobindo's note.]

detachable—and what is meant then by cutting out and taking one element and leaving the rest? If we take over a Western ideal, we take it over from a living form which strikes us; we imitate that form, are subjugated by its spirit and natural tendencies, and the good and bad intertwined in the living growth come in upon us together and take united possession. In fact, we have been for a long time so imitating the West, trying to become like it or partly like it and have fortunately failed, for that would have meant creating a bastard or two-natured culture; but two-natured, as Tennyson[3] makes his Lucretius say, is no-natured and a bastard culture is no sound, truth-living culture. An entire return upon ourselves is our only way of salvation.

There is much to be said here, it seems to me, both in the way of Confirmation and of modification. But let us be clear about the meaning of our terms. That the attempt in the last century which still in some directions continues—to imitate European civilisation and to make ourselves a sort of brown Englishmen, to throw our ancient culture into the dust-bin and put on the livery or uniform of the West was a mistaken and illegitimate endeavour, I heartily agree. At the same time a certain amount of imitation, a great amount even, was, one might almost say, a biological necessity, at any rate a psychological necessity of the situation. Not only when a lesser meets a greater culture, but when a culture which has fallen into a state of comparative inactivity, sleep, contraction, is faced with, still more when it receives the direct shock of a waking, active, tremendously creative civilisation, finds thrown upon it novel and successful powers and functionings, sees an immense succession and development of new ideas and formations, it is impelled by the very instinct of life to take over these ideas and

---

[3] Alfred, Lord Tennyson (1809-92), leading Victorian poet. Lucretius is the central character in Tennyson's monologue of the same title, published in 1868.

forms, to annex, to enrich itself, even to imitate and reproduce, and in one way or in another take large account and advantage of these new forces and opportunities.

That is a phenomenon which has happened repeatedly in history, in a greater or a lesser degree, in part or in totality. But if there is only a mechanical imitation, if there is a subordination and servitude, the inactive or weaker culture perishes, it is swallowed up by the invading leviathan. And even short of that, in proportion as there is a leaning towards these undesirable things, it languishes, is unsuccessful in its attempt at annexation, loses besides the power of its own spirit. To recover its own centre, find its own base and do whatever it has to do in its own strength and genius is certainly the one way of salvation. But even then a certain amount of acceptance, of forms too—some imitation, if all taking over of forms must be called imitation—is inevitable. We have, for instance, taken over in literature the form of the novel, the short story, the critical essay among a number of other adoptions, in science not only the discoveries and inventions, but the method and instrumentation of inductive research, in politics the press, the platform, the forms and habits of agitation, the public association. I do not suppose that anyone seriously thinks of renouncing or exiling these modern additions to our life— though they are not all of them by any means unmixed blessings—on the ground that they are foreign importations. But the question is what we do with them and whether we can bring them to be instruments and by some characteristic modification moulds of our own spirit. If so, there has been an acceptance and an assimilation; if not there has been merely a helpless imitation.

But the taking over of forms is not the heart of the question. When I speak of acceptance and assimilation, I am thinking of certain influences, ideas, energies brought forward with a great living force by Europe, which can awaken and enrich our own cultural activities and cultural being if we succeed in dealing with them with a victorious power and originality, if we can bring them into our characteristic way of being and transform them by its shaping action. That was in fact what our own ancestors did, never losing their originality, never effacing their uniqueness, because always vigorously creating from within, with whatever knowledge or artistic suggestion from outside they thought worthy of acceptance or capable of an Indian treatment. But I would certainly repel the formula of taking the good and leaving the bad as a crudity, one of those facile formulas which catch the superficial mind but are unsound in conception. Obviously, if we 'take over' anything, the good and the bad in it will come in together pell-mell. If we take over for instance that terrible, monstrous and compelling thing, that giant Asuric creation, European industrialism—unfortunately we are being forced by circumstances to do it—whether we take it in its form or its principle, we may under more favourable conditions develop by it our wealth and economic resources, but assuredly we shall get too its social discords and moral plagues and cruel problems, and I do not see how we shall avoid becoming the slaves of the economic aim in life and losing the spiritual principle of our culture.

But, besides, these terms good and bad in this connection mean nothing definite, give us no help. If I must use them, where they can have only a relative significance, in a matter not of ethics, but of an interchange between life and life, I must first give them this general significance that whatever helps me to find myself more intimately, nobly, with a greater and sounder possibility of self-expressive creation, is good; whatever carries me out of my orientation, whatever weakens and belittles my power, richness, breadth and height of self-being, is bad for me. If the distinction is so understood, it will be evident, I think, to any serious and critical mind which tries to fathom things, that the real point is not the taking over of this or that formal detail, which has only a sign value, for example, widow remarriage, but a dealing with great effective ideas, such as are the ideas, in the external field of life, of social and political liberty, equality, democracy. If I accept any of these ideas it is not because they are modern or European, which is in itself no recommendation, but because they are human, because they present fruitful view-points to the spirit, because they are things of the greatest importance in the future development of the life of man. What I mean by acceptance of the effective idea of democracy—the thing itself, never fully worked out, was present as an element in ancient Indian as in ancient European polity and society—is that I find its inclusion in our future way of living, in some shape, to be a necessity of our growth. What I mean by assimilation, is that we must not take it crudely in the European forms, but must go back to whatever corresponds to it, illumines its sense, justifies its highest purport in our own spiritual conception of life and existence, and in that light work out its extent, degree, form, relation to other ideas, application. To everything I would apply the same principle, to each in its own kind, after its proper *dharma,* in its right measure of importance, its spiritual, intellectual, ethical, aesthetic, dynamic utility.

I take it as a self-evident law of individual being applicable to group-individuality, that it is neither desirable nor possible to exclude everything that comes in to us from outside. I take it as an equally self-evident law that a living organism, which grows not by accretion, but by self-development and assimilation, must recast the things it takes in to suit the law and form and characteristic action of its biological or psychological body, reject what would be deleterious or poisonous to it—and what is that but the non-assimilable?— take only what can be turned into useful stuff of self-expression. It is, to use an apt Sanskritic phrase employed in the Bengali tongue, *ātmasātkaraṇa,* an assimilative appropriation, a making the thing settle into oneself and turn into the characteristic form of our self-being. The impossibility of entire rejection arises from the very fact of our being a term of diversity in a unity, not really separate from all other existence, but in relation with all that surrounds us, because in life this relation expresses itself very largely by a process of interchange. The undesirability of total rejection, even if it were entirely possible, arises from the fact that interchange with the environment is necessary to a healthy persistence and growth; the living organism which rejects all such interchange, would speedily languish and die of lethargy and inanition.

Mentally, vitally and physically I do not grow by a pure self-development from within in a virgin isolation; I am not a separate self-existent being proceeding from a past to a new becoming in a world of its own where no one is but itself, nothing works but its own inner powers and musings. There is in every individualised existence a double action, a self-development from within which is its greatest intimate power of being and by which it is itself, and a reception of impacts from outside which it has to accommodate to its own individuality and make into the material of self-growth and self-power. The two operations are not mutually exclusive, nor is the second harmful to the first except when the inner genius is too weak to deal victoriously with its environmental world; on the contrary the reception of impacts stimulates in a vigorous and healthy being its force for self-development and is an aid to a greater and more pronouncedly characteristic self-determination. As we rise in the scale we find that the power of original development from within, of conscious self-determination increases more and more, while in those who live most powerfully in themselves it reaches striking, sometimes almost divine proportions. But at the same time we see that the allied power of seizing upon the impacts and suggestions of the outside world grows in proportion; those who live most powerfully in themselves, can also most largely use the world and all its material for the Self—and, it must be added, most successfully help the world and enrich it out of their own being. The man who most finds and lives from the inner self, can most embrace the universal and become one with it; the *svarāṭ*, independent, self-possessed and self-ruler, can most be the *samrāṭ*, possessor and shaper of the world in which he lives, can most too grow one with all in the Atman. That is the truth this developing existence teaches us, and it is one of the greatest secrets of the old Indian spiritual knowledge.

Therefore to live in one's self, determining one's self-expression from one's own centre of being in accordance with one's own law of being, svadharma, is the first necessity. Not to be able to do that means disintegration of the life; not to do it sufficiently means languor, weakness, inefficiency, the danger of being oppressed by the environing forces and overborne; not to be able to do it wisely, intuitively, with a strong use of one's inner material and inner powers, means confusion, disorder and finally decline and loss of vitality. But also not to be able to use the material that the life around offers us, not to lay hold on it with an intuitive selection and a strong mastering assimilation is a serious deficiency and a danger to the existence. To a healthy individuality the external impact or entering energy, idea, influence may act as an irritant awakening the inner being to a sense of discord, incompatibility or peril, and then there is a struggle, an impulse and process of rejection; but even in this struggle, in this process of rejection there is some resultant of change and growth, some increment of the power and material of life; the energies of the being are stimulated and helped by the attack. It may act as a stimulus, awakening a new action of the self-consciousness and a sense of fresh possibility— by comparison, by suggestion, by knocking at locked doors and arousing slumbering energies. It may come in as a possible material which has then to be reshaped to a form of the inner energy, harmonised with the inner being, reinterpreted in the light of its own characteristic self-consciousness. In a great change of environment or a close meeting with a mass of invading influences all these processes work together and there is possibly much temporary perplexity and difficulty, many doubtful and perilous movements, but also the opportunity of a great self-developing transformation or an immense and vigorous renascence.

The group-soul differs from the individual only in being more self-sufficient by reason of its being an assemblage of many individual selves and capable within of many group variations. There is a constant inner interchange which may for a long time suffice to maintain the vitality, growth, power of developing activity, even when there is a restricted interchange with the rest of humanity. Greek civilisation—after growing under the influence of Egyptian, Phoenician and other oriental influences—separated itself sharply from the non-Hellenic 'barbarian' cultures and was able for some centuries to live within itself by a rich variation and internal interchange. There was the same phenomenon in ancient India of a culture living intensely from within in a profound differentiation from all surrounding cultures, its vitality rendered possible by an even greater richness of internal interchange and variation. Chinese civilisation offers a third instance. But at no time did Indian culture exclude altogether external influences; on the contrary a very great power of selective assimilation, subordination and transformation of external elements was a characteristic of its processes; it protected itself from any considerable or overwhelming invasion, but laid hands on and included whatever struck or impressed it and in the act of inclusion subjected it to a characteristic change which harmonised the new element with the spirit of its own culture. But nowadays any such strong separative aloofness as distinguished the ancient civilisations, is no longer possible; the races of mankind have come too close to each other, are being thrown together in a certain unavoidable life unity. We are confronted with the more difficult problem of living in the full stress of this greater interaction and imposing on its impacts the law of our being.

Any attempt to remain exactly what we were before the European invasion or to ignore in future the claims of a modern environment and necessity is foredoomed to an obvious failure. However much we may deplore some of the characteristics of that intervening period in which we were dominated by the Western standpoint or move away from the standpoint back to our own characteristic way of seeing existence, we cannot get rid of a certain element of inevitable change it has produced upon us, any more than a man can go back in life to what he was some years ago and recover entire and unaffected by a past mentality. Time and its influences have not only passed over him, but carried him forward in their stream. We cannot go backward to a past form of our being, but we can go forward to a large repossession of ourselves in which we shall make a better, more living, more real, more self-possessed use of the intervening experience. We can still think in the essential sense of the great spirit and ideals of our past, but the form of our thinking, our speaking, our development of them has changed by the very fact of new thought and experience; we see them not only in the old, but in new lights, we support them by the added strength of new view-points, even the old words we use acquire for us a modified, more extended and richer significance. Again, we cannot be 'ourselves alone' in any narrow formal sense, because we must necessarily take account of the modern world around us and get full knowledge of it, otherwise we cannot live. But all such taking account of things, all added knowledge modifies our subjective being. My mind, with all that depends on it, is modified by what it observes and works upon, modified when it takes in from it fresh materials of thought, modified when it is wakened by its stimulus to new activities, modified even when it denies and rejects; for even an old thought or truth which I affirm against an opposing idea, becomes a new thought to me in the effort of affirmation and rejection, clothes itself with new aspects and issues. My life is modified in the same way by the life influences it has to encounter and confront. Finally, we cannot avoid dealing with the great governing ideas and problems of the modern world. The modern world is still mainly European, a world dominated by the European mind and Western civilisation. We claim to set right this undue preponderance, to reassert the Asiatic and, for ourselves, the Indian mind and to preserve and develop the great values of Asiatic and of Indian civilisation. But the Asiatic or the Indian mind can only assert itself successfully by meeting these problems and by giving them a solution which will justify its own ideals and spirit.

The principle I have affirmed results both from the necessity of our nature and the necessity of things, of life—fidelity to our own spirit, nature, ideals, the creation of our own characteristic forms in the new age and the new environment, but also a strong and masterful dealing with external influences which need not be and in the nature of the situation cannot be a total rejection; therefore there must be an element of successful assimilation. There remains the very difficult question of the application of the principle—the degree, the way, the guiding perceptions. To think that out we must look at each province of culture and, keeping always firm hold on a perception of what the Indian spirit is and the Indian ideal is, see how they can work upon the present situation and possibilities in each of these provinces and lead to a new victorious creation. In such thinking it will not do to be too dogmatic. Each capable Indian mind must think it out or, better, work it out in its own light and power—as the Bengal artists are working it out in their own sphere—and contribute some illumination or effectuation. The spirit of the Indian renascence will take care of the rest, that power of the universal Time-Spirit which has begun to move in our midst for the creation of a new and greater India.

On the Vedas,
Upanishads, and the Gita

The Secret of the Veda: The Problem and Its Solution[1]

Is there at all or is there still a secret of the Veda? According to current conceptions the heart of that ancient mystery has been plucked out and revealed to the gaze of all, or rather no real secret ever existed. The hymns of the Veda are the sacrificial compositions of a primitive and still barbarous race written around a system of ceremonial and propitiatory rites, addressed to personified Powers of Nature and replete with a confused mass of half-formed myth and crude astronomical allegories yet in the making. Only in the later hymns do we perceive the first appearance of deeper psychological and moral ideas—borrowed, some think, from the hostile Dravidians, the 'robbers' and 'Veda-haters' freely cursed in the hymns themselves—and, however acquired, the first seed of the later Vedantic speculations. This modern theory is in accord with the received idea of a rapid human evolution from the quite recent savage; it is supported by an imposing apparatus of critical research and upheld by a number of Sciences, unhappily still young and still largely conjectural in their methods and shifting in their results—Comparative Philology, Comparative Mythology and the Science of Comparative Religion.

---

[1] This first chapter of *The Secret of the Veda* was published in the inaugural issue of the *Arya*, 15 August 1914.

It is my object in these chapters to suggest a new view of the ancient problem. I do not propose to use a negative and destructive method directed against the received solutions, but simply to present, positively and constructively, a larger and, in some sort, a complementary hypothesis built upon broader foundations—a hypothesis which, in addition, may shed light on one or two important problems in the history of ancient thought and cult left very insufficiently solved by the ordinary theories.

We have in the Rig Veda—the true and only Veda in the estimation of European scholars—a body of sacrificial hymns couched in a very ancient language which presents a number of almost insoluble difficulties. It is full of ancient forms and words which do not appear in later speech and have often to be fixed in some doubtful sense by intelligent conjecture; a mass even of the words that it has in common with classical Sanskrit seem to bear or at least to admit another significance than in the later literary tongue; and a multitude of its vocables, especially the most common, those which are most vital to the sense, are capable of a surprising number of unconnected significances which may give, according to our preference in selection, quite different complexions to whole passages, whole hymns and even to the whole thought of the Veda. In the course of several thousands of years there have been at least three considerable attempts, entirely differing from each other in their methods and results, to fix the sense of these ancient litanies. One of these is prehistoric in time and exists only by fragments in the Brahmanas and Upanishads; but we possess in its entirety the traditional interpretation of the Indian scholar Sayana[2] and we have in our own day the interpretation constructed after an immense labour of comparison and conjecture by modern European scholarship. Both of them present one characteristic in common, the extraordinary incoherence and poverty of sense

---

[2] Fourteenth-century author of a widely-respected commentary on the Vedas.

which their results stamp upon the ancient hymns. The separate lines can be given, whether naturally or by force of conjecture, a good sense or a sense that hangs together; the diction that results, if garish in style, if loaded with otiose and decorative epithets, if developing extraordinarily little of meaning in an amazing mass of gaudy figure and verbiage, can be made to run into intelligible sentences; but when we come to read the hymns as a whole we seem to be in the presence of men who, unlike the early writers of other races, were incapable of coherent and natural expression or of connected thought. Except in the briefer and simpler hymns, the language tends to be either obscure or artificial; the thoughts are either unconnected or have to be forced and beaten by the interpreter into a whole. The scholar in dealing with his text is obliged to substitute for interpretation a process almost of fabrication. We feel that he is not so much revealing the sense as hammering and forging rebellious material into some sort of shape and consistency.

Yet these obscure and barbarous compositions have had the most splendid good fortune in all literary history. They have been the reputed source not only of some of the world's richest and profoundest religions, but of some of its subtlest metaphysical philosophies. In the fixed tradition of thousands of years they have been revered as the origin and standard of all that can be held as authoritative and true in Brahmana and Upanishad, in Tantra and Purana, in the doctrines of great philosophical schools and in the teachings of famous saints and sages. The name borne by them was Veda, the knowledge—the received name for the highest spiritual truth of which the human mind is capable. But if we accept the current interpretations, whether Sayana's or the modern theory, the whole of this sublime and sacred reputation is a colossal fiction. The hymns are, on the contrary, nothing more than the naive superstitious fancies of untaught and materialistic barbarians concerned only with the most external gains and enjoyments and ignorant of all but the most elementary moral notions or religious aspirations. Nor do occasional passages, quite out of harmony with their general spirit, destroy this total impression. The true foundation or starting-point of the later religions and philosophies is the Upanishads, which have then to be conceived as a revolt of philosophical and speculative minds against the ritualistic materialism of the Vedas.

But this conception, supported by misleading European parallels, really explains nothing. Such profound and ultimate thoughts, such systems of subtle and elaborate psychology as are found in the substance of the Upanishads, do not spring out of a previous void. The human mind in its progress marches from knowledge to knowledge, or it renews and enlarges previous knowledge that has been obscured and overlaid, or it seizes on old imperfect clues and is led by them to new discoveries. The thought of the Upanishads supposes great origins anterior to itself, and these in the ordinary theories are lacking. The hypothesis, invented to fill the gap, that these ideas were borrowed by barbarous Aryan invaders from the civilised Dravidians, is a conjecture supported only by other conjectures. It is indeed coming to be doubted whether the whole story of an Aryan invasion through the Punjab is not a myth of the philologists.

Now, in ancient Europe the schools of intellectual philosophy were preceded by the secret doctrines of the mystics; Orphic and Eleusinian mysteries prepared the rich soil of mentality out of which sprang Pythagoras and Plato.[3] A similar starting-point is at least probable for the later march of thought in India. Much indeed of the forms and symbols of thought which we find in the

---

[3] Orphic mysteries were secret religious rites associated with the Greek god Dionysus. Eleusinian mysteries were religious rites involving the legends of Demeter, Persephone and Dionysus. Pythagoras (c. 582-507 bc) and Plato (427-347 bc) were major Greek philosophers whose writings contain certain mystical elements.

Upanishads, much of the substance of the Brahmanas supposes a period in India in which thought took the form or the veil of secret teachings such as those of the Greek mysteries.

Another hiatus left by the received theories is the gulf that divides the material worship of external Nature-Powers in the Veda from the developed religion of the Greeks and from the psychological and spiritual ideas we find attached to the functions of the Gods in the Upanishads and Puranas. We may accept for the present the theory that the earliest fully intelligent form of human religion is necessarily—since man on earth begins from the external and proceeds to the internal,—a worship of outward Nature-Powers invested with the consciousness and the personality that he finds in his own being.

Agni in the Veda is avowedly Fire; Surya is the Sun, Parjanya the Raincloud, Usha the Dawn; and if the material origin or function of some other Gods is less trenchantly clear, it is easy to render the obscure precise by philological inferences or ingenious speculation. But when we come to the worship of the Greeks not much later in date than the Veda, according to modern ideas of chronology, we find a significant change. The material attributes of the Gods are effaced or have become subordinate to psychological conceptions. The impetuous God of Fire has been converted into a lame God of Labour; Apollo, the Sun, presides over poetical and prophetic inspiration; Athene, who may plausibly be identified as in origin a Dawn-Goddess, has lost all memory of her material functions and is the wise, strong and pure Goddess of Knowledge; and there are other deities also, Gods of War, Love, Beauty, whose material functions have disappeared if they ever existed. It is not enough to say that this change was inevitable with the progress of human civilisation: the process also of the change demands inquiry and elucidation. We see the same revolution effected in the Puranas partly by the substitution of other divine names and figures, but also in part by the same obscure process that we observe in the evolution of Greek mythology. The river Saraswati has become the Muse and Goddess of Learning; Vishnu and Rudra of the Vedas are now the supreme Godhead, members of a divine Triad and expressive separately of the conservative and destructive process in the cosmos. In the Isha Upanishad we find an appeal to Surya as a God of revelatory knowledge by whose action we can arrive at the highest truth. This, too, is his function in the sacred Vedic formula of the Gayatri which was for thousands of years repeated by every Brahmin in his daily meditation; and we may note that this formula is a verse from the Rig Veda, from a hymn of the Rishi Vishwamitra.[4] In the same Upanishad, Agni is invoked for purely moral functions as the purifier from sin, the leader of the soul by the good path to the divine Bliss, and he seems to be identified with the power of the will and responsible for human actions. In other Upanishads the Gods are clearly the symbols of sense-functions in man. Soma, the plant which yielded the mystic wine for the Vedic sacrifice, has become not only the God of the moon, but manifests himself as mind in the human being. These evolutions suppose some period, posterior to the early material worship or superior Pantheistic Animism attributed to the Vedas and prior to the developed Puranic mythology, in which the gods became invested with deeper psychological functions, a period which may well have been the Age of the Mysteries. As things stand, a gap is left or else has been created by our exclusive preoccupation with the naturalistic element in the religion of the Vedic Rishis.

I suggest that the gulf is of our own creation and does not really exist in the ancient sacred writings. The hypothesis I propose is that the Rig Veda is itself the one considerable document that remains to us from the early period of human thought of which the historic Eleusinian and Orphic mysteries were the failing remnants, when the spiritual and psychological knowledge of the

---

[4] One of the seven ancient Rishis, he occupies a prominent place in the Rig Veda.

race was concealed, for reasons now difficult to determine, in a veil of concrete and material figures and symbols which protected the sense from the profane and revealed it to the initiated. One of the leading principles of the mystics was the sacredness and secrecy of self-knowledge and the true knowledge of the Gods. This wisdom was, they thought, unfit, perhaps even dangerous to the ordinary human mind or in any case liable to perversion and misuse and loss of virtue if revealed to vulgar and unpurified spirits. Hence they favoured the existence of an outer worship, effective but imperfect, for the profane, an inner discipline for the initiate, and clothed their language in words and images which had, equally, a spiritual sense for the elect, a concrete sense for the mass of ordinary worshippers. The Vedic hymns were conceived and constructed on this principle. Their formulas and ceremonies are, overtly, the details of an outward ritual devised for the Pantheistic Nature-Worship which was then the common religion, covertly the sacred words, the effective symbols of a spiritual experience and knowledge and a psychological discipline of self-culture which were then the highest achievement of the human race. The ritual system recognised by Sayana may, in its externalities, stand; the naturalistic sense discovered by European scholarship may, in its general conceptions, be accepted; but behind them there is always the true and still hidden secret of the Veda—the secret words, *ninyā vacāṁ si,* which were spoken for the purified in soul and the awakened in knowledge. To disengage this less obvious but more important sense by fixing the import of Vedic terms, the sense of Vedic symbols and the psychological functions of the Gods is thus a difficult but necessary task, for which these chapters and the translations that accompany them are only a preparation.

The hypothesis, if it proves to be valid, will have three advantages. It will elucidate simply and effectively the parts of the Upanishads that remain yet unintelligible or ill-understood as well as much of the origins of the Puranas. It will explain and justify rationally the whole ancient tradition of India; for it will be found that, in sober truth, the Vedanta, Purana, Tantra, the philosophical schools and the great Indian religions do go back in their source to Vedic origins. We can see there in their original seed or in their early or even primitive forms the fundamental conceptions of later Indian thought. Thus, a natural starting-point will be provided for a sounder study of Comparative Religion in the Indian field. Instead of wandering amid insecure speculations or having to account for impossible conversions and unexplained transitions we shall have a clue to a natural and progressive development satisfying to the reason. Incidentally, some light may be thrown on the obscurities of early cult and myth in other ancient nations. Finally, the incoherencies of the Vedic texts will at once be explained and disappear. They exist in appearance only, because the real thread of the sense is to be found in an inner meaning. That thread found, the hymns appear as logical and organic wholes and the expression, though alien in type to our modern ways of thinking and speaking, becomes, in its own style, just and precise and sins rather by economy of phrase than by excess, by over-pregnancy rather than by poverty of sense. The Veda ceases to be merely an interesting remnant of barbarism and takes rank among the most important of the world's early Scriptures.

A Retrospect of Vedic Theory[1]

Veda, then, is the creation of an age anterior to our intellectual philosophies. In that original epoch thought proceeded by other methods than those of our logical reasoning and speech accepted modes of expression which in our modern habits would be inadmissible. The wisest then depended on inner experience and the suggestions of the intuitive mind for all knowledge that ranged beyond mankind's ordinary perceptions and daily activities. Their aim was illumination, not logical conviction, their ideal the inspired seer, not the accurate reasoner. Indian tradition has faithfully preserved this account of the origin of the Vedas. The Rishi was not the individual composer of the hymn, but the seer (*dr.s.ṭā*) of an eternal truth and an impersonal knowledge. The language of Veda itself is *śruti*, a rhythm not composed by the intellect but heard, a divine Word that came vibrating out of the Infinite to the inner audience of the man who had previously made himself fit for the impersonal knowledge. The words themselves, *dr.s.ṭi* and *śruti*, sight and hearing, are Vedic expressions; these and cognate words signify, in the esoteric terminology of the hymns, revelatory knowledge and the contents of inspiration.

In the Vedic idea of the revelation there is no suggestion of the miraculous or the supernatural. The Rishi who employed these faculties had acquired them by a progressive self-culture.

---

[1] Chapter II of *The Secret of the Veda.*

Knowledge itself was a travelling and a reaching, or a finding and a winning; the revelation came only at the end, the light was the prize of a final victory. There is continually in the Veda this image of the journey, the soul's march on the path of Truth. On that path, as it advances, it also ascends; new vistas of power and light open to its aspiration; it wins by a heroic effort its enlarged spiritual possessions.

From the historical point of view the Rig Veda may be regarded as a record of a great advance made by humanity by special means at a certain period of its collective progress. In its esoteric, as well as its exoteric significance, it is the Book of Works, of the inner and the outer sacrifice; it is the spirit's hymn of battle and victory as it discovers and climbs to planes of thought and experience inaccessible to the natural or animal man, man's praise of the divine Light, Power and Grace at work in the mortal. It is far, therefore, from being an attempt to set down the results of intellectual or imaginative speculation, nor does it consist of the dogmas of a primitive religion. Only, out of the sameness of experience and out of the impersonality of the knowledge received, there arise a fixed body of conceptions constantly repeated and a fixed symbolic language which, perhaps, in that early human speech, was the inevitable form of these conceptions because alone capable by its combined concreteness and power of mystic suggestion of expressing that which for the ordinary mind of the race was inexpressible. We have, at any rate, the same notions repeated from hymn to hymn with the same constant terms and figures and frequently in the same phrases with an entire indifference to any search for poetical originality or any demand for novelty of thought and freshness of language. No pursuit of aesthetic grace, richness or beauty induces these mystic poets to vary the consecrated form which had become for them a sort of divine algebra transmitting the eternal formulae of the Knowledge to the continuous succession of the initiates.

The hymns possess indeed a finished metrical form, a constant subtlety and skill in their technique, great variations of style and poetical personality; they are not the work of rude, barbarous and primitive craftsmen, but the living breath of a supreme and conscious Art forming its creations in the puissant but well-governed movement of a self-observing inspiration. Still, all these high gifts have deliberately been exercised within one unvarying framework and always with the same materials. For the art of expression was to the Rishis only a means, not an aim; their principal preoccupation was strenuously practical, almost utilitarian, in the highest sense of utility. The hymn was to the Rishi who composed it a means of spiritual progress for himself and for others. It rose out of his soul, it became a power of his mind, it was the vehicle of his self-expression in some important or even critical moment of his life's inner history. It helped him to express the god in him, to destroy the devourer, the expresser of evil; it became a weapon in the hands of the Aryan striver after perfection, it flashed forth like Indra's lightning against the Coverer on the slopes, the Wolf on the path, the Robber by the streams.

The invariable fixity of Vedic thought when taken in conjunction with its depth, richness and subtlety, gives rise to some interesting speculations. For we may reasonably argue that such a fixed form and substance would not easily be possible in the beginnings of thought and psychological experience or even during their early progress and unfolding. We may therefore surmise that our actual Sanhita represents the close of a period, not its commencement, nor even some of its successive stages. It is even possible that its most ancient hymns are a comparatively modern development or version of a more ancient[2] lyric evangel

---

[2] The Veda itself speaks constantly of 'ancient' and 'modern' Rishis, (*pūrvebhiḥ . . . nūtanaiḥ*), the former remote enough to be regarded as a kind of demigods, the first founders of knowledge. [Sri Aurobindo's note]

couched in the freer and more pliable forms of a still earlier human speech. Or the whole voluminous mass of its litanies may be only a selection by Veda Vyasa out of a more richly vocal Aryan past. Made, according to the common belief, by Krishna of the Isle, the great traditional sage, the colossal compiler (Vyasa),[3] with his face turned towards the commencement of the Iron Age,[4] towards the centuries of increasing twilight and final darkness, it is perhaps only the last testament of the Ages of Intuition, the luminous Dawns of the Forefathers, to their descendants, to a human race already turning in spirit towards the lower levels and the more easy and secure gains—secure perhaps only in appearance—of the physical life and of the intellect and the logical reason.

But these are only speculations and inferences. Certain it is that the old tradition of a progressive obscuration and loss of the Veda as the law of the human cycle has been fully justified by the event. The obscuration had already proceeded far before the opening of the next great age of Indian spirituality, the Vedantic, which struggled to preserve or recover what it yet could of the ancient knowledge. It could hardly have been otherwise. For the system of the Vedic mystics was founded upon experiences difficult to ordinary mankind and proceeded by the aid of faculties which in most of us are rudimentary and imperfectly developed and, when active at all, are mixed and irregular in their operation. Once the first intensity of the search after truth had passed, periods of fatigue and relaxation were bound to intervene in which the old truths would be partially lost. Nor once lost, could they easily be recovered by scrutinising the sense of the ancient hymns; for those hymns were couched in a language that was deliberately ambiguous.

---

[3] Krishna Dvaipayana (c 5th cent. BC), traditionally considered the author and the compiler of the Vedas and the author of the *Mahabharata*.

[4] According to Hindu mythology, the degenerate 'Iron Age,' the last of the four ages in one cycle of creation.

A tongue unintelligible to us may be correctly understood once a clue has been found; a diction that is deliberately ambiguous, holds its secret much more obstinately and successfully, for it is full of lures and of indications that mislead. Therefore when the Indian mind turned again to review the sense of Veda, the task was difficult and the success only partial.

One source of light still existed, the traditional knowledge handed down among those who memorised and explained the Vedic text or had charge of the Vedic ritual—two functions that had originally been one; for in the early days the priest was also the teacher and seer. But the clearness of this light was already obscured. Even Purohits of repute performed the rites with a very imperfect knowledge of the power and the sense of the sacred words which they repeated. For the material aspects of Vedic worship had grown like a thick crust over the inner knowledge and were stifling what they had once served to protect. The Veda was already a mass of myth and ritual. The power had begun to disappear out of the symbolic ceremony; the light had departed from the mystic parable and left only a surface of apparent grotesqueness and naïveté.

The Brahmanas and the Upanishads are the record of a powerful revival which took the sacred text and ritual as a starting-point for a new statement of spiritual thought and experience. This movement had two complementary aspects, one, the conservation of the forms, another the revelation of the soul of Veda—the first represented by the Brahmanas,[5] the second by the Upanishads.

The Brahmanas labour to fix and preserve the minutiae of the Vedic ceremony, the conditions of their material effectuality, the

---

[5] Necessarily, these and other appreciations in the chapter are brief and summary views of certain main tendencies. The Brahmanas for instance have their philosophical passages. [Sri Aurobindo's note]

symbolic sense and purpose of their different parts, movements, implements, the significance of texts important in the ritual, the drift of obscure allusions, the memory of ancient myths and traditions. Many of their legends are evidently posterior to the hymns, invented to explain passages which were no longer understood; others may have been part of the apparatus of original myth and parable employed by the ancient symbolists or memories of the actual historical circumstances surrounding the composition of the hymns. Oral tradition is always a light that obscures; a new symbolism working upon an old that is half lost, is likely to overgrow rather than reveal it; therefore the Brahmanas, though full of interesting hints, help us very little in our research; nor are they a safe guide to the meaning of separate texts when they attempt an exact and verbal interpretation.

The Rishis of the Upanishads followed another method. They sought to recover the lost or waning knowledge by meditation and spiritual experience and they used the text of the ancient mantras as a prop or an authority for their own intuitions and perceptions; or else the Vedic Word was a seed of thought and vision by which they recovered old truths in new forms. What they found, they expressed in other terms more intelligible to the age in which they lived. In a certain sense their handling of the texts was not disinterested; it was not governed by the scholar's scrupulous desire to arrive at the exact intention of the words and the precise thought of the sentences in their actual framing. They were seekers of a higher than verbal truth and used words merely as suggestions for the illumination towards which they were striving. They knew not or they neglected the etymological sense and employed often a method of symbolic interpretation of component sounds in which it is very difficult to follow them. For this reason, while the Upanishads are invaluable for the light they shed on the principal ideas and on the psychological system of the ancient Rishis, they help us as little as the Brahmanas in determining the accurate sense of the texts which they quote. Their real work was to found Vedanta rather than to interpret Veda.

For this great movement resulted in a new and more permanently powerful statement of thought and spirituality, Veda culminating in Vedanta. And it held in itself two strong tendencies which worked towards the disintegration of the old Vedic thought and culture. First, it tended to subordinate more and more completely the outward ritual, the material utility of the mantra and the sacrifice to a more purely spiritual aim and intention. The balance, the synthesis preserved by the old Mystics between the external and the internal, the material and the spiritual life was displaced and disorganised. A new balance, a new synthesis was established, leaning finally towards asceticism and renunciation, and maintained itself until it was in its turn displaced and disorganised by the exaggeration of its own tendencies in Buddhism. The sacrifice, the symbolic ritual became more and more a useless survival and even an encumbrance; yet, as so often happens, by the very fact of becoming mechanical and ineffective the importance of everything that was most external in them came to be exaggerated and their minutiae irrationally enforced by that part of the national mind which still clung to them. A sharp practical division came into being, effective though never entirely recognised in theory, between Veda and Vedanta, a distinction which might be expressed in the formula, 'the Veda for the priests, the Vedanta for the sages.'

The second tendency of the Vedantic movement was to disencumber itself progressively of the symbolic language, the veil of concrete myth and poetic figure, in which the Mystics had shrouded their thought and to substitute a clearer statement and more philosophical language. The complete evolution of this tendency rendered obsolete the utility not only of the Vedic ritual but of the Vedic text. Upanishads, increasingly clear and direct in their language, became the fountainhead of the highest

Indian thought and replaced the inspired verses of Vasishtha and Vishwamitra.[6] The Vedas, becoming less and less the indispensable basis of education, were no longer studied with the same zeal and intelligence; their symbolic language, ceasing to be used, lost the remnant of its inner sense to new generations whose whole manner of thought was different from that of the Vedic forefathers. The Ages of Intuition were passing away into the first dawn of the Age of Reason.

Buddhism completed the revolution and left of the externalities of the ancient world only some venerable pomps and some mechanical usages. It sought to abolish the Vedic sacrifice and to bring into use the popular vernacular in place of the literary tongue. And although the consummation of its work was delayed for several centuries by the revival of Hinduism in the Puranic religions, the Veda itself benefited little by this respite. In order to combat the popularity of the new religion it was necessary to put forward instead of venerable but unintelligible texts Scriptures written in an easy form of a more modern Sanskrit. For the mass of the nation the Puranas pushed aside the Veda and the forms of new religious systems took the place of the ancient ceremonies. As the Veda had passed from the sage to the priest, so now it began to pass from the hands of the priest into the hands of the scholar. And in that keeping it suffered the last mutilation of its sense and the last diminution of its true dignity and sanctity.

Not that the dealings of Indian scholarship with the hymns, beginning from the pre-Christian centuries, have been altogether a record of loss. Rather it is to the scrupulous diligence and conservative tradition of the Pandits that we owe the preservation of Veda at all after its secret had been lost and the hymns themselves

---

[6] Again this expresses the main tendency and is subject to qualification. The Vedas are also quoted as authorities; but as a whole it is the Upanishads that become the Book of Knowledge, the Veda being rather the Book of Works. [Sri Aurobindo's note]. Vasishta and Vishwamitra were Vedic Rishis.

had ceased in practice to be a living Scripture. And even for the recovery of the lost secret the two millenniums of scholastic orthodoxy have left us some invaluable aids, a text determined scrupulously to its very accentuation, the important lexicon of Yaska[7] and Sayana's great commentary which in spite of its many and often startling imperfections remains still for the scholar an indispensable first step towards the formation of a sound Vedic learning.

---

[7] Yaska, (c 4th cent. CE) author of the *Nirukta*, the oldest surviving gloss on the Vedic hymns.

Selected Hymns[1]

The Colloquy of Indra and Agastya Rig Veda 1.70[2]

Indrah:
na nūnamasti no svah kastaveda yaddbhutam
anyasya cittamabhi sancarenyamutadhinam vi nasyati ||1 ||

1. It is not now, nor is It tomorrow; who knoweth that which is Supreme and Wonderful? It has motion and action in the consciousness of another, but when It is approached by the thought, It vanishes.

Agastya:
Kiṃ na indra jughaṃsasi bhrataro mimtastva
tebhih kalpasva sadhuyā mā nah samarane vadhiḥ ||2||

---

[1] From *The Secret of the Veda.*

[2] These translations are offered here only in their results for the interest of the general reader and as an illustration of the theory advanced. Their philological and critical justification would be interesting only to a limited circle. A few indications, however, may at a later stage be given which will illustrate the method. [Sri Aurobindo's note]

Agastya

2. Why dost thou seek to smite us, O Indra? The Maruts are thy
   brothers. By them accomplish perfection; slay us not in our
   struggle.

Indra:
Kiṃ no bhrātaragustya sakhā sannati manyane
vid-mā he te yathā manosmabhyaminna ditsasi ||3||
aram krnvantu vedim samagnimindhatām puruḥ
tatrā mrtasya cetanaṃ yajnaṃ te tanavā vahai ||4||

Indra

3. Why, O my brother Agastya, art thou my friend, yet settest thy
   thought beyond me? For well do I know how to us thou willest
   not to give thy mind.

4. Let them make ready the Altar, let them set Agni in blaze
   in front. It is there, the awakening of the consciousness to
   Immortality. Let us two extend for thee thy effective sacrifice.

Agastyah:
tvamīṣive vasupate tvaṃ mitrā nāṃ mitrapate dhéṣṭah:
indra tvaṃ marudbhiḥ saṃ vadasvādha prāṣāna
rtuthā havīṃṣi ||5||

5. O Lord of substance over all substances of being, thou art the
   master in force! O Lord of Love over the powers of love, thou
   art the strongest to hold in status! Do thou, O Indra, agree with
   the Maruts, then enjoy the offerings in the ordered method of
   the Truth.

Commentary

The governing idea of the hymn belongs to a stage of spiritual
progress when the human soul wishes by the sheer force of

Thought to hasten forward beyond in order to reach prematurely the source of all things without full development of the being in all its progressive stages of conscious activity. The effort is opposed by the gods who preside over the universe of man and of the world and a violent struggle takes place in the human consciousness between the individual soul in its egoistic eagerness and the universal Powers which seek to fulfil the divine purpose of the Cosmos.

The seer Agastya at such a moment confronts in his inner experience Indra,[3] Lord of Swar, the realm of pure intelligence, through which the ascending soul passes into the divine Truth.

Indra speaks first of that unknowable Source of things towards which Agastya is too impatiently striving. That is not to be found in Time. It does not exist in the actualities of the present, nor in the eventualities of the future. It neither is now nor becomes hereafter. Its being is beyond Space and Time and therefore in Itself cannot be known by that which is in Space and Time. It manifests itself by Its forms and activities in the consciousness of that which is not Itself and through those activities it is meant that It should be realised. But if one tries to approach It and study It in Itself, It disappears from the thought that would seize It and is as if It were not.

Agastya still does not understand why he is so violently opposed in a pursuit which is the eventual aim of all being and which all his thoughts and feelings demand. The Maruts are the powers of Thought which by the strong and apparently destructive motion of their progress break down that which is established and help to the attainment of new formations. Indra, the Power of pure Intelligence, is their brother, kin to them in his nature although elder in being. He should by their means effect the perfection towards which Agastya is striving and not turn enemy nor slay

---

[3] Agastya was a Vedic sage and Indra the chief of the Vedic gods.

his friend in this terrible struggle towards the goal. Indra replies that Agastya is his friend and brother— brother in the soul as children of one Supreme Being, friends as comrades in a common effort and one in the divine love that unites God and man—and by this friendship and alliance has attained to the present stage in his progressive perfection; but now he treats Indra as an inferior Power and wishes to go beyond without fulfilling himself in the domain of the God. He seeks to divert his increased thought-powers towards his own object instead of delivering them up to the universal Intelligence so that it may enrich its realisations in humanity through Agastya and lead him forward by the way of the Truth. Let the egoistic endeavour cease, the great sacrifice be resumed, the flame of the divine Force, Agni, be kindled in front as head of the sacrifice and leader of the march. Indra and Agastya together, the universal Power and the human soul, will extend in harmony the effective inner action on the plane of the pure Intelligence so that it may enrich itself there and attain beyond. For it is precisely by the progressive surrender of the lower being to the divine activities that the limited and egoistic consciousness of the mortal awakens to the infinite and immortal state which is its goal.

Agastya accepts the will of the God and submits. He agrees to perceive and fulfil the Supreme in the activities of Indra. From his own realm Indra is supreme lord over the substances of being as manifested through the triple world of mind, life and body and has therefore power to dispose of its formations towards the fulfilment, in the movement of Nature, of the divine Truth that expresses itself in the universe—supreme lord over love and delight manifested in the same triple world and has therefore power to fix those formations harmoniously in the status of Nature. Agastya gives up all that is realised in him into the hands of Indra, as offerings of the sacrifice, to be held by him in the fixed parts of Agastya's consciousness and directed in the motional towards fresh formations. Indra is once more to enter into friendly parley with the upward aspiring powers of Agastya's being and to establish agreement between the seer's thoughts and the illumination that comes to us through the pure Intelligence. That power will then enjoy in Agastya the offerings of the sacrifice according to the right order of things as formulated and governed by the Truth which is beyond.

The Discovery of the Absolute Brahman[1]

The idea of transcendental Unity, Oneness, and Stability behind all the flux and variety of phenomenal life is the basal idea of the Upanishads: this is the pivot of all Indian metaphysics, the sum and goal of our spiritual experience. To the phenomenal world around us stability and singleness seem at first to be utterly alien; nothing but passes and changes, nothing but has its counterparts, contrasts, harmonised and dissident parts; and all are perpetually shifting and rearranging their relative positions and affections. Yet if one thing is certain, it is that the sum of all this change and motion is absolutely stable, fixed and unvarying; that all this heterogeneous multitude of animate and inanimate things are fundamentally homogeneous and one. Otherwise nothing could endure, nor could there be any certainty in existence. And this unity, stability, unvarying fixity which reason demands, and ordinary experience points to, is being ascertained slowly but surely by the investigations of Science. We can no longer escape from the growing conviction that however the parts may change and shift and appear to perish, yet the sum and whole remains unchanged, undiminished and imperishable; however multitudinous, mutable and mutually irreconcilable forms and compounds may be, yet the grand substratum is one, simple and enduring; death itself is

---

[1] This is the first of a series of articles that Sri Aurobindo wrote when he was in Baroda (1893-1906) and published posthumously in the *Advent* in 1953.

not a reality but a seeming, for what appears to be destruction, is merely transformation and a preparation for rebirth. Science may not have appreciated the full import of her own discoveries; she may shrink from an unflinching acceptance of the logical results to which they lead; and certainly she is as yet far from advancing towards the great converse truths which they for the present conceal—for instance the wonderful fact that not only is death a seeming, but life itself is a seeming, and beyond life and death there lies a condition which is truer and therefore more permanent than either. But though Science dreams not as yet of her goal, her feet are on the road from which there is no turning back—the road which Vedanta on a different plane has already trod before it.

Here then is a great fundamental fact which demands from philosophy an adequate explanation of itself;—that all variations resolve themselves into an unity; that within the flux of things and concealed by it is an indefinable, immutable Something, at once the substratum and sum of all, which Time cannot touch, motion perturb, nor variation increase or diminish; and that this substratum and sum has been from all eternity and will be for all eternity. A fundamental fact to which all Thought moves, and yet is it not, when narrowly considered, an acute paradox? For how can the sum of infinite variations be a sempiternally fixed amount which has never augmented or decreased and can never augment or decrease? How can that whole be fixed and eternal of which every smallest part is eternally varying and perishing? Given a bewildering whirl of motion, how does the result come to be not merely now or as a result, but from beginning to end a perfect fixity? Impossible, unless either there be a guiding Power, for which at first sight there seems to be no room in the sempiternal chain of causation; or unless that sum and substratum be the one reality, imperishable because not conditioned by Time, indivisible because not conditioned by Space, immutable because not conditioned by causality—in a word absolute and transcendent and *therefore* eternal, unalterable and undecaying. Motion and change and death and division would then be merely transitory phenomena, masks and seemings of the One and Absolute, the as yet undefined and perhaps indefinable It which alone *is*.

To such a conclusion Indian speculation had turned at a very early period of its conscious strivings—uncertainly at first and with many gropings and blunders. The existence of some Oneness which gives order and stability to the multitudinous stir of the visible world, the Aryan thinkers were from the first disposed to envisage and they sought painfully to arrive at the knowledge of that Oneness in its nature or its essentiality. The living Forces of the Cosmos which they had long worshipped, yet always with a floating but persistent perception of an Unity in their multitude, melted on closer analysis into a single concept, a single Force or Presence, one and universal. The question then arose, Was that Force or Presence intelligent or non-intelligent? God or Nature? 'He alone,' hazarded the Rig Veda, 'knoweth, or perhaps He knoweth not.' Or might it not be that the Oneness which ties together and governs phenomena and rolls out the evolution of the worlds, is really the thing we call *Time*, since of the three original conditions of phenomenal existence, Time, Space and Causality, Time is a necessary part of the conception of Causality and can hardly be abstracted from the conception of Space, but neither Space nor Causality seems necessary to the conception of Time? Or if it be not Time, might it not be *svabhāva*, the essential Nature of Things taking various conditions and forms? Or perhaps *Chance*, some blind principle working out an unity and law in things by infinite experiment— this too might be possible. Or since from eternal uncertainty eternal certainty cannot come, might it not be *Fate*, a fixed and unalterable law in things in subjection to which this world evolves itself in a preordained procession of phenomena from which it cannot deviate? Or perhaps in the original atomic fountain of things certain *Elements* might be discovered which by perpetual and infinite combinations and permutations keep the universe to its workings? But if so, these elements must themselves proceed from something which imposes on them the law of their being, and what could that be but the *Womb,* the matrix of original and indestructible Matter, the plasm which moulds the universe and out of which it is moulded? And yet in whatever scheme of things the mind might ultimately rest, some room surely must be made for these conscious, thinking and knowing *Egos* of living beings, of whom knowledge and thought seem to be the essential selves and without whom this world of perceivable and knowable things could not be perceived and known—and if not perceived and known, might it not be that without them it could not even exist?

Such were the gurges [sic; surges] of endless speculation in which the old Aryan thinkers, tossed and perplexed, sought for some firm standing-ground, some definite clue which might save them from being beaten about like stumbling blind men led by a guide as blind. They sought at first to liberate themselves from the tyranny of appearances by the method which Kapila, the ancient prehistoric Master of Thought, had laid down for mankind, the method called Sankhya or the law of Enumeration. The method of Kapila consisted in guidance by pure discriminative reason and it took its name from one of its principal rules, the law of enumeration and generalisation. They enumerated first the immediate Truths-in-Things which they could distinguish or deduce from things obviously phenomenal, and from these by generalisation they arrived at a much smaller number of ulterior Truths-in-Things of which the immediate were merely aspects. And then having enumerated these ulterior Truths-in-Things, they were able by generalisation to reduce them to a very small number of ultimate Truths-in-Things, the Tattwas (literally That-nesses) of the developed Sankhya philosophy. And these Tattwas once enumerated with some approach to certainty, was it not possible

to generalise yet one step farther? The Sankhya did so generalise
and by this supreme and final generalisation arrived at the very
last step on which, in its own unaided strength, it could take safe
footing. This was the great principle of Prakriti, the single eternal
indestructible principle and origin of Matter which by perpetual
evolution rolls out through aeons and aeons the unending
panorama of things.[2] And for whose benefit? Surely for those
conscious knowing and perceiving Egos, the army of witnesses,
who, each in his private space of reasoning and perceiving Mind
partitioned off by an enveloping medium of gross matter, sit for
ever as spectators in the theatre of the Universe! For ever, thought
the Sankhyas, since the Egos, though their partitions are being
continually broken down and built anew and the spaces occupied
never remain permanently identical, yet seem themselves to be no
less eternal and indestructible than Prakriti.

This then was the wide fixed lake of ascertained philosophical
knowledge into which the method of Sankhya, pure intellectual
reasoning on definite principles, led in the mind of ancient India.
Branchings off, artificial canals from the reservoir were not,
indeed, wanting. Some by resolving that army of witnesses into a
single Witness, arrived at the dual conception of God and Nature,
Purusha and Prakriti, Spirit and Matter, Ego and Non-ego.
Others, more radical, perceived Prakriti as the creation, shadow
or aspect of Purusha, so that God alone remained, the spiritual or
ideal factor eliminating by inclusion the material or real. Solutions
were also attempted on the opposite side; for some eliminated the
conscious Egos themselves as mere seemings; not a few seem to
have thought that each ego is only a series of successive shocks
of consciousness and the persistent sense of identity no more

---

[2] Note that Matter here not only includes gross matter with which Western
Science is mainly concerned, but subtle matter, the material in which thought
and feeling work, and causal matter in which the fundamental operations of
the Will-to-live are conducted. [Sri Aurobindo's note]

than an illusion due to the unbroken continuity of the shocks. If these shocks of consciousness are borne in on the brain from the changes of Prakriti in the multitudinous stir of evolution, then is consciousness one out of the many terms of Prakriti itself, so that Prakriti alone remains as the one reality, the material or real factor eliminating by inclusion the spiritual or ideal. But if we deny, as many did, that Prakriti is an ultimate reality apart from the perceptions of Purushas and yet apply the theory of a false notion of identity created by successive waves of sensation, we arrive at the impossible and sophistic position of the old Indian Nihilists whose reason by a singular suicide landed itself in Nothingness as the cradle and bourne, nay, the very stuff and reality of all existence. And there was a third direction in which thought tended and which led it to the very threshold of Vedanta; for this also was a possible speculation that Prakriti and Purusha might both be quite real and yet not ultimately different aspects or sides of each other and so, after all, of a Oneness higher than either. But these speculations, plausible or imperfect, logical or sophistic, were yet mere speculations; they had no basis either in observed fact or in reliable experience. Two certainties seemed to have been arrived at, Prakriti was testified to by a close analysis of phenomenal existence; it was the basis of the phenomenal world which without a substratum of original matter could not be accounted for and without a fundamental oneness and indestructibility in that substratum could not be what observation showed it to be, subject, namely, to fixed laws and evidently invariable in its sum and substance. On the other hand Purushas were testified to by the eternal persistence of the sense of individuality and identity whether during life or after death[3] and by the necessity of a

---

[3] Survival of the human personality after death has always been held in India to be a proved fact beyond all dispute; the Charvaka denial of it was condemned as mere irrational and wilful folly. Note however that survival after death

perceiving cause for the activity of Prakriti; they were the receptive and contemplative Egos within the sphere of whose consciousness Prakriti, stirred to creative activity by their presence, performed her long drama of phenomenal Evolution.

But meanwhile the seers of ancient India had, in their experiments and efforts at spiritual training and the conquest of the body, perfected a discovery which in its importance to the future of human knowledge dwarfs the divinations of Newton and Galileo; even the discovery of the inductive and experimental method in Science was not more momentous; for they discovered down to its ultimate processes the method of Yoga and by the method of Yoga they rose to three crowning realisations. They realised first as a fact the existence under the flux and multitudinousness of things of that supreme Unity and immutable Stability which had hitherto been posited only as a necessary theory, an inevitable generalisation. They came to know that It is the one reality and all phenomena merely its seemings and appearances, that It is the true Self of all things and phenomena are merely its clothes and trappings. They learned that It is absolute and transcendent and, because absolute and transcendent, therefore eternal, immutable, imminuable [sic] and indivisible. And looking back on the past progress of speculation they perceived that this also was the goal to which pure intellectual reasoning would have led them. For that which is in Time must be born and perish; but the Unity and Stability of things is eternal and must therefore transcend Time. That which is in Space must increase and diminish, have parts and relations, but the Unity and Stability of things is imminuable, not augmentable, independent of the changefulness of its parts and untouched by the shifting of their relations, and must therefore transcend Space—and if it transcends Space, cannot really have

---

does not necessarily to the Indian mind imply immortality, but only raises a presumption in its favour. [Sri Aurobindo's note]

parts, since Space is the condition of material divisibility; divisibility therefore must be, like death, a seeming and not a reality. Finally that which is subject to Causality, is necessarily subject to Change; but the Unity and Stability of things is immutable, the same now as it was aeons ago and will be aeons hereafter, and must therefore transcend Causality.

This then was the first realisation through Yoga, *nityo'nityānām*, the One Eternal in many transient.

At the same time they realised one truth more—a surprising truth; they found that the transcendent absolute Self of things was also the Self of living beings, the Self too of man, that highest of the beings living in the material plane on earth. The Purusha or conscious Ego in man which had perplexed and baffled the Sankhyas, turned out to be precisely the same in his ultimate being as Prakriti the apparently non-conscious source of things; the non-consciousness of Prakriti, like so much else, was proved a seeming and no reality, since behind the inanimate form a conscious Intelligence at work is to the eyes of the Yogin luminously self-evident.

This then was the second realisation through Yoga, *cetanaś cetanā nām*, the One Consciousness in many Consciousnesses.

Finally at the base of these two realisations was a third, the most important of all to our race—that the Transcendent Self in individual man is as complete *because identically the same* as the Transcendent Self in the Universe; for the Transcendent is indivisible and the sense of separate individuality is only one of the fundamental seemings on which the manifestation of phenomenal existence perpetually depends. In this way the Absolute which would otherwise be beyond knowledge, becomes knowable; and the man who knows his whole Self knows the whole Universe. This stupendous truth is enshrined to us in the two famous formulae of Vedanta, *so'ham*, He am I, and *aham brahma asmi*, I am Brahman, the Eternal.

Based on these four grand truths, *nityo'nityā nām, cetanaś cetanā nām, so'harn, aharn brahma asmi,* as upon four mighty pillars the lofty philosophy of the Upanishads raises its front among the distant stars.

Our Demand and Need from the Gita[1]

The world abounds with scriptures sacred and profane, with revelations and half-revelations, with religions and philosophies, sects and schools and systems. To these the many minds of a half-ripe knowledge or no knowledge at all attach themselves with exclusiveness and passion and will have it that this or the other book is alone the eternal Word of God and all others are either impostures or at best imperfectly inspired, that this or that philosophy is the last word of the reasoning intellect and other systems are either errors or saved only by such partial truth in them as links them to the one true philosophical cult. Even the discoveries of physical Science have been elevated into a creed and in its name religion and spirituality banned as ignorance and superstition, philosophy as frippery and moonshine. And to these bigoted exclusions and vain wranglings even the wise have often lent themselves, misled by some spirit of darkness that has mingled with their light and overshadowed it with some cloud of intellectual egoism or spiritual pride. Mankind seems now indeed inclined to grow a little modester and wiser; we no longer slay our fellows in the name of God's truth or because they have minds differently trained or differently constituted from ours; we are

---

[1] The first chapter of *Essays on the Gita* published in the *Arya* in August 1916. The entire book was published in one volume by the Sri Aurobindo Library, New York, in 1950.

less ready to curse and revile our neighbour because he is wicked or presumptuous enough to differ from us in opinion; we are ready even to admit that Truth is everywhere and cannot be our sole monopoly; we are beginning to look at other religions and philosophies for the truth and help they contain and no longer merely in order to damn them as false or criticise what we conceive to be their errors. But we are still apt to declare that our truth gives us *the* supreme knowledge which other religions or philosophies have missed or only imperfectly grasped so that they deal either with subsidiary and inferior aspects of the truth of things or can merely prepare less evolved minds for the heights to which we have arrived. And we are still prone to force upon ourselves or others the whole sacred mass of the book or gospel we admire, insisting that all shall be accepted as eternally valid truth and no iota or underline or diaeresis denied its part of the plenary inspiration.

It may therefore be useful in approaching an ancient Scripture, such as the Veda, Upanishads or Gita, to indicate precisely the spirit in which we approach it and what exactly we think we may derive from it that is of value to humanity and its future. First of all, there is undoubtedly a Truth one and eternal which we are seeking, from which all other truth derives, by the light of which all other truth finds its right place, explanation and relation to the scheme of knowledge. But precisely for that reason it cannot be shut up in a single trenchant formula, it is not likely to be found in its entirety or in all its bearings in any single philosophy or scripture or uttered altogether and for ever by any one teacher, thinker, prophet or Avatar. Nor has it been wholly found by us if our view of it necessitates the intolerant exclusion of the truth underlying other systems; for when we reject passionately, we mean simply that we cannot appreciate and explain. Secondly, this Truth, though it is one and eternal, expresses itself in Time and through the mind of man; therefore every Scripture must necessarily contain two elements, one temporary, perishable, belonging to the ideas of the period and country in which it was produced, the other eternal and imperishable and applicable in all ages and countries. Moreover, in the statement of the Truth the actual form given to it, the system and arrangement, the metaphysical and intellectual mould, the precise expression used must be largely subject to the mutations of Time and cease to have the same force; for the human intellect modifies itself always; continually dividing and putting together it is obliged to shift its divisions continually and to rearrange its syntheses; it is always leaving old expression and symbol for new or, if it uses the old, it so changes its connotation or at least its exact content and association that we can never be quite sure of understanding an ancient book of this kind precisely in the sense and spirit it bore to its contemporaries. What is of entirely permanent value is that which besides being universal has been experienced, lived and seen with a higher than the intellectual vision.

I hold it therefore of small importance to extract from the Gita its exact metaphysical connotation as it was understood by the men of the time—even if that were accurately possible. That it is not possible, is shown by the divergence of the original commentaries which have been and are still being written upon it; for they all agree in each disagreeing with all the others, each finds in the Gita its own system of metaphysics and trend of religious thought. Nor will even the most painstaking and disinterested scholarship and the most luminous theories of the historical development of Indian philosophy save us from inevitable error. But what we can do with profit is to seek in the Gita for the actual living truths it contains, apart from their metaphysical form, to extract from it what can help us or the world at large and to put it in the most natural and vital form and expression we can find that will be suitable to the mentality and helpful to the spiritual needs of our present-day humanity. No doubt in this attempt we may mix a good deal of error born of our own individuality and of the ideas in which we live, as did greater men before us, but if we steep ourselves in the spirit of this great Scripture and, above all, if we have tried to live in that spirit, we may be sure of finding in it as much real truth as we are capable of receiving as well as the spiritual influence and actual help that, personally, we were intended to derive from it. And that is after all what Scriptures were written to give; the rest is academical disputation or theological dogma. Only those Scriptures, religions, philosophies which can be thus constantly renewed, relived, their stuff of permanent truth constantly reshaped and developed in the inner thought and spiritual experience of a developing humanity, continue to be of living importance to mankind. The rest remain as monuments of the past, but have no actual force or vital impulse for the future.

In the Gita there is very little that is merely local or temporal and its spirit is so large, profound and universal that even this little can easily be universalised without the sense of the teaching suffering any diminution or violation; rather by giving an ampler scope to it than belonged to the country and epoch, the teaching gains in depth, truth and power. Often indeed the Gita itself suggests the wider scope that can in this way be given to an idea in itself local or limited. Thus it dwells on the ancient Indian system and idea of sacrifice as an interchange between gods and men—a system and idea which have long been practically obsolete in India itself and are no longer real to the general human mind; but we find here a sense so entirely subtle, figurative and symbolic given to the word 'sacrifice' and the conception of the gods is so little local or mythological, so entirely cosmic and philosophical that we can easily accept both as expressive of a practical fact of psychology and general law of Nature and so apply them to the modern conceptions of interchange between life and life and of ethical sacrifice and self-giving as to widen and deepen these and cast over them a more spiritual aspect and the light of a profounder and more far-reaching Truth. Equally the idea of action according to the Shastra, the fourfold order of society, the allusion to the relative position of the four orders or the comparative spiritual disabilities of Shudras and women seem at first sight local and temporal, and, if they are too much pressed in their literal sense, narrow so much at least of the teaching, deprive it of its universality and spiritual depth and limit its validity for mankind at large. But if we look behind to the spirit and sense and not at the local name and temporal institution, we see that here too the sense is deep and true and the spirit philosophical, spiritual and universal. By Shastra we perceive that the Gita means the law imposed on itself by humanity as a substitute for the purely egoistic action of the natural unregenerate man and a control on his tendency to seek in the satisfaction of his desire the standard and aim of his life. We see too that the fourfold order of society is merely the concrete form of a spiritual truth which is itself independent of the form; it rests on the conception of right works as a rightly ordered expression of the nature of the individual being through whom the work is done, that nature assigning him his line and scope in life according to his inborn quality and his self-expressive function. Since this is the spirit in which the Gita advances its most local and particular instances, we are justified in pursuing always the same principle and looking always for the deeper general truth which is sure to underlie whatever seems at first sight merely local and of the time. For we shall find always that the deeper truth and principle is implied in the grain of the thought even when it is not expressly stated in its language.

Nor shall we deal in any other spirit with the element of philosophical dogma or religious creed which either enters into the Gita or hangs about it owing to its use of the philosophical terms and religious symbols current at the time. When the Gita speaks of Sankhya and Yoga, we shall not discuss beyond the limits of what is just essential for our statement, the relations of the Sankhya of the Gita with its one Purusha and strong Vedantic colouring to the non-theistic or 'atheistic' Sankhya that has come down to us bringing with it its scheme of many Purushas and one Prakriti, nor of the Yoga of the Gita, many-sided, subtle, rich and flexible to the theistic doctrine and the fixed, scientific, rigorously defined and graded system of the Yoga of Patanjali. In the Gita the Sankhya and Yoga are evidently only two convergent parts of the same Vedantic truth or rather two concurrent ways of approaching its realisation, the one philosophical, intellectual, analytic, the other intuitional, devotional, practical, ethical, synthetic, reaching knowledge through experience. The Gita recognises no real difference in their teachings. Still less need we discuss the theories which regard the Gita as the fruit of some particular religious system or tradition. Its teaching is universal whatever may have been its origins.

The philosophical system of the Gita, its arrangement of truth, is not that part of its teaching which is the most vital, profound, eternally durable; but most of the material of which the system is composed, the principal ideas suggestive and penetrating which are woven into its complex harmony, are eternally valuable and valid; for they are not merely the luminous ideas or striking speculations of a philosophic intellect, but rather enduring truths of spiritual experience, verifiable facts of our highest psychological possibilities which no attempt to read deeply the mystery of existence can afford to neglect. Whatever the system may be, it is not, as the commentators strive to make it, framed or intended to support any exclusive school of philosophical thought or to put forward predominantly the claims of any one form of Yoga. The language of the Gita, the structure of thought, the combination and balancing of ideas belong neither to the temper of a sectarian teacher nor to the spirit of a rigorous analytical dialectics cutting off one angle of the truth to exclude all the others; but rather there is a wide, undulating, encircling movement of ideas which is the manifestation of a vast synthetic mind and a rich synthetic experience. This is one of those great syntheses in which Indian spirituality has been as rich as in its creation of the more intensive, exclusive movements of knowledge and religious realisation that follow out with an absolute concentration one clue, one path to its extreme issues. It does not cleave asunder, but reconciles and unifies.

The thought of the Gita is not pure Monism although it sees in one unchanging, pure, eternal Self the foundation of all cosmic existence, nor Mayavada although it speaks of the Maya of the three modes of Prakriti omnipresent in the created world; nor is it qualified Monism although it places in the One his eternal supreme Prakriti manifested in the form of the Jiva and lays most stress on dwelling in God rather than dissolution as the supreme state of spiritual consciousness; nor is it Sankhya although it explains the created world by the double principle of Purusha and Prakriti; nor is it Vaishnava Theism although it presents to us Krishna, who is the Avatara of Vishnu according to the Puranas, as the supreme Deity and allows no essential difference nor any actual superiority of the status of the indefinable relationless Brahman over that of this Lord of beings who is the Master of the universe and the Friend of all creatures. Like the earlier spiritual synthesis of the Upanishads this later synthesis at once spiritual and intellectual avoids naturally every such rigid determination as would injure its universal comprehensiveness. Its aim is precisely the opposite to that of the polemist commentators who found this Scripture established as one of the three highest Vedantic authorities and attempted to turn it into a weapon of offence and defence against other schools and systems. The Gita is not a weapon for dialectical warfare; it is a gate opening on the whole world of spiritual truth and experience and the view it gives us embraces all the provinces of that supreme region. It maps out, but it does not cut up or build walls or hedges to confine our vision. There have been other syntheses in the long history of Indian thought. We start with the Vedic synthesis of the psychological being of man in its highest flights and widest rangings of divine knowledge, power, joy, life and glory with the cosmic existence of the gods, pursued behind the symbols of the material universe into those superior planes which are hidden from the physical sense and the material mentality. The crown of this synthesis was in the experience of the Vedic Rishis something divine, transcendent and blissful in whose unity the increasing soul of man and the eternal divine fullness of the cosmic godheads meet perfectly and fulfil themselves. The Upanishads take up this crowning experience of the earlier seers and make it their starting-point for a high and profound synthesis of spiritual knowledge; they draw together into a great harmony all that had been seen and experienced by the inspired and liberated knowers of the Eternal throughout a great and fruitful period of spiritual seeking. The Gita starts from this Vedantic synthesis and upon the basis of its essential ideas builds another harmony of the three great means and powers, Love, Knowledge and Works, through which the soul of man can directly approach and cast itself into the Eternal. There is yet another, the Tantric,[2] which though less subtle and spiritually profound, is even more bold and forceful than the synthesis of the Gita—for it seizes even upon the obstacles to the spiritual life and compels them to become the means for a richer spiritual conquest and enables us to embrace the whole of Life in our divine scope as the Lila[3] of the Divine; and in some directions it is more immediately rich and fruitful, for it brings forward into the foreground along with divine knowledge, divine works and an enriched devotion of divine Love, the secrets also of the Hatha and Raja Yogas, the use of the body and of mental askesis for the opening up of the divine life on all its planes,

---

[2] All the Puranic tradition, it must be remembered, draws the richness of its contents from the Tantra. [Sri Aurobindo's note]

[3] The cosmic Play. [Sri Aurobindo's note]

to which the Gita gives only a passing and perfunctory attention. Moreover it grasps at that idea of the divine perfectibility of man, possessed by the Vedic Rishis but thrown into the background by the intermediate ages, which is destined to fill so large a place in any future synthesis of human thought, experience and aspiration.

We of the coming day stand at the head of a new age of development which must lead to such a new and larger synthesis. We are not called upon to be orthodox Vedantins of any of the three schools or Tantrics or to adhere to one of the theistic religions of the past or to entrench ourselves within the four corners of the teaching of the Gita. That would be to limit ourselves and to attempt to create our spiritual life out of the being, knowledge and nature of others, of the men of the past, instead of building it out of our own being and potentialities. We do not belong to the past dawns, but to the noons of the future. A mass of new material is flowing into us; we have not only to assimilate the influences of the great theistic religions of India and of the world and a recovered sense of the meaning of Buddhism, but to take full account of the potent though limited revelations of modern knowledge and seeking; and, beyond that, the remote and dateless past which seemed to be dead is returning upon us with an effulgence of many luminous secrets long lost to the consciousness of mankind but now breaking out again from behind the veil. All this points to a new, a very rich, a very vast synthesis; a fresh and widely embracing harmonisation of our gains is both an intellectual and a spiritual necessity of the future. But just as the past syntheses have taken those which preceded them for their starting-point, so also must that of the future, to be on firm ground, proceed from what the great bodies of realised spiritual thought and experience in the past have given. Among them the Gita takes a most important place.

Our object, then, in studying the Gita will not be a scholastic or academical scrutiny of its thought, nor to place its philosophy in the history of metaphysical speculation, nor shall we deal with it in the manner of the analytical dialectician. We approach it for help and light and our aim must be to distinguish its essential and living message, that in it on which humanity has to seize for its perfection and its highest spiritual welfare.

The Core of the Teaching[1]

We know the divine Teacher, we see the human disciple; it remains to form a clear conception of the doctrine. A clear conception fastening upon the essential idea, the central heart of the teaching is especially necessary here because the Gita with its rich and many-sided thought, its synthetical grasp of different aspects of the spiritual life and the fluent winding motion of its argument lends itself, even more than other scriptures, to one-sided misrepresentations born of a partisan intellectuality. The unconscious or half-conscious wresting of fact and word and idea to suit a preconceived notion or the doctrine or principle of one's preference is recognised by Indian logicians as one of the most fruitful sources of fallacy; and it is perhaps the one which it is most difficult for even the most conscientious thinker to avoid. For the human reason is incapable of always playing the detective upon itself in this respect; it is its very nature to seize upon some partial conclusion, idea, principle, become its partisan and make it the key to all truth, and it has an infinite faculty of doubling upon itself so as to avoid detecting in its operations this necessary and cherished weakness. The Gita lends itself easily to this kind of error, because it is easy, by throwing particular emphasis on one of its aspects or even on some salient and emphatic text and putting all the rest of the eighteen chapters into the background or making them a

---

[1] Chapter IV of *Essays on the Gita*.

subordinate and auxiliary teaching, to turn it into a partisan of our own doctrine or dogma.

Thus, there are those who make the Gita teach, not works at all, but a discipline of preparation for renouncing life and works: the indifferent performance of prescribed actions or of whatever task may lie ready to the hands, becomes the means, the discipline; the final renunciation of life and works is the sole real object. It is quite easy to justify this view by citations from the book and by a certain arrangement of stress in following out its argument, especially if we shut our eyes to the peculiar way in which it uses such a word as *sannyāsa*, renunciation; but it is quite impossible to persist in this view on an impartial reading in face of the continual assertion to the very end that action should be preferred to inaction and that superiority lies with the true, the inner renunciation of desire by equality and the giving up of works to the supreme Purusha. Others again speak of the Gita as if the doctrine of devotion were its whole teaching and put in the background its monistic elements and the high place it gives to quietistic immergence in the one self of all. And undoubtedly its emphasis on devotion, its insistence on the aspect of the Divine as Lord and Purusha and its doctrine of the Purushottama, the Supreme Being who is superior both to the mutable Being and to the Immutable and who is what in His relation to the world we know as God, are the most striking and among the most vital elements of the Gita. Still, this Lord is the Self in whom all knowledge culminates and the Master of sacrifice to whom all works lead as well as the Lord of Love into whose being the heart of devotion enters, and the Gita preserves a perfectly equal balance, emphasising now knowledge, now works, now devotion, but for the purposes of the immediate trend of the thought, not with any absolute separate preference of one over the others. He in whom all three meet and become one, He is the Supreme Being, the Purushottama.

But at the present day, since in fact the modern mind began to recognise and deal at all with the Gita, the tendency is to subordinate its elements of knowledge and devotion, to take advantage of its continual insistence on action and to find in it a scripture of the Karmayoga, a Light leading us on the path of action, a Gospel of Works. Undoubtedly, the Gita is a Gospel of Works, but of works which culminate in knowledge, that is, in spiritual realisation and quietude, and of works motived by devotion, that is, a conscious surrender of one's whole self first into the hands and then into the being of the Supreme, and not at all of works as they are understood by the modern mind, not at all an action dictated by egoistic and altruistic, by personal, social, humanitarian motives, principles, ideals. Yet this is what present-day interpretations seek to make of the Gita. We are told continually by many authoritative voices that the Gita, opposing in this the ordinary ascetic and quietistic tendency of Indian thought and spirituality, proclaims with no uncertain sound the gospel of human action, the ideal of disinterested performance of social duties, nay, even, it would seem, the quite modern ideal of social service. To all this I can only reply that very patently and even on the very surface of it the Gita does nothing of the kind and that this is a modern misreading, a reading of the modern mind into an ancient book, of the present-day European or Europeanised intellect into a thoroughly antique, a thoroughly Oriental and Indian teaching. That which the Gita teaches is not a human, but a divine action; not the performance of social duties, but the abandonment of all other standards of duty or conduct for a selfless performance of the divine will working through our nature; not social service, but the action of the Best, the God-possessed, the Master-men done impersonally for the sake of the world and as a sacrifice to Him who stands behind man and Nature.

In other words, the Gita is not a book of practical ethics, but of the spiritual life. The modern mind is just now the European mind, such as it has become after having abandoned not only the philosophic idealism of the highest Graeco-Roman culture from which it started, but the Christian devotionalism of the Middle Ages; these it has replaced by or transmuted into a practical idealism and social, patriotic and philanthropic devotion. It has got rid of God or kept Him only for Sunday use and erected in His place man as its deity and society as its visible idol. At its best it is practical, ethical, social, pragmatic, altruistic, humanitarian. Now all these things are good, are especially needed at the present day, are part of the divine Will or they would not have become so dominant in humanity. Nor is there any reason why the divine man, the man who lives in the Brahmic consciousness, in the God-being should not be all of these things in his action; he will be, if they are the best ideal of the age, the Yugadharma, and there is no yet higher ideal to be established, no great radical change to be effected. For he is, as the Teacher points out to his disciple, the best who has to set the standard for others; and in fact Arjuna is called upon to live according to the highest ideals of his age and the prevailing culture, but with knowledge, with understanding of that which lay behind, and not as ordinary men, with a following of the merely outward law and rule.

But the point here is that the modern mind has exiled from its practical motive-power the two essential things, God or the Eternal and spirituality or the God-state, which are the master conceptions of the Gita. It lives in humanity only, and the Gita would have us live in God, though for the world in God; in its life, heart and intellect only, and the Gita would have us live in the spirit; in the mutable Being who is 'all creatures', and the Gita would have us live also in the Immutable and the Supreme; in the changing march of Time, and the Gita would have us live in the Eternal. Or if these higher things are now beginning to be vaguely envisaged, it is only to make them subservient to man and society; but God and spirituality exist in their own right and not as adjuncts. And in practice the lower in us must learn to exist for the higher, in order that the higher also may in us consciously exist for the lower, to draw it nearer to its own altitudes.

Therefore it is a mistake to interpret the Gita from the standpoint of the mentality of today and force it to teach us the disinterested performance of duty as the highest and all-sufficient law. A little consideration of the situation with which the Gita deals will show us that this could not be its meaning.

For the whole point of the teaching, that from which it arises, that which compels the disciple to seek the Teacher, is an inextricable clash of the various related conceptions of duty ending in the collapse of the whole useful intellectual and moral edifice erected by the human mind. In human life some sort of a clash arises fairly often, as for instance between domestic duties and the call of the country or the cause, or between the claim of the country and the good of humanity or some larger religious or moral principle. An inner situation may even arise, as with the Buddha, in which all duties have to be abandoned, trampled on, flung aside in order to follow the call of the Divine within. I cannot think that the Gita would solve such an inner situation by sending Buddha back to his wife and father and the government of the Sakya State, or would direct a Ramakrishna to become a Pundit in a vernacular school and disinterestedly teach little boys their lessons, or bind down a Vivekananda to support his family and for that to follow dispassionately the law or medicine or journalism. The Gita does not teach the disinterested performance of duties but the following of the divine life, the abandonment of all dharmas, *sarvadharmān,* to take refuge in the Supreme alone, and the divine activity of a Buddha, a Ramakrishna, a Vivekananda is perfectly in consonance with this teaching. Nay, although the Gita prefers action to inaction, it does not rule out the renunciation of works, but accepts it as one of the ways to the Divine. If that can only be attained by renouncing works and life and all duties and the call is strong within us, then into the bonfire they must go, and there is no help for it. The call of God is imperative and cannot be weighed against any other considerations.

But here there is this farther difficulty that the action which Arjuna must do is one from which his moral sense recoils. It is his duty to fight, you say? But that duty has now become to his mind a terrible sin. How does it help him or solve his difficulty, to tell him that he must do his duty disinterestedly, dispassionately? He will want to know which is his duty or how it can be his duty to destroy in a sanguinary massacre his kin, his race and his country. He is told that he has right on his side, but that does not and cannot satisfy him, because his very point is that the justice of his legal claim does not justify him in supporting it by a pitiless massacre destructive to the future of his nation. Is he then to act dispassionately in the sense of not caring whether it is a sin or what its consequences may be so long as he does his duty as a soldier? That may be the teaching of a State, of politicians, of lawyers, of ethical casuists; it can never be the teaching of a great religious and philosophical Scripture which sets out to solve the problem of life and action from the very roots. And if that is what the Gita has to say on a most poignant moral and spiritual problem, we must put it out of the list of the world's Scriptures and thrust it, if anywhere, then into our library of political science and ethical casuistry.

Undoubtedly, the Gita does, like the Upanishads, teach the equality which rises above sin and virtue, beyond good and evil, but only as a part of the Brahmic consciousness and for the man who is on the path and advanced enough to fulfil the supreme rule. It does not preach indifference to good and evil for the ordinary life of man, where such a doctrine would have the most pernicious consequences. On the contrary it affirms that the doers of evil shall not attain to God. Therefore if Arjuna simply seeks to fulfil in the best way the ordinary law of man's life, disinterested performance of what he feels to be a sin, a thing of Hell, will not help him, even though that sin be his duty as a soldier. He must refrain from what his conscience abhors though a thousand duties were shattered to pieces.

We must remember that duty is an idea which in practice rests upon social conceptions. We may extend the term beyond its proper connotation and talk of our duty to ourselves or we may, if we like, say in a transcendent sense that it was Buddha's duty to abandon all, or even that it is the ascetic's duty to sit motionless in a cave! But this is obviously to play with words. Duty is a relative term and depends upon our relation to others. It is a father's duty, as a father, to nurture and educate his children; a lawyer's to do his best for his client even if he knows him to be guilty and his defence to be a lie; a soldier's to fight and shoot to order even if he kill his own kin and countrymen; a judge's to send the guilty to prison and hang the murderer. And so long as these positions are accepted, the duty remains clear, a practical matter of course even when it is not a point of honour or affection, and overrides the absolute religious or moral law. But what if the inner view is changed, if the lawyer is awakened to the absolute sinfulness of falsehood, the judge becomes convinced that capital punishment is a crime against humanity, the man called upon to the battlefield feels, like the conscientious objector of today or as a Tolstoy would feel, that in no circumstances is it permissible to take human life any more than to eat human flesh? It is obvious that here the moral law which is above all relative duties must prevail; and that law depends on no social relation or conception of duty but on the awakened inner perception of man, the moral being.

There are in the world, in fact, two different laws of conduct each valid on its own plane, the rule principally dependent on external status and the rule independent of status and entirely dependent on the thought and conscience. The Gita does not teach us to subordinate the higher plane to the lower, it does not ask the awakened moral consciousness to slay itself on the altar of duty as a sacrifice and victim to the law of the social status. It calls us higher and not lower; from the conflict of the two planes it bids us ascend to a supreme poise above the mainly practical, above the purely ethical, to the Brahmic consciousness. It replaces the conception of social duty by a divine obligation. The subjection to external law gives place to a certain principle of inner self-determination of action proceeding by the soul's freedom from the tangled law of works. And this, as we shall see—the Brahmic consciousness, the soul's freedom from works and the determination of works in the nature by the Lord within and above us—is the kernel of the Gita's teaching with regard to action.

The Gita can only be understood, like any other great work of the kind, by studying it in its entirety and as a developing argument. But the modern interpreters, starting from the great writer Bankim Chandra Chatterji who first gave to the Gita this new sense of a Gospel of Duty, have laid an almost exclusive stress on the first three or four chapters and in those on the idea of equality, on the expression *kartavyam karma,* the work that is to be done, which they render by duty, and on the phrase, 'Thou hast a right to action, but none to the fruits of action,' which is now popularly quoted as the great word, *mahāvākya,* of the Gita. The rest of the eighteen chapters with their high philosophy are given a secondary importance, except indeed the great vision in the eleventh. This is natural enough for the modern mind which is, or has been till yesterday, inclined to be impatient of metaphysical subtleties and far-off spiritual seekings, eager to get to work and, like Arjuna himself, mainly concerned for a workable law of works, a *dharma.* But it is the wrong way to handle this Scripture.

The equality which the Gita preaches is not disinterestedness— the great command to Arjuna given *after* the foundation and main structure of the teaching have been laid and built, 'Arise, slay thy enemies, enjoy a prosperous kingdom,' has not the ring of an uncompromising altruism or of a white, dispassionate abnegation;

it is a state of inner poise and wideness which is the foundation of spiritual freedom. With that poise, in that freedom we have to do the 'work that is to be done,' a phrase which the Gita uses with the greatest wideness including in it all works, *sarvakarmāṇi*, and which far exceeds, though it may include, social duties or ethical obligations. What is the work to be done is not to be determined by the individual choice; nor is the right to the action and the rejection of claim to the fruit the great word of the Gita, but only a preliminary word governing the first state of the disciple when he begins ascending the hill of Yoga. It is practically superseded at a subsequent stage. For the Gita goes on to affirm emphatically that the man is not the doer of the action; it is Prakriti, it is Nature, it is the great Force with its three modes of action that works through him, and he must learn to see that it is *not* he who does the work. Therefore the 'right to action' is an idea which is only valid so long as we are still under the illusion of being the doer; it must necessarily disappear from the mind like the claim to the fruit, as soon as we cease to be to our own consciousness the doer of our works. All pragmatic egoism, whether of the claim to fruits or of the right to action, is then at an end.

But the determinism of Prakriti is not the last word of the Gita. The equality of the will and the rejection of fruits are only means for entering with the mind and the heart and the understanding into the divine consciousness and living in it; and the Gita expressly says that they are to be employed as a means as long as the disciple is unable so to live or even to seek by practice the gradual development of this higher state. And what is this Divine, whom Krishna declares himself to be? It is the Purushottama beyond the Self that acts not, beyond the Prakriti that acts, foundation of the one, master of the other, the Lord of whom all is the manifestation, who even in our present subjection to Maya sits in the heart of His creatures governing the works of Prakriti, He by whom the armies on the field of Kurukshetra have already been slain while yet they live and who uses Arjuna only as an instrument or immediate occasion of this great slaughter. Prakriti is only His executive force. The disciple has to rise beyond this Force and its three modes or *Guṇas;* he has to become *triguṇātīta.* Not to her has he to surrender his actions, over which he has no longer any claim or 'right', but into the being of the Supreme. Reposing his mind and understanding, heart and will in Him, with self-knowledge, with God-knowledge, with world-knowledge, with a perfect equality, a perfect devotion, an absolute self-giving, he has to do works as an offering to the Master of all self-energisings and all sacrifice. Identified in will, conscious with that consciousness, That shall decide and initiate the action. This is the solution which the Divine Teacher offers to the disciple.

What the great, the supreme word of the Gita is, its *mahā vākya,* we have not to seek; for the Gita itself declares it in its last utterance, the crowning note of the great diapason. 'With the Lord in thy heart take refuge with all thy being; by His grace thou shalt attain to the supreme peace and the eternal status. So have I expounded to thee a knowledge more secret than that which is hidden. Further hear the most secret, the supreme word that I shall speak to thee. Become My-minded, devoted to Me, to Me do sacrifice and adoration; infallibly, thou shalt come to Me, for dear to Me art thou. Abandoning all laws of conduct seek refuge in Me alone. I will release thee from all sin; do not grieve.'

The argument of the Gita resolves itself into three great steps by which action rises out of the human into the divine plane leaving the bondage of the lower for the liberty of a higher law. First, by the renunciation of desire and a perfect equality works have to be done as a sacrifice by man as the doer, a sacrifice to a deity who is the supreme and only Self, though by him not yet realised in his own being. This is the initial step. Secondly, not only the desire of the fruit, but the claim to be the doer of works has to be renounced in the realisation of the Self as the equal, the inactive, the immutable principle and of all works as simply the operation of universal Force, of the Nature-Soul, Prakriti, the unequal, active, mutable power. Lastly, the supreme Self has to be seen as the supreme Purusha governing this Prakriti, of whom the soul in Nature is a partial manifestation, by whom all works are directed, in a perfect transcendence, through Nature. To him love and adoration and the sacrifice of works have to be offered; the whole being has to be surrendered to Him and the whole consciousness raised up to dwell in this divine consciousness so that the human soul may share in His divine transcendence of Nature and of His works and act in a perfect spiritual liberty.

The first step is Karmayoga, the selfless sacrifice of works, and here the Gita's insistence is on action. The second is Jnanayoga, the self-realisation and knowledge of the true nature of the self and the world; and here the insistence is on knowledge; but the sacrifice of works continues and the path of Works becomes one with but does not disappear into the path of Knowledge. The last step is Bhaktiyoga, adoration and seeking of the supreme Self as the Divine Being, and here the insistence is on devotion; but the knowledge is not subordinated, only raised, vitalised and fulfilled, and still the sacrifice of works continues; the double path becomes the triune way of knowledge, works and devotion. And the fruit of the sacrifice, the one fruit still placed before the seeker, is attained, union with the divine Being and oneness with the supreme divine Nature.

The Life Divine

The Human Aspiration[1]

For all problems of existence are essentially problems of harmony. They arise from the perception of an unsolved discord and the instinct of an undiscovered agreement or unity. To rest content with an unsolved discord is possible for the practical and more animal part of man, but impossible for his fully awakened mind, and usually even his practical parts only escape from the general necessity either by shutting out the problem or by accepting a rough, utilitarian and unillumined compromise. For essentially, all Nature seeks a harmony, life and matter in their own sphere as much as mind in the arrangement of its perceptions. The greater the apparent disorder of the materials offered or the apparent disparateness, even to irreconcilable opposition, of the elements that have to be utilised, the stronger is the spur, and it drives towards a more subtle and puissant order than can normally be the result of a less difficult endeavour. The accordance of active Life with a material of form in which the condition of activity itself seems to be inertia, is one problem of opposites that Nature has solved and seeks always to solve better with greater complexities; for its perfect solution would be the material immortality of a

---

1 From the opening chapter of *The Life Divine*, originally published in the *Arya*, vol. I, 15 August 1914. Published in instalments in the Arya from 15 August 1914 to January 1919, *The Life Divine* was thoroughly revised, enlarged, and published in book form in 1939 (Book One) and 1940 (Book Two, Vols. I and II).

fully organised mind-supporting animal body. The accordance of conscious mind and conscious will with a form and a life in themselves not overtly self-conscious and capable at best of a mechanical or subconscious will is another problem of opposites in which she has produced astonishing results and aims always at higher marvels; for there her ultimate miracle would be an animal consciousness no longer seeking but possessed of Truth and Light, with the practical omnipotence which would result from the possession of a direct and perfected knowledge. Not only, then, is the upward impulse of man towards the accordance of yet higher opposites rational in itself, but it is the only logical completion of a rule and an effort that seem to be a fundamental method of Nature and the very sense of her universal strivings.

We speak of the evolution of Life in Matter, the evolution of Mind in Matter; but evolution is a word which merely states the phenomenon without explaining it. For there seems to be no reason why Life should evolve out of material elements or Mind out of living form, unless we accept the Vedantic solution that Life is already involved in Matter and Mind in Life because in essence Matter is a form of veiled Life, Life a form of veiled Consciousness. And then there seems to be little objection to a farther step in the series and the admission that mental consciousness may itself be only a form and a veil of higher states which are beyond Mind. In that case, the unconquerable impulse of man towards God, Light, Bliss, Freedom, Immortality presents itself in its right place in the chain as simply the imperative impulse by which Nature is seeking to evolve beyond Mind, and appears to be as natural, true and just as the impulse towards Life which she has planted in certain forms of Matter or the impulse towards Mind which she has planted in certain forms of Life. As there, so here, the impulse exists more or less obscurely in her different vessels with an ever-ascending series in the power of its will-to-be; as there, so here, it is gradually evolving and bound fully to evolve the necessary organs and faculties. As the impulse towards Mind ranges from the more sensitive reactions of Life in the metal and the plant up to its full organisation in man, so in man himself there is the same ascending series, the preparation, if nothing more, of a higher and divine life. The animal is a living laboratory in which Nature has, it is said, worked out man. Man himself may well be a thinking and living laboratory in whom and with whose conscious co-operation she wills to work out the superman, the god. Or shall we not say, rather, to manifest God? For if evolution is the progressive manifestation by Nature of that which slept or worked in her, involved, it is also the overt realisation of that which she secretly is. We cannot, then, bid her pause at a given stage of her evolution, nor have we the right to condemn with the religionist as perverse and presumptuous or with the rationalist as a disease or hallucination any intention she may evince or effort she may make to go beyond. If it be true that Spirit is involved in Matter and apparent Nature is secret God, then the manifestation of the divine in himself and the realisation of God within and without are the highest and most legitimate aim possible to man upon earth.

Thus the eternal paradox and eternal truth of a divine life in an animal body, an immortal aspiration or reality inhabiting a mortal tenement, a single and universal consciousness representing itself in limited minds and divided egos, a transcendent, indefinable, timeless and spaceless Being who alone renders time and space and cosmos possible, and in all these the higher truth realisable by the lower term, justify themselves to the deliberate reason as well as to the persistent instinct or intuition of mankind. Attempts are sometimes made to have done finally with questionings which have so often been declared insoluble by logical thought and to persuade men to limit their mental activities to the practical and immediate problems of their material existence in the universe; but such evasions are never permanent in their effect. Mankind returns from them with a more vehement impulse of inquiry or a more violent hunger for an immediate solution. By that hunger mysticism profits and new religions arise to replace the old that have been destroyed or stripped of significance by a scepticism which itself could not satisfy because, although its business was inquiry, it was unwilling sufficiently to inquire. The attempt to deny or stifle a truth because it is yet obscure in its outward workings and too often represented by obscurantist superstition or a crude faith, is itself a kind of obscurantism. The will to escape from a cosmic necessity because it is arduous, difficult to justify by immediate tangible results, slow in regulating its operations, must turn out eventually to have been no acceptance of the truth of Nature but a revolt against the secret, mightier will of the great Mother. It is better and more rational to accept what she will not allow us as a race to reject and lift it from the sphere of blind instinct, obscure intuition and random aspiration into the light of reason and an instructed and consciously self-guiding will. And if there is any higher light of illumined intuition or self-revealing truth which is now in man either obstructed and inoperative or works with intermittent glancings as if from behind a veil or with occasional displays as of the northern lights in our material skies, then there also we need not fear to aspire. For it is likely that such is the next higher state of consciousness of which Mind is only a form and veil, and through the splendours of that light may lie the path of our progressive self-enlargement into whatever highest state is humanity's ultimate resting-place.

The Two Negations[1]

He energised conscious-force (in the austerity of thought) and came to the knowledge that Matter is the Brahman. For from Matter all existences are born; born, by Matter they increase and enter into Matter in their passing hence. Then he went to Varuna, his father, and said, "Lord, teach me of the Brahman." But he said to him: "Energise (again) the conscious-energy in thee; for the Energy is Brahman."

Taittiriya Upanishad. (III. 1) Taittiriya Upanishad. (III. 2)

The affirmation of a divine life upon earth and an immortal sense in mortal existence can have no base unless we recognise not only eternal Spirit as the inhabitant of this bodily mansion, the wearer of this mutable robe, but accept Matter of which it is made, as a fit and noble material out of which He weaves constantly His garbs, builds recurrently the unending series of His mansions.

Nor is this, even, enough to guard us against a recoil from life in the body unless, with the Upanishads, perceiving behind their appearances the identity in essence of these two extreme terms of existence, we are able to say in the very language of those ancient writings, "Matter also is Brahman", and to give its full value to the vigorous figure by which the physical universe is described as the

---

[1] From Book I, Chapter II of *The Life Divine.*

external body of the Divine Being. Nor,—so far divided apparently are these two extreme terms,—is that identification convincing to the rational intellect if we refuse to recognise a series of ascending terms (Life, Mind, Supermind and the grades that link Mind to Supermind) between Spirit and Matter. Otherwise the two must appear as irreconcilable opponents bound together in an unhappy wedlock and their divorce the one reasonable solution. To identify them, to represent each in the terms of the other, becomes an artificial creation of Thought opposed to the logic of facts and possible only by an irrational mysticism.

If we assert only pure Spirit and a mechanical unintelligent substance or energy, calling one God or Soul and the other Nature, the inevitable end will be that we shall either deny God or else turn from Nature. For both Thought and Life, a choice then becomes imperative. Thought comes to deny the one as an illusion of the imagination or the other as an illusion of the senses; Life comes to fix on the immaterial and flee from itself in a disgust or a self-forgetting ecstasy, or else to deny its own immortality and take its orientation away from God and towards the animal. Purusha and Prakriti, the passively luminous Soul of the Sankhyas and their mechanically active Energy, have nothing in common, not even their opposite modes of inertia; their antinomies can only be resolved by the cessation of the inertly driven Activity into the immutable Repose upon which it has been casting in vain the sterile procession of its images. Shankara's wordless, inactive Self and his Maya of many names and forms are equally disparate and irreconcilable entities; their rigid antagonism can terminate only by the dissolution of the multitudinous illusion into the sole Truth of an eternal Silence.

The materialist has an easier field; it is possible for him by denying Spirit to arrive at a more readily convincing simplicity of statement, a real Monism, the Monism of Matter or else of Force. But in this rigidity of statement it is impossible for him to persist permanently. He too ends by positing an unknowable as inert, as remote from the known universe as the passive Purusha or the silent Atman. It serves no purpose but to put off by a vague concession the inexorable demands of Thought or to stand as an excuse for refusing to extend the limits of inquiry.

Therefore, in these barren contradictions the human mind cannot rest satisfied. It must seek always a complete affirmation; it can find it only by a luminous reconciliation. To reach that reconciliation it must traverse the degrees which our inner consciousness imposes on us and, whether by objective method of analysis applied to Life and Mind as to Matter or by subjective synthesis and illumination, arrive at the repose of the ultimate unity without denying the energy of the expressive multiplicity. Only in such a complete and catholic affirmation can all the multiform and apparently contradictory data of existence be harmonised and the manifold conflicting forces which govern our thought and life discover the central Truth which they are here to symbolise and variously fulfil. Then only can our Thought, having attained a true centre, ceasing to wander in circles, work like the Brahman of the Upanishad, fixed and stable even in its play and its worldwide coursing, and our life, knowing its aim, serve it with a serene and settled joy and light as well as with a rhythmically discursive energy.

But when that rhythm has once been disturbed, it is necessary and helpful that man should test separately, in their extreme assertion, each of the two great opposites. It is the mind's natural way of returning more perfectly to the affirmation it has lost. On the road it may attempt to rest in the intervening degrees, reducing all things into the terms of an original Life-Energy or of sensation or of Ideas; but these exclusive solutions have always an air of unreality. They may satisfy for a time the logical reason which deals only with pure ideas, but they cannot satisfy the mind's sense of actuality. For the mind knows that there is something behind itself which is not the Idea; it knows, on the other hand, that there is something within itself which is more than the vital Breath. Either Spirit or Matter can give it for a time some sense of ultimate reality; not so any of the principles that intervene. It must, therefore, go to the two extremes before it can return fruitfully upon the whole. For by its very nature, served by a sense that can perceive with distinctness only the parts of existence and by a speech that, also, can achieve distinctness only when it carefully divides and limits, the intellect is driven, having before it this multiplicity of elemental principles, to seek unity by reducing all ruthlessly to the terms of one. It attempts practically, in order to assert this one, to get rid of the others. To perceive the real source of their identity without this exclusive process, it must either have overleaped itself or must have completed the circuit only to find that all equally reduce themselves to That which escapes definition or description and is yet not only real but attainable. By whatever road we may travel, That is always the end at which we arrive and we can only escape it by refusing to complete the journey.

The Triple Transformation[1]

As the crust of the outer nature cracks, as the walls of inner
separation break down, the inner light gets through, the inner
fire burns in the heart, the substance of the nature and the stuff
of consciousness refine to a greater subtlety and purity, and the
deeper psychic experiences, those which are not solely of an inner
mental or inner vital character, become possible in this subtler,
purer, finer substance; the soul begins to unveil itself, the psychic
personality reaches its full stature. The soul, the psychic entity,
then manifests itself as the central being which upholds mind and
life and body and supports all the other powers and functions of
the Spirit; it takes up its greater function as the guide and ruler of
the nature. A guidance, a governance begins from within which
exposes every movement to the light of Truth, repels what is false,
obscure, opposed to the divine realisation: every region of the being,
every nook and corner of it, every movement, formation, direction,
inclination of thought, will, emotion, sensation, action, reaction,
motive, disposition, propensity, desire, habit of the conscious or
subconscious physical, even the most concealed, camouflaged,
mute, recondite, is lighted up with the unerring psychic light,
their confusions dissipated, their tangles disentangled, their
obscurities, deceptions, self-deceptions precisely indicated and
removed; all is purified, set right, the whole nature harmonised,

---

[1] From Book II, Chapter XXV of *The Life Divine*.

modulated in the psychic key, put in spiritual order. This process may be rapid or tardy according to the amount of obscurity and resistance still left in the nature, but it goes on unfalteringly so long as it is not complete. As a final result the whole conscious being is made perfectly apt for spiritual experience of every kind, turned to wards spiritual truth of thought, feeling, sense, action, tuned to the right responses, delivered from the darkness and stubbornness of the tamasic inertia, the turbidities and turbulences and impurities of the rajasic passion and restless unharmonised kinetism, the enlightened rigidities and sattwic limitations or poised balancements of constructed equilibrium which are the character of the Ignorance.

This is the first result, but the second is a free inflow of all kinds of spiritual experience, experience of the Self, experience of the Ishwara and the Divine Shakti, experience of cosmic consciousness, a direct touch with cosmic forces and with the occult movements of universal Nature, a psychic sympathy and unity and inner communication and interchanges of all kinds with other beings and with Nature, illuminations of the mind by knowledge, illuminations of the heart by love and devotion and spiritual joy and ecstasy, illuminations of the sense and the body by higher experience, illuminations of dynamic action in the truth and largeness of a purified mind and heart and soul, the certitudes of the divine light and guidance, the joy and power of the divine force working in the will and the conduct. These experiences are the result of an opening outward of the inner and inmost being and nature; for then there comes into play the soul's power of unerring inherent consciousness, its vision, its touch on things which is superior to any mental cognition; there is there, native to the psychic consciousness in its pure working, an immediate sense of the world and its beings, a direct inner contact with them and a direct contact with the Self and with the Divine,—a direct knowledge, a direct sight of Truth and of all truths, a direct penetrating spiritual emotion and feeling, a direct intuition of right will and right action, a power to rule and to create an order of the being not by the gropings of the superficial self, but from within, from the inner truth of self and things and the occult realities of Nature.

Some of these experiences can come by an opening of the inner mental and vital being, the inner and larger and subtler mind and heart and life within us, without any full emergence of the soul, the psychic entity, since there too there is a power of direct contact of consciousness but the experience might then be of a mixed character; for there could be an emergence not only of the subliminal knowledge but of the subliminal ignorance. An insufficient expansion of the being, a limitation by mental idea, by narrow and selective emotion or by the form of the temperament so that there would be only an imperfect self-creation and action and not the free soul-emergence, could easily occur. In the absence of any or of a complete psychic emergence, experiences of certain kinds, experiences of a greater knowledge and force, a surpassing of the ordinary limits, might lead to a magnified ego and even bring about instead of an outflowering of what is divine or spiritual an uprush of the titanic or demoniac, or might call in agencies and powers which, though not of this disastrous type, are of a powerful but inferior cosmic character. But the rule and guidance of the soul brings into all experience the tendency of light, of integration, of harmony and intimate rightness which is native to the psychic essence. A psychic or, more widely speaking, a psycho-spiritual transformation of this kind would be already a vast change of our mental human nature.

But all this change and all this experience, though psychic and spiritual in essence and character, would still be, in its parts of life-effectuation, on the mental, vital and physical level; its dynamic spiritual outcome would be a flowering of the soul in mind and life and body, but in act and form it would be circumscribed within the limitations—however enlarged, uplifted and rarefied—of an inferior instrumentation. It would be a reflected and modified manifestation of things whose full reality, intensity, largeness, oneness and diversity of truth and power and delight are above us, above mind and therefore above any perfection, within mind's own formula, of the foundations or superstructure of our present nature. A highest spiritual transformation must intervene on the psychic or psycho-spiritual change; the psychic movement inward to the inner being, the Self or Divinity within us, must be completed by an opening upward to a supreme spiritual status or a higher existence. This can be done by our opening into what is above us, by an ascent of consciousness into the ranges of overmind and supramental nature in which the sense of self and spirit is ever unveiled and permanent and in which the self-luminous instrumentation of the self and spirit is not restricted or divided as in our mind-nature, life-nature, body-nature. This also the psychic change makes possible; for as it opens us to the cosmic consciousness now hidden from us by many walls of limiting individuality, so also it opens us to what is now superconscient to our normality because it is hidden from us by the strong, hard and bright lid of mind,—mind constricting, dividing and separative. The lid thins, is slit, breaks asunder or opens and disappears under the pressure of the psycho-spiritual change and the natural urge of the new spiritualised consciousness towards that of which it is an expression here. This effectuation of an aperture and its consequences may not at all take place if there is only a partial psychic emergence satisfied with the experience of the Divine Reality in the normal degrees of the spiritualised mind but if there is any awakening to the existence of these higher supernormal levels, then an aspiration towards them may break the lid or operate a rift in it. This may happen long before the psycho-spiritual change is complete or even before it has well begun or proceeded far, because the psychic personality has become aware and has an eager concentration towards the superconscience. An early illumination from above or a rending of the upper velamen can come as an outcome of aspiration or some inner readiness, or it may even come uncalled-for or not called for by any conscious part of the mind,—perhaps by a secret subliminal necessity or by an action or pressure from the higher levels, by something which is felt as the touch of the Divine Being, the touch of the Spirit,— and its results can be exceedingly powerful. But if it is brought about by a premature pressure from below, it can be attended with difficulties and dangers which are absent when the full psychic emergence precedes this first admission to the superior ranges of our spiritual evolution. The choice, however, does not always rest with our will, for the operations of the spiritual evolution in us are very various, and according to the line it has followed will be the turn taken at any critical phase by the action of the Consciousness-Force in its urge towards a higher self-manifestation and formation of our existence.

If the rift in the lid of mind is made, what happens is an opening of vision to something above us or a rising up towards it or a descent of its powers into our being. What we see by the opening of vision is an Infinity above us, an eternal Presence or an infinite Existence, an infinity of consciousness, an infinity of bliss,—a boundless Self, a boundless Light, a boundless Power, a boundless Ecstasy. It may be that for a long time all that is obtained is the occasional or frequent or constant vision of it and a longing and aspiration, but without anything further, because, although something in the mind, heart or other part of the being has opened to this experience, the lower nature as a whole is too heavy and obscure as yet for more. But there may be, instead of this first wide awareness from below or subsequently to it, an ascension of the mind to heights above: the nature of these heights we may not know or clearly discern, but some consequence of the ascent is felt; there is often too an awareness of infinite ascension and return but no record or translation of that higher state. This is because it has been superconscient to mind and therefore mind, when it rises into it, is unable at first to retain there its power of conscious discernment and defining experience. But when this power begins to awake and act, when mind becomes by degrees conscious in what was to it superconscient, then there begins a knowledge and experience of superior planes of existence. The experience is in accord with that which is brought to us by the first opening of vision: the mind rises into a higher plane of pure self, silent, tranquil, illimitable; or it rises into regions of light or of felicity, or into planes where it feels an infinite Power or a divine Presence or experiences the contact of a divine Love or Beauty or the atmosphere of a wider and greater and luminous Knowledge. In the return the spiritual impression abides; but the mental record is often blurred and remains as a vague or a fragmentary memory; the lower consciousness from which the ascent took place falls back to what it was, with only the addition of an unkept or a remembered but no longer dynamic experience. In time the ascent comes to be made at will and the consciousness brings back and retains some effect or some gain of its temporary sojourn in these higher countries of the spirit. These ascents take place for many in trance, but are perfectly possible in a concentration of the waking consciousness or, where that consciousness has become sufficiently psychic, at any unconcentrated moment by an upward attraction or affinity. But these two types of contact with the superconscient, though they can be powerfully illuminating, ecstatic or liberating, are by themselves insufficiently effective: for the full spiritual transformation more is needed, a permanent ascension from the lower into the higher consciousness and an effectual permanent descent of the higher into the lower nature.

This is the third motion, the descent which is essential for bringing the permanent ascension, an increasing inflow from above, an experience of reception and retention of the descending spirit or its powers and elements of consciousness. This experience of descent can take place as a result of the other two movements or automatically before either has happened, through a sudden rift in the lid or a percolation, a downpour or an influx. A light descends and touches or envelops or penetrates the lower being, the mind, the life or the body; or a presence or a power or a stream of knowledge pours in waves or currents, or there is a flood of bliss or a sudden ecstasy; the contact with the superconscient has been established. For such experiences repeat themselves till they become normal, familiar and well-understood, revelatory of their contents and their significance which may have at first been involved and wrapped into secrecy by the figure of the covering experience. For a knowledge from above begins to descend, frequently, constantly, then uninterruptedly, and to manifest in the mind's quietude or silence; intuitions and inspirations, revelations born of a greater sight, a higher truth and wisdom, enter into the being, a luminous intuitive discrimination works which dispels all darkness of understanding or dazzling confusions, puts all in order; a new consciousness begins to form, the mind of a high wide self-existent thinking knowledge or an illumined or an intuitive or an overmental consciousness with new forces of thought or sight and a greater power of direct spiritual realisation which is more than thought or sight, a greater becoming in the spiritual substance of our present being; the heart and the sense become subtle, intense, large to embrace all existence, to see God, to feel and hear and touch the Eternal, to make a deeper and closer unity of self and the world in a transcendent realisation. Other decisive experiences, other changes of consciousness determine themselves which are corollaries and consequences of this fundamental change. No limit can be fixed to this revolution; for it is in its nature an invasion by the Infinite.

The Ascent to the Supermind[1]

Overmind and its delegated powers, taking up and penetrating mind and the life and body dependent upon mind, would subject all to a greatening process; at each step of this process a greater power and a higher intensity of gnosis less and less mixed with the loose, diffused, diminishing and diluting stuff of mind could establish itself: but all gnosis is in its origin power of supermind, so that this would mean a greater and greater influx of a half-veiled and indirect supramental light and power into the nature. This would continue until the point was reached at which overmind would begin itself to be transformed into supermind; the supramental consciousness and force would take up the transformation directly into its own hands, reveal to the terrestrial mind, life, bodily being their own spiritual truth and divinity and, finally, pour into the whole nature the perfect knowledge, power, significance of the supramental existence. The soul would pass beyond the borders of the Ignorance and cross its original line of departure from the supreme Knowledge: it would enter into the integrality of the supramental gnosis; the descent of the gnostic Light would effectuate a complete transformation of the Ignorance.

This or something more largely planned on these lines might be regarded as the schematic, logical or ideal account of the spiritual transformation, a structural map of the ascent to the supramental

---

[1] From Book II, Chapter XXVI of *The Life Divine*.

summit, looked at as a succession of separate steps, each accomplished before the passage to the next commences. It would be as if the soul, putting forth an organised natural individuality, were a traveller mounting the degrees of consciousness cut out in universal Nature, each ascent carrying it totally as a definite integer, as a separate body of conscious being, from one state of its existence to the next in order. This is so far correct that a sufficient integration of one status has to be complete before an ascent to the next higher station can be entirely secure: this clear succession might also be the course followed by a few even in the early stages of this evolution, and it might become too a normal process after the whole stair-flight of the evolution had been built and made safe. But evolutionary Nature is not a logical series of separate segments; it is a totality of ascending powers of being which interpenetrate and dovetail and exercise in their action on each other a power of mutual modification. When the higher descends into the lower consciousness, it alters the lower but is also modified and diminished by it; when the lower ascends, it is sublimated but at the same time qualifies the sublimating substance and power. This interaction creates an abundant number of different intermediate and interlocked degrees of the force and consciousness of being, but it also makes it difficult to bring about a complete integration of all the powers under the full control of any one power. For this reason there is not actually a series of simple clear-cut and successive stages in the individual's evolution; there is instead a complexity and a partly determinate, partly confused comprehensiveness of the movement. The soul may still be described as a traveller and climber who presses towards his high goal by step on step, each of which he has to build up as an integer but must frequently re descend in order to rebuild and make sure of the supporting stair so that it may not crumble beneath him: but the evolution of the whole consciousness has rather the movement of an ascending ocean of Nature; it can be compared to a tide or a mounting flux, the leading fringe of which touches the higher degrees of a cliff or hill while the rest is still below. At each stage the higher parts of the nature may be provisionally but incompletely organised in the new consciousness while the lower are in a state of flux or formation, partly moving in the old way though influenced and beginning to change, partly belonging to the new kind but still imperfectly achieved and not yet firm in the change. Another image might be that of an army advancing in columns which annexes new ground, while the main body is still behind in a territory overrun but too large to be effectively occupied, so that there has to be a frequent halt and partial return to the traversed areas for consolidation and assurance of the hold on the occupied country and assimilation of its people. A rapid conquest might be possible, but it would be of the nature of an encampment or a domination established in a foreign country; it would not be the assumption, total assimilation, integration needed for the entire supramental change.

This entails certain consequences which modify the clear successions of the evolution and prevent it from following the cleanly determined and firmly arranged course which our logical intelligence demands from Nature but seldom gets from her. As life and mind begin to appear when the organisation of Matter is sufficient to admit them but the more complex and perfect organisation of Matter comes with the evolution of life and mind, as mind appears when life is sufficiently organised to admit of a developed vibration of consciousness but life receives its full organisation and development only after mind can act upon it, as the spiritual evolution begins when man as mind is capable of the movements of spirituality but mind also rises to its own highest perfection by the growth of the intensities and luminosities of the spirit, so it is with this higher evolution of the ascending powers of the Spirit. As soon as there is a sufficient spiritual development, something of intuition, illumination of the being, the movements of the higher spiritual grades of Consciousness begins to manifest,—sometimes one, sometimes the other or all together, and they do not wait for each power in the series to complete itself before a higher power comes into action. An Overmind light and power may descend in some sort, create a partial form of itself in the being and take a leading part or supervise or intervene while the intuitive and illumining mind and higher mind are still incomplete; these would then remain in the whole, acting along with the greater Power, often penetrated or sublimated by it or rising into it to form a greater or overmind intuition, a greater or overmind illumination, a greater or overmind spiritual thinking. This intricate action takes place because each descending power by its intensity of pressure on the nature and uplifting effect makes the being already capable of a still higher invasion before that earlier power itself is complete in its self-formation; but also it happens because the work of assumption and transformation of the lower nature can with difficulty be done if a higher and higher intervention does not take place. The illumination and the higher thought need the help of the intuition, the intuition needs the help of the overmind to combat the darkness or ignorance in which they labour and to give them their own fullness. Still, it is not possible in the end for the overmind status and integration to be complete until the higher mind and the illumined mind have been integrated and taken up into the intuition and the intuition itself subsequently integrated and taken up into the all-enlarging and all-sublimating overmind energy. The law of the gradation has to be satisfied even in the complexity of the process of evolutionary Nature.

The Divine Life[1]

But these are evidently problems of the transition, of the evolution before the full and victorious reversal of the manifesting Force has taken place and the life of the gnostic being becomes as much as that of the mental being an established part of the terrestrial world-order. If we suppose the gnostic consciousness to be established in the earth-life, the power and knowledge at its disposal would be much greater than the power and knowledge of mental man, and the life of a community of gnostic beings, supposing it to be separate, would be as safe against attack as the organised life of man against any attack by a lower species. But as this knowledge and the very principle of the gnostic nature would ensure a luminous unity in the common life of gnostic beings, so also it would be sufficient to ensure a dominating harmony and reconciliation between the two types of life. The influence of the supramental principle on earth would fall upon the life of the Ignorance and impose harmony on it within its limits. It is conceivable that the gnostic life would be separate, but it would surely admit within its borders as much of human life as was turned towards spirituality and in progress towards the heights; the rest might organise itself mainly on the mental principle and on the old foundations, but, helped and influenced by a recognisable greater knowledge, it would be likely to do so on lines of a completer harmonisation of which the

---

[1] From Book II, Chapter XXVIII, which concludes *The Life Divine*.

human collectivity is not yet capable. Here also, however, the mind can only forecast probabilities and possibilities; the supramental principle in Supernature would itself determine according to the truth of things the balance of a new world-order.

A gnostic Supernature transcends all the values of our normal ignorant Nature; our standards and values are created by ignorance and therefore cannot determine the life of Super nature. At the same time our present nature is a derivation from Supernature and is not a pure ignorance but a half-knowledge; it is therefore reasonable to suppose that whatever spiritual truth there is in or behind its standards and values will reappear in the higher life, not as standards, but as elements transformed, uplifted out of the ignorance and raised into the true harmony of a more luminous existence. As the universalised spiritual individual sheds the limited personality, the ego, as he rises beyond mind to a completer knowledge in Supernature, the conflicting ideals of the mind must fall away from him, but what is true behind them will remain in the life of Supernature. The gnostic consciousness is a consciousness in which all contradictions are cancelled or fused into each other in a higher light of seeing and being, in a unified self-knowledge and world-knowledge. The gnostic being will not accept the mind's ideals and standards; he will not be moved to live for himself, for his ego, or for humanity or for others or for the community or for the State; for he will be aware of something greater than these half-truths, of the Divine Reality, and it is for that he will live, for its will in himself and in all, in a spirit of large universality, in the light of the will of the Transcendence. For the same reason there can be no conflict between self-affirmation and altruism in the gnostic life, for the self of the gnostic being is one with the self of all, no conflict between the ideal of individualism and the collective ideal, for both are terms of a greater Reality and only in so far as either expresses the Reality or their fulfilment serves the will of the Reality, can they have a value for his spirit. But at the same time what is true in the mental ideals and dimly figured in them will be fulfilled in his existence; for while his consciousness exceeds the human values so that he cannot substitute mankind or the community or the State or others or himself for God, the affirmation of the Divine in himself and a sense of the Divine in others and the sense of oneness with humanity, with all other beings, with all the world because of the Divine in them and a lead towards a greater and better affirmation of the growing Reality in them will be part of his life action. But what he shall do will be decided by the Truth of the Knowledge and Will in him, a total and infinite Truth that is not bound by any single mental law or standard but acts with freedom in the whole reality, with respect for each truth in its place and with a clear knowledge of the forces at work and the intention in the manifesting Divine Nisus at each step of cosmic evolution and in each event and circumstance.

All life for the achieved spiritual or gnostic consciousness must be the manifestation of the realised truth of spirit; only what can transform itself and find its own spiritual self in that greater Truth and fuse itself into its harmony can be accorded a life-acceptance. What will so survive the mind cannot determine, for the supramental gnosis will itself bring down its own truth and that truth will take up whatever of itself has been put forth in our ideals and realisations of mind and life and body. The forms it has taken there may not survive, for they are not likely to be suitable without change or replacement in the new existence; but what is real and abiding in them or even in their forms will undergo the transformation necessary for survival. Much that is normal to human life would disappear. In the light of gnosis the many mental idols, constructed principles and systems, conflicting ideals which man has created in all domains of his mind and life, could command no acceptance or reverence; only the truth, if any, which these specious images conceal, could have a chance of entry as elements of a harmony founded on a much wider basis. It is evident that in a life governed by the gnostic consciousness war with its spirit of antagonism and enmity, its brutality, destruction and ignorant violence, political strife with its perpetual conflict, frequent oppression, dishonesties, turpitudes, selfish interests, its ignorance, ineptitude and muddle could have no ground for existence. The arts and the crafts would exist, not for any inferior mental or vital amusement, entertainment of leisure and relieving excitement or pleasure, but as expressions and means of the truth of the spirit and the beauty and delight of existence. Life and the body would be no longer tyrannous masters demanding nine tenths of existence for their satisfaction, but means and powers for the expression of the spirit. At the same time, since matter and the body are accepted, the control and the right use of physical things would be a part of the realised life of the spirit in the manifestation in earth-nature.

It is almost universally supposed that spiritual life must necessarily be a life of ascetic spareness, a pushing away of all that is not absolutely needed for the bare maintenance of the body; and this is valid for a spiritual life which is in its nature and intention a life of withdrawal from life. Even apart from that ideal, it might be thought that the spiritual turn must always make for an extreme simplicity, because all else would be a life of vital desire and physical self-indulgence. But from a wider standpoint this is a mental standard based on the law of the Ignorance of which desire is the motive; to overcome the Ignorance, to delete the ego, a total rejection not only of desire but of all the things that can satisfy desire may intervene as a valid principle. But this standard or any mental standard cannot be absolute nor can it be binding as a law on the consciousness that has arisen above desire; a complete purity and self-mastery would be in the very grain of its nature and that would remain the same in poverty or in riches: for if it could be shaken or sullied by either, it would not be real or would not be complete. The one rule of the gnostic life would be the self-expression of the Spirit, the will of the Divine Being; that will, that self-expression could manifest through extreme simplicity or through extreme complexity and opulence or in their natural balance,—for beauty and plenitude, a hidden sweetness and laughter in things, a sunshine and gladness of life are also powers and expressions of the Spirit. In all directions the Spirit within determining the law of the nature would determine the frame of the life and its detail and circumstance. In all there would be the same plastic principle; a rigid standardisation, however necessary for the mind's arrangement of things, could not be the law of the spiritual life. A great diversity and liberty of self-expression based on an underlying unity might well become manifest; but everywhere there would be harmony and truth of order.

A life of gnostic beings carrying the evolution to a higher supramental status might fitly be characterised as a divine life; for it would be a life in the Divine, a life of the beginnings of a spiritual divine light and power and joy manifested in material Nature. That might be described, since it surpasses the mental human level, as a life of spiritual and supramental Supermanhood. But this must not be confused with past and present ideas of Supermanhood; for Supermanhood in the mental idea consists of an overtopping of the normal human level, not in kind but in degree of the same kind, by an enlarged personality, a magnified and exaggerated ego, an increased power of mind, an increased power of vital force, a refined or dense and massive exaggeration of the forces of the human Ignorance; it carries also, commonly implied in it, the idea of a forceful domination over humanity by the superman. That would mean a superman hood of the Nietzschean type; it might be at its worst the reign of the "blonde beast" or the dark beast or of any and every beast, a return to barbaric strength and ruthlessness and force: but this would be no evolution, it would be a reversion to an old strenuous barbarism. Or it might signify the emergence of the Rakshasa or Asura out of a tense effort of humanity to surpass and transcend itself, but in the wrong direction. A violent and turbulent exaggerated vital ego satisfying itself with a supreme tyrannous or anarchic strength of self-fulfilment would be the type of a Rakshasic supermanhood: but the giant, the ogre or devourer of the world, the Rakshasa, though he still survives, belongs in spirit to the past; a larger emergence of that type would be also a retrograde evolution. A mighty exhibition of an overpowering force, a self-possessed, self-held, even, it may be, an ascetically self-restrained mind-capacity and life-power, strong, calm or cold or formidable in collected vehemence, subtle, dominating, a sublimation at once of the mental and vital ego, is the type of the Asura. But earth has had enough of this kind in her past and its repetition can only prolong the old lines; she can get no true profit for her future, no power of self-exceeding, from the Titan, the Asura: even a great or supernormal power in it could only carry her on larger circles of her old orbit. But what has to emerge is something much more difficult and much more simple; it is a self-realised being, a building of the spiritual self, an intensity and urge of the soul and the deliverance and sovereignty of its light and power and beauty,—not an egoistic supermanhood seizing on a mental and vital domination over humanity, but the sovereignty of the Spirit over its own instruments, its possession of itself and its possession of life in the power of the spirit, a new consciousness in which humanity itself shall find its own self-exceeding and self-fulfilment by the revelation of the divinity that is striving for birth within it. This is the sole true supermanhood and the one real possibility of a step forward in evolutionary Nature.

This new status would indeed be a reversal of the present law of human consciousness and life, for it would reverse the whole principle of the life of the Ignorance. It is for the taste of the Ignorance, its surprise and adventure, one might say, that the soul has descended into the Inconscience and assumed the disguise of Matter, for the adventure and the joy of creation and discovery, an adventure of the spirit, an adventure of the mind and life and the hazardous surprises of their working in Matter, for the discovery and conquest of the new and the unknown; all this constitutes the enterprise of life and all this, it might seem, would cease with the cessation of the Ignorance. Man's life is made up of the light and the darkness, the gains and losses, the difficulties and dangers, the pleasures and pains of the Ignorance, a play of colours moving on a soil of the general neutrality of Matter which has as its basis the nescience and insensibility of the Inconscient. To the normal life-being an existence without the reactions of success and frustration, vital joy and grief, peril and passion, pleasure and pain, the vicissitudes and uncertainties of fate and struggle and battle and endeavour, a joy of novelty and surprise and creation projecting itself into the unknown, might seem to be void of variety and therefore void of vital savour. Any life surpassing these things tends to appear to it as something featureless and empty or cast in the figure of an immutable sameness; the human mind's picture of heaven is the incessant repetition of an eternal monotone. But this is a misconception; for an entry into the gnostic consciousness would be an entry into the Infinite. It would be a self-creation bringing out the Infinite infinitely into form of being, and the interest of the Infinite is much greater and multitudinous as well as more imperishably delightful than the interest of the finite. The evolution in the Knowledge would be a more beautiful and glorious manifestation with more vistas ever unfolding themselves and more intensive in all ways than any evolution could be in the Ignorance. The delight of the Spirit is ever new, the forms of beauty it takes innumerable, its godhead ever young and the taste of delight, rasa, of the Infinite eternal and inexhaustible. The gnostic manifestation of life would be more full and fruitful and its interest more vivid than the creative interest of the Ignorance; it would be a greater and happier constant miracle.

If there is an evolution in material Nature and if it is an evolution of being with consciousness and life as its two key-terms and powers, this fullness of being, fullness of consciousness, fullness of life must be the goal of development towards which we are tending and which will manifest at an early or later stage of our destiny. The self, the spirit, the reality that is disclosing itself out of the first inconscience of life and matter, would evolve its complete truth of being and consciousness in that life and matter. It would return to itself—or, if its end as an individual is to return into its Absolute, it could make that return also,—not through a frustration of life but through a spiritual completeness of itself in life. Our evolution in the Ignorance with its chequered joy and pain of self-discovery and world discovery, its half fulfilments, its constant finding and missing, is only our first state. It must lead inevitably towards an evolution in the Knowledge, a self-finding and self-unfolding of the Spirit, a self-revelation of the Divinity in things in that true power of itself in Nature which is to us still a Supernature.

A New Global Agenda

The Turn towards Unity: Its
Necessity and Dangers[1]

The surfaces of life are easy to understand; their laws, characteristic movements, practical utilities are ready to our hand and we can seize on them and turn them to account with a sufficient facility and rapidity. But they do not carry us very far. They suffice for an active superficial life from day to day, but they do not solve the great problems of existence. On the other hand, the knowledge of life's profundities, its potent secrets, its great, hidden, all-determining laws is exceedingly difficult to us. We have found no plummet that can fathom these depths; they seem to us a vague, indeterminate movement, a profound obscurity from which the mind recoils willingly to play with the fret and foam and facile radiances of the surface. Yet it is these depths and their unseen forces that we ought to know if we would understand existence; on the surface we get only Nature's secondary rules and practical bye-laws which help us to tide over the difficulties of the moment and to organise empirically without understanding them her continual transitions.

Nothing is more obscure to humanity or less seized by its understanding, whether in the power that moves it or the sense of the aim towards which it moves, than its own communal and

---

[1] Chapter I of *The Ideal of Human Unity*. First published in the *Arya* in 1915. The book was published in 1919 and reissued in 1950 with slight revisions.

collective life. Sociology does not help us, for it only gives us the general story of the past and the external conditions under which communities have survived. History teaches us nothing; it is a confused torrent of events and personalities or a kaleidoscope of changing institutions. We do not seize the real sense of all this change and this continual streaming forward of human life in the channels of Time. What we do seize are current or recurrent phenomena, facile generalisations, partial ideas. We talk of democracy, aristocracy and autocracy, collectivism and individualism, imperialism and nationalism, the State and the commune, capitalism and labour; we advance hasty generalisations and make absolute systems which are positively announced today only to be abandoned perforce tomorrow; we espouse causes and ardent enthusiasms whose triumph turns to an early disillusionment and then forsake them for others, perhaps for those that we have taken so much trouble to destroy. For a whole century mankind thirsts and battles after liberty and earns it with a bitter expense of toil, tears and blood; the century that enjoys without having fought for it turns away as from a puerile illusion and is ready to renounce the depreciated gain as the price of some new good. And all this happens because our whole thought and action with regard to our collective life is shallow and empirical; it does not seek for, it does not base itself on a firm, profound and complete knowledge. The moral is not the vanity of human life, of its ardours and enthusiasms and of the ideals it pursues, but the necessity of a wiser, larger, more patient search after its true law and aim.

Today the ideal of human unity is more or less vaguely making its way to the front of our consciousness. The emergence of an ideal in human thought is always the sign of an intention in Nature, but not always of an intention to accomplish; sometimes it indicates only an attempt which is predestined to temporary failure. For Nature is slow and patient in her methods. She takes up ideas and half carries them out, then drops them by the wayside to resume them in some future era with a better combination. She tempts humanity, her thinking instrument, and tests how far it is ready for the harmony she has imagined; she allows and incites man to attempt and fail, so that he may learn and succeed better another time. Still the ideal, having once made its way to the front of thought, must certainly be attempted, and this ideal of human unity is likely to figure largely among the determining forces of the future; for the intellectual and material circumstances of the age have prepared and almost impose it, especially the scientific discoveries which have made our earth so small that its vastest kingdoms seem now no more than the provinces of a single country.

But this very commodity of the material circumstances may bring about the failure of the ideal; for when material circumstances favour a great change, but the heart and mind of the race are not really ready—especially the heart—failure may be predicted, unless indeed men are wise in time and accept the inner change along with the external readjustment. But at present the human intellect has been so much mechanised by physical Science that it is likely to attempt the revolution it is beginning to envisage principally or solely through mechanical means, through social and political adjustments. Now it is not by social and political devices, or at any rate not by these chiefly or only, that the unity of the human race can be enduringly or fruitfully accomplished.

It must be remembered that a greater social or political unity is not necessarily a boon in itself; it is only worth pursuing in so far as it provides a means and a framework for a better, richer, more happy and puissant individual and collective life. But hitherto the experience of mankind has not favoured the view that huge aggregations, closely united and strictly organised, are favourable to a rich and puissant human life. It would seem rather that collective life is more at ease with itself, more genial, varied, fruitful when it can concentrate itself in small spaces and simpler organisms.

If we consider the past of humanity so far as it is known to us, we find that the interesting periods of human life, the scenes in which it has been most richly lived and has left behind it the most precious fruits, were precisely those ages and countries in which humanity was able to organise itself in little independent centres acting intimately upon each other but not fused into a single unity. Modern Europe owes two-thirds of its civilisation to three such supreme moments of human history, the religious life of the congeries of tribes which called itself Israel and, subsequently, of the little nation of the Jews, the many-sided life of the small Greek city states, the similar, though more restricted artistic and intellectual life of mediaeval Italy. Nor was any age in Asia so rich in energy, so well worth living in, so productive of the best and most enduring fruits as that heroic period of India when she was divided into small kingdoms, many of them no larger than a modern district. Her most wonderful activities, her most vigorous and enduring work, that which, if we had to make a choice, we should keep at the sacrifice of all else, belonged to that period; the second best came afterwards in larger, but still comparatively small nations and kingdoms like those of the Pallavas, Chalukyas, Pandyas, Cholas and Cheras. In comparison she received little from the greater empires that rose and fell within her borders, the Moghul, the Gupta or the Maurya—little indeed except political and administrative organisation, some fine art and literature and a certain amount of lasting work in other kinds, not always of the best quality. Their impulse was rather towards elaborate organisation than original, stimulating and creative.

Nevertheless, in this regime of the small city state or of regional cultures there was always a defect which compelled a tendency towards large organisations. The defect was a characteristic of impermanence, often of disorder, especially of defencelessness against the onslaught of larger organisations, even of an insufficient capacity for widespread material well-being. Therefore this earlier form of collective life tended to disappear and give place to the organisation of nations, kingdoms and empires.

And here we notice, first, that it is the groupments of smaller nations which have had the most intense life and not the huge States and colossal empires. Collective life diffusing itself in too vast spaces seems to lose intensity and productiveness. Europe has lived in England, France, the Netherlands, Spain, Italy, the small States of Germany—all her later civilisation and progress evolved itself there, not in the huge mass of the Holy Roman or the Russian Empire. We see a similar phenomenon in the social and political field when we compare the intense life and activity of Europe in its many nations acting richly upon each other, rapidly progressing by quick creative steps and sometimes by bounds, with the great masses of Asia, her long periods of immobility in which wars and revolutions seem to be small, temporary and usually unproductive episodes, her centuries of religious, philosophic and artistic reveries her tendency towards an increasing isolation and a final stagnancy of the outward life.

Secondly, we note that in this organisation of nations and kingdoms those which have had the most vigorous life have gained it by a sort of artificial concentration of the vitality into some head, centre or capital, London, Paris, Rome. By this device Nature, while acquiring the benefits of a larger organisation and more perfect unity, preserves to some extent that equally precious power of fruitful concentration in a small space and into a closely packed activity which she had possessed in her more primitive system of the city state or petty kingdom. But this advantage was purchased by the condemnation of the rest of the organisation, the district, the provincial town, the village to a dull, petty and somnolent life in strange contrast with the vital intensity of the *urbs* or metropolis.

The Roman Empire is the historic example of an organisation of unity which transcended the limits of the nation, and its advantages and disadvantages are there perfectly typified. The advantages are admirable organisation, peace, widespread security, order and material well-being; the disadvantage is that the individual, the city, the region sacrifice their independent life and become mechanical parts of a machine; life loses its colour, richness, variety, freedom and victorious impulse towards creation. The organisation is great and admirable, but the individual dwindles and is overpowered and overshadowed; and eventually by the smallness and feebleness of the individual the huge organism inevitably and slowly loses even its great conservative vitality and dies of an increasing stagnation. Even while outwardly whole and untouched, the structure has become rotten and begins to crack and dissolve at the first shock from outside. Such organisations, such periods are immensely useful for conservation, even as the Roman Empire served to consolidate the gains of the rich centuries that preceded it. But they arrest life and growth.

We see, then, what is likely to happen if there were a social, administrative and political unification of mankind, such as some have begun to dream of nowadays. A tremendous organisation would be needed under which both individual and regional life would be crushed, dwarfed, deprived of their necessary freedom like a plant without rain and wind and sunlight, and this would mean for humanity, after perhaps one first outburst of satisfied and joyous activity, a long period of mere conservation, increasing stagnancy and ultimately decay.

Yet the unity of mankind is evidently a part of Nature's eventual scheme and must come about. Only it must be under other conditions and with safeguards which will keep the race intact in the roots of its vitality, richly diverse in its oneness.

The Inadequacy of the State Idea[1]

What after all, is this State idea, this idea of the organised community to which the individual has to be immolated? Theoretically, it is the subordination of the individual to the good of all that is demanded; practically, it is his subordination to a collective egoism, political, military, economic, which seeks to satisfy certain collective aims and ambitions shaped and imposed on the great mass of the individuals by a smaller or larger number of ruling persons who are supposed in some way to represent the community. It is immaterial whether these belong to a governing class or emerge as in modern States from the mass partly by force of character, but much more by force of circumstances; nor does it make any essential difference that their aims and ideals are imposed nowadays more by the hypnotism of verbal persuasion than by overt and actual force. In either case there is no guarantee that this ruling class or ruling body represents the best mind of the nation or its noblest aims or its highest instincts.

Nothing of the kind can be asserted of the modern politician in any part of the world; he does not represent the soul of a people or its aspirations. What he does usually represent is all the average pettiness, selfishness, egoism, self-deception that is about him and these he represents well enough as well as a great deal of mental incompetence and moral conventionality, timidity

---

[1] Chapter IV of *The Ideal of Human Unity.*

and pretence. Great issues often come to him for decision, but he does not deal with them greatly; high words and noble ideas are on his lips, but they become rapidly the claptrap of a party. The disease and falsehood of modern political life is patent in every country of the world and only the hypnotised acquiescence of all, even of the intellectual classes, in the great organised sham, cloaks and prolongs the malady, the acquiescence that men yield to everything that is habitual and makes the present atmosphere of their lives. Yet it is by such minds that the good of all has to be decided, to such hands that it has to be entrusted, to such an agency calling itself the State that the individual is being more and more called upon to give up the government of his activities. As a matter of fact, it is in no way the largest good of all that is thus secured, but a great deal of organised blundering and evil with a certain amount of good which makes for real progress, because Nature moves forward always in the midst of all stumblings and secures her aims in the end more often in spite of man's imperfect mentality than by its means.

But even if the governing instrument were better constituted and of a higher mental and moral character, even if some way could be found to do what ancient civilisations by their enforcement of certain high ideals and disciplines tried to do with their ruling classes, still the State would not be what the State idea pretends that it is. Theoretically, it is the collective wisdom and force of the community made available and organised for the general good. Practically, what controls the engine and drives the train is so much of the intellect and power available in the community as the particular machinery of State organisation will allow to come to the surface; but it is also caught in the machinery and hampered by it and hampered as well by the large amount of folly and selfish weakness that comes up in the emergence. Doubtless, this is the best that can be done under the circumstances, and Nature, as always, utilises it for the best. But things would be much worse if there were not a field left for a less trammelled individual effort doing what the State cannot do, deploying and using the sincerity, energy, idealism of the best individuals to attempt that which the State has not the wisdom or courage to attempt, getting that done which a collective conservatism and imbecility would either leave undone or actively suppress and oppose. It is this energy of the individual which is the really effective agent of collective progress. The State sometimes comes in to aid it and then, if its aid does not mean undue control, it serves a positively useful end. As often it stands in the way and then serves either as a brake upon progress or supplies the necessary amount of organised opposition and friction always needed to give greater energy and a more complete shape to the new thing which is in process of formation. But what we are now tending towards is such an increase of organised State power and such a huge irresistible and complex State activity as will either eliminate free individual effort altogether or leave it dwarfed and cowed into helplessness. The necessary corrective to the defects, limitations and inefficiency of the State machine will disappear.

The organised State is neither the best mind of the nation nor is it even the sum of the communal energies. It leaves out of its organised action and suppresses or unduly depresses the working force and thinking mind of important minorities, often of those which represent that which is best in the present and that which is developing for the future. It is a collective egoism much inferior to the best of which the community is capable. What that egoism is in its relation to other collective egoisms we know, and its ugliness has recently been forced upon the vision and the conscience of mankind. The individual has usually something at least like a soul, and, at any rate, he makes up for the deficiencies of the soul by a system of morality and an ethical sense, and for the deficiencies of these again by the fear of social opinion or, failing that, a fear of the communal law which he has ordinarily either to obey or at least to circumvent; and even the difficulty of circumventing is a check on all except the most violent or the most skilful. But the State is an entity which, with the greatest amount of power, is the least hampered by internal scruples or external checks. It has no soul or only a rudimentary one. It is a military, political and economic force; but it is only in a slight and undeveloped degree, if at all, an intellectual and ethical being. And unfortunately the chief use it makes of its undeveloped intellect is to blunt by fictions, catchwords and recently by State philosophies, its ill-developed ethical conscience. Man within the community is now at least a half-civilised creature, but his international existence is still primitive. Until recently the organised nation in its relations with other nations was only a huge beast of prey with appetites which sometimes slept when gorged or discouraged by events, but were always its chief reason for existence. Self-protection and self-expansion by the devouring of others were its *dharma*. At the present day there is no essential improvement; there is only a greater difficulty in devouring. A 'sacred egoism' is still the ideal of nations, and therefore there is neither any true and enlightened consciousness of human opinion to restrain the predatory State nor any effective international law. There is only the fear of defeat and the fear, recently, of a disastrous economic disorganisation; but experience after experience has shown that these checks are ineffective.

In its inner life this huge State egoism was once little better than in its outer relations.[2] Brutal, rapacious, cunning, oppressive, intolerant of free action, free speech and opinion, even of freedom of conscience in religion, it preyed upon individuals and classes within as upon weaker nations outside. Only the necessity of

---

[2] I am speaking of the intermediate age between ancient and modern times. In ancient times the State had, in some countries at least, ideals and a conscience with regard to the community, but very little in its dealings with other States. [Sri Aurobindo's note]

keeping alive and rich and strong in a rough sort of way the community on which it lived, made its action partially and crudely beneficent. In modern times there has been much improvement in spite of deterioration in certain directions. The State now feels the necessity of justifying its existence by organising the general economic and animal well-being of the community and even of all individuals. It is beginning to see the necessity of assuring the intellectual and, indirectly, the moral development of the whole community. This attempt of the State to grow into an intellectual and moral being is one of the most interesting phenomena of modern civilisation. Even the necessity of intellectualising and moralising it in its external relations has been enforced upon the conscience of mankind by the European catastrophe. But the claim of the State to absorb all free individual activities, a claim which it increasingly makes as it grows more clearly conscious of its new ideals and its possibilities, is, to say the least of it, premature and, if satisfied, will surely end in a check to human progress, a comfortably organised stagnancy such as overtook the Graeco-Roman world after the establishment of the Roman Empire. The call of the State to the individual to immolate himself on its altar and to give up his free activities into an organised collective activity is therefore something quite different from the demand of our highest ideals. It amounts to the giving up of the present form of individual egoism into another, a collective form, larger but not superior, rather in many ways inferior to the best individual egoism. The altruistic ideal, the discipline of self-sacrifice, the need of a growing solidarity with our fellows and a growing collective soul in humanity are not in dispute. But the loss of self in the State is not the thing that these high ideals mean, nor is it the way to their fulfilment. Man must learn not to suppress and mutilate, but to fulfil himself in the fulfilment of mankind, even as he must learn not to mutilate or destroy, but to complete his ego by expanding it out of its limitations and losing it in something greater which it now tries to represent. But the deglutition of the free individual by a huge State machine is quite another consummation. The State is a convenience, and a rather clumsy convenience, for our common development; it ought never to be made an end in itself.

The second claim of the State idea that this supremacy and universal activity of the organised State machine is the best means of human progress, is also an exaggeration and a fiction. Man lives by the community; he needs it to develop himself individually as well as collectively. But is it true that a State-governed action is the most capable of developing the individual perfectly as well as of serving the common ends of the community? It is not true. What is true is that it is capable of providing the co-operative action of the individuals in the community with all necessary conveniences and of removing from it disabilities and obstacles which would otherwise interfere with its working. Here the real utility of the State ceases. The non-recognition of the possibilities of human cooperation was the weakness of English individualism; the turning of a utility for co-operative action into an excuse for rigid control by the State is the weakness of the Teutonic idea of collectivism. When the State attempts to take up the control of the co-operative action of the community, it condemns itself to create a monstrous machinery which will end by crushing out the freedom, initiative and serious growth of the human being.

The State is bound to act crudely and in the mass; it is incapable of that free, harmonious and intelligently or instinctively varied action which is proper to organic growth. For the State is not an organism; it is a machinery, and it works like a machine, without tact, taste, delicacy or intuition. It tries to manufacture, but what humanity is here to do is to grow and create. We see this flaw in State-governed education. It is right and necessary that education should be provided for all and in providing for it the State is eminently useful; but when it controls the education, it turns it into a routine, a mechanical system in which individual initiative, individual growth and true development as opposed to a routine instruction become impossible. The State tends always to uniformity, because uniformity is easy to it and natural variation is impossible to its essentially mechanical nature; but uniformity is death, not life. A national culture, a national religion, a national education may still be useful things provided they do not interfere with the growth of human solidarity on the one side and individual freedom of thought and conscience and development on the other; for they give form to the communal soul and help it to add its quota to the sum of human advancement; but a State education, a State religion, a State culture are unnatural violences. And the same rule holds good in different ways and to a different extent in other directions of our communal life and its activities.

The business of the State, so long as it continues to be a necessary element in human life and growth, is to provide all possible facilities for co-operative action, to remove obstacles, to prevent all really harmful waste and friction—a certain amount of waste and friction is necessary and useful to all natural action—and, removing avoidable injustice, to secure for every individual a just and equal chance of self-development and satisfaction to the extent of his powers and in the line of his nature. So far the aim in modern socialism is right and good. But all unnecessary interference with the freedom of man's growth is or can be harmful. Even co-operative action is injurious if, instead of seeking the good of all compatibly with the necessities of individual growth—and without individual growth there can be no real and permanent good of all—it immolates the individual to a communal egoism and prevents so much free room and initiative as is necessary for the flowering of a more perfectly developed humanity. So long as humanity is not full-grown, so long as it needs to grow and is capable of a greater perfectibility, there can be no static good of all independent of the growth of the individuals composing the all. All collectivist ideals which seek unduly to subordinate the individual, really envisage a static condition whether it be a present status or one it soon hopes to establish, after which all attempt at serious change would be regarded as an offence of impatient individualism against the peace, just routine and security of the happily established communal order. Always it is the individual who progresses and compels the rest to progress; the instinct of the collectivity is to stand still in its established order. Progress, growth, realisation of wider being, give his greatest sense of happiness to the individual; status, secure ease, to the collectivity. And so it must be as long as the latter is more a physical and economic entity than a self-conscious collective soul.

It is therefore quite improbable that in the present conditions of the race a healthy unity of mankind can be brought about by State machinery, whether it be by a grouping of powerful and organised States enjoying carefully regulated and legalised relations with each other or by the substitution of a single World-State for the present half chaotic half-ordered comity of nations—be the form of that World-State a single Empire like the Roman or a federated unity. Such an external or administrative unity may be intended in the near future of mankind in order to accustom the race to the idea of a common life, to its habit, to its possibility; but it cannot be really healthy, durable or beneficial over all the true line of human destiny unless something be developed, more profound, internal and real. Otherwise the experience of the ancient world will be repeated on a larger scale and in other circumstances. The experiment will break down and give place to a new reconstructive age of confusion and anarchy. Perhaps this experience also is necessary for mankind; yet it ought to be possible for us now to avoid it by subordinating mechanical means to our true development through a moralised and even a spiritualised humanity united in its inner soul and not only in its outward life and body.

The Ideal of Human Unity: Summary and Conclusion[1]

In other words—and this is the conclusion at which we arrive—while it is possible to construct a precarious and quite mechanical unity by political and administrative means, the unity of the human race, even if achieved, can only be secured and can only be made real if the religion of humanity, which is at present the highest active ideal of mankind, spiritualises itself and becomes the general inner law of human life.

The outward unity may well achieve itself—possibly, though by no means certainly, in a measurable time—because that is the inevitable final trend of the working of Nature in human society which makes for larger and yet larger aggregations and cannot fail to arrive at a total aggregation of mankind in a closer international system.

This working of Nature depends for its means of fulfilment upon two forces which combine to make the larger aggregation inevitable. First, there is the increasing closeness of common interests or at least the interlacing and interrelation of interests in a larger and yet larger circle which makes old divisions an obstacle and a cause of weakness, obstruction and friction, and the clash and collision that comes out of this friction a ruinous calamity to all, even to the victor who has to pay a too heavy price

---

[1] Chapter XXXV of *The Ideal of Human Unity*.

for his gains; and even these expected gains, as war becomes more complex and disastrous, are becoming more and more difficult to achieve and the success problematical. An increasing perception of this community or interrelation of interests and a growing unwillingness to face the consequences of collision and ruinous struggle must push men to welcome any means for mitigating the divisions which lead to such disasters. If the trend to the mitigation of divisions is once given a definite form, that commences an impetus which drives towards closer and closer union. If she cannot arrive by these means, if the incoherence is too great for the trend of unification to triumph, Nature will use other means, such as war and conquest or the temporary domination of the powerful State or empire or the menace of such a domination which will compel those threatened to adopt a closer system of union. It is these means and this force of outward necessity which she used to create nation-units and national empires, and, however modified in the circumstances and workings, it is at bottom the same force and 'the same means which she is using to dri e mankind towards international unification.

But, secondly, there is the force of a common uniting sentiment. This may work in two ways; it may come before as an originating or contributory cause or it may come afterwards as a cementing result. In the first case, the sentiment of a larger unity springs up among units which were previously divided and leads them to seek after a form of union which may then be brought about principally by the force of the sentiment and its idea or by that secondarily as an aid to other and more outward events and causes. We may note that in earlier times this sentiment was insufficiently effective, as among the petty clans or regional nations; unity had ordinarily to be effected by outward circumstances and generally by the grossest of them, by war and conquest, by the domination of the most powerful among many warring or contiguous peoples. But in later times the force of the sentiment of unity, supported as it has been by a clearer political idea, has become more effective. The larger national aggregates have grown up by a simple act of federation or union, though this has sometimes had to be preceded by a common struggle for liberty or a union in war against a common enemy; so have grown into one the United States, Italy, Germany, and more peacefully the Australian and South African federations. But in other cases, especially in the earlier national aggregations, the sentiment of unity has grown up largely or entirely as the result of the formal, outward or mechanical union. But whether to form or to preserve the growth of the sentiment, the psychological factor is indispensable; without it there can be no secure and lasting union. Its absence, the failure to create such a sentiment or to make it sufficiently living, natural, forcible has been the cause of the precariousness of such aggregates as Austro-Hungary and of the ephemeral character of the empires of the past, even as it is likely to bring about, unless circumstances change, the collapse or disintegration of the great present-day empires.

The trend of forces towards some kind of international world-organisation eventuating in a possible far-off unification, which is now just beginning to declare itself as an idea or aspiration though the causes which made it inevitable have been for some time at work, is enforced by the pressure of need and environment, by outward circumstances. At the same time, there is a sentiment helped and stimulated by these outward circumstances, a cosmopolitan, international sentiment, still rather nebulous and vaguely ideal, which may accelerate the growth of the formal union. In itself this sentiment would be an insufficient cement for the preservation of any mechanical union which might be created; for it could not easily be so close and forcible a sentiment as national feeling. It would have to subsist on the conveniences of union as its only substantial provender. But the experience of the past shows that this mere necessity of convenience is in the end not strong enough to resist the pressure of unfavourable circumstances and the reassertion of old or the effective growth of new centrifugal forces. There is, however, at work a more powerful force, a sort of intellectual religion of humanity, clear in the minds of the few, vaguely felt in its effects and its disguises by the many, which has largely helped to bring about much of the trend of the modern mind and the drift of its developing institutions. This is a psychological force which tends to break beyond the formula of the nation and aspires to replace the religion of the country and even, in its more extreme forms, to destroy altogether the national sentiment and to abolish its divisions so as to create the single nation of mankind.

We may say, then, that this trend must eventually realise itself, however great may be the difficulties; and they are really enormous, much greater than those which attended the national formation. If the present unsatisfactory condition of international relations should lead to a series of cataclysms, either large and world-embracing like the present war or, though each more limited in scope, yet in their sum world-pervading and necessarily, by the growing interrelation of interests, affecting even those who do not fall directly under their touch, then mankind will finally be forced in self-defence to a new, closer and more stringently unified order of things. Its choice will be between that and a lingering suicide. If the human reason cannot find out the way, Nature herself is sure to shape these upheavals in such a way as to bring about her end. Therefore—whether soon or in the long run, whether brought about by its own growing sentiment of unity, stimulated by common interest and convenience, or by the evolutionary pressure of circumstances—we may take it that an eventual unification or at least some formal organisation of human life on earth is, the incalculable being always allowed for, practically inevitable.

I have tried to show from the analogy of the past evolution of the nation that this international unification must culminate or at least is likely to culminate in one of two forms. There is likely to be either a centralised World-State or a looser world-union which may be either a close federation or a simple confederacy of the peoples for the common ends of mankind. The last form is the most desirable, because it gives sufficient scope for the principle of variation which is necessary for the free play of life and the healthy progress of the race. The process by which the World-State may come starts with the creation of a central body which will at first have very limited functions, but, once created, must absorb by degrees all the different utilities of a centralised international control, as the State, first in the form of a monarchy and then of a parliament, has been absorbing by degrees the whole control of the life of the nation, so that we are now within measurable distance of a centralised socialistic State which will leave no part of the life of its individuals unregulated. A similar process in the World-State will end in the taking up and the regulation of the whole life of the peoples into its hands; it may even end by abolishing national individuality and turning the divisions that it has created into mere departmental groupings, provinces and districts of the one common State. Such an eventuality may seem now a fantastic dream or an unrealisable idea; but it is one which, under certain conditions that are by no means beyond the scope of ultimate possibility, may well become feasible and even, after a certain point is reached, inevitable. A federal system and still more a confederacy would mean, on the other hand, the preservation of the national basis and a greater or less freedom of national life, but the subordination of the separate national to the larger common interests and of full separate freedom to the greater international necessities.

It may be questioned whether past analogies are a safe guide in a problem so new and whether something else might not be evolved more intimately and independently arising from it and suitable to its complexities. But mankind even in dealing with its new problems works upon past experience and therefore upon past motives and analogies. Even when it seizes on new ideas, it goes to the past for the form it gives to them. Behind the apparent changes of the most radical revolutions we see this unavoidable principle of continuity surviving in the heart of the new order. Moreover, these alternatives seem the only way in which the two forces in presence can work out their conflict, either by the disappearance of the one, the separative national instinct, or by an accommodation between them. On the other hand, it is quite possible that human thought and action may take so new a turn as to bring in a number of unforeseen possibilities and lead to a quite different ending.

And one might upon these lines set one's imagination to work and produce perhaps a Utopia of a better kind. Such constructive efforts of the human imagination have their value and often a very great value; but any such speculations would evidently have been out of place in the study I have attempted. Assuredly, neither of the two alternatives and none of the three forms considered are free from serious objections. A centralised World-State would signify the triumph of the idea of mechanical unity or rather of uniformity. It would inevitably mean the undue depression of an indispensable element in the vigour of human life and progress, the free life of the individual, the free variation of the peoples. It must end, if it becomes permanent and fulfils all its tendencies, either in a death in life, a stagnation, or by the insurgence of some new saving but revolutionary force or principle which would shatter the whole fabric into pieces. The mechanical tendency is one to which the logical reason of man, itself a precise machine, is easily addicted and its operations are obviously the easiest to manage and the most ready to hand; its full evolution may seem to the reason desirable, necessary, inevitable, but its end is predestined. A centralised socialistic State may be a necessity of the future, once it is founded, but a reaction from it will be equally an eventual necessity of the future. The greater its pressure, the more certainly will it be met by the spread of the spiritual, the intellectual, the vital and practical principle of Anarchism in revolt against that mechanical pressure. So, too, a centralised mechanical World-State must rouse in the end a similar force against it and might well terminate in a crumbling up and disintegration, even in the necessity for a repetition of the cycle of humanity ending in a better attempt to solve the problem. It could be kept in being only if humanity agreed to allow all the rest of its life to be regularised for it for the sake of peace and stability and took refuge for its individual freedom in the spiritual life, as happened once under the Roman Empire. But even that would be only a temporary solution. A federal system also would tend inevitably to establish one general type for human life, institutions and activities; it would allow only a play of minor variations. But the need of variation in living Nature could not always rest satisfied with that scanty sustenance. On the other hand, a looser confederacy might well be open to the objection that it would give too ready a handle for centrifugal forces, were such to arise in new strength. A loose confederation could not be permanent; it must turn in one direction or the other, end either in a close and rigid centralisation or at last by a break-up of the loose unity into its original elements.

The saving power needed is a new psychological factor which will at once make a united life necessary to humanity and force it to respect the principle of freedom. The religion of humanity seems to be the one growing force which tends in that direction; for it makes for the sense of human oneness, it has the idea of the race, and yet at the same time it respects the human individual and the natural human grouping. But its present intellectual form seems hardly sufficient. The idea, powerful in itself and in its effects, is yet not powerful enough to mould the whole life of the race in its image. For it has to concede too much to the egoistic side of human nature, once all and still nine-tenths of our being, with which its larger idea is in conflict. On the other side, because it leans principally on the reason, it turns too readily to the mechanical solution. For the rational idea ends always as a captive of its machinery, becomes a slave of its own too binding process. A new idea with another turn of the logical machine revolts against it and breaks up its machinery, but only to substitute in the end another mechanical system, another credo, formula and practice.

A spiritual religion of humanity is the hope of the future. By this is not meant what is ordinarily called a universal religion, a system, a thing of creed and intellectual belief and dogma and outward rite. Mankind has tried unity by that means; it has failed and deserved to fail, because there can be no universal religious system, one in mental creed and vital form. The inner spirit is indeed one, but more than any other the spiritual life insists on freedom and variation in its self-expression and means of development. A religion of humanity means the growing realisation that there is a secret Spirit, a divine Reality, in which we are all one, that humanity is its highest present vehicle on earth, that the human race and the human being are the means by which it will progressively reveal itself here. It implies a growing attempt to live out this knowledge and bring about a kingdom of this divine Spirit upon earth. By its growth within us oneness with our fellow-men will become the leading principle of all our life, not merely a principle of cooperation but a deeper brotherhood, a real and an inner sense of unity and equality and a common life. There must be the realisation by the individual that only in the life of his fellow-men is his own life complete. There must be the realisation by the race that only on the free and full life of the individual can its own perfection and permanent happiness be founded. There must be too a discipline and a way of salvation in accordance with this religion, that is to say, a means by which it can be developed by each man within himself, so that it may be developed in the life of the race. To go into all that this implies would be too large a subject to be entered upon here; it is enough to point out that in this direction lies the eventual road. No doubt, if this is only an idea like the rest, it will go the way of all ideas. But if it is at all a truth of our being, then it must be the truth to which all is moving and in it must be found the means of a fundamental, an inner, a complete, a real human unity which would be the one secure base of a unification of human life. A spiritual oneness which would create a psychological oneness not dependent upon any intellectual or outward uniformity and compel a oneness of life not bound up with its mechanical means of unification, but ready always to enrich its secure unity by a free inner variation and a freely varied outer self-expression, this would be the basis for a higher type of human existence.

Could such a realisation develop rapidly in mankind, we might then solve the problem of unification in a deeper and truer way from the inner truth to the outer forms. Until then, the attempt to bring it about by mechanical means must proceed. But the higher hope of humanity lies in the growing number of men who will realise this truth and seek to develop it in themselves, so that when the mind of man is ready to escape from its mechanical bent—perhaps when it finds that its mechanical solutions are all temporary and disappointing—the truth of the Spirit may step in and lead humanity to the path of its highest possible happiness and perfection.

The Cycle of Society[1]

Modern Science, obsessed with the greatness of its physical discoveries and the idea of the sole existence of Matter, has long attempted to base upon physical data even its study of Soul and Mind and of those workings of Nature in man and animal in which a knowledge of psychology is as important as any of the physical sciences. Its very psychology founded itself upon physiology and the scrutiny of the brain and nervous system. It is not surprising therefore that in history and sociology attention should have been concentrated on the external data, laws, institutions, rites, customs, economic factors and developments, while the deeper psychological elements so important in the activities of a mental, emotional, ideative being like man have been very much neglected. This kind of science would explain history and social development as much as possible by economic necessity or motive—by economy understood in its widest sense. There are even historians who deny or put aside as of a very subsidiary importance the working of the idea and the influence of the thinker in the development of human institutions. The French Revolution, it is thought, would have happened just as it did and when it did, by economic necessity, even if Rousseau and Voltaire had never written and the eighteenth-

---

[1] First published in the *Arya* on 15 August 1916 as the opening chapter of a larger work called *The Psychology of Social Development*. Published in book form with slight revisions in 1949 with the present title, *The Human Cycle*.

century philosophic movement in the world of thought had never worked out its bold and radical speculations.

Recently, however, the all-sufficiency of Matter to explain Mind and Soul has begun to be doubted and a movement of emancipation from the obsession of physical science has set in, although as yet it has not gone beyond a few awkward and rudimentary stumblings. Still there is the beginning of a perception that behind the economic motives and causes of social and historical development there are profound psychological, even perhaps soul factors; and in pre-war Germany, the metropolis of rationalism and materialism but the home also, for a century-and-a-half, of new thought and original tendencies good and bad, beneficent and disastrous, a first psychological theory of history was conceived and presented by an original intelligence. The earliest attempts in a new field are seldom entirely successful, and the German historian, originator of this theory, seized on a luminous idea, but was not able to carry it very far or probe very deep. He was still haunted by a sense of the greater importance of the economic factor, and like most European science his theory related classified and organised phenomena much more successfully than it explained them. Nevertheless, its basic idea formulated a suggestive and illuminating truth, and it is worthwhile following up some of the suggestions it opens out in the light especially of Eastern thought and experience.

The theorist, Lamprecht,[2] basing himself on European and particularly on German history, supposed that human society progresses through certain distinct psychological stages which he terms respectively symbolic, typal and conventional, individualist and subjective. This development forms, then, a sort of psychological cycle through which a nation or a civilisation is bound to proceed. Obviously, such classifications are likely to err by rigidity and to substitute a mental straight line for the coils and

---

[2] Karl Lamprecht (1856-1915), German historian and social theorist.

zigzags of Nature. The psychology of man and his societies is too complex, too synthetical of many-sided and intermixed tendencies to satisfy any such rigorous and formal analysis. Nor does this theory of a psychological cycle tell us what is the inner meaning of its successive phases or the necessity of their succession or the term and end towards which they are driving. But still to understand natural laws whether of Mind or Matter it is necessary to analyse their working into its discoverable elements, main constituents, dominant forces, though these may not actually be found anywhere in isolation. I will leave aside the Western thinker's own dealings with his idea. The suggestive names he has offered us, if we examine their intrinsic sense and value, may yet throw some light on the thickly veiled secret of our historic evolution, and this is the line on which it would be most useful to investigate.

Undoubtedly, wherever we can seize human society in what to us seems its primitive beginnings or early stages—no matter whether the race is comparatively cultured or savage or economically advanced or backward—we do find a strongly symbolic mentality that governs or at least pervades its thought, customs and institutions. Symbolic, but of what? We find that this social stage is always religious and actively imaginative in its religion; for symbolism and a widespread imaginative or intuitive religious feeling have a natural kinship and especially in earlier or primitive formations they have gone always together. When man begins to be predominantly intellectual, sceptical, ratiocinative he is already preparing for an individualist society and the age of symbols and the age of conventions have passed or are losing their virtue. The symbol then is of something which man feels to be present behind himself and his life and his activities—the Divine, the Gods, the vast and deep unnameable, a hidden, living and mysterious nature of things. All his religious and social institutions, all the moments and phases of his life are to him symbols in which he seeks to express what he knows or guesses of the mystic influences that are behind his life and shape and govern or at the least intervene in its movements.

If we look at the beginnings of Indian society, the far-off Vedic age which we no longer understand, for we have lost that mentality, we see that everything is symbolic. The religious institution of sacrifice governs the whole society and all its hours and moments, and the ritual of the sacrifice is at every turn and in every detail, as even a cursory study of the Brahmanas and Upanishads ought to show us, mystically symbolic. The theory that there was nothing in the sacrifice except a propitiation of Nature-gods for the gaining of worldly prosperity and of Paradise, is a misunderstanding by a later humanity which had already become profoundly affected by an intellectual and practical bent of mind, practical even in its religion and even in its own mysticism and symbolism, and therefore could no longer enter into the ancient spirit. Not only the actual religious worship but also the social institutions of the time were penetrated through and through with the symbolic spirit. Take the hymn of the Rig Veda which is supposed to be a marriage hymn for the union of a human couple and was certainly used as such in the later Vedic ages. Yet the whole sense of the hymn turns about the successive marriages of *Suryā,* daughter of the Sun, with different gods and the human marriage is quite a subordinate matter overshadowed and governed entirely by the divine and mystic figure and is spoken of in the terms of that figure. Mark, however, that the divine marriage here is not, as it would be in later ancient poetry, a decorative image or poetical ornamentation used to set off and embellish the human union; on the contrary, the human is an inferior figure and image of the divine. The distinction marks off the entire contrast between that more ancient mentality and our modern regard upon things. This symbolism influenced for a long time Indian ideas of marriage and is even now conventionally remembered though no longer understood or effective.

We may note also in passing that the Indian ideal of the relation between man and woman has always been governed by the symbolism of the relation between the Purusha and Prakriti (in the Veda Nṛ and Gnā), the male and female divine Principles in the universe. Even, there is to some degree a practical correlation between the position of the female sex and this idea. In the earlier Vedic times when the female principle stood on a sort of equality with the male in the symbolic cult, though with a certain predominance for the latter, woman was as much the mate as the adjunct of man; in later times when the Prakriti has become subject in idea to the Purusha, the woman also depends entirely on the man, exists only for him and has hardly even a separate spiritual existence. In the Tantrik Shakta religion which puts the female principle highest, there is an attempt which could not get itself translated into social practice—even as this Tantrik cult could never entirely shake off the subjugation of the Vedantic idea— to elevate woman and make her an object of profound respect and even of worship.

Or let us take, for this example will serve us best, the Vedic institution of the fourfold order, *caturvarna*, miscalled the system of the four castes, for caste is a conventional, *varṇa* a symbolic and typal institution. We are told that the institution of the four orders of society was the result of an economic evolution complicated by political causes. Very possibly;[3] but the important point is that it was not so regarded and could not be so regarded by the men of that age. For while we are satisfied when we have found the practical and material causes of a social phenomenon and do not care to look farther, they cared little or only subordinately for its material factors and looked always

---

[3] It is at least doubtful. The Brahmin class at first seem to have exercised all sorts of economic functions and not to have confined themselves to those of the priesthood. [Sri Aurobindo's note]

first and foremost for its symbolic, religious or psychological significance. This appears in the Purushasukta of the Veda, where the four orders are described as having sprung from the body of the creative Deity, from his head, arms, thighs and feet. To us this is merely a poetical image and its sense is that the Brahmins were the men of knowledge, the Kshatriyas the men of power, the Vaishyas the producers and support of society, the Shudras its servants. As if that were all, as if the men of those days would have so profound a reverence for mere poetical figures like this of the body of Brahma or that other of the marriages of *Suryā,* would have built upon them elaborate systems of ritual and sacred ceremony, enduring institutions, great demarcations of social type and ethical discipline. We read always our own mentality into that of these ancient forefathers and it is therefore that we can find in them nothing but imaginative barbarians. To us poetry is a revel of intellect and fancy, imagination a plaything and caterer for our amusement, our entertainer, the nautch-girl of the mind. But to the men of old the poet was a seer, a revealer of hidden truths, imagination no dancing courtesan but a priestess in God's house commissioned not to spin fictions but to image difficult and hidden truths; even the metaphor or simile in the Vedic style is used with a serious purpose and expected to convey a reality, not to suggest a pleasing artifice of thought. The image was to these seers a revelative symbol of the unrevealed and it was used because it could hint luminously to the mind what the precise intellectual word, apt only for logical or practical thought or to express the physical and the superficial, could not at all hope to manifest. To them this symbol of the Creator's body was more than an image, it expressed a divine reality. Human society was for them an attempt to express in life the cosmic Purusha who has expressed himself otherwise in the material and the supraphysical universe. Man and the cosmos are both of them symbols and expressions of the same hidden Reality.

From this symbolic attitude came the tendency to make everything in society a sacrament, religious and sacrosanct, but as yet with a large and vigorous freedom in all its forms—a freedom which we do not find in the rigidity of 'savage' communities because these have already passed out of the symbolic into the conventional stage though on a curve of degeneration instead of a curve of growth. The spiritual idea governs all; the symbolic religious forms which support it are fixed in principle; the social forms are lax, free and capable of infinite development. One thing, however, begins to progress towards a firm fixity and this is the psychological type. Thus we have first the symbolic idea of the four orders, expressing—to employ an abstractly figurative language which the Vedic thinkers would not have used nor perhaps understood, but which helps best our modern understanding—the Divine as knowledge in man, the Divine as power, the Divine as production, enjoyment and mutuality, the Divine as service, obedience and work. These divisions answer to four cosmic principles, the Wisdom that conceives the order and principle of things, the Power that sanctions, upholds and enforces it, the Harmony that creates the arrangement of its parts, the Work that carries out what the rest direct. Next, out of this idea there developed a firm but not yet rigid social order based primarily upon temperament and psychic type[4] with a corresponding ethical discipline and secondarily upon the social and economic function.[5] But the function was determined by its suitability to the type and its helpfulness to the discipline; it was not the primary or sole factor. The first, the symbolic stage of this evolution is predominantly religious and spiritual; the other elements, psychological, ethical, economic, physical are there but subordinated to the spiritual and religious idea. The second stage,

---

4   *guṇa.* [Sri Aurobindo's note]
5   *karma.* [Sri Aurobindo's note]

which we may call the typal, is predominantly psychological and ethical; all else, even the spiritual and religious, is subordinate to the psychological idea and to the ethical ideal which expresses it. Religion becomes then a mystic sanction for the ethical motive and discipline, *Dharma;* that becomes its chief social utility, and for the rest it takes a more and more other-worldly turn. The idea of the direct expression of the divine Being or cosmic Principle in man ceases to dominate or to be the leader and in the forefront; it recedes, stands in the background and finally disappears from the practice and in the end even from the theory of life.

This typal stage creates the great social ideals which remain impressed upon the human mind even when the stage itself is passed. The principal active contribution it leaves behind when it is dead is the idea of social honour; the honour of the Brahmin which resides in purity, in piety, in a high reverence for the things of the mind and spirit and a disinterested possession and exclusive pursuit of learning and knowledge; the honour of the Kshatriya which lives in courage, chivalry, strength, a certain proud self-restraint and self-mastery, nobility of character and the obligations of that nobility; the honour of the Vaishya which maintains itself by rectitude of dealing, mercantile Fidelity, sound production, order, liberality and philanthropy; the honour of the Shudra which gives itself in obedience, subordination, faithful service, a disinterested attachment. But these more and more cease to have a living root in the clear psychological idea or to spring naturally out of the inner life of the man; they become a convention, though the most noble of conventions. In the end they remain more as a tradition in the thought and on the lips than a reality of the life.

For the typal passes naturally into the conventional stage. The conventional stage of human society is born when the external supports, the outward expressions of the spirit or the ideal become more important than the ideal, the body or even the clothes more important than the person. Thus in the evolution of caste, the outward supports of the ethical fourfold order—birth, economic function, religious ritual and sacrament, family custom—each began to exaggerate enormously its proportions and its importance in the scheme. At first, birth does not seem to have been of the first importance in the social order, for faculty and capacity prevailed; but afterwards, as the type fixed itself, its maintenance by education and tradition became necessary and education and tradition naturally fixed themselves in a hereditary groove. Thus the son of a Brahmin came always to be looked upon conventionally as a Brahmin; birth and profession were together the double bond of the hereditary convention at the time when it was most firm and faithful to its own character. This rigidity once established, the maintenance of the ethical type passed from the first place to a secondary or even a quite tertiary importance. Once the very basis of the system, it came now to be a not indispensable crown or pendent tassel, insisted upon indeed by the thinker and the ideal code-maker but not by the actual rule of society or its practice. Once ceasing to be indispensable, it came inevitably to be dispensed with except as an ornamental fiction. Finally, even the economic basis began to disintegrate; birth, family custom and remnants, deformations, new accretions of meaningless or fanciful religious sign and ritual, the very scarecrow and caricature of the old profound symbolism, became the riveting links of the system of caste in the iron age of the old society. In the full economic period of caste the priest and the Pundit masquerade under the name of the Brahmin, the aristocrat and feudal baron under the name of the Kshatriya, the trader and money-getter under the name of the Vaishya, the half-fed labourer and economic serf under the name of the Shudra. When the economic basis also breaks down, then the unclean and diseased decrepitude of the old system has begun; it has become a name, a shell, a sham and must either be dissolved in the crucible of an individualist period of society or else fatally affect with weakness and falsehood the system of life that clings to it. That in visible fact is the last and present state of the caste system in India.

The tendency of the conventional age of society is to fix, to arrange firmly, to formalise, to erect a system of rigid grades and hierarchies, to stereotype religion, to bind education and training to a traditional and unchangeable form, to subject thought to infallible authorities, to cast a stamp of finality on what seems to it the finished life of man. The conventional period of society has its golden age when the spirit and thought that inspired its forms are confined but yet living, not yet altogether walled in, not yet stifled to death and petrified by the growing hardness of the structure in which they are cased. That golden age is often very beautiful and attractive to the distant view of posterity by its precise order, symmetry, fine social architecture, the admirable subordination of its parts to a general and noble plan. Thus at one time the modern litterateur, artist or thinker looked back often with admiration and with something like longing to the mediaeval age of Europe; he forgot in its distant appearance of poetry, nobility, spirituality the much folly, ignorance, iniquity, cruelty and oppression of those harsh ages, the suffering and revolt that simmered below these fine surfaces, the misery and squalor that was hidden behind that splendid façade. So too the Hindu orthodox idealist looks back to a perfectly regulated society devoutly obedient to the wise yoke of the Shastra, and that is his golden age—a nobler one than the European in which the apparent gold was mostly hard burnished copper with a thin gold-leaf covering it, but still of an alloyed metal, not the true Satya Yuga. In these conventional periods of society there is much indeed that is really fine and sound and helpful to human progress, but still they are its copper age and not the true golden; they are the age when the Truth we strive to arrive at is not realised, not accomplished,[6] but the exiguity of it eked out or its full appearance imitated by an artistic form, and what we have of the reality has begun to fossilise and is doomed to be lost in a hard mass of rule and order and convention.

For always the form prevails and the spirit recedes and diminishes. It attempts indeed to return, to revive the form, to modify it, anyhow to survive and even to make the form survive; but the time-tendency is too strong. This is visible in the history of religion; the efforts of the saints and religious reformers become progressively more scattered, brief and superficial in their actual effects, however strong and vital the impulse. We see this recession in the growing darkness and weakness of India in her last millennium; the constant effort of the most powerful spiritual personalities kept the soul of the people alive but failed to resuscitate the ancient free force and truth and vigour or permanently revivify a conventionalised and stagnating society; in a generation or two the iron grip of that conventionalism has always fallen on the new movement and annexed the names of its founders. We see it in Europe in the repeated moral tragedy of ecclesiasticism and Catholic monasticism. Then there arrives a period when the gulf between the convention and the truth becomes intolerable and the men of intellectual power arise, the great 'swallowers of formulas', who, rejecting robustly or fiercely or with the calm light of reason symbol and type and convention, strike at the walls of the prison-house and seek by the individual reason, moral sense or emotional desire the Truth that society has lost or buried in its whited sepulchres. It is then that the individualistic age of religion and thought and society is created; the Age of Protestantism has begun, the Age of Reason, the Age of Revolt, Progress, Freedom. A partial and external freedom, still betrayed by the conventional

---

[6] The Indian names of the golden age are *Satya*, the Age of the Truth, and *Kṛta*, the Age when the law of the Truth is accomplished. [Sri Aurobindo's note]

age that preceded it into the idea that the Truth can be found in outsides, dreaming vainly that perfection can be determined by machinery, but still a necessary passage to the subjective period of humanity through which man has to circle back towards the recovery of his deeper self and a new upward line or a new revolving cycle of civilisation.

The Human Mind[1]

The true basis of education is the study of the human mind, infant, adolescent and adult. Any system of education founded on theories of academical perfection, which ignores the instrument of study, is more likely to hamper and impair intellectual growth than to produce a perfect and perfectly equipped mind. For the educationist has to do, not with dead material like the artist or sculptor, but with an infinitely subtle and sensitive organism. He cannot shape an educational masterpiece out of human wood or stone; he has to work in the elusive substance of mind and respect the limits imposed by the fragile human body.

There can be no doubt that the current educational system of Europe is a great advance on many of the methods of antiquity, but its defects are also palpable. It is based on an insufficient knowledge of human psychology, and it is only safeguarded in Europe from disastrous results by the refusal of the ordinary student to subject himself to the processes it involves, his habit of studying only so much as he must to avoid punishment or to pass an immediate test, his resort to active habits and vigorous physical exercise. In India the disastrous effects of the system on body, mind and character are only too apparent. The first problem in a national system of education is to give an education as comprehensive as

---

[1] The opening essay in *A System of National Education,* first serialized in the *Karmayogin* in 1909-1910 and published as a book in 1921.

the European and more thorough, without the evils of strain and cramming. This can only be done by studying the instruments of knowledge and finding a system of teaching which shall be natural, easy and effective. It is only by strengthening and sharpening these instruments to their utmost capacity that they can be made effective for the increased work which modern conditions require. The muscles of the mind must be thoroughly trained by simple and easy means; then, and not till then, great feats of intellectual strength can be required of them.

The first principle of true teaching is that nothing can be taught. The teacher is not an instructor or taskmaster, he is a helper and guide. His business is to suggest and not to impose. He does not actually train the pupil's mind, he only shows him how to perfect his instruments of knowledge and helps and encourages him in the process. He does not impart knowledge to him, he shows him how to acquire knowledge for himself. He does not call forth the knowledge that is within; he only shows him where it lies and how it can be habituated to rise to the surface. The distinction that reserves this principle for the teaching of adolescent and adult minds and denies its application to the child, is a conservative and unintelligent doctrine. Child or man, boy or girl, there is only one sound principle of good teaching. Difference of age only serves to diminish or increase the amount of help and guidance necessary; it does not change its nature.

The second principle is that the mind has to be consulted in its own growth. The idea of hammering the child into the shape desired by the parent or teacher is a barbarous and ignorant superstition. It is he himself who must be induced to expand in accordance with his own nature. There can be no greater error than for the parent to arrange beforehand that his son shall develop particular qualities, capacities, ideas, virtues, or be prepared for a pre-arranged career. To force the nature to abandon its own *dharma* is to do it permanent harm, mutilate its growth and deface its perfection. It is a selfish tyranny over a human soul and a wound to the nation, which loses the benefit of the best that a man could have given it and is forced to accept instead something imperfect and artificial, second-rate, perfunctory and common. Every man has in him something divine, something his own, a chance of strength and perfection in however small a sphere, which God offers him to take or refuse. The task is to find it, develop it, use it. The chief aim of education should be to help the growing soul to draw out that in itself which is best and make it perfect for a noble use.

The third principle of education is to work from the near to the far, from that which is to that which shall be. The basis of a man's nature is almost always, in addition to his soul's past, his heredity, his surroundings, his nationality, his country, the soil from which he draws sustenance, the air which he breathes, the sights, sounds, habits to which he is accustomed. They mould him not the less powerfully because insensibly. From that then we must begin. We must not take up the nature by the roots from the earth in which it must grow or surround the mind with images and ideas of a life which is alien to that in which it must physically move. If anything has to be brought in from outside, it must be offered, not forced on the mind. A free and natural growth is the condition of genuine development. There are souls which naturally revolt from their surroundings and seem to belong to another age and clime. Let them be free to follow their bent; but the majority languish, become empty, become artificial, if artificially moulded into an alien form. It is God's arrangement for mankind that they should belong to a particular nation, age, society, that they should be children of the past, possessors of the present, creators of the future. The past is our foundation, the present our material, the future our aim and summit. Each must have its due and natural place in a national system of education.

Integral Yoga and Its Sadhana

The Yoga and Its Objects[1]

The yoga we practise is not for ourselves alone, but for the Divine; its aim is to work out the will of the Divine in the world, to effect a spiritual transformation and to bring down a divine nature and a divine life into the mental, vital and physical nature and life of humanity. Its object is not personal Mukti, although Mukti is a necessary condition of the yoga, but the liberation and transformation of the human being. It is not personal Ananda, but the bringing down of the divine Ananda—Christ's kingdom of heaven, our Satyayuga—upon the earth. Of *mokṣa* we have no personal need; for the soul is *nityamukta* and bondage is an illusion. We play at being bound, we are not really bound. We can be free when God wills; for he, our supreme Self, is the master of the game, and without his grace and permission no soul can leave the game. It is often God's will in us to take through the mind the *bhoga* of ignorance, of the dualities, of joy and grief, of pleasure and pain, of virtue and sin, of enjoyment and renunciation: for long ages, in many countries, he never even thinks of the yoga but plays out this play century after century without wearying of it. There is nothing evil in this, nothing which we need condemn or from which we need shrink—it is God's play. The wise man is he who recognises this truth and knowing his freedom, yet plays out

---

[1] The first draft of this essay was probably composed before 1913; first published by Sadhana Press, Chandranagore in 1921.

God's play, waiting for his command to change the methods of the game.

The command is now. God always keeps for himself a chosen country in which the higher knowledge is through all chances and dangers, by the few or the many, continually preserved, and for the present, in this Chaturyuga at least, that country is India. Whenever he chooses to take the full pleasure of ignorance, of the dualities, of strife and wrath and tears and weakness and selfishness, the tamasic and rajasic pleasures, of the play of the Kali in short, he dims the knowledge in India and puts her down into weakness and degradation so that she may retire into herself and not interfere with this movement of his Lila. When he wants to rise up from the mud and Narayana in man to become once again mighty and wise and blissful, then he once more pours out the knowledge on India and raises her up so that she may give the knowledge with its necessary consequences of might, wisdom and bliss to the whole world. When there is the contracted movement of knowledge, the yogins in India withdraw from the world and practise yoga for their own liberation and delight or for the liberation of a few disciples; but when the movement of knowledge again expands and the soul of India expands with it, they come forth once more and work in the world and for the world. Yogins like Janaka, Ajatashatru and Kartavirya once more sit on the thrones of the world and govern the nations.

God's Lila in man moves always in a circle, from Satyayuga to Kali and through Kali to the Satya, from the Age of Gold to the Age of Iron and back again through the Iron to the Gold. In modern language the Satyayuga is a period of the world in which a harmony, stable and sufficient, is created and man realises for a time, under certain conditions and limitations, the perfection of his being. The harmony exists in his nature, by the force of a settled purity; but afterwards it begins to break down and man upholds it, in the Treta, by force of will, individual and collective; it breaks down further and he attempts to uphold it in the Dwapara by intellectual regulation and common consent and rule; then in the Kali it finally collapses and is destroyed. But the Kali is not merely evil; in it the necessary conditions are progressively built up for a new Satya, another harmony, a more advanced perfection. In the period of the Kali which has passed, still endures in its effects, but is now at an end, there has been a general destruction of the ancient knowledge and culture. Only a few fragments remain to us in the Vedas, Upanishads and other sacred works and in the world's confused traditions. But the time is at hand for a first movement upward, the first attempt to build up a new harmony and perfection. That is the reason why so many ideas are abroad for the perfection of human society, knowledge, religion and morals. But the true harmony has not yet been found.

It is only India that can discover the harmony, because it is only by a change—not a mere readjustment—of man's present nature that it can be developed, and such a change is not possible except by yoga. The nature of man and of things is at present a discord, a harmony that has got out of tune. The whole heart and action and mind of man must be changed, but from within, not from without, not by political and social institutions, not even by creeds and philosophies, but by realisation of God in ourselves and the world and a remoulding of life by that realisation. This can only be effected by Purnayoga, a yoga not devoted to a particular purpose, even though that purpose be Mukti or Ananda, but to the fulfilment of the divine humanity in ourselves and others. For this purpose the practices of Hatha and Raja Yoga are not sufficient and even the Trimarga[2] will not serve; we must go higher and resort to the Adhyatmayoga. The principle of Adhyatmayoga is, in knowledge, the realisation of all things that we see or do not see but are aware of—men, things, ourselves, events, gods, titans, angels—

---

[2] The three paths of Karma, Bhakti and Jnana yoga.

as one divine Brahman, and in action and attitude, an absolute self-surrender to the Paratpara Purusha, the transcendent, infinite and universal Personality who is at once personal and impersonal, finite and infinite, self-limiting and illimitable, one and many, and informs with his being not only the Gods above, but man and the worm and the clod below. The surrender must be complete. Nothing must be reserved, no desire, no demand, no opinion, no idea that this must be, that cannot be, that this should be and that should not be—all must be given. The heart must be purified of all desire, the intellect of all self-will, every duality must be renounced, the whole world seen and unseen must be recognised as one supreme expression of concealed Wisdom, Power and Bliss, and the entire being given up, as an engine is passive in the hands of the driver, for the divine Love, Might and perfect Intelligence to do its work and fulfil its divine Lila. *Ahaṅkāra* must be blotted out in order that we may have, as God intends us ultimately to have, the perfect bliss, the perfect calm and knowledge and the perfect activity of the divine existence. If this attitude of perfect self-surrender can be even imperfectly established, all necessity of Yogic *kriyā* inevitably ceases. For then God himself in us becomes the sadhaka and the siddha and his divine power works in us, not by our artificial processes, but by a working of Nature which is perfectly informed, all-searching and infallibly efficient. Even the most powerful Rajayogic *saṁyama,* the most developed *prāṇāyām*, the most strenuous meditation, the most ecstatic Bhakti, the most self-denying action, mighty as they are and efficacious, are comparatively weak in their results when set beside this supreme working. For those are all limited to a certain extent by our capacity, but this is illimitable in potency because it is God's capacity. It is only limited by his will which knows what is best for the world and for each of us in the world and apart from it.

The first process of the yoga is to make the *sankalpa*. Of *ātmasamarpaṇa*. Put yourself with all your heart and all your strength into God's hands. Make no conditions, ask for nothing, not even for *siddhi* in the yoga, for nothing at all except that in you and through you his will may be directly performed. To those who demand from him, God gives what they demand, but to those who give themselves and demand nothing, he gives everything that they might otherwise have asked or needed and in addition he gives himself and the spontaneous boons of his love.

The next process is to stand aside and watch the working of the divine power in yourself. This working is often attended with disturbance and trouble in the system, therefore faith is necessary, though perfect faith is not always possible at once; for whatever impurity is in you, harboured openly or secretly lurking, is likely to rise at first and be repeated so long as it is not exhaustively swept out, and doubt in this age is an almost universal impurity. But even when doubt assails, stand by and wait for it to pass, availing yourself if possible of the *satsaṅga* of those who are already advanced on the path, but when that is absent, still holding fast to the principle of the yoga, self-surrender. When distressed within or assailed from without, remember the words of the Gita,

> 'By giving thyself up in heart and mind to Me, thou shalt cross over all difficulties and perils by My grace,'[3]
> and again,
> 'Abandon all *dharmas* (all law, rule, means and codes of every kind whether formed by previous habit and belief or imposed from outside) and take refuge in Me alone; I will deliver thee from all sin and evil, do not grieve.'[4]

'I will deliver'—you have not to be troubled or struggle yourself as if the responsibility were yours or the result depended on your

---

[3]   *maccittaḥ sarvadurgāṇi matprasādāt tariṣyasi.* [Sri Aurobindo's note]

[4]   ³*sarvadharmān parityajya māmekam śaraṇam vraja aham tvā sarvapāpebhyo mokṣayiṣyāmi mā śucaḥ.* [Sri Aurobindo's note]

efforts, a mightier than you is busy with the matter. Neither disease nor calamity nor the rising of sin and impurity in you should cause any alarm. Hold fast only to him. 'I will deliver thee from all sin and evil.' But the release does not come by a sudden miracle, it comes by a process of purification and these things are a part of the process. They are like the dust that rises in clouds when a room long uncleaned is at last swept out. Though the dust seem to choke you, yet persevere, *mā śucaḥ*.[5]

In order to stand aside, you must know yourself as the Purusha who merely watches, consents to God's work, holds up the Adhar and enjoys the fruits that God gives. The work itself is done by God as Shakti, by Kali, and is offered up by her as a *yajña* to Sri Krishna; you are the *yajamāna* who sees the sacrifice done, whose presence is necessary to every movement of the sacrifice and who tastes its results. This separation of yourself, this renunciation of the *kartṛtva-abhimāna* (the idea of yourself as the doer) is easier if you know what the Adhar is. Above the *buddhi* which is the highest function of mind is the higher *buddhi,* or *vijñāna,* the seat of the *satyadharma,* truth of knowledge, truth *bhāva,* truth of action, and above this ideal faculty is the *ānanda* or cosmic bliss in which the divine part of you dwells. It is of this *vijñāna* and this *ānanda* that Christ spoke as the kingdom of God that is within you. We at present are awake, *jāgrat,* in the lower movements but *suṣupta,* fast asleep, in the *vijñāna* and *ānanda;* we have to awaken these levels of consciousness within us and their awakening and unmixed activity is the *siddhi* of the yoga. For when that happens, we gain the condition of being which is called in the Gita dwelling in God, of which Sri Krishna speaks when he says, *mayi nivasiṣyasyeva,* 'Verily thou shalt dwell in Me.' Once it is gained, we are free and blessed and have everything towards which we strive.

---

[5] 'Do not grieve'. *(Gita 18.66)*

The third process of the yoga is to perceive all things as God. First, as a rule, in the process of knowledge one comes to see pervading all space and time one divine impersonal Existence, *sad-ātman,* without movement, distinction or feature, *śāntam alakṣaṇam,* in which all names and forms seem to stand with a very doubtful or a very minor reality. In this realisation the One may seem to be the only reality and everything else *māyā,* a purposeless and inexplicable illusion. But afterwards, if you do not stop short and limit yourself by the impersonal realisation, you will come to see the same *ātman* not only containing and supporting all created things, but informing and filling them, and eventually you will be able to understand that even the names and forms are Brahman. You will then be able to live more and more in the knowledge which the Upanishads and the Gita hold up as the rule of life; you will see the Self in all existing things and all existing things in the Self, *ātmānam sarvabhūteṣu sarvabhūtāni cātmani;*[6] you will be aware of all things as Brahman, *sarva-mkhalvida-mbrahma.*[7] But the crowning realisation of this yoga is when you become aware of the whole world as the expression, play or Lila of an infinite divine personality, when you see in all, not the impersonal *sad-ātman* which is the basis of manifest existence—although you do not lose that knowledge— but Sri Krishna who at once is, bases and transcends all manifest and unmanifest existence, *avyakto vyaktāt paraḥ.*[8] For behind the *sad-ātman* is the silence of the Asat which the Buddhist Nihilists realised as the *śūnyam* and beyond that silence is the *parātpara puruṣa*[9] *(puruṣo vareṇya ādityavarṇas tamasaḥ parastāt).*[10] It is he

---

[6] 'The Self existing in all things and all things existing in the Self' (*Iso Upanishad* 6; *Gita* 6.29).

[7] 'Verily, all this that is Brahman' (*Chandogya Upanishad* 3.14.1).

[8] Unmanifest, supreme beyond manifestation.

[9] The purusha higher than the highest.

[10] 'The excellent purusha, of the colour of the sun, beyond darkness' (*Svetaswatara Upanishad* 3.8; *Gita* 8.9).

who has made this world out of his being and is immanent in and sustains it as the infinite-finite Ishwara, *ananta* and *sānta*, Shiva and Narayana, Sri Krishna the *līlāmaya* who draws all of us to him by his love, compels all of us by his masteries and plays his eternal play of joy and strength and beauty in the manifold world.

The world is only a play of his being, knowledge and delight, *sat, cit* and *ānanda*. Matter itself, you will one day realise, is not material, it is not substance but form of consciousness, *guṇa*, the result of quality of being perceived by sense-knowledge. Solidity itself is only a combination of the *guṇas, saṁhati* and *dhṛti*, cohesion and permanence, a state of conscious being, nothing else. Matter, life, mind and what is beyond mind, it is all Sri Krishna the *anantaguṇa* Brahman playing in the world as the Sachchidananda. When we have this realisation, when we dwell in it securely and permanently, all possibilities of grief and sin, fear, delusion, internal strife and pain are driven puissantly from our being. We realise in our experience the truth of the Upanishads,

'He who possesses the delight of the Brahman has no fear from anything in the world,'[11] and that other in the Isha Upanishad, 'When all created things become one with a man's self by his getting the knowledge (*vijñāna*), thereafter what bewilderment can he have or what grief, when in all things he sees their oneness?'[12] The whole world then appears to us in a changed aspect, as an ocean of beauty, good, light, bliss, exultant movement on a basis of eternal strength and peace. We see all things as *śubha, śiva, maṅgala, ānandamaya*. We become one in soul with all beings, *sarvabhūtātmabhūtātmā*, and, having steadfastly this experience, are able by contact, by oneness, by the reaching out of love, to

---

[11] *ānandam brahmaṇo vidvān na bibheti kutaścana.* [Sri Aruobindo's note]
[12] *yasmin sarvāṇi bhūtāni ātmaivābhud vijānataḥ tatra ko mohaḥ kaḥ śokaḥ ekatvam anupaśyataḥ.* [Sri Aurobindo's note]

communicate it to others, so that we become a centre of the radiation of this divine state, *brāhmī sthiti,* throughout our world.

It is not only in things animate but in things inanimate also that we must see Narayana, experience Shiva, throw our arms around Shakti. When our eyes, that are now blinded by the idea of Matter, open to the supreme Light, we shall find that nothing is inanimate, but all contains, expressed or unexpressed, involved or evolved, secret or manifest or in course of manifestation, not only that state of involved consciousness which we call *annam* or Matter, but also life, mind, knowledge, bliss, divine force and being—*prāṇa, manas, vijñāna, ānanda, cit, sat.* In all things the self-conscious personality of God broods and takes the delight of his *guṇas.* Flowers, fruits, earth, trees, metals, all things have a joy in them of which you will become aware, because in all Sri Krishna dwells, *praviśya,* having entered into them, not materially or physically,—because there is no such thing, Space and Time being only conventions and arrangements of perception, the perspective in God's creative Art—but by *cit,* the divine awareness in his transcendent being.

'All this world and every object in this world of Prakriti has been created as a habitation for the Lord.'[13]

Nor is it enough to see him in all things and beings, *sarva-bhuteṣu;* you must see him in all events, actions, thoughts, feelings, in yourself and others, throughout the world. For this realisation two things are necessary: first, that you should give up to him the fruit of all your actions, secondly, that you should give up to him the actions themselves. Giving up the fruits of action does not mean that you must have the *vairāgya* for the fruits, turn away from them or refuse to act with a given end before you. It means that you must act, not because you want this or that to happen or think it necessary that this or that should happen and your action

---

[13] *īśā vāsyam idam sarvam yat kiñca jagatyām jagat.* [Sri Aurobindo's note]

needed to bring it about, but because it is *kartavyam,* demanded by the Master of your being and must be done with whatever result God is pleased to give. You must put aside what you want and wish to know what God wants; distrust what your heart, your passions or your habitual opinions prefer to hold as right and necessary, and passing beyond them, like Arjuna in the Gita, seek only to know what God has set down as right and necessary. Be strong in the faith that whatever is right and necessary will inevitably happen as the result of your due fulfilment of the *kartavyam karma,* even if it is not the result that you preferred or expected. The power that governs the world is at least as wise as you and it is not absolutely necessary that you should be consulted or indulged in its management; God is seeing to it.

But what is the *kartavya karma?* It is very difficult to say—*gahanā karmaṇo gatiḥ.*[14] Most people would translate *kartavya karma* by the English word and idea, *duty,* if asked to define it, they would say it is the right and moral action, what people understand by right and morality, what you yourself conscientiously think to be right or else what the good of society, the nation or mankind demands of you. But the man who remains bound by these personal or social ideas of duty, necessary as they are for the ignorant to restrain and tame their clamorous desires or their personal egoism, will be indeed what is called a good man, but he will never attain to the fulfilment of this yoga. He will only replace the desire for one kind of fruit by the desire for another kind; he will strive, even more passionately perhaps, for these higher results and be more bitterly grieved by not attaining them. There is no passion so terrible as the passion of the altruist, no egoism so hard to shake as the fixed egoism of virtue, precisely because it is justified in its own eyes and justified in the sight of men and cannot see the necessity for yielding to a higher law. Even if there

---

[14] 'Thick and tangled is the way of works' *(Gita* 4.17).

is no grieving over the results, there will be the labour and strife of the rajasic karta, struggling and fighting, getting eager and getting exhausted, not trigunātīta, always under bondage to the *guṇas*.

It was under the domination of these ideas of personal virtue and social duty that Arjuna refused to fight. Against his reasonings Sri Krishna sets two different ideas, one inferior for the use of the man bound but seeking liberation, another superior for the liberated man, the Shastra and surrender not only of the fruits of the work but of the work itself to God. The virtue of the Shastra is that it sets up a standard outside ourselves, different from our personal desires, reasonings, passions and prejudices, outside our selfishness and self-will, by living up to which in the right spirit we can not only acquire self-control but by reducing even the sattwic *ahaṅkāra* to a minimum prepare ourselves for liberation. In the old days the Shastra was the Vedic Dharma based upon a profound knowledge of man's psychology and the laws of the world, revealing man to himself and showing him how to live according to his nature; afterwards it was the law of the Smritis which tried to do the same thing more roughly by classifying men according to the general classes of which the Vedas speak, the *cāturvarṇya;* today it is little more than blind mechanical custom and habitual social observance, a thing not sattwic but tamasic, not a preparatory discipline for liberation, but a mere bondage.

Even the highest Shastra can be misused for the purposes of egoism, the egoism of virtue and the egoism of prejudice and personal opinion. At its best it is a great means towards the preparation of liberation. It is *śabda-brahma*. But we must not be satisfied with mere preparation, we must, as soon as our eyes are opened, hasten on to actual freedom. The liberated soul and the sadhaka of liberation who has surrendered even his actions to God, gets beyond the highest Shastra, *śabdabrahmāti-vartate*.[15]

---

[15] 'Passes beyond the range of sabdabrahman' (*Gita* 6.44).

The best foundation for the surrender of action is the realisation that Prakriti is doing all our actions at God's command and God through our *svabhāva* determines the action. From that moment the action belongs to him, it is not yours nor the responsibility yours; there is indeed no responsibility, no bondage of Karma, for God has no responsibility, but is in every way master and free. Our actions become not only like the Shastric man's svabhavaniyata regulated by nature and therefore *dharma,* but the svabhāva itself is controlled like a machine by God. It is not easy for us, full as we are of the Sanskaras of ignorance, to arrive at this stage of knowledge, but there are three stages by which it can be rapidly done. The first is to live in the spirit of the *śloka,*

'According as I am appointed by Thee, O Hrishikesha! seated in my heart, so I act.'[16]

When this has entered into your daily life, it will be easier to accomplish the second stage and live in the knowledge of the Gita,

'God stands in the heart of all beings, whirling round all, as on a wheel, by the Maya of the three *guṇas.*'[17]

You will then be able to perceive the action of the three *guṇas* in you and watch the machinery at its work, no longer saying, *tathā karomi,* I do, but *guṇā vartanta eva,* it is merely the *guṇās* that work. One great difficulty in these stages, especially before you can distinguish the action of the *guṇas,* is the perception of the impurity of the *svabhāva,* the haunting idea of sin and virtue. You must always remember that, since you have put yourself in God's hands,

---

[16] *tvayā hṛṣīkesa hṛdi sthitena yathā niyukto'smi tathā karomi.* [Sri Aurobindo's note]

[17] *īśvaraḥ sarvabhūtā nām hṛddeśe'rjuna tiṣṭhati bhrāmayan sarvabhūtā ni yantrārūḍhā ni māyayā.* [Sri Aurobindo's note]

he will work out the impurities and you have only to be careful, as you cannot be attached either to *pāpa* or *puṇya*, sin or virtue. For he has repeatedly given the *abhayavacana*, the assurance of safety. '*Pratijānīhi*,' he says in the Gita, ' *na me bhaktaḥ praṇaśyati*, he who is devoted to Me cannot perish.'[18]

The third stage comes out of the second, by full realisation of God, or of itself by the grace of God. Not only will the Purusha stand apart and be *triguṇātita*, beyond the three *guṇas*, but the Prakriti, though using the *guṇas*, will be free from their bondage. Sattwa, as we know it, will disappear into pure *prakāśa* and *jyoti*, and the nature will live in a pure, free and infinite self-existing illumination. Tamas, as we know it, will disappear into pure *śama* or *śānti*, and the nature will take its firm stand on an infinite and ineffable rest and peace. Rajas, as we know it, will disappear into pure *tapas*, and the nature will flow in a free and infinite ocean of divine force. On that foundation of calm and in that heaven of light, action will occur as the spontaneous objective expression of God's knowledge, which is one with God's will. This is the condition of infinity, *ānantya*, in which this struggle of bound and limited sattwa, rajas and tamas is replaced by a mighty harmony of three, *prakāśa*, *tapas* and *śama*. And even before you reach that condition, on the way to it, you will find that some mighty force not your own, not situated in your body though possessing and occupying it, is thinking for you, feeling for you, acting for you, your very body as well as your mind and heart being moved by that force and not by yourself. You will enjoy that thought, feeling, action, but will neither possess nor be possessed by it—*karmāṇi pravilīyante*, your actions will disappear[19] without leaving in you mark or trace, as a wave disappears from the surface of the sea, as water falls from the lotus leaf. Your mind, heart, body will not

---

[18] *Gita*. (9.31.)

[19] *Gita* (4.23.)

be yours, but God's; you yourself will be only a centre of being, knowledge and bliss through which God works in that Adhar. This is the condition in which one is utterly *taccittaḥ*, given up in all his conscious being to God, in which there is utter fulfilment of the description, 'One whose state of being is free from egoism and whose understanding receives no stain.'[20]

This is the surrender of action to which Sri Krishna gives so much importance.

> 'Laying down all actions upon Me, with thy whole conscious being in *adhyātmayoga*, become free from desire and the sense of belongings; fight, let the fever of thy soul pass from thee.'[21]

For this great and complete liberation it is necessary that you should be *niḥspṛha*, *nirdvandva* and *nirahaṅkāra*, without the longing and reaching after things, free from the *saṃskāra* of the dualities and free from egoism; for these three things are the chief enemies of self-surrender. If you are *nirdvandva*, you can be *niḥspṛha*, but hardly otherwise, for every *dvandva* creates in the mind by the very nature of the mind some form of *rāgadveṣa*, like and dislike, attraction and repulsion, whether they are the lowest dualities that appeal to the mind through the body, hunger and thirst, heat and cold, physical pleasure and pain, or the middle sorts that appeal to it through the feelings and desires, success and failure, victory and defeat, fortune and misfortune, pleasure and displeasure, joy and grief, hate and love, or the highest which appeal to the mind through the discriminating *buddhi*, virtue and sin, reason and unreason, error and truth. These things can only be put under

---

[20] *yasya nāhaṅkṛto bhāvo buddhir yasya na lipyate.* [Sri Aurobindo's note]

[21] *mayi sarvāṇi karmāṇi san nyasyādhyātmacetasā nirāśīrnirmamo bhūtvā yudhyasva vigatajvaraḥ.* [Sri Aurobindo's note]

our feet by complete knowledge, the knowledge that sees God in all things and thus comes to understand the relations of things to each other in his great cosmic purpose, by complete Bhakti which accepts all things with joy,—thus abolishing the *dvandvas*, because they come from the Beloved or by perfect action offering up all works as a sacrifice to God with an entire indifference to these dualities of success, failure, honour, disgrace, etc., which usually pursue all Karma. Such knowledge, such Bhakti, such Karma come inevitably as the eventual result of the *sankalpa* of self-surrender and the practice of it.

But it is *ahankāra* that by making the relation and effect of things on ourselves or on things connected with us the standard of life, makes the dvandvas a chain for our bondage. *Ahankāra* in its action on our life and sadhana will be seen to be of three kinds, rajasic, tamasic and sattwic. Rajas binds by desire and the craving in the nature for occupation and activity, it is always reaching after action and the fruit of action; it is in order that we may be free from the rajasic *ahankāra* that we have the command, 'Do not do works from the desire of fruit,' *mākarmaphalaheturbhūḥ*, and the command to give up our actions to God.[22] Tamas binds by weakness and the craving in the nature for ease and inaction; it is always sinking into idleness, depression, confusion of mind, fear, disappointment, despondency and despair; it is in order that we may get rid of the tamasic *ahankāra* that we are given the command, 'Let there be no attachment to inaction,' and the instruction to pursue the yoga always, whether we seem to advance or seem to be standing still or seem even to be going back, always with a calm faith and patient and cheerful perseverance, *anirvinnacetasā*.[23] Sattwa binds by knowledge and pleasure; it is always attaching itself to some imperfect realisation, to the idea

---

[22] *Gita* 2.47.
[23] 'With a consciousness free from despondency' (*Gita* 6.23).

of one's own virtue, the correctness of one's own opinions and principles or at its highest, as in the case of Arjuna, opposing some personal idea of altruism, justice or virtue against the surrender of our will that God demands of us. It is for the escape from the sattwic *ahaṅkāra* that we have to pass beyond the attachment to the duality of virtue and sin, *ubhe sukṛtaduṣkṛte.*[24]

Each of the *guṇas* working on the *ahaṅkāra* has its particular danger for the sadhaka who has made the *saṅkalpa* of self-surrender, but has not yet attained to the full accomplishment of the surrender. The danger of the *rajoguṇa* is when the sadhaka is assailed by the pride that thinks, 'I am a great sadhaka, I have advanced so far, I am a great instrument in God's hands,' and similar ideas, or when he attaches himself to the work as God's work which must be carried out, putting himself into it and troubling himself about it as if he had more interest in God's work than God himself and could manage it better. Many, while they are acting all the while in the spirit of rajasic *ahaṅkāra,* persuade themselves that God is working through them and they have no part in the action. This is because they are satisfied with the mere intellectual assent to the idea without waiting for the whole system and life to be full of it. A continual remembrance of God in others and renunciation of individual eagerness *(spṛhā)* are needed and a careful watching of our inner activities until God by the full light of self-knowledge, *jñānadīpena bhāsyata,*[25] dispels all further chance of self-delusion.

The danger of *tamoguṇa* is twofold, first, when the Purusha thinks, identifying himself with the tamas in him, 'I am weak, sinful, miserable, ignorant, good-for-nothing, inferior to this man and inferior to that man, *adhama,* what will God do through me?' as if God were limited by the temporary capacities or incapacities

---

[24] *Gita* 2.50.
[25] *Gita* 10.11.

of his instruments and it were not true that he can make the dumb to talk and the lame to cross the hills,[26] and again when the sadhaka tastes the relief, the tremendous relief of a negative *śānti* and, feeling himself delivered from all troubles and in possession of peace, turns away from life and action and becomes attached to the peace and ease of inaction. Remember always that you too are Brahman and the divine Shakti is working in you; reach out always to the realisation of God's omnipotence and his delight in the Lila. He bids Arjuna work *lokasaṅgrahārthāya,*[27] for keeping the world together, for he does not wish the world to sink back into Prakriti, but insists on your acting as he acts, 'These worlds would be overpowered by tamas and sink into Prakriti if I did not do actions.'[28]

To be attached to inaction is to give up our action not to God but to our tamasic *ahaṅkāra.*

The danger of the *sattvaguṇa* is when the sadhaka becomes attached to any one-sided conclusion of his reason, to some particular *kriyā* or movement of the sadhana, to the joy of any particular *siddhi* of the yoga, perhaps the sense of purity or the possession of some particular power or the Ananda of the contact with God or the sense of freedom and hungers after it, becomes attached to that only and would have nothing else. Remember that the yoga is not for yourself; for these things, though they are part of the *siddhi,* are not the object of the *siddhi,* for you have decided at the beginning to make no claim upon God but take what he gives you freely and, as for the Ananda, the selfless soul will even forego the joy of God's presence, when that is God's will. You must be free even from the highest sattwic *ahaṅkāra,* even from the subtle ignorance of *mumukṣutva,* the desire of liberation, and

---

[26] *mūkam karoti vācālam paṅgrum laṅghayate girim* [Sri Aurobindo's note]

[27] *Gita* 3.20

[28] *utsīdeyur ime lokā na kuryām karma cedaham.* [Sri Aurobindo's note] *Gita* 3.24.

take all joy and delight without attachment. You will then be the *siddha* or perfect man of the Gita.

These then are the processes of the yoga, (1) the *saṅkalpa* of *ātmasamarpaṇa*, (2) the standing apart from the Adhar by self-knowledge, (3) the vision of God everywhere and in all things and in all happenings, the surrender of the fruits of action and action itself to God, and the freedom thereby from ignorance, from *ahaṅkāra*, from the *dvandvas*, from desire, so that you are *śuddha, mukta, siddha*, full of Ananda, pure, free, perfect and blissful in your being. But the processes will be worked out, once the *saṅkalpa* is made, by God's Shakti, by a mighty process of Nature. All that is indispensable on your part is the *anumati* and *smṛti*. Anumati is consent, you must give a temporary consent to the movements of the yoga, to all that happens inside or outside you as part of the circumstances of the sadhana, not exulting at the good, not fretting at the evil, not struggling in your heart to keep the one or get rid of the other, but always keeping in mind and giving a permanent assent to that which has to be finally effected. The temporary consent is passive submission to the methods and not positive acceptance of the results. The permanent consent is an anticipatory acceptance of the results, a sort of effortless and desireless exercise of will. It is the constant exercise of this desireless will, an intent aspiration and constant remembrance of the path and its goal which are the *dhṛti* and *utsāha* needed, the necessary steadfastness and zeal of the sadhaka; *vyākulatā* or excited, passionate eagerness is more intense, but less widely powerful, and it is disturbing and exhausting, giving intense pleasure and pain in the pursuit but not so vast a bliss in the acquisition. The followers of this path must be like the men of the early yugas, *dhīrāḥ*, the great word of praise in the Upanishads. In the remembrance, the *smṛti* or *smaraṇa*, you must be *apramatta*, free from negligence. It is by the loss of the *smṛti* owing to the rush and onset of the *guṇas* that the yogin becomes *bhraṣṭa*, falls from his firm seat, wanders from his path. But you need not be distressed when the *pramāda* comes and the state of fall or clouded condition seems to persist, for there is no fear for you of a permanent fall since God himself has taken entire charge of you and if you stumble, it is because it is best for you to stumble, as a child by frequent stumbling and falling learns to walk. The necessity of *apramattatā* disappears when you can replace the memory of the yoga and its objects by the continual remembrance of God in all things and happenings, the *nitya anusmaraṇa* of the Gita. For those who can make the full surrender from the beginning there is no question; their path is utterly swift and easy.

It is said in the *Sanatsujatiya* that four things are necessary for *siddhi*—*śāstra, utsāha, guru* and *kāla*—the teaching of the path, zeal in following it, the Guru and time. Your path is that which I am pointing out, the *utsāha* needed is this *anumati* and this *nitya smaraṇa*, the Guru is God himself and for the rest only time is needed. That God himself is the Guru, you will find when knowledge comes to you; you will see how every little circumstance within you and without you has been subtly planned and brought about by infinite wisdom to carry out the natural process of the yoga, how the internal and external movements are arranged and brought together to work on each other, so as to work out the imperfection and work in the perfection. An almighty love and wisdom are at work for your uplifting. Therefore never be troubled by the time that is being taken, even if it seems very long, but when imperfections and obstructions arise, be *apramatta, dhīra*, have the *utsāha*, and leave God to do the rest. Time is necessary. It is a tremendous work that is being done in you, the alteration of your whole human nature into a divine nature, the crowding of centuries of evolution into a few years. You ought not to grudge the time. There are other paths that offer more immediate results or at any rate, by offering you some definite *kriyā* you can work at yourself, give your *ahaṅkāra* the satisfaction of feeling that you are doing something, so many more *prāṇāyāmas* today, so much longer a time for the *āsana,* so many more repetitions of the *japa,* so much done, so much definite progress marked. But once you have chosen this path, you must cleave to it. Those are human methods, not the way that the infinite Shakti works, which moves silently, sometimes imperceptibly to its goal, advances here, seems to pause there, then mightily and triumphantly reveals the grandiose thing that it has done. Artificial paths are like canals hewn by the intelligence of man; you travel easily, safely, surely, but from one given place to another. This path is the broad and trackless ocean by which you can travel widely to all parts of the world and are admitted to the freedom of the infinite. All that you need are the ship, the steering-wheel, the compass, the motive-power and a skilful captain. Your ship is the *Brahma-vidyā,* faith is your steering-wheel, self-surrender your compass, the motive-power is she who makes, directs and destroys the worlds at God's command and God himself is your captain. But he has his own way of working and his own time for everything. Watch his way and wait for his time. Understand also the importance of accepting the Shastra and submitting to the Guru and do not do like the Europeans who insist on the freedom of the individual intellect to follow its own fancies and preferences which it calls reasonings, even before it is trained to discern or fit to reason. It is much the fashion nowadays to indulge in metaphysical discussions and philosophical subtleties about Maya and Advaita and put them in the forefront, making them take the place of spiritual experience. Do not follow that fashion or confuse yourself and waste time on the way by questionings which will be amply and luminously answered when the divine knowledge of the *vijñāna* awakes in you. Metaphysical knowledge has its place, but as a handmaid to spiritual experience, showing it the way sometimes but much more dependent on it and living upon its bounty. By itself it is mere *pāṇḍitya,* a dry and barren thing and more often a stumbling-block than a help. Having accepted this path, follow its Shastra without unnecessary doubt and questioning, keeping the mind plastic to the light of the higher knowledge, gripping firmly what is experienced, waiting for light where things are dark to you, taking without pride what help you can from the living guides who have already trod the path, always patient, never hastening to narrow conclusions, but waiting for a more complete experience and a fuller light, relying on the Jagadguru who helps you from within.

It is necessary to say something about the *māyāvāda* and the modern teachings about the Advaita because they are much in the air at the present moment and, penetrated with ideas from European rationalism and agnosticism for which Shankara would have been astonished to find himself made responsible, perplex many minds. Remember that one-sided philosophies are always a partial statement of truth. The world, as God has made it, is not a rigid exercise in logic but, like a strain of music, an infinite harmony of many diversities, and his own existence, being free and absolute, cannot be logically defined. Just as the best religion is that which admits the truth of all religions, so the best philosophy is that which admits the truth of all philosophies and gives each its right place. Maya is one realisation, an important one which Shankara overstressed because it was most vivid to his own experience. For yourself leave the word for subordinate use and fix rather on the idea of Lila, a deeper and more penetrating word than Maya. Lila includes the idea of Maya and exceeds it; nor has it that association of the vanity of all things, useless to you who have elected to remain and play with Sri Krishna in Mathura and Brindavan.

God is one but he is not bounded by his unity. We see him here as one who is always manifesting as many, not because he cannot help it, but because he so wills, and outside manifestation he is *anirdeśyam*, indefinable, and cannot be described as either one or many. That is what the Upanishads and other sacred books consistently teach; he is *ekamevādvitīyam,* One and there is not other, but also and consequently he is 'this man, yonder woman, that blue-winged bird, this scarlet-eyed.' He is *sānta,* he is *ananta;* the Jiva is he. 'I am the *aśvattha* tree,' says Sri Krishna in the Gita, 'I am death, I am Agni Vaishwanara, I am the heat that digests food, I am Vyasa, I am Vasudeva, I am Arjuna.' All that is the play of his *caitanya* in his infinite being, his manifestations, and therefore all are real. Maya means nothing more than the freedom of Brahman from the circumstances through which he expresses himself. He is in no way limited by that which we see or think about him. That is the Maya from which we must escape, the Maya of ignorance which takes things as separately existent and not God, not *caitanya,* the illimitable for the really limited, the free for the bound. Do you remember the story of Sri Krishna and the Gopis, how Narada found him differently occupied in each house to which he went, present to each Gopi in a different body, yet always the same Sri Krishna? Apart from the devotional meaning of the story, which you know, it is a good image of his World-Lila. He is *sarva,* everyone, each Purusha with his apparently different Prakriti and action is he, and yet at the same time he is the Purushottama who is with Radha, the Para Prakriti, and can withdraw all these into himself when he wills and put them out again when he wills. From one point of view they are one with him, from another one yet different, from yet another always different because they always exist, latent in him or expressed at his pleasure. There is no profit in disputing about these standpoints. Wait until you see God and know yourself and him and then debate and discussion will be unnecessary.

The goal marked out for us is not to speculate about these things, but to experience them. The call upon us is to grow into the image of God, to dwell in him and with him and be a channel of his joy and might and an instrument of his works. Purified from all that is *aśubha,* transfigured in soul by his touch, we have to act in the world as dynamos of that divine electricity and send it thrilling and radiating through mankind, so that wherever one of us stands, hundreds around may become full of his light and force, full of God and full of Ananda. Churches, Orders, theologies, philosophies have failed to save mankind because they have busied themselves with intellectual creeds, dogmas, rites and institutions, with *ācāraśuddhi* and *darśana,* as if these could save mankind, and have neglected the one thing needful, the power and purification of the soul. We must go back to the one thing needful, take up again Christ's gospel of the purity and perfection of mankind, Mahomed's gospel of perfect submission, self-surrender and servitude to God, Chaitanya's gospel of the perfect love and joy of God in man, Ramakrishna's gospel of the unity of all religions and the divinity of God in man, and, gathering all these streams into one mighty river, one purifying and redeeming Ganges, pour it over the death-in-life of a materialistic humanity as Bhagirath led down the Ganges and flooded with it the ashes of his fathers, so that there may be a resurrection of the soul in mankind and the Satyayuga for a while return to the world. Nor is this the whole object of the Lila or the Yoga; the reason for which the Avatars descend is to raise up man again and again, developing in him a higher and ever higher humanity, a greater and yet greater development of divine being, bringing more and more of heaven again and again upon the earth until our toil is done, our work accomplished and Sachchidananda fulfilled in all even here, even in this material universe. Small is his work, even if he succeeds, who labours for his own salvation or the salvation of a few; infinitely great is he even if he fail or succeed only partially or for a season, who lives only to bring about peace of soul, joy, purity and perfection among all mankind.

The Object of Our Yoga

The object of our Yoga is self-perfection, not self-annulment.

There are two paths set for the feet of the Yogin, withdrawal from the universe and perfection in the Universe; the first comes by asceticism, the second is effected by tapasya; the first receives us when we lose God in Existence, the second is attained when we fulfil existence in God. Let ours be the path of perfection, not of abandonment; let our aim be victory in the battle, not the escape from all conflict.

Buddha and Shankara supposed the world to be radically false and miserable; therefore escape from the world was to them the only wisdom. But this world is Brahman, the world is God, the world is Satyam, the world is Ananda; it is our misreading of the world through mental egoism that is a falsehood and our wrong relation with God in the world that is a misery. There is no other falsity and no other cause of sorrow. God created the world in Himself through Maya; but the Vedic meaning of Maya is not illusion, it is wisdom, knowledge, capacity, wide extension in consciousness, *prajñā prasṛtā purāṇī.*[1] Omnipotent Wisdom created the world, it is not the organised blunder of some Infinite Dreamer; omniscient Power manifests or conceals it in Itself or Its

---

[1] Written circa 1913, first published in *The Hour of God* (1959).
    'Wisdom that went forth from the beginning' (Svetasvatara Upanishad 4.18).

own delight, it is not a bondage imposed by His own ignorance on the free and absolute Brahman.

If the world were Brahman's self-imposed nightmare, to awake from it would be the natural and only goal of our supreme endeavour; or if life in the world were irrevocably bound to misery, a means of escape from this bondage would be the sole secret worth discovering. But perfect truth in world-existence is possible, for God here sees all things with the eye of truth; and perfect bliss in the world is possible, for God enjoys all things with the sense of unalloyed freedom. We also can enjoy this truth and bliss, called by the Veda *amṛtam,* Immortality, if by casting away our egoistic existence into perfect unity with His being we consent to receive the divine perception and the divine freedom.

The world is a movement of God in His own being; we are the centres and knots of divine consciousness which sum up and support the processes of His movement. The world is His play with His own self-conscious delight, He who alone exists, infinite, free and perfect; we are the self-multiplications of that conscious delight, thrown out into being to be His playmates. The world is a formula, a rhythm, a symbol-system expressing God to Himself in His own consciousness—it has no material existence but exists only in His consciousness and self-expression; we, like God, are in our inward being That which is expressed, but in our outward being terms of that formula, notes of that rhythm, symbols of that system. Let us lead forward God's movement, play out His play, work out His formula, execute His harmony, express Him through ourselves in His system. This is our joy and our self-fulfilment; to this end we who transcend exceed the universe have entered into universe-existence.

Perfection has to be worked out, harmony has to be accomplished. Imperfection, limitation, death, grief, ignorance, matter, are only the first terms of the formula—unintelligible till we have worked out the wider terms and reinterpreted the formulary; they are the initial discords of the musician's tuning. Out of imperfection we have to construct perfection, out of limitation to discover infinity, out of death to find immortality, out of grief to recover divine bliss, out of ignorance to rescue divine self-knowledge, out of matter to reveal Spirit. To work out this end for ourselves and for humanity is the object of our Yogic practice.

The Integral Knowledge and the Aim of Life; Four Theories of Existence[1]

When all the desires that cling to the heart are loosed away from it, then the mortal becomes immortal, even here he possesses the Eternal.

Brihadaranyaka Upanishad.[2]

He becomes the Eternal and departs into the Eternal.

Brihadaranyaka Upanishad.[3]

This bodiless and immortal Life and Light is the Brahman.

Brihadaranyaka Upanishad.[4]

Long and narrow is the ancient Path—I have touched it, I have found it—the Path by which the wise, knowers of the

---

[1] Chapter XVI of *The Life Divine*; the book was published in instalments in the *Arya* from 15 August 1914 to January 1919. It was 'thoroughly revised and enlarged' and published in book form in 1939 (Book One) and 1940 (Book Two, Vols. I and II). See the separate section on *The Life Divine* in this anthology for more.

[2] IV. 4. 7

[3] IV. 4. 6.

[4] IV 4. 7.

Eternal, attaining to salvation, depart hence to the high world of Paradise.

Brihadaranyaka Upanishad.[5]

I am a son of Earth, the soil is my mother . . . May she lavish on me her manifold treasure, her secret riches . . . May we speak the beauty of thee, O Earth, that is in thy villages and forests and assemblies and war and battles.

Atharva Veda.[6]

May Earth, sovereign over the past and the future, make for us a wide world . . . Earth that was the water on the Ocean and whose course the thinkers follow by the magic of their knowledge, she who has her heart of immortality covered up by the Truth in the supreme ether, may she establish for us light and power in that most high kingdom.

Atharva Veda.[7]

O Flame, thou foundest the mortal in a supreme immortality for increase of inspired Knowledge day by day; for the seer who has thirst for the dual birth, thou createst divine bliss and human joy.

Rig Veda.[8]

---

[5] IV. 4.8. [Sri Aurobindo's gloss]
[6] XII. 1.12, 44, 56
[7] XII. 1. 1, 8.
[8] I. 31.7.

O Godhead, guard for us the Infinite and lavish the finite.

Rig Veda.[9]

But before we examine the principles and process of the evolutionary ascent of Consciousness, it is necessary to restate what our theory of integral knowledge affirms as fundamental truths of the Reality and its manifestation and what it admits as effectual sides and dynamic aspects but is unable to accept as sufficient for a total explanation of existence and the universe. For truth of knowledge must base truth of life and determine the aim of life; the evolutionary process itself is the development of a Truth of existence concealed here in an original Inconscience and brought out from it by ah emerging Consciousness which rises from gradation to gradation of its self-unfolding until it can manifest in itself the integral reality of things and a total self-knowledge. On the nature of that Truth from which it starts and which it has to manifest must depend the course of the evolutionary development—the steps of its process and their significance.

First, we affirm an Absolute as the origin and support and secret Reality of all things. The Absolute Reality is indefinable and ineffable by mental thought and mental language; it is self-existent and self-evident to itself, as all absolutes are self-evident, but our mental affirmatives and negatives, whether taken separatively or together, cannot limit or define it. But at the same time there is a spiritual consciousness, a spiritual knowledge, a knowledge by identity which can seize the Reality in its fundamental aspects and its manifested powers and figures. All that is comes within this description and, if seen by this knowledge in its own truth or its occult meaning, can be regarded as an expression of the Reality

---

[9] IV. 2. 11.
[Sri Aurobindo's gloss]

and itself a reality. This manifested reality is self-existent in these fundamental aspects; for all the basic realities are a bringing out of something that is eternal and inherently true in the Absolute; but all that is not fundamental, all that is temporary is phenomenal, is form and power dependent on the reality it expresses and is real by that and by its own truth of significance, the truth of what it carries in it, because it is that and not something fortuitous, not baseless, illusory, a vain constructed figure. Even what deforms and disguises, as falsehood deforms and disguises truth, evil deforms and disguises good, has a temporal reality as true consequences of the Inconscience; but these contrary figures, though real in their own field, are not essential but only contributory to the manifestation and serve it as a temporal form or power of its movement. The universal then is real by virtue of the Absolute of which it is a self-manifestation, and all that it contains is real by virtue of the universal to which it gives a form and figure.

The Absolute manifests itself in two terms, a Being and a Becoming. The Being is the fundamental reality; the Becoming is an effectual reality: it is a dynamic power and result, a creative energy and working out of the Being, a constantly persistent yet mutable form, process, outcome of its immutable formless essence. All theories that make the Becoming sufficient to itself are therefore half-truths, valid for some knowledge of the manifestation acquired by an exclusive concentration upon what they affirm and envisage, but otherwise valid only because the Being is not separate from the Becoming but present in it, constituted of it, inherent in its every infinitesimal atom and in its boundless expansion and extension. Becoming can only know itself wholly when it knows itself as Being; the soul in the Becoming arrives at self-knowledge and immortality when it knows the Supreme and Absolute and possesses the nature of the Infinite and Eternal. To do that is the supreme aim of our existence; for that is the truth of our being and must therefore be the inherent aim, the necessary outcome of our becoming: this truth of our being becomes in the soul a necessity of manifestation, in matter a secret energy, in life an urge and tendency, a desire and a seeking, in mind a will, aim, endeavour, purpose; to manifest what is from the first occult within it is the whole hidden trend of evolutionary Nature.

Therefore we accept the truth on which the philosophies of the supracosmic Absolute take their stand; Illusionism itself, even if we contest its ultimate conclusions, can still be accepted as the way in which the soul in mind, the mental being, has to see things in a spiritual-pragmatic experience when it cuts itself off from the Becoming in order to approach and enter into the Absolute. But also, since the Becoming is real and is inevitable in the very self-power of the Infinite and Eternal, this too is not a complete philosophy of existence. It is possible for the soul in the Becoming to know itself as the Being and possess the Becoming, to know itself as the Infinite in essence but also as the Infinite self-expressed in the finite, the timeless Eternal regarding itself and its works in the founding status and the developing motion of Time-eternity. This realisation is the culmination of the Becoming; it is the fulfilment of the Being in its dynamic reality. This too then must be part of the total truth of things, for it alone gives a full spiritual significance to the universe and justifies the soul in manifestation; an explanation of things that deprives cosmic and individual existence of all significance cannot be the whole explanation or the solution it proposes the sole true issue.

The next affirmation which we put forward is that the fundamental reality of the Absolute is to our spiritual perception a Divine Existence, Consciousness and Delight of Being which is a supracosmic Reality, self-existent, but also the secret truth underlying the whole manifestation; for the fundamental truth of Being must necessarily be the fundamental truth of Becoming. All is a manifestation of That; for it dwells even in all that seem to be its opposites and its hidden compulsion on them to disclose it is the cause of evolution, on Inconscience to develop from itself its secret consciousness, on the apparent Non-Being to reveal in itself the occult spiritual existence, on the insensible neutrality of Matter to develop a various delight of being which must grow, setting itself free from its minor terms, its contrary dualities of pain and pleasure, into the essential delight of existence, the spiritual Ananda.

The Being is one, but this oneness is infinite and contains in itself an infinite plurality or multiplicity of itself: the One is the All; it is not only an essential Existence, but an All-Existence. The infinite multiplicity of the One and the eternal unity of the Many are the two realities or aspects of one reality on which the manifestation is founded. By reason of this fundamental verity of the manifestation the Being presents itself to our cosmic experience in three poises—the supracosmic Existence, the cosmic Spirit and the individual Self in the Many. But the multiplicity permits of a phenomenal division of consciousness, an effectual Ignorance in which the Many, the individuals, cease to become aware of the eternal self-existent Oneness and are oblivious of the oneness of the cosmic Self in which and by which they live, move and have their being. But, by force of the secret Unity, the soul in becoming is urged by its own unseen reality and by the occult pressure of evolutionary Nature to come out of this state of Ignorance and recover eventually the knowledge of the one Divine Being and its oneness with it and at the same time to recover its spiritual unity with all individual beings and the whole universe. It has to become aware not only of itself in the universe but of the universe in itself and of the Being of cosmos as its greater self; the individual has to universalise himself and in the same movement to become aware of his supracosmic transcendence. This triple aspect of the reality must be included in the total truth of the soul and of the cosmic manifestation, and this necessity must determine the ultimate trend of the process of evolutionary Nature.

All views of existence that stop short of the Transcendence and ignore it must be incomplete accounts of the truth of being. The pantheistic view of the identity of the Divine and the Universe is a truth, for all this that is is the Brahman: but it stops short of the whole truth when it misses and omits the supracosmic Reality. On the other side, every view that affirms the cosmos only and dismisses the individual as a by-product of the cosmic Energy, errs by laying too much emphasis on one apparent factual aspect of the world-action; it is true only of the natural individual and is not even the whole truth of that: for the natural individual, the nature-being, is indeed a product of the universal Energy, but is at the same time a nature-personality of the soul, an expressive formation of the inner being and person, and this soul is not a perishable cell or a dissoluble portion of the cosmic Spirit, but has its original immortal reality in the Transcendence. It is a fact that the cosmic Being expresses itself through the individual being, but also it is a truth that the Transcendental Reality expresses itself through both the individual existence and the Cosmos; the soul is an eternal portion of the Supreme and not a fraction of Nature. But equally any view that sees the universe as existent only in the individual consciousness must very evidently be a fragmentary truth: it is justified by a perception of the universality of the spiritual individual and his power of embracing the whole universe in his consciousness; but neither the cosmos nor the individual consciousness is the fundamental truth of existence; for both depend upon and exist by the transcendental Divine Being.

This Divine Being, Sachchidananda, is at once impersonal and personal: it is an Existence and the origin and foundation of all truths, forces, powers, existences, but it is also the one transcendent Conscious Being and the All-Person of whom all conscious beings are the selves and personalities; for He is their highest Self and the universal indwelling Presence. It is a necessity for the soul in the universe—and therefore the inner trend of the evolutionary

Energy and its ultimate intention—to know and to grow into this truth of itself, to become one with the Divine Being, to raise its nature to the Divine Nature, its existence into the Divine Existence, its consciousness into the Divine Consciousness, its delight of being into the divine Delight of Being, and to receive all this into its becoming, to make the becoming an expression of that highest Truth, to be possessed inwardly of the Divine Self and Master of its existence and to be at the same time wholly possessed by Him and moved by His Divine Energy and live and act in a complete self-giving and surrender. On this side the dualistic and theistic views of existence which affirm the eternal real existence of God and the Soul and the eternal real existence and cosmic action of the Divine Energy, express also a truth of the integral existence; but their formulation falls short of the whole truth if it denies the essential unity of God and Soul or their capacity for utter oneness or ignores what underlies the supreme experience of the merger of the soul in the Divine Unity through love, through union of consciousness, through fusion of existence in existence.

The manifestation of the Being in our universe takes the shape of an involution which is the starting-point of an evolution—Matter the nethermost stage, Spirit the summit. In the descent into involution there can be distinguished seven principles of manifested being, seven gradations of the manifesting Consciousness of which we can get a perception or a concrete realisation of their presence and immanence here or a reflected experience. The first three are the original and fundamental principles and they form universal states of consciousness to which we can rise; when we do so, we can become aware of supreme planes or levels of fundamental manifestation or self-formulation of the spiritual reality in which is put in front the unity of the Divine Existence, the power of the Divine Consciousness, the bliss of the Divine Delight of existence—not concealed or disguised as here, for we can possess them in their full independent reality. A fourth principle of supramental truth-consciousness is associated with them; manifesting unity in infinite multiplicity, it is the characteristic power of self-determination of the Infinite. This quadruple power of the supreme existence, consciousness and delight constitutes an upper hemisphere of manifestation based on the Spirit's eternal self-knowledge. If we enter into these principles or into any plane of being in which there is the pure presence of the Reality, we find in them a complete freedom and knowledge. The other three powers and planes of being, of which we are even at present aware, form a lower hemisphere of the manifestation, a hemisphere of Mind, Life and Matter. These are in themselves powers of the superior principles; but wherever they manifest in a separation from their spiritual sources, they undergo as a result a phenomenal lapse into a divided in place of the true undivided existence: this lapse, this separation creates a state of limited knowledge exclusively concentrated on its own limited world-order and oblivious of all that is behind it and of the underlying unity, a state therefore of cosmic and individual Ignorance.

In the descent into the material plane of which our natural life is a product, the lapse culminates in a total Inconscience out of which an involved Being and Consciousness have to emerge by a gradual evolution. This inevitable evolution first develops, as it is bound to develop, Matter and a material universe; in Matter, Life appears and living physical beings; in Life, Mind manifests and embodied thinking and living beings; in Mind, ever increasing its powers and activities in forms of Matter, the Supermind or Truth-Consciousness must appear, inevitably, by the very force of what is contained in the Inconscience and the necessity in Nature to bring it into manifestation. Supermind appearing manifests the Spirit's self-knowledge and whole-knowledge in a supramental living being and must bring about by the same law, by an inherent necessity and inevitability, the dynamic manifestation here of the divine Existence, Consciousness and Delight of existence. It is this that is the significance of the plan and order of the terrestrial evolution; it is this necessity that must determine all its steps and degrees, its principle and its process. Mind, Life and Matter are the realised powers of the evolution and well-known to us; Supermind and the triune aspects of Sachchidananda are the secret principles which are not yet put in front and have still to be realised in the forms of the manifestation, and we know them only by hints and a partial and fragmentary action still not disengaged from the lower movement and therefore not easily recognisable. But their evolution too is part of the destiny of the soul in the Becoming,— there must be a realisation and dynamisation in earth-life and in Matter not only of Mind but of all that is above it, all that has descended indeed but is still concealed in earth-life and Matter.

Our theory of the integral knowledge admits Mind as a creative principle, a power of the Being, and assigns it its place in the manifestation; it similarly accepts Life and Matter as powers of the Spirit and in them also is a creative Energy. But the view of things that makes Mind the sole or the supreme creative principle and the philosophies that assign to Life or Matter the same sole reality or predominance, are expressions of a half-truth and not the integral knowledge. It is true that when Matter first emerges it becomes the dominant principle; it seems to be and is within its own field the basis of all things, the constituent of all things, the end of all things: but Matter itself is found to be a result of something that is not Matter, of Energy, and this Energy cannot be something self-existent and acting in the Void, but can turn out and, when deeply scrutinised, seems likely to turn out to be the action of a secret Consciousness and Being: when the spiritual knowledge and experience emerge, this becomes a certitude—it is seen that the creative Energy in Matter is a movement of the power of the Spirit. Matter itself cannot be the original and ultimate reality. At the same time the view that divorces Matter and Spirit and puts them as opposites is unacceptable; Matter is a form of

Spirit, a habitation of Spirit, and here in Matter itself there can be a realisation of Spirit.

It is true again that Life when it emerges becomes dominant, turns Matter into an instrument for its manifestation, and begins to look as if it were itself the secret original principle which breaks out into creation and veils itself in the forms of Matter; there is a truth in this appearance and this truth must be admitted as a part of the integral knowledge. Life, though not the original Reality, is yet a form, a power of it which is missioned here as a creative urge in Matter. Life, therefore, has to be accepted as the means of our activity and the dynamic mould into which we have here to pour the Divine Existence; but it can so be accepted only because it is a form of a Divine Energy which is itself greater than the Life-force. The Life-principle is not the whole foundation and origin of things; its creative working cannot be perfected and sovereignly fulfilled or even find its true novement until it knows itself as an energy of the Divine Being and elevates and subtilises its action into a free channel for the outpourings of the superior Nature.

Mind in its turn, when it emerges, becomes dominant; it uses Life and Matter as means of its expression, a field for its own growth and sovereignty, and it begins to work as if it were the true reality and the creator even as it is the witness of existence. But Mind also is a limited and derivative power; it is an outcome of Overmind or it is here a luminous shadow thrown by the divine Supermind: it can only arrive at its own perfection by admitting the light of a larger knowledge; it must transform its own more ignorant, imperfect and conflicting powers and values into the divinely effective potencies and harmonious values of the supramental truth-consciousness. All the powers of the lower hemisphere with their structures of the Ignorance can find their true selves only by a transformation in the light that descends to us from the higher hemisphere of an eternal self-knowledge.

All these three lower powers of being build upon the Inconscient and seem to be originated and supported by it: the black dragon of the Inconscience sustains with its vast wings and its back of darkness the whole structure of the material universe; its energies unroll the flux of things, its obscure intimations seem to be the starting-point of consciousness itself and the source of all life-impulse. The Inconscient, in consequence of this origination and predominance, is taken now by a certain line of enquiry as the real origin and creator. It has indeed to be accepted that an inconscient force, an inconscient substance are the starting-point of the evolution, but it is a conscious Spirit and not an inconscient Being that is emerging in the evolution. The Inconscient and its primary works are penetrated by a succession of higher and higher powers of being and are made subject to Consciousness so that its obstructions to the evolution, its circles of restriction, are slowly broken, the Python coils of its obscurity shot through by the arrows of the Sun-God; so are the limitations of our material substance diminished until they can be transcended and mind, life and body can be transformed through a possession of them by the greater law of divine Consciousness, Energy and Spirit. The integral knowledge admits the valid truths of all views of existence, valid in their own field, but it seeks to get rid of their limitations and negations and to harmonise and reconcile these partial truths in a larger truth which fulfils all the many sides of our being in the one omnipresent Existence.

At this point we must take a step farther and begin to regard the metaphysical truth we have so stated as a determinant not only of our thought and inner movements but of our life-direction, a guide to a dynamic solution of our self-experience and world-experience. Our metaphysical knowledge, our view of the fundamental truth of the universe and the meaning of existence, should naturally be the determinant of our whole conception of life and attitude to it; the aim of life, as we conceive it, must be structured on that basis. Metaphysical philosophy is an attempt to fix the fundamental realities and principles of being as distinct from its processes and the phenomena which result from those processes. But it is on the fundamental realities that the processes depend: our own process of life, its aim and method, should be in accordance with the truth of being that we see; otherwise our metaphysical truth can be only a play of the intellect without any dynamic importance. It is true that the intellect must seek after truth for its own sake without any illegitimate interference of a preconceived idea of life-utility. But still the truth, once discovered, must be realisable in our inner being and our outer activities: if it is not, it may have an intellectual but not an integral importance; a truth for the intellect, for our life it would be no more than the solution of a thought-puzzle or an abstract unreality or a dead letter. Truth of being must govern truth of life; it cannot be that the two have no relation or interdependence. The highest significance of life to us, the fundamental truth of existence, must be also the accepted meaning of our own living, our aim, our ideal.

There are, roughly, from this viewpoint, four main theories, or categories of theory, with their corresponding mental attitudes and ideals in accordance with four different conceptions of truth of existence. These we may call- the supracosmic, the cosmic and terrestrial, the supraterrestrial or other-worldly, and the integral or synthetic or composite, the theories that try to reconcile the three factors—or any two of them—which the other views tend to isolate. In this last category would fall our view of our existence here as a Becoming with the Divine Being for its origin and its object, a progressive manifestation, a spiritual evolution with the supracosmic for its source and support, the other-worldly for a condition and connecting link and the cosmic and terrestrial for its field, and with human mind and life for its nodus and turning-point of release towards a higher and a highest perfection. Our regard then must be on the three first to see where they depart from the integralising view of life and how far the truths they stand on fit into its structure.

In the supracosmic view of things the supreme Reality is alone entirely real. A certain illusoriness, a sense of the vanity of cosmic existence and individual being is a characteristic turn of this seeing of things, but it is not essential, not an indispensable adjunct to its main thought-principle. In the extreme forms of its world-vision human existence has no real meaning; it is a mistake of the soul or a delirium of the will to live, an error or ignorance which somehow overcasts the absolute Reality. The only true truth is the supracosmic; or, in any case, the Absolute, the Parabrahman is the origin and goal of all existence, all else is an interlude without any abiding significance. If so, it would follow that the one thing to be done, the one wise and needful way of our being is to get away from all living, whether terrestrial or celestial, as soon as our inner evolution or some hidden law of the spirit makes that possible. True, the illusion is real to itself, the vanity pretends to be full of purpose; its laws and facts—they are only facts and not truths, empirical and not real realities—are binding on us so long as we rest in the error. But from any standpoint of real knowledge, in any view of the true truth of things, all this self-delusion would seem to be little better than the laws of a cosmic madhouse; so long as we are mad and have to remain in the madhouse, we are perforce subject to its rules and we must make, according to our temperament, the best or the worst of them, but always our proper aim is to get cured of our insanity and depart into light and truth and freedom. Whatever mitigations may be made in the severity of this logic, whatever concessions validating life and personality for the time being, yet from this viewpoint the true law of living must be whatever rule can help us soonest to get back to self-knowledge and lead by the most direct road to Nirvana; the true ideal must be an extinction of the individual and the universal, a self-annulment in the Absolute. This ideal of self-extinction which is boldly and clearly proclaimed by the Buddhists, is in Vedantic thought a self-finding: but the self-finding of the individual by his growth into his true being in the Absolute would only be possible if both are interrelated realities; it could not apply to the final world-abolishing self-affirmation of the Absolute in an unreal or temporary individual by the annulment of the false personal being and by the destruction of all individual and cosmic existence for that individual consciousness—however much these errors may go on, helplessly inevitable, in the world of Ignorance permitted by the Absolute, in a universal, eternal and indestructible Avidya.

But this idea of the total vanity of life is not altogether an inevitable consequence of the supracosmic theory of existence. In the Vedanta of the Upanishads, the Becoming of Brahman is accepted as a reality; there is room therefore for a truth of the Becoming: there is in that truth a right law of life, a permissible satisfaction of the hedonistic element in our being, its delight of temporal existence, an effective utilisation of its practical energy, of the executive force of consciousness in it; but, the truth and law of its temporal becoming once fulfilled, the soul has to turn back to its final self-realisation, for its natural highest fulfilment is a release, a liberation into its original being, its eternal self, its timeless reality. There is a circle of becoming starting from eternal Being and ending in it; or, from the point of view of the Supreme as a personal or superpersonal Reality, there is a temporary play, a game of becoming and living in the universe. Here, evidently, there is no other significance of life than the will of the Being to become, the will of consciousness and the urge of its force towards becoming, its delight of becoming; for the individual, when that is withdrawn from him or fulfilled in him and no longer active, the becoming ceases: but otherwise the universe persists or always comes back into manifestation, because the will to become is eternal and must be so since it is the inherent will of an eternal Existence. It may be said that one defect in this view of things is the absence of any fundamental reality of the individual, of any abiding value and significance of his natural or his spiritual activity: but it can be replied that this demand for a permanent personal significance, for a personal eternity, is an error of our ignorant surface consciousness; the individual is a temporary becoming of the Being, and that is a quite sufficient value and significance. It may be added that in a pure or an absolute Existence there can be no values and significances: in the universe values exist and are indispensable, but only as relative and temporary buildings; there can be no absolute values, no eternal and self-existent significances in a Time-structure. This sounds conclusive enough and it seems that nothing more can be said about the matter. And yet the question remains over; for the stress on our individual being, the demand on it, the value put on individual perfection and salvation is too great to be dismissed as a device for a minor operation, the coiling and uncoiling of an insignificant spiral amid the vast circlings of the Eternal's becoming in the universe. The cosmic-terrestrial view which we may take next as the exact opposite of the supracosmic, considers cosmic existence as real; it goes farther and accepts it as the only reality, and its view is confined, ordinarily, to life in the material universe. God, if God exists, is an eternal Becoming; or if God does not exist, then Nature—whatever view we may take of Nature, whether we regard it as a play of Force with Matter or a great cosmic Life or even admit a universal impersonal Mind in Life and Matter—is a perennial becoming. Earth is the field or it is one of the temporary fields, man is the highest possible form or only one of the temporary forms of the Becoming. Man individually may be altogether mortal; mankind also may survive only for a certain short period of the earth's existence; earth itself may bear life only for a rather longer period of its duration in the solar system; that system may itself one day come to an end or at least cease to be an active or productive factor in the Becoming; the universe we live in may itself dissolve or contract again into the

seed-state of its Energy: but the principle of Becoming is eternal—
or at least as eternal as anything can be in the obscure ambiguity
of existence. It is indeed possible to suppose a persistence of man
the individual as a psychic entity in Time, a continuous terrestrial
or cosmic ensouling or reincarnation without any after-life or
other-life elsewhere: in that case one may either suppose an ideal
of constantly increasing perfection or approach to perfection or
a growth towards an enduring felicity somewhere in the universe
as the aim of this endless Becoming. But in an extreme terrestrial
view this is with difficulty tenable. Certain speculations of human
thought have tended in this direction, but they have not taken
a substantial body. A perpetual persistence in the Becoming is
usually associated with the acceptance of a greater supraterrestrial
existence.

In the ordinary view of a sole terrestrial life or a restricted
transient passage in the material universe—for possibly there may
be thinking living beings in other planets—an acceptance of man's
mortality and a passive endurance of it or an active dealing with a
limited personal or collective life and life-aims are the only choice
possible. The one high and reasonable course for the individual
human being—unless indeed he is satisfied with pursuing his
personal purposes or somehow living his life until it passes out
of him—is to study the laws of the Becoming and take the best
advantage of them to realise, rationally or intuitionally, inwardly
or in the dynamism of life, its potentialities in himself or for
himself or in or for the race of which he is a member; his business
is to make the most of such actualities as exist and to seize on or
to advance towards the highest possibilities that can be developed
here or are in the making. Only mankind as a whole can do this
with entire effect, by the mass of individual and collective action,
in the process of time, in the evolution of the race-experience: but
the individual man can help towards it in his own limits, can do
all these things for himself to a certain extent in the brief space

of life allotted to him; but, especially, his thought and action can be a contribution towards the present intellectual, moral and vital welfare and the future progress of the race. He is capable of a certain nobility of being; an acceptance of his inevitable and early individual annihilation does not preclude him from making a high use of the will and thought which have been developed in him or from directing them to great ends which shall or may be worked out by humanity. Even the temporary character of the collective being of humanity does not so very much matter—except in the most materialist view of existence; for so long as the universal Becoming takes the form of human body and mind, the thought, the will it has developed in its human creature will work itself out and to follow that intelligently is the natural law and best rule of human life. Humanity and its welfare and progress during its persistence on earth provide the largest field and the natural limits for the terrestrial aim of our being; the superior persistence of the race and the greatness and importance of the collective life should determine the nature and scope of our ideals. But if the progress or welfare of humanity be excluded as not our business or as a delusion, the individual is there; to achieve his greatest possible perfection or make the most of his life in whatever way his nature demands will then be life's significance.

The supraterrestrial view admits the reality of the material cosmos and it accepts the temporary duration of earth and human life as the first fact we have to start from; but it adds to it a perception of other worlds or planes of existence which have an eternal or at least a more permanent duration; it perceives behind the mortality of the bodily life of man the immortality of the soul within him. A belief in the immortality, the eternal persistence of the individual human spirit apart from the body is the keyword of this conception of life. That of itself necessitates its other belief in higher planes of existence than the material or terrestrial, since for a disembodied spirit there can be no abiding place in a world whose every operation depends upon some play of force, whether spiritual, mental, vital or material, in and with the forms of Matter. There arises from this view of things the idea that the true home of man is beyond and that the earth-life is in some way or other only an episode of his immortality or a deviation from a celestial and spiritual into a material existence.

But what then is the character, the origin and the end of this deviation? There is first the idea of certain religions, long persistent but now greatly shaken or discredited, that man is a being primarily created as a material living body upon earth into which a newly born divine soul is breathed or else with which it is associated by the fiat of an almighty Creator. A solitary episode, this life is his one opportunity from which he departs to a world of eternal bliss or to a world of eternal misery either according as the general or preponderant balance of his acts is good or evil or according as he accepts or rejects, knows or ignores a particular creed, mode of worship, divine mediator, or else according to the arbitrary predestining caprice of his Creator. But that is the supraterrestrial theory of life in its least rational form of questionable creed or dogma. Taking the idea of the creation of a soul by the physical birth as our starting-point, we may still suppose that by a natural law, common to all, the rest of its existence has to be pursued beyond in a supraterrestrial plane, when the soul has shaken off from it its original matrix of matter like a butterfly escaped from the chrysalis and disporting itself in the air on its light and coloured wings. Or we may suppose preferably a pre-terrestrial existence of the soul, a fall or descent into matter and a reascension into celestial being. If we admit the soul's pre-existence, there is no reason to exclude this last possibility as an occasional spiritual occurrence—a being belonging to another plane of existence may, conceivably, assume for some purpose the human body and nature: but this is not likely to be the universal principle of earth-existence or a sufficient rationale for the creation of the material universe.

It is also sometimes supposed that the solitary life on earth is a stage only and the development of the being nearer to its original glory occurs in a succession of worlds which are so many other stages of its growth, stadia of its journey. The material universe, or earth especially, will then be a sumptuously appointed field created by a divine power, wisdom or caprice for the enacting of this interlude. According to the view we choose to take of the matter, we shall see in it a place of ordeal, a field of development or a scene of spiritual fall and exile. There is too an Indian view which regards the world as a garden of the divine Lila, a play of the divine Being with the conditions of cosmic existence in this world of an inferior Nature; the soul of man takes part in the Lila through a protracted series of births, but it is destined to reascend at last into the proper plane of the Divine Being and there enjoy an eternal proximity and communion: this gives a certain rationale to the creative process and the spiritual adventure which is either absent or not clearly indicated in the other accounts of this kind of soul-movement or soul-cycle. Always there are three essential characteristics in all these varying statements of the common principle; first, the belief in the individual immortality of the human spirit; secondly, as a necessary consequence, the idea of its sojourn on earth as a temporary passage or a departure from its highest eternal nature and of a heaven beyond as its proper habitation; thirdly, an emphasis on the development of the ethical and spiritual being as the means of ascension and therefore the one proper business of life in this world of Matter.

These are the three fundamental ways of seeing, each with its mental attitude towards life, that can be adopted with regard to our existence; the rest are usually midway stations or else variations or composites which attempt to adapt themselves more freely to the complexity of the problem. For, practically, it is impossible for man taken as a race, whatever a few individuals may succeed in doing, to guide his life permanently or wholly by the leading motive of any of these three attitudes, uniquely, to the exclusion of the others' claim upon his nature. A confused amalgam of two or more of them, a conflict or division of his life-motives between them or some attempt at synthesis is his way of dealing with the various impulses of his complex being and the intuitions of his mind to which they appeal for their sanction. Almost all men normally devote the major part of their energy to the life on earth, to the terrestrial needs, interests, desires, ideals of the individual and the race. It could not be otherwise; for the care of the body, the sufficient development and satisfaction of the vital and the mental being of man, the pursuit of high individual and large collective ideals which start from the idea of an attainable human perfection or nearer approach to perfection through his normal development, are imposed upon us by the very character of our terrestrial being; they are part of its law, its natural impulse and rule, its condition of growth, and without these things man could not attain to his full manhood. Any view of our being which neglects, unduly belittles or intolerantly condemns them, is therefore by that very fact, whatever its other truth or merit or utility, or whatever its suitability to individuals of a certain temperament or in a certain stage of spiritual evolution, unfit to be the general and complete rule of human living. Nature takes good care that the race shall not neglect these aims which are a necessary part of her evolution; for they fall within the method and stages of the divine plan in us, and a vigilance for her first steps and for the maintenance of their mental and material ground is a preoccupation which she cannot allow to go into the background, since these things belong to the foundation and body of her structure.

But also she has implanted in us a sense that there is something in our composition which goes beyond this first terrestrial nature of humanity. For this reason the race cannot accept or follow for a very long time any view of being which ignores this higher and subtler sense and labours to confine us entirely to a purely terrestrial way of living. The intuition of a beyond, the idea and feeling of a soul and spirit in us which is other than the mind, life and body or is greater, not limited by their formula, returns upon us and ends by resuming possession. The ordinary man satisfies this sense easily enough by devoting to it his exceptional moments or the latter part of his life when age shall have blunted the zest of his earthly nature, or by recognising it as something behind or above his normal action to which he can more or less imperfeclyy direct his natural being: the exceptional man turns to the supraterrestrial as the one aim and law of living and diminishes or mortifies as much as possible his earthly parts in the hope of developing his celestial nature. There have been epochs in which the supraterrestrial view has gained a very powerful hold and there has been a vacillation between an imperfect human living which cannot take its large natural expansion and a sick ascetic longing for the celestial life which also does not acquire in more than a few its best pure and happy movement. This is a sign of the creation of some false war in the being by the setting up of a standard or a device that ignores the law of evolutionary capacity or an overstress that misses the reconciling equation which must exist somewhere in a divine dispensation of our nature.

But, finally, there must open in us, as our mental life deepens and subtler knowledge develops, the perception that the terrestrial and the supraterrestrial are not the only terms of being; there is something which is supracosmic and the highest remote origin of our existence. This perception is easily associated by spiritual enthusiasm, by the height and ardour of the soul's aspiration, by the philosophic aloofness or the strict logical intolerance of our intellect, by the eagerness of our will or by a sick disgust in our vital being discouraged by the difficulties or disappointed by the results of life—by any or all of these motive-forces—with a sense of the entire vanity and unreality of all else than this remote Supreme, the vanity of human life, the unreality of cosmic existence, the bitter ugliness and cruelty of earth, the insufficiency of heaven, the aimlessness of the repetition of births in the body. Here again the ordinary man cannot really live with these ideas; they can only give at most a greyness and restless dissatisfaction to the life in which he must still continue: but the exceptional man abandons all to follow the truth he has seen and for him they can be the needed food of his spiritual impulse or a stimulus to the one achievement that is now for him the one thing that matters. Periods and countries there have been, in which this view of being has become very powerful; a considerable part of the race has swerved aside to the life of the ascetic—not always with a real call to it—the rest adhered to the normal life but with an underlying belief in its unreality, a belief which can bring about by too much reiteration and insistence an unnerving of the life-impulse and an increasing littleness of its motives, or even, by a subtle reaction, an absorption in an ordinary narrow living through a missing of our natural response to the Divine Being's larger joy in cosmic existence and a failure of the great progressive human idealism by which we are spurred to a collective self-development and a noble embrace of the battle and the labour. Here again there is a sign of some insufficiency in the statement of the supracosmic Reality, perhaps an overstatement or a mistaken opposition, a missing of the divine equation, of the total sense of creation and the enure will of the Creator.

That equation can only be found if we recognise the purport of our whole complex human nature in its right place in the cosmic movement; what is needed is to give its full legitimate value to each part of our composite being and many-sided aspiration and find out the key of their unity as well as their difference. The finding must be by a synthesis or an integration and, since development is clearly the law of the human soul, it is most likely to be discovered by an evolutionary synthesis. A synthesis of this kind was attempted in the ancient Indian culture. It accepted four legitimate motives of human living—man's vital interests and needs, his desires, his ethical and religious aspiration, his ultimate spiritual aim and destiny—in other words, the claims of his vital, physical and emotional being, the claims of his ethical and religious being governed by a knowledge of the law of God and Nature and man, and the claims of his spiritual longing for the Beyond for which he seeks satisfaction by an ultimate release from an ignorant mundane existence. It provided for a period of education and preparation based on this idea of life, a period of normal living to satisfy human desires and interests under the moderating rule of the ethical and religious part in us, a period of withdrawal and spiritual preparation, and a last period of renunciation of life and release into the spirit. Evidently, if applied as a universal rule, this prescribed norm, this delineation of the curve of our journey, would miss the fact that it is impossible for all to trace out the whole circle of development in a single short lifetime; but it was modified by the theory of a complete evolution pursued through a long succession of rebirths before one could be fit for a spiritual liberation. This synthesis with its spiritual insight, largeness of view, symmetry, completeness did much to raise the tone of human life; but eventually it collapsed: its place was occupied by an exaggeration of the impulse of renunciation which destroyed the symmetry of the system and cut it into two movements of life in opposition to each other, the normal life of interests and desires with an ethical and religious colouring and the abnormal or supernormal inner life founded on renunciation. The old synthesis in fact contained in itself the seed of this exaggeration and could not but lapse into it: for if we regard the escape from life as our desirable end, if we omit to hold up any high offer of life-fulfilment, if life has not a divine significance in it, the impatience of the human intellect and will must end by driving at a short cut and getting rid as much as possible of any more tedious and dilatory processes; if it cannot do that or if it is incapable of following the short cut, it is left with the ego and its satisfactions but with nothing greater to be achieved here. Life is split into the spiritual and the mundane and there can only be an abrupt transition, not a harmony or reconciliation of these parts of our nature.

A spiritual evolution, an unfolding here of the Being within from birth to birth, of which man becomes the central instrument and human life at its highest offers the critical turning-point, is the link needed for the reconciliation of life and spirit; for it allows us to take into account the total nature of man and to recognise the legitimate place of his triple attraction, to earth, to heaven and to the supreme Reality. But a complete solution of its oppositions can be arrived at only on this basis that the lower consciousness of mind, life and body cannot arrive at its full meaning until it is taken up, restated, transformed by the light and power and joy of the higher spiritual consciousness, while the higher too does not stand in its full right relation to the lower by mere rejection, but by this assumption and domination, this taking up of its unfulfilled values, this restatement and transformation—a spiritualising and supramentalising of the mental, vital and physical nature. The terrestrial ideal, which has been so powerful in the modern mind, restored man and his life on earth and the collective hope of the race to a prominent position and created an insistent demand for a solution; this is the good it has accomplished. But by overdoing and exclusiveness it unduly limited man's scope, it ignored that which is the highest and in the end the largest thing in him, and by this limitation it missed the full pursuit of its own object. If mind were the highest thing in man and Nature, then indeed this frustration might not result; still, the limitation of scope would be there, a narrow possibility, a circumscribed prospect. But if mind is only a partial unfolding of consciousness and there are powers beyond of which Nature in our race is capable, then not only does our hope upon earth, let alone what is beyond it, depend upon their development, but this becomes the one proper road of our evolution.

Mind and life themselves cannot grow into their fullness except by the opening up of the larger and greater consciousness to which mind only approaches. Such a larger and greater consciousness is the spiritual, for the spiritual consciousness is not only higher than the rest but more embracing. Universal as well as transcendent, it can take up mind and life into its light and give them the true and utmost realisation of all for which they are seeking: for it has a greater instrumentality of knowledge, a fountain of deeper power and will, an unlimited reach and intensity of love and joy and beauty. These are the things for which our mind, life and body are seeking, knowledge, power and joy, and to reject that by which all these arrive at their utmost plenitude is to shut them out from their own highest consummation. An opposite exaggeration demanding only some colourless purity of spiritual existence nullifies the creative action of the spirit and excludes from us all that the Divine manifests in its being: it leaves room only for an evolution without sense or fulfilment— for a cutting off of all that has been evolved is the sole culmination; it turns the process of our being into the meaningless curve of a plunge into Ignorance and return out of it or erects a wheel of cosmic Becoming with only an escape-issue. The intermediary, the supraterrestrial aspiration cuts short the fulfilment of the being above by not proceeding to its highest realisation of oneness and diminishes it below by not allowing a proper amplitude of sense to its presence in the material universe and its acceptance of life in an earthly body. A large relation of unity, an integration, restores the balance, illumines the whole truth of being and links together the steps of Nature.

In this integration the supracosmic Reality stands as the supreme Truth of being; to realise it is the highest reach of our consciousness. But it is this highest Reality which is also the cosmic being, the cosmic consciousness, the cosmic will and life: it has put these things forth, not outside itself but in its own being, not as an opposite principle but as its own self-unfolding and self-expression. Cosmic being is not a meaningless freak or phantasy or a chance error; there is a divine significance and truth in it: the manifold self-expression of the spirit is its high sense, the Divine itself is the key of its enigma. A perfect self-expression of the spirit is the object of our terrestrial existence. This cannot be achieved if we have not grown conscious of the supreme Reality; for it is only by the touch of the Absolute that we can arrive at our own absolute. But neither can it be done to the exclusion of the cosmic Reality: we must become universal, for without an opening into universality the individual remains incomplete. The individual separating himself from the All to reach the Highest, loses himself in the supreme heights; including in himself the cosmic consciousness, he recovers his wholeness of self and still keeps his supreme gain of transcendence; he fulfils it and himself in the cosmic completeness. A realised unity of the transcendent, the universal and the individual is an indispensable condition for the fullness of the self-expressing spirit: for the universe is the field of its totality of self-expression, while it is through the individual that its evolutionary self-unfolding here comes to its acme. But this supposes not only a real being of the individual, but the revelation of our secret eternal oneness with the Supreme and with all cosmic existence. In his self-integration the soul of the individual must awake to universality and to transcendence.

The supraterrestrial existence is also a truth of being; for the material is not the only plane of our existence; other planes of consciousness there are to which we can attain and which have already their hidden links with us: not to reach up to whatever greater regions of the soul are open to us, not to have the experience of them, not to know and manifest their law in ourselves is to fall short of the height and fullness of our being. But worlds of a higher consciousness are not the only possible scene and habitation of the perfected soul; nor can we find in any unchanging typal world the final or total sense of the Spirit's self-expression in the cosmos: the material world, this earth, this human life are a part of the Spirit's self-expression and have their divine possibility; that possibility is evolutionary and it contains the possibilities of all the other worlds in it, unrealised but realisable. Earth-life is not a lapse into the mire of something undivine, vain and miserable, offered by some Power to itself as a spectacle or to the embodied soul as a thing to be suffered and then cast away from it: it is the scene of the evolutionary unfolding of the being which moves towards the revelation of a supreme spiritual light and power and joy and oneness, but includes in it also the manifold diversity of the self-achieving spirit. There is an all-seeing purpose in the terrestrial creation; a divine plan is working itself out through its contradictions and perplexities which are a sign of the many-sided achievement towards which are being led the soul's growth and the endeavour of Nature.

It is true that the soul can ascend into worlds of a greater consciousness beyond the earth, but it is also true that the power of these worlds, the power of a greater consciousness has to develop itself here; the embodiment of the soul is the means for that embodiment. All the higher powers of Consciousness exist because they are powers of the Supreme Reality. Our terrestrial being has also the same truth; it is a becoming of the One Reality which has to embody in itself these greater powers. Its present appearance is a veiled and partial figure and to limit ourselves to that first figure, to the present formula of an imperfect humanity, is to exclude our divine potentialities; we have to bring a wider meaning into our human life and manifest in it the much more that we secretly are. Our mortality is only justified in the light of our immortality; our earth can know and be all itself only by opening to the heavens; the individual can see himself aright and use his world divinely only when he has entered into greater planes of being and seen the light of the Supreme and lived in the being and power of the Divine and Eternal.

An integration of this kind would not be possible if a spiritual evolution were not the sense of our birth and terrestrial existence; the evolution of mind, life and spirit in Matter is the sign that this integration, this completed manifestation of a secret self contained in it is its significance. A complete involution of all that the Spirit is and its evolutionary self-unfolding are the double term of our material existence. There is a possibility of self-expression by an always unveiled luminous development of the being, a possibility also of various expression in perfect types fixed and complete in their own nature: that is the principle of becoming in the higher worlds; they are typal and not evolutionary in their life principle; they exist each in its own perfection, but within the limits of a stationary world-formula. But there is also a possibility of self-expression by self-finding, a deployment which takes the form and goes through the progression of a self-veiling and an adventure of self-recover)': that is the principle of becoming in this universe of which an involution of consciousness and concealment of the spirit in Matter is the first appearance.

An involution of spirit in the Inconscience is the beginning; an evolution in the Ignorance with its play of the possibilities of a partial developing knowledge is the middle, and the cause of the anomalies of our present nature—our imperfection is the sign of a transitional state, a growth not yet completed, an effort that is finding its way; a consummation in a deployment of the spirit's self-knowledge and the self-power of its divine being and consciousness is the culmination: these are the three stages of this cycle of the spirit's progressive self-expression in life. The two stages that have already their play seem at first sight to deny the possibility of the later consummating stage of the cycle, but logically they imply its emergence; for if the inconscience has evolved consciousness, the partial consciousness already reached must surely evolve into complete consciousness. It is a perfected and divinised life for which the earth-nature is seeking, and this seeking is a sign of the Divine Will in Nature. Other seekings also there are and these too find their means of self-fulfilment; a withdrawal into the supreme peace or ecstasy, a withdrawal into the bliss of the Divine Presence are open to the soul in earth-existence: for the Infinite in its manifestation has many possibilities and is not confined by its formulations. But neither of these withdrawals can be the fundamental intention in the Becoming itself here; for then an evolutionary progression would not have been undertaken—such a progression here can only have for its aim a self-fulfilment here: a progressive manifestation of this kind can only have for its soul of significance the revelation of Being in a perfect Becoming.

Life and Yoga

There are two necessities of Nature's workings which seem always to intervene in the greater forms of human activity, whether they belong to our ordinary fields of movement or seek those exceptional spheres and fulfilments which appear to us high and divine. Every such form tends towards a harmonised complexity and totality which again breaks apart into various channels of special effort and tendency, only to unite once more in a larger and more puissant synthesis. Secondly, development into forms is an imperative rule of effective manifestation; yet all truth and practice too strictly formulated becomes old and loses much, if not all, of its virtue; it must be constantly renovated by fresh streams of the spirit revivifying the dead or dying vehicle and changing it, if it is to acquire a new life. To be perpetually reborn is the condition of a material immortality. We are in an age, full of the throes of travail, when all forms of thought and activity that have in themselves any strong power of utility or any secret virtue of persistence are being subjected to a supreme test and given their opportunity of rebirth. The world today presents the aspect of a huge cauldron of Medea[1] in which all things are being cast, shredded into pieces, experimented on, combined and recombined either to perish

---

[1] This opening chapter of *The Synthesis of Yoga* was published in the *Arya* in August 1914. The book was first published posthumously in 1955.
A sorceress in Greek mythology, celebrated in the plays of Euripides, Seneca, Corneille and others.

and provide the scattered material of new forms or to emerge rejuvenated and changed for a fresh term of existence. Indian Yoga, in its essence a special action or formulation of certain great powers of Nature, itself specialised, divided and variously formulated, is potentially one of these dynamic elements of the future life of humanity. The child of immemorial ages, preserved by its vitality and truth into our modern times, it is now emerging from the secret schools and ascetic retreats in which it had taken refuge and is seeking its place in the future sum of living human powers and utilities. But it has first to rediscover itself, bring to the surface the profoundest reason of its being in that general truth and that unceasing aim of Nature which it represents, and find by virtue of this new self-knowledge and self-appreciation its own recovered and larger synthesis. Reorganising itself, it will enter more easily and powerfully into the reorganised life of the race which its processes claim to lead within into the most secret penetralia and upward to the highest altitudes of its own existence and personality.

In the right view both of life and of Yoga all life is either consciously or subconsciously a Yoga. For we mean by this term a methodised effort towards self-perfection by the expression of the potentialities latent in the being and a union of the human individual with the universal and transcendent Existence we see partially expressed in man and in the Cosmos. But all life, when we look behind its appearances, is a vast Yoga of Nature attempting to realise her perfection in an ever increasing expression of her potentialities and to unite herself with her own divine reality. In man, her thinker, she for the first time upon this Earth devises self-conscious means and willed arrangements of activity by which this great purpose may be more swiftly and puissantly attained. Yoga, as Swami Vivekananda has said, may be regarded as a means of compressing one's evolution into a single life or a few years or even a few months of bodily existence. A given system of Yoga, then, can be no more than a selection or a compression, into narrower but more energetic forms of intensity, of the general methods which are already being used loosely, largely, in a leisurely movement, with a profuser apparent waste of material and energy but with a more complete combination by the great Mother in her vast upward labour. It is this view of Yoga that can alone form the basis for a sound and rational synthesis of Yogic methods. For then Yoga ceases to appear something mystic and abnormal which has no relation to the ordinary processes of the World-Energy or the purpose she keeps in view in her two great movements of subjective and objective self-fulfilment; it reveals itself rather as an intense and exceptional use of powers that she has already manifested or is progressively organising in her less exalted but more general operations.

Yogic methods have something of the same relation to the customary psychological workings of man as has the scientific handling of the natural force of electricity or of steam to the normal operations of steam and electricity. And they, too, are formed upon a knowledge developed and confirmed by regular experiment, practical analysis and constant result. All Raja Yoga, for instance, depends on this perception and experience that our inner elements, combinations, functions, forces, can be separated or dissolved, can be new-combined and set to novel and formerly impossible workings or can be transformed and resolved into a new general synthesis by fixed internal processes. Hatha Yoga similarly depends on this perception and experience that the vital forces and functions to which our life is normally subjected and whose ordinary operations seem set and indispensable, can be mastered and the operations changed or suspended with results that would otherwise be impossible and that seem miraculous to those who have not seized the rationale of their process. And if in some other of its forms this character of Yoga is less apparent, because they are more intuitive and less mechanical, nearer, like the Yoga of

Devotion, to a supernal ecstasy or, like the Yoga of Knowledge, to a supernal infinity of consciousness and being, yet they too start from the use of some principal faculty in us by ways and for ends not contemplated in its everyday spontaneous workings. All methods grouped under the common name of Yoga are special psychological processes founded on a fixed truth of Nature and developing, out of normal functions, powers and results which were always latent but which her ordinary movements do not easily or do not often manifest.

But as in physical knowledge the multiplication of scientific processes has its disadvantages, as that tends, for instance, to develop a victorious artificiality which overwhelms our natural human life under a load of machinery and to purchase certain forms of freedom and mastery at the price of an increased servitude, so the preoccupation with Yogic processes and their exceptional results may have its disadvantages and losses. The Yogin tends to draw away from the common existence and lose his hold upon it; he tends to purchase wealth of spirit by an impoverishment of his human activities, the inner freedom by an outer death. If he gains God, he loses life, or if he turns his efforts outward to conquer life, he is in danger of losing God. Therefore we see in India that a sharp incompatibility has been created between life in the world and spiritual growth and perfection, and although the tradition and ideal of a victorious harmony between the inner attraction and the outer demand remains, it is little exemplified. In fact, when a man turns his vision and energy inward and enters on the path of Yoga, he is supposed to be lost inevitably to the great stream of our collective existence and the secular effort of humanity. So strongly has the idea prevailed, so much has it been emphasized by prevalent philosophies and religions that to escape from life is now commonly considered as not only the necessary condition, but the general object of Yoga. No synthesis of Yoga can be satisfying which does not, in its aim, reunite God and

Nature in a liberated and perfected human life or, in its method, not only permit but favour the harmony of our inner and outer activities and experiences in the divine consummation of both. For man is precisely that term and symbol of a higher Existence descended into the material world in which it is possible for the lower to transfigure itself and put on the nature of the higher and the higher to reveal itself in the forms of the lower. To avoid the life which is given him for the realisation of that possibility, can never be either the indispensable condition or the whole and ultimate object of his supreme endeavour or of his most powerful means of self-fulfilment. It can only be a temporary necessity under certain conditions or a specialised extreme effort imposed on the individual so as to prepare a greater general possibility for the race. The true and full object and utility of Yoga can only be accomplished when the conscious Yoga in man becomes, like the subconscious Yoga in Nature, outwardly conterminous with life itself and we can once more, looking out both on the path and the achievement, say in a more perfect and luminous sense: 'All life is Yoga.'

The Synthesis[1]

By the very nature of the principal Yogic schools each covering in its operations a part of the complex human integer and attempting to bring out its highest possibilities, it will appear that a synthesis of all of them largely conceived and applied might well result in an integral Yoga. But they are so disparate in their tendencies, so highly specialised and elaborated in their forms, so long confirmed in the mutual opposition of their ideas and methods that we do not easily find how we can arrive at their right union.

An undiscriminating combination in block would not be a synthesis, but a confusion. Nor would successive practice of each of them in turn be easy in the short span of our human life and with our limited energies, to say nothing of the waste of labour implied in so cumbrous a process. Sometimes, indeed, Hatha Yoga and Raja Yoga are thus successively practised. And in a recent unique example, in the life of Ramakrishna Paramahansa, we see a colossal spiritual capacity, first driving straight to the divine realisation, taking, as it were, the kingdom of heaven by violence, and then seizing upon one Yogic method after another and extracting the substance out of it with an incredible rapidity, always to return to the heart of the whole matter, the realisation and possession of God by the power of love, by the extension of inborn spirituality into various experience and by the spontaneous play of an intuitive

---

[1] Chapter V of the *Synthesis of Yoga*.

knowledge. Such an example cannot be generalised. Its object also was special and temporal, to exemplify in the great and decisive experience of a master-soul the truth, now most necessary to humanity, towards which a world long divided into jarring sects and schools is with difficulty labouring, that all sects are forms and fragments of a single integral truth and all disciplines labour in their different ways towards one supreme experience. To know, be and possess the Divine is the one thing needful and it includes or leads up to all the rest; towards this sole good we have to drive and this attained, all the rest that the divine Will chooses for us, all necessary form and manifestation, will be added.

The synthesis we propose cannot, then, be arrived at either by combination in mass or by successive practice. It must therefore be effected by neglecting the forms and outsides of the Yogic disciplines and seizing rather on some central principle common to all which will include and utilise in the right place and proportion their particular principles, and on some central dynamic force which is the common secret of their divergent methods and capable therefore of organising a natural selection and combination of their varied energies and different utilities. This was the aim which we set before ourselves at first when we entered upon our comparative examination of the methods of Nature and the methods of Yoga and we now return to it with the possibility of hazarding some definite solution.

We observe, first, that there still exists in India a remarkable Yogic system which is in its nature synthetical and starts from a great central principle of Nature, a great dynamic force of Nature; but it is a Yoga apart, not a synthesis of other schools. This system is the way of the Tantra. Owing to certain of its developments Tantra has fallen into discredit with those who are not Tantrics; and especially owing to the developments of its left-hand path, the Vamamarga, which not content with exceeding the duality of virtue and sin and instead of replacing them by spontaneous lightness of action seemed to make a method of self-indulgence, a method of unrestrained social immorality. Nevertheless, in its origin Tantra was a great and puissant system founded upon ideas which were at least partially true. Even its twofold division into the right-hand and left-hand paths, Dakshinamarga and Varnamarga, started from a certain profound perception. In the ancient symbolic sense of the words Dakshina and Varna, it was the distinction between the way of Knowledge and the way of Ananda—Nature in man liberating itself by right discrimination in power and practice of its own energies, elements and potentialities and Nature in man liberating itself by joyous acceptance in power and practice of its own energies, elements and potentialities. But in both paths there was in the end an obscuration of principles, a deformation of symbols and a fall.

If, however, we leave aside, here also, the actual methods and practices and seek for the central principle, we find, first, that Tantra expressly differentiates itself from the Vedic methods of Yoga. In a sense, all the schools we have hitherto examined are Vedantic in their principle; their force is in knowledge, their method is knowledge, though it is not always discernment by the intellect, but may be, instead, the knowledge of the heart expressed in love and faith or a knowledge in the will working out through action. In all the lord of the Yoga is the Purusha, the Conscious Soul that knows, observes, attracts, governs. But in Tantra it is rather Prakriti, the Nature-Soul, the Energy, the Will-in-Power executive in the universe. It was by learning and applying the intimate secrets of this Will-in-Power, its method, its Tantra, that the Tantric Yogin pursued the aims of his discipline—mastery, perfection, liberation, beatitude. Instead of drawing back from manifested Nature and its difficulties, he confronted them, seized and conquered. But in the end, as is the general tendency of Prakriti, Tantric Yoga largely lost its principle in its machinery and became a thing of formulae and occult mechanism still powerful when rightly used but fallen from the clarity of their original intention.

We have in this central Tantric conception one side of the truth, the worship of the Energy, the Shakti, as the sole effective force for all attainment. We get the other extreme in the Vedantic conception of the Shakti as a power of Illusion and in the search after the silent inactive Purusha as the means of liberation from the deceptions created by the active Energy. But in the integral conception the Conscious Soul is the Lord, the Nature-Soul is his executive Energy. Purusha is of the nature of Sat, conscious self-existence pure and infinite; Shakti or Prakriti is of the nature of Chit—it is power of the Purusha's self-conscious existence, pure and infinite. The relation of the two exists between the poles of rest and action. When the Energy is absorbed in the bliss of conscious self-existence, there is rest; when the Purusha pours itself out in the action of its Energy, there is action, creation and the enjoyment or Ananda of becoming. But if Ananda is the creator and begetter of all becoming, its method is Tapas or force of the Purusha's consciousness dwelling upon its own infinite potentiality in existence and producing from it truths of conception or real Ideas, *vijñāna,* which, proceeding from an omniscient and omnipotent Self-Existence, have the surety of their own fulfilment and contain in themselves the nature and law of their own becoming in the terms of mind, life and matter. The eventual omnipotence of Tapas and the infallible fulfilment of the Idea are the very foundation of all Yoga. In man we render these terms by Will and Faith—a will that is eventually self-effective because it is of the substance of Knowledge and a faith that is the reflex in the lower consciousness of a Truth or real Idea yet unrealised in the manifestation. It is this self-certainty of the Idea which is meant by the Gita when it says, *Yo yacchraddhah sa eva sah,* 'whatever is a man's faith or the sure Idea in him, that he becomes.'

We see, then, what from the psychological point of view—and Yoga is nothing but practical psychology—is the conception of Nature from which we have to start. It is the self-fulfilment of the Purusha through his Energy. But the movement of Nature is twofold, higher and lower, or, as we may choose to term it, divine and undivine. The distinction exists indeed for practical purposes only; for there is nothing that is not divine, and in a larger view it is as meaningless, verbally, as the distinction between natural and supernatural, for all things that are are natural. All things are in Nature and all things are in God. But, for practical purposes, there is a real distinction. The lower Nature, that which we know and are and must remain so long as the faith in us is not changed, acts through limitation and division, is of the nature of Ignorance and culminates in the life of the ego; but the higher Nature, that to which we aspire, acts by unification and transcendence of limitation, is of the nature of Knowledge and culminates in the life divine. The passage from the lower to the higher is the aim of Yoga; and this passage may effect itself by the rejection of the lower and escape into the higher—the ordinary view-point—or by the transformation of the lower and its elevation to the higher Nature. It is this, rather, that must be the aim of an integral Yoga.

But in either case it is always through something in the lower that we must rise into the higher existence, and the schools of Yoga each select their own point of departure or their own gate of escape. They specialise certain activities of the lower Prakriti and turn them towards the Divine. But the normal action of Nature in us is an integral movement in which the full complexity of all our elements is affected by and affects all our environments. The whole of life is the Yoga of Nature. The Yoga that we seek must also be an integral action of Nature, and the whole difference between the Yogin and the natural man will be this, that the Yogin seeks to substitute in himself for the integral action of the lower Nature working in and by ego and division the integral action of the higher Nature working in and by God and unity. If indeed our aim be only an escape from the world to God, synthesis is unnecessary and a waste of time; for then our sole practical aim must be to find out one path out of the thousand that lead to God, one shortest possible of short cuts, and not to linger exploring different paths that end in the same goal. But if our aim be a transformation of our integral being into the terms of God-existence, it is then that a synthesis becomes necessary.

The method we have to pursue, then, is to put our whole conscious being into relation and contact with the Divine and to call Him in to transform our entire being into His, so that in a sense God Himself, the real Person in us, becomes the Sadhaka of the Sadhana[2] as well as the Master of the Yoga by whom the lower personality is used as the centre of a divine transfiguration and the instrument of its own perfection. In effect, the pressure of the Tapas, the force of consciousness in us dwelling in the Idea of the divine Nature upon that which we are in our entirety, produces its own realisation. The divine and all-knowing and all-effecting descends upon the limited and obscure, progressively illumines and energises the whole lower nature and substitutes its own action for all the terms of the inferior human light and mortal activity.

In psychological fact this method translates itself into the progressive surrender of the ego with its whole field and all its apparatus to the Beyond-ego with its vast and incalculable but always inevitable workings. Certainly, this is no short cut or easy Sadhana. It requires a colossal faith, an absolute courage and above all an unflinching patience. For it implies three stages of which only the last can be wholly blissful or rapid—the attempt of the ego to enter into contact with the Divine, the wide, full and therefore laborious preparation of the whole lower Nature by the

---

[2] *Sadhanā,* the practice by which perfection, *sidhi,* is attained; *sādhaka,* the Yogin who seeks by that practice the Siddhi. [Sri Aurobindo's note]

divine working to receive and become the higher Nature, and the eventual transformation. In fact, however, the divine Strength, often unobserved and behind the veil, substitutes itself for our weakness and supports us through all our failings of faith, courage and patience. It 'makes the blind to see and the lame to stride over the hills.' The intellect becomes aware of a Law that beneficently insists and a succour that upholds; the heart speaks of a Master of all things and Friend of man or a universal Mother who upholds through all stumblings. Therefore this path is at once the most difficult imaginable and yet, in comparison with the magnitude of its effort and object, the most easy and sure of all.

There are three outstanding features of this action of the higher when it works integrally on the lower nature. In the first place, it does not act according to a fixed system and succession as in the specialised methods of Yoga, but with a sort of free, scattered and yet gradually intensive and purposeful working determined by the temperament of the individual in whom it operates, the helpful materials which his nature offers and the obstacles which it presents to purification and perfection. In a sense, therefore, each man in this path has his own method of Yoga. Yet are there certain broad lines of working common to all which enable us to construct not indeed a routine system, but yet some kind of Shastra or scientific method of the synthetic Yoga.

Secondly, the process, being integral, accepts our nature such as it stands organised by our past evolution and without rejecting anything essential compels all to undergo a divine change. Everything in us is seized by the hands of a mighty Artificer and transformed into a clear image of that which it now seeks confusedly to present. In that ever-progressive experience we begin to perceive how this lower manifestation is constituted and that everything in it, however seemingly deformed or petty or vile, is the more or less distorted or imperfect figure of some element or action in the harmony of the divine Nature. We begin to understand what the Vedic Rishis meant when they spoke of the human forefathers fashioning the gods as a smith forges the crude material in his smithy.

Thirdly, the divine Power in us uses all life as the means of this integral Yoga. Every experience and outer contact with our world-environment, however trifling or however disastrous, is used for the work, and every inner experience, even to the most repellent suffering or the most humiliating fall, becomes a step on the path to perfection. And we recognise in ourselves with opened eyes the method of God in the world, His purpose of light in the obscure, of might in the weak and fallen, of delight in what is grievous and miserable. We see the divine method to be the same in the lower and in the higher working; only in the one it is pursued tardily and obscurely through the subconscious in Nature, in the other it becomes swift and self-conscious and the instrument confesses the hand of the Master.

All life is a Yoga of Nature seeking to manifest God within itself. Yoga marks the stage at which this effort becomes capable of self-awareness and therefore of right completion in the individual. It is a gathering up and concentration of the movements dispersed and loosely combined in the lower evolution.

An integral method and an integral result. First, an integral realisation of Divine Being; not only a realisation of the One in its indistinguishable unity, but also in its multitude of aspects which are also necessary to the complete knowledge of it by the relative consciousness; not only realisation of unity in the Self, but of unity in the infinite diversity of activities, worlds and creatures.

Therefore, also, an integral liberation. Not only the freedom born of unbroken contact of the individual being in all its parts with the Divine, *sāyujyamukti,* by which it becomes, free even in its separation, even in the duality; not only the *sālokyamukti* by which the whole conscious existence dwells in the same status of being as the Divine, in the state of Sachchidananda; but also the acquisition of the divine nature by the transformation of this lower being into the human image of the divine, *sādharmyamukti*, and the complete and final release of all, the liberation of the consciousness from the transitory mould of the ego and its unification with the One Being, universal both in the world and the individual and transcendentally one both in the world and beyond all universe.

By this integral realisation and liberation, the perfect harmony of the results of Knowledge, Love and Works. For there is attained the complete release from ego and identification in being with the One in all and beyond all. But since the attaining consciousness is not limited by its attainment, we win also the unity in Beatitude and the harmonised diversity in Love, so that all relations of the play remain possible to us even while we retain on the heights of our being the eternal oneness with the Beloved. And by a similar wideness, being capable of a freedom in spirit that embraces life and does not depend upon withdrawal from life, we are able to become without egoism, bondage or reaction the channel in our mind and body for a divine action poured out freely upon the world.

The divine existence is of the nature not only of freedom, but of purity, beatitude and perfection. An integral purity which shall enable, on the one hand, the perfect reflection of the divine Being in ourselves and on the other the perfect outpouring of its Truth and Law in us in the terms of life and through the right functioning of the complex instrument we are in our outer parts, is the condition of an integral liberty. Its result is an integral beatitude, in which there becomes possible at once the Ananda of all that is in the world seen as symbols of the Divine and the Ananda of that which is not-world. And it prepares the integral perfection of our humanity as a type of the Divine in the conditions of the human manifestation, a perfection founded on a certain free universality of being, of love and joy, of play of knowledge and of play of will in power and will in unegoistic action. This integrality also can be attained by the integral Yoga.

Perfection includes perfection of mind and body, so that the highest results of Raja Yoga and Hatha Yoga should be contained in the widest formula of the synthesis finally to be effected by mankind. At any rate a full development of the general mental and physical faculties and experiences attainable by humanity through Yoga must be included in the scope of the integral method. Nor would these have any *raison d'etre* unless employed for an integral mental and physical life. Such a mental and physical life would be in its nature a translation of the spiritual existence into its right mental and physical values. Thus we would arrive at a synthesis of the three degrees of Nature and of the three modes of human existence which she has evolved or is evolving. We would include in the scope of our liberated being and perfected modes of activity the material life, our base, and the mental life, our intermediate instrument.

Nor would the integrality to which we aspire be real or even possible, if it were confined to the individual. Since our divine perfection embraces the realisation of ourselves in being, in life and in love through others as well as through ourselves, the extension of our liberty and of its results in others would be the inevitable outcome as well as the broadest utility of our liberation and perfection. And the constant and inherent attempt of such an extension would be towards its increasing and ultimately complete generalisation in mankind.

The divinising of the normal material life of man and of his great secular attempt of mental and moral self-culture in the individual and the race by this integralisation of a widely perfect spiritual existence would thus be the crown alike of our individual and of our common effort. Such a consummation being no other than the kingdom of heaven within reproduced in the kingdom of heaven without, would be also the true fulfilment of the great dream cherished in different terms by the world's religions.

The widest synthesis of perfection possible to thought is the sole effort entirely worthy of those whose dedicated vision perceives that God dwells concealed in humanity.

From: Letters on Yoga[1]

[A New Consciousness on Earth]

What we are doing, if and when we succeed, will be a beginning, not a completion. It is the foundation of a new consciousness on earth—a consciousness with infinite possibilities of manifestation. The eternal progression is in the manifestation and beyond it there is no progression.

If the redemption of the soul from the physical vesture be the object, then there is no need of supramentalisation. Spiritual Mukti and Nirvana are sufficient. If the object is to rise to supraphysical planes, then also there is no need of supramentalisation. One can enter into some heaven above by devotion to the Lord of that heaven. But that is no progression. The other worlds are typal worlds, each fixed in its own kind and type and law. Evolution takes place on the earth and therefore the earth is the proper field for progression. The beings of the other worlds do not progress from one world to another. They remain fixed to their own type.

The purely monistic Vedantist says, all is Brahman, life is a dream, an unreality, only Brahman exists. One has Nirvana or Mukti, then one lives only till the body falls—after that there is no such thing as life.

[1] From *Letters on Yoga,* Part I. Most of these and the following letters were written to disciples in the 1930s. The first three series were published by Sri Aurobindo Circle, Bombay, in 1947. The titles are the editor's.

They do not believe in transformation, because mind, life and body are an ignorance, an illusion—the only reality is the featureless relationless Self or Brahman. Life is a thing of relations; in the pure Self, all life and relations disappear. What would be the use or the possibility of transforming an illusion that can never be anything else (however transformed) than an illusion? There is no such thing for them as a 'Nirvanic life'.

It is only some yogas that aim at a transformation of any kind except that of ignorance into knowledge. The idea varies,—sometimes a divine knowledge or power or else a divine purity or an ethical perfection or a divine love.

What has to be overcome is the opposition of the Ignorance that does not want the transformation of the nature. If that can be overcome, then old spiritual ideas will not form an obstacle. It is not intended to supramentalise humanity at large, but to establish the principle of the supramental consciousness in the earth-evolution. If that is done, all that is needed will be evolved by the supramental Power itself. It is not therefore important that the mission should be widespread. What is important is that the thing should be done at all in however small a number; that is the only difficulty.

If the transformation of the body is complete, that means no subjection to death—it does not mean that one will be bound to keep the same body for all time. One creates a new body for oneself when one wants to change, but how it will be done cannot be said now. The present method is by physical birth—some occultists suppose that a time will come when that will not be necessary—but the question must be left for the supramental evolution to decide.

The questions about the supermind cannot be answered profitably now. Supermind cannot be described in terms that the mind will understand, because the terms will be mental and mind will understand them in a mental way and mental sense and miss their true import. It would therefore be a waste of time and energy which should be devoted to the preliminary work—psychicisation and spiritualisation of the being and nature without which no supramentalisation is possible. Let the whole dynamic nature led by the psychic make itself full of the dynamic spiritual light, peace, purity, knowledge, force; let it afterwards get experience of the intermediate spiritual planes and know, feel and act in their sense; then it will be possible to speak last of the supramental transformation.

Shankara's[2] Explanation of the Universe

It is rather difficult to say nowadays what really was Shankara's philosophy: there are numberless exponents and none of them agrees with any of the others. I have read accounts given by some scores of his exegetes and each followed his own line. We are even told by some that he was no Mayavadin at all, although he has always been famed as the greatest exponent of the theory of Maya, but rather, the greatest Realist in philosophical history. One eminent follower of Shankara even declared that my philosophy and Shankara's were identical, a statement which rather took my breath away. One used to think that Shankara's philosophy was this that the Supreme Reality is a spaceless and timeless Absolute (Parabrahman) which is beyond all feature or quality, beyond all action or creation, and that the world is a creation of Maya, not absolutely unreal, but real only in time and while one lives in time; once we get into a knowledge of the Reality, we perceive that Maya and the world and all in it have no abiding or true existence. It is, if not nonexistent, yet false, *jaganmithyā;* it is a mistake of the consciousness, it is and it is not; it is an irrational and inexplicable

---

[2] Shankaracharya, eighth century philosopher and theologian, considered the foremost exponent of Advaita Vedanta, and one of the greatest synthesizers of Hindu thought.

mystery in its origin, though we can see its process or at least how it keeps itself imposed on the consciousness. Brahman is seen in Maya as Ishwara upholding the works of Maya and the apparendy individual soul is really nothing but Brahman itself. In the end, however, all this seems to be a myth of Maya, *mithyā,* and not anything really true. If that is Shankara's philosophy, it is to me unacceptable and incredible, however brilliantly ingenious it may be and however boldly and incisively reasoned; it does not satisfy my reason and it does not agree with my experience.

I don't know exactly what is meant by this *yuktivāda*. If it is meant that it is merely for the sake of arguing down opponents, then this part of the philosophy has no fundamental validity; Shankara's theory destroys itself. Either he meant it as a sufficient explanation of the universe or he did not. If he did, it is no use dismissing it as Yuktivada. I can understand that thorough-going Mayavadin's declaration that the whole question is illegitimate, because Maya and the world do not really exist; in fact, the problem how the world came to existence is only a part of Maya, is like Maya unreal and does not truly arise; but if an explanation is to be given, it must be a real, valid and satisfying explanation. If there are two planes and in putting the question we are confusing the two planes, that argument can only be of value if both planes have some kind of existence and the reasoning and explanation are true in the lower plane but cease to have any meaning for a consciousness which has passed out of it.

Advaita

People are apt to speak of the Advaita as if it were identical with Mayavada monism, just as they speak of Vedanta as if it were identical with Advaita only; that is not the case. There are several forms of Indian philosophy which base themselves upon the One Reality, but they admit also the reality of the world, the reality of the Many, the reality of the differences of the Many as well as the sameness of the One *(bhedābheda).* But the Many exist in the One and by the One, the differences are variations in manifestation of that which is fundamentally ever the same. This we actually see as the universal law of existence where oneness is always the basis with an endless multiplicity and difference in the oneness; as, for instance, there is one mankind but many kinds of man, one thing called leaf or flower but many forms, patterns, colours of leaf and flower.

Through this we can look back into one of the fundamental secrets of existence, the secret which is contained in the one Reality itself. The oneness of the Infinite is not something limited, fettered to its unity; it is capable of an infinite multiplicity. The Supreme Reality is an Absolute not limited by either oneness or multiplicity but simultaneously capable of both; for both are its aspects, although the oneness is fundamental and the multiplicity depends upon the oneness. There is possible a realistic as well as an illusionist Advaita. The philosophy of *The Life Divine* is such a realistic Advaita. The world is a manifestation of the Real and therefore is itself real. The reality is the infinite and eternal Divine, infinite and eternal Being, Consciousness-Force and Bliss. This Divine by his power has created the world or rather manifested it in his own infinite Being. But here in the material world or at its basis he has hidden himself in what seem to be his opposites, Non-Being, Inconscience and Insentience. This is what we nowadays call the Inconscient which seems to have created the material universe by its inconscient Energy, but this is only an appearance, for we find in the end that all the dispositions of the world can only have been arranged by the working of a supreme secret Intelligence. The Being which is hidden in what seems to be an inconscient void emerges in the world first in Matter, then in Life, then in Mind and finally as the Spirit. The apparently inconscient Energy which creates is in fact the Consciousness-Force of the Divine and its aspect of consciousness, secret in Matter, begins to emerge in Life, finds something more of itself in Mind and finds its true self in a spiritual consciousness and finally a supramental Consciousness through which we become aware of the Reality, enter into it and unite ourselves with it. This is what we call evolution which is an evolution of Consciousness and an evolution of the Spirit in things and only outwardly an evolution of species. Thus also, the delight of existence emerges from the original insentience, first in the contrary forms of pleasure and pain, and then has to find itself in the bliss of the Spirit or, as it is called in the Upanishads, the bliss of the Brahman. That is the central idea in the explanation of the universe put forward in *The Life Divine*.

Nirguna and Saguna

In a realistic Advaita there is no need to regard the Saguna as a creation from the Nirguna or even secondary or subordinate to it: both are equal aspects of the one Reality, its position of silent status and rest and its position of action and dynamic force; a silence of eternal rest and peace supports an eternal action and movement. The one Reality, the Divine Being, is bound by neither, since it is in no way limited; it possesses both. There is no incompatibility between the two, as there is none between the Many and the One, the sameness and the difference. They are all eternal aspects of the universe which could not exist if either of them were eliminated, and it is reasonable to suppose that they both came from the Reality which has manifested the universe and are both real. We can only get rid of the apparent contradiction—which is not really a contradiction but only a natural concomitance—by treating one or the other as an illusion. But it is hardly reasonable to suppose that the eternal Reality allows the existence of an eternal illusion with which it has nothing to do or that it supports and enforces on being a vain cosmic illusion and has no power for any other and real action. The force of the Divine is always there in silence as in action, inactive in silence, active in the manifestation. It is hardly possible to suppose that the Divine Reality has no power or force or that its only power is to create a universal falsehood, a cosmic lie—*mithiyā*.

Nirvana

What then is Nirvana? In orthodox Buddhism it does mean a disintegration, not of the soul—for that does not exist—but of a mental compound or stream of associations or *saṁ skāras* which we mistake for ourself. In illusionist Vedanta it means, not a disintegration but a disappearance of a false and unreal individual self into the one real Self or Brahman; it is the idea and experience of individuality that so disappears and ceases, we may say a false light that is extinguished *(nirvāṇa)* in the true Light. In spiritual experience it is sometimes the loss of all sense of individuality in a boundless cosmic consciousness; what was the individual remains only as a centre or a channel for the flow of a cosmic consciousness and a cosmic force and action. Or it may be the experience of the loss of individuality in a transcendent being and consciousness in which the sense of cosmos as well as the individual disappears. Or again, it may be in a transcendence which is aware of and supports the cosmic action. But what do we mean by the individual? What we usually call by that name is a natural ego, a device of Nature which holds together her action in the mind and body. This ego has to be extinguished, otherwise there is no complete liberation possible; but the individual self or soul is not this ego. The individual soul is the spiritual being which is sometimes described as an eternal portion of the Divine, but can also be described as the Divine himself supporting his manifestation as the Many. This is the true spiritual individual which appears in its complete truth when we get rid of the ego and our false separative sense of individuality, realise our oneness with the transcendent and cosmic Divine and with all beings. It is this which makes possible the Divine Life. Nirvana is a step towards it; the disappearance of the false separative individuality is a necessary condition for our realising and living in our true eternal being, living divinely in the Divine. But this we can do in the world and in life.

Rebirth

If evolution is a truth and is not only a physical evolution of species, but an evolution of consciousness, it must be a spiritual and not only a physical fact. In that case, it is the individual who evolves and grows into a more and more developed and perfect consciousness and obviously that cannot be done in the course of a brief single human life. If there is the evolution of a conscious individual, then there must be rebirth. Rebirth is a logical necessity and a spiritual fact of which we can have the experience. Proofs of rebirth, sometimes of an overwhelmingly convincing nature, are not lacking, but as yet they have not been carefully registered and brought together.

Integral Yoga and Other Paths

By transformation I do not mean some change of the nature — I do not mean, for instance, sainthood or ethical perfection or yogic siddhis (like the Tantrik's) or a transcendental (cinmaya) body. I use transformation in a special sense, a change of consciousness radical and complete and of a certain specific kind which is so conceived as to bring about a strong and assured step forward in the spiritual evolution of the being of a greater and higher kind and of a larger sweep and completeness than what took place when a mentalised being first appeared in a vital and material animal world. If anything short of that takes place or at least if a real beginning is not made on that basis, a fundamental progress towards this fulfilment, then my object is not accomplished. A partial realisation, something mixed and inconclusive, does not meet the demand I make on life and yoga.

Light of realisation is not the same thing as Descent. Realisation by itself does not necessarily transform the being as a whole; it may bring only an opening or heightening or widening of the consciousness at the top so as to realise something in the Purusha part without any radical change in the parts of Prakriti. One may have some light of realisation at the spiritual summit of the consciousness but the parts below remain what they were. I have seen any number of instances of that. There must be a descent of the light not merely into the mind or part of it but into all the being down to the physical and below before a real transformation can take place. A light in the mind may spiritualise or otherwise change the mind or part of it in one way or another, but it need not change the vital nature; a light in the vital may purify and enlarge the vital movements or else silence and immobilise the vital being, but leave the body and the physical consciousness as it was, or even leave it inert or shake its balance. And the descent of Light is not enough, it must be the descent of the whole higher consciousness, its Peace, Power, Knowledge, Love, Ananda. Moreover, the descent may be enough to liberate, but not to perfect, or it may be enough to make a great change in the inner being, while the outer remains an imperfect instrument, clumsy, sick or unexpressive. Finally, transformation effected by the sadhana cannot be complete unless it is a supramentalisation of the being. Psychicisation is not enough, it is only a beginning; spiritualisation and the descent of the higher consciousness is not enough, it is only a middle term; the ultimate achievement needs the action of the supramental Consciousness and Force. Something less than that may very well be considered enough by the individual, but it is not enough for the earth-consciousness to take the definitive stride forward it must take at one time or another.

I have never said that my yoga was something brand new in all its elements. I have called it the integral yoga and that means that it takes up the essence and many processes of the old yogas —its newness is in its aim, standpoint and the totality of its method. In the earlier stages which is all I deal with in books like the *Riddle* or the *Lights* or in the new book to be published[3] there is nothing in it that distinguishes it from the old yogas except the aim underlying its comprehensiveness, the spirit in its movements and the ultimate significance it keeps before it—also the scheme of its psychology and its workings: but as that was not and could not be developed systematically or schematically in these letters, it has not been grasped by those who are not already acquainted with it by mental familiarity or some amount of practice. The detail or method of the later stages of the yoga which go into little known or untrodden regions, I have not made public and I do not at present intend to do so.

I know very well also that there have been seemingly allied ideals and anticipations—the perfectibility of the race, certain Tantric sadhanas, the effort after a complete physical siddhi by certain schools of yoga, etc., etc. I have alluded to these things myself and have put forth the view that the spiritual past of the race has been a preparation of Nature not merely for attaining the Divine beyond the world, but also for this very step forward which the evolution of the earth-consciousness has still to make. I do not therefore care in the least—even though these ideals were, up to some extent parallel, yet not identical with mine—whether this yoga and its aim and method are accepted as new or not; that is in itself a trifling matter. That it should be recognised as true in itself by those who can accept or practise it and should make

---

[3] *Bases of Yoga.* [Sri Aurobindo's note]

itself true by achievement is the one thing important; it does not matter if it is called new or a repetition or revival of the old which was forgotten. I laid emphasis on it as new in a letter to certain sadhakas so as to explain to them that a repetition of the aim and idea of the old yogas was not enough in my eyes, that I was putting forward a thing to be achieved that has not yet been achieved, not yet clearly visualised, even though it is the natural but still secret outcome of all the past spiritual endeavour.

It is new as compared with the old yogas:

1. Because it aims not at a departure out of world and life into Heaven or Nirvana, but at a change of life and existence, not as something subordinate or incidental, but as a distinct and central object. If there is a descent in other yogas, yet it is only an incident on the way or resulting from the ascent— the ascent is the real thing. Here the ascent is the first step, but it is a means for the descent. It is the descent of the new consciousness attained by the ascent that is the stamp and seal of the sadhana. Even the Tantra and Vaishnavism end in the release from life; here the object is the divine fulfilment of life.

2. Because the object sought after is not an individual achievement of divine realisation for the sake of the individual, but something to be gained for the earth-consciousness here, a cosmic, not solely a supra-cosmic achievement. The thing to be gained also is the bringing in of a Power of Conciousness (the supramental) not yet organised or active directly in earth-nature, even in the spiritual life, but yet to be organised and made directly active.

3. Because a method has been preconized for achieving this purpose which is as total and integral as the aim set before it, viz., the total and integral change of the consciousness and nature, taking up old methods but only as a part action and present aid to others that are distinctive. I have not found this

method (as a whole) or anything like it professed or realised in the old yogas. If I had, I should not have wasted my time in hewing out a road and in thirty years of search and inner creation when I could have hastened home safely to my goal in an easy canter over paths already blazed out, laid down, perfectly mapped, macadamised, made secure and public. Our yoga is not a retreading of old walks, but a spiritual adventure.

The Supramental Transformation

Certitudes

In the deep there is a greater deep, in the heights a greater height. Sooner shall man arrive at the borders of infinity than at the fullness of his own being. For that being is infinity, is God.

I aspire to infinite force, infinite knowledge, infinite bliss. Can I attain it? Yes, but the nature of infinity is that it has no end. Say not therefore that I attain it. I become it. Only so can man attain God by becoming God.

But before attaining he can enter into relations with Him. To enter into relations with God is Yoga, the highest rapture and the noblest utility. There are relations within the compass of the humanity we have developed. These are called prayer, worship, adoration, sacrifice, thought, faith, science, philosophy. There are other relations beyond our developed capacity, but within the compass of the humanity we have yet to develop. Those are the relations that are attained by the various practices we usually call Yoga.

We may not know Him as God, we may know Him as Nature, our Higher Self, Infinity, some ineffable goal. It was so that Buddha approached Him; so approaches Him the rigid Adwaitin. He is accessible even to the Atheist. To the materialist He disguises

Himself in matter. For the Nihilist He waits ambushed in the bosom of Annihilation.

ये यथा मां प्रपद्यन्ते तांस्तथैव भजाम्यहम् |
मम वर्त्मानुवर्तन्ते मनुष्याः पार्थ सर्वशः ||[1]

---

[1] Written between 1911-1913 and first published in *The Hour of God* (1959). From the Bhagavad Gita (4.11), meaning 'Whosoever, through whatsoever path worships me, I accept them in the same manner.'

The Superman

The ideal of the Superman has been brought recently into much notice, some not very fruitful discussion and a good deal of obloquy. It is apt to be resented by average humanity because men are told or have a lurking consciousness that here is a claim of the few to ascend to heights of which the many are not capable, to concentrate moral and spiritual privileges and enjoy a domination, powers and immunities hurtful to a diffused dignity and freedom in mankind. So considered, supermanhood is nothing more important than a deification of the rare or solitary ego that has out-topped others in the force of our common human qualities. But this presentation is narrow and a travesty. The gospel of true supermanhood gives us a generous ideal for the progressive human race and should not be turned into an arrogant claim for a class or individuals. It is a call to man to do what no species has yet done or aspired to do in terrestrial history, evolve itself consciously into the next superior type already half foreseen by the continual cyclic development of the world-idea in Nature's fruitful musings. And when we so envisage it, this conception ranks surely as one of the most potent seeds that can be cast by thought into the soil of our human growth.

Nietzsche[1] first cast it, the mystic of Will-worship, the troubled, profound, half-luminous Hellenising Slav with his strange clarities,

---

[1] First published in the *Arya* in April 1915 under the title 'The Type of the Superman'.
Friedrich Nietzsche (1844-1900), German philosopher and cultural critic who exerted a great influence on European thought.

his violent half-ideas, his rare gleaming intuitions that came marked with the stamp of an absolute truth and sovereignty of light. But Nietzsche was an apostle who never entirely understood his own message. His prophetic style was like that of the Delphic oracles[2] which spoke constantly the word of the Truth but turned it into untruth in the mind of the hearer. Not always indeed; for sometimes he rose beyond his personal temperament and individual mind, his European inheritance and environment, his revolt against the Christ-idea, his war against current moral values and spoke out the Word as he had heard it, the Truth as he had seen it, bare, luminous, impersonal and therefore flawless and imperishable. But for the most part this message that had come to his inner hearing vibrating out of a distant Infinite like a strain caught from the lyre of far-off Gods, did get, in his effort to appropriate and make it nearer to him, mixed up with a somewhat turbulent surge of collateral ideas that drowned much of the pure original note.

Especially, in his concept of the Superman he never cleared his mind of a preliminary confusion. For if a sort of human godhead is the goal to which the race must advance, the first difficulty is that we have to decide to which of two very different types of divinity the idea in us should owe allegiance. For the deity within may confront us either with the clear, joyous and radiant countenance of the God or the stern convulsed visage of the Titan. Nietzsche hymned the Olympian but presented him with the aspect of the Asura. His hostile preoccupation with the Christ-idea of the crucified God and its consequences was perhaps responsible for this distortion, as much as his subjection to the imperfect ideas of the Greeks. He presents to us sometimes a superman who fiercely and arrogantly repels the burden of simple sorrow and service,

---

[2] Delphi was the site of the most important temple of Apollo; here Pythia, who was the medium and oracle of the god, delivered his cryptic messages.

not one who arises victorious over mortality and suffering, his ascension vibrant with the triumph-song of a liberated humanity. To lose the link of Nature's moral evolution is a capital fault in the apostle of supermanhood; for only out of the unavoidable line of the evolution can that emerge in the bosom of a humanity long tested, ripened and purified by the fire of egoistic and altruistic suffering.

God and Titan, Deva and Asura, are indeed close kin in their differences; nor could either have been spared in the evolution. Yet do they inhabit opposite poles of a common existence and common nature. The one descends from the light and the infinity, satisfied, to the play; the other ascends from the obscurity and the vagueness, angry, to the struggle. All the acts of the God derive from the universal and tend to the universal. He was born out of a victorious harmony. His qualities join pure and gracious hands and link themselves together naturally and with delight as in the pastoral round of Brindavan, divine Krishna dominating and holding together its perfect circles. To evolve in the sense of the God is to grow in intuition, in light, in joy, in love, in happy mastery; to serve by rule and to rule by service; to be able to be bold and swift and even violent without hurt or wickedness and mild and kindly and even self-indulgent without laxity or vice or weakness; to make a bright and happy whole in oneself and, by sympathy, with mankind and all creatures. And in the end it is to evolve a large impersonal personality and to heighten sympathy into constant experience of world-oneness. For such are the Gods, conscious always of their universality and therefore divine.

Certainly, power is included. To be the divine man is to be self-ruler and world-ruler; but in another than the external sense. This is a rule that depends upon a secret sympathy and oneness which knows the law of another's being and of the world's being and helps or, if need be, compels it to realise its own greatest possibilities, but by a divine and essentially an inner compulsion. It is to take all qualities, energies, joys, sorrows, thoughts, knowledge, hopes, aims of the world around us into ourselves and return them enriched and transmuted in a sublime commerce and exploitation. Such an empire asks for no vulgar ostentation or golden trappings. The gods work oftenest veiled by light or by the storm-drift; they do not disdain to live among men even in the garb of the herdsman or the artisan; they do not shrink from the cross and the crown of thorns either in their inner evolution or their outward fortunes. For they know that the ego must be crucified and how shall men consent to this if God and the gods have not shown them the way? To take all that is essential in the human being and uplift it to its most absolute term so that it may become an element of light, joy, power for oneself and others, this is divinity. This, too, should be the drift of supermanhood.

But the Titan will have nothing of all this; it is too great and subtle for his comprehension. His instincts call for a visible, tangible mastery and a sensational domination. How shall he feel sure of his empire unless he can feel something writhing helpless under his heel—if in agony, so much the better? What is exploitation to him, unless it diminishes the exploited? To be able to coerce, exact, slay, overtly, irresistibly, it is this that fills him with the sense of glory and dominion. For he is the son of division and the strong flowering of the Ego. To feel the comparative limitation of others is necessary to him that he may imagine himself immeasurable; for he has not the real, self-existent sense of infinity which no outward circumstance can abrogate. Contrast, division, negation of the wills and lives of others are essential to his self-development and self-assertion. The Titan would unify by devouring, not by harmonising; he must conquer and trample what is not himself either out of existence or into subservience so that his own image may stand out stamped upon all things and dominating all his environment.

In Nature, since it started from division and egoism, the Titan had to come first; he is here in us as the elder god, the first ruler of man's heaven and earth. Then arrives the God and delivers and harmonises. Thus the old legend tells us that the Deva and the Asura laboured together to churn the ocean of life for the supreme draught of immortality, but, once it had been won, Vishnu kept it for the God and defrauded the fiercer and more violent worker. And this seems unjust; for the Asura has the heavier and less grateful portion of the burden. He begins and leads; he goes his way hewing, shaping, planting: the God follows, amends, concludes, reaps. He prepares fiercely and with anguish against a thousand obstacles the force that we shall use: the other enjoys the victory and the delight. And therefore to the great God Shiva the stained and stormy Titan is very dear—Shiva who took for himself the fierce, dark and bitter poison first churned up from the sea of life and left to others the nectar. But the choice that Shiva made with knowledge and from love, the Titans made from darkness and passion—desirous really of something very different and deceived by their stormy egoism. Therefore the award of Vishnu stands; to the God shall fall the crown and the immortality and not, unless he divinise himself, to the proud and strenuous Asura.

For what is supermanhood but a certain divine and harmonious absolute of all that is essential in man? He is made in God's image, but there is this difference between the divine Reality and its human representative that everything which in the one is unlimited, spontaneous, absolute, harmonious, self-possessed becomes in the other limited, relative, laboured, discordant, deformed, possessed by struggle, kept by subservience to one's possessions, lost by the transience and insecurity which come from wrong holding. But in this constant imperfection there is always a craving and an aspiration towards perfection. Man, limited, yearns to the Infinite; relative, is attracted in all things towards their absolute; artificial in Nature, drives towards a higher ease, mastery and naturalness that must for ever be denied to her inconscient forces and half-conscient animals; full of discords, he insists upon harmony; possessed by Nature and to her enslaved, is yet convinced of his mission to possess and master her. What he aspires to, is the sign of what he may be. He has to pass by a sort of transmutation of the earthly metal he now is out of flawed manhood into some higher symbol. For Man is Nature's great term of transition in which she grows conscious of her aim; in him she looks up from the animal with open eyes towards her divine ideal.

But God is complex, not simple; and the temptation of the human intellect is to make a short cut to the divine nature by the exclusive worship of one of its principles. Knowledge, Love whose secret word is Delight, Power and Unity are some of the Names of God. But though they are all divine, yet to follow any of them exclusively is to invite, after the first energy is over, His departure from us and denial; for even unity, exclusively pursued, ceases to be a true oneness. Yet this error we perpetually commit. Is it Love in whose temple we adore? Then we shut its gates upon Power as a child of the world and the devil and bid Knowledge carry elsewhere her lack of sweetness and remoteness from the heart's fervour. We erect an idol of Power and would pass all else through the fire of Moloch before its sombre and formidable image, expelling Love with scorn as a nurse of weaklings and degrading Knowledge to the position of a squire or even a groom of Force. Or we cultivate Knowledge with a severe aloofness and austerity to find at last the lotus of the heart dulled and fading— happy if its more divine faculties are not already atrophied—and ourselves standing impotent with our science while the thunders of Rudra crash through and devastate the world we have organised so well by our victorious and clear-minded efficiency. Or we run after a vague and mechanical zero we call unity and when we have sterilised our secret roots and dried up the wells of Life within us, discover, unwise unifiers, that we have achieved death and not a greater existence. And all this happens because we will not recognise the complexity of the riddle we are set here to solve. It is a great and divine riddle; but it is no knot of Gordius,[3] nor is its all-wise Author a dead king that he should suffer us to mock his intention and cut through to our will with the fierce impatience of the hasty mortal conqueror.

None of these oppositions is more constant than that of Power and Love: yet neither of these deities can be safely neglected. What can be more divine than Love? But followed exclusively it is impotent to solve the world's discords. The worshipped Avatar of love and the tender saint of saints leave behind them a divine but unfollowed example, a luminous and imperishable but ineffective memory. They have added an element to the potentialities of the heart, but the race cannot utilise it effectively for life because it has not been harmonised with the rest of the qualities that are essential to our fullness. Shall we therefore turn round and give ourselves to Power with its iron hands of action and its hard and clear practical intellect? The men of power may say that they have done a more tangible work for their race than the souls of Love, but it is a vain advantage. For they have not even tried to raise us beyond our imperfect humanity. They have erected a temporary form or given a secular impetus. An empire has been created, an age or a century organised, but the level of humanity has not been raised nearer to the secret of a Caesar or a Napoleon. Love fails because it hastily rejects the material of the world's discords or only tramples them underfoot in an unusual ecstasy; Power because it seeks only to organise an external arrangement. The world's discords have to be understood, seized, transmuted. Love must call Power and Knowledge into the temple and seat them beside her in a unified

---

[3] King Gordius was the founder of the city of Gordium, the capital of Phrygia. The knot in question, the famous Gordian knot, was said to have been cut by Alexander the Great in 333 bcE.

equality; Power must bow its neck to the yoke of Light and Love before it can do any real good to the race.

Unity is the secret, a complex, understanding and embracing unity. When the full heart of Love is tranquillised by knowledge into a calm ecstasy and vibrates with strength, when the strong hands of Power labour for the world in a radiant fullness of joy and light, when the luminous brain of knowledge accepts and transforms the heart's obscure inspirations and lends itself to the workings of the high-seated Will, when all these gods are founded together on a soul of sacrifice that lives in unity with all the world and accepts all things to transmute them, then is the condition of man's integral self-transcendence. This and not a haughty, strong and brilliant egoistic self-culture enthroning itself upon an enslaved humanity is the divine way of supermanhood.

The Experiment of Human Life[1]

The experiment of human life on an earth is not now for the first time enacted. It has been conducted a million times before and the long drama will again a million times be repeated. In all that we do now, our dreams, our discoveries, our swift or difficult attainments we profit subconsciously by the experience of innumerable precursors and our labour will be fecund in planets unknown to us and in worlds yet uncreated. The plan, the peripeties, the denouement differ continually, yet are always governed by the conventions of an eternal Art. God, Man, Nature are the three perpetual symbols.

The idea of eternal recurrence affects with a shudder of alarm the mind entrenched in the minute, the hour, the years, the centuries, all the finite's unreal defences. But the strong soul conscious of its own immortal stuff and the inexhaustible ocean of its ever-flowing energies is seized by it with the thrill of an inconceivable rapture. It hears behind the thought the childlike laughter and ecstasy of the Infinite.

God, Man, Nature, what are these three? Whence flow their divergences? To what ineffable union advances the ever-increasing sum of their contacts? Let us look beyond the hours and moments; let us tear down the hedge of the years and the concept-wall of

---

[1] Written c. 1915, possibly meant for the *Arya* but not published there. Included in *Essays Divine and Human* (1994).

centuries and millenniums and break out beyond the limits of our prison-house. For all things seek to concentrate our view on the temporal interests, conceptions and realisations of our humanity. We have to look beyond them to know that which they serve and represent. Nothing in the world can be understood by itself, but only by that which is beyond it. If we would know all, we must turn our gaze to that which is beyond all. That being known all else is comprehended.

The Hour of God[1]

There are moments when the Spirit moves among men and the breath of the Lord is abroad upon the waters of our being; there are others when it retires and men are left to act in the strength or the weakness of their own egoism. The first are periods when even a little effort produces great results and changes destiny; the second are spaces of time when much labour goes to the making of a little result. It is true that the latter may prepare the former, may be the little smoke of sacrifice going up to heaven which calls down the rain of God's bounty. Unhappy is the man or the nation which, when the divine moment arrives, is found sleeping or unprepared to use it, because the lamp has not been kept trimmed for the welcome and the ears are sealed to the call. But thrice woe to them who are strong and ready, yet waste the force or misuse the moment; for them is irreparable loss or a great destruction. In the hour of God cleanse thy soul of all self-deceit and hypocrisy and vain self-flattering that thou mayst look straight into thy spirit and hear that which summons it. All insincerity of nature, once thy defence against the eye of the Master and the light of the ideal, becomes now a gap in thy armour and invites the blow. Even if thou conquer for the moment, it is the worse for thee, for the blow shall come afterwards and cast thee down in the midst of thy triumph. But being pure cast aside all fear; for the hour is often

---

[1] Written c. 1918, first published posthumously in *The Hour of God* (1959).

terrible, a fire and a whirlwind and a tempest, a treading of the winepress of the wrath of God; but he who can stand up in it on the truth of his purpose is he who shall stand; even though he fall, he shall rise again, even though he seem to pass on the wings of the wind, he shall return. Nor let worldly prudence whisper too closely in thy ear; for it is the hour of the unexpected, the incalculable, the immeasurable. Mete not the power of the Breath by thy petty instruments, but trust and go forward.

But most keep thy soul clear, even if for a while, of the clamour of the ego. Then shall a fire march before thee in the night and the storm be thy helper and thy flag shall wave on the highest height of the greatness that was to be conquered.

The Real Difficulty[1]

The real difficulty is always in ourselves, not in our surroundings. There are three things necessary in order to make men invincible, Will, Disinterestedness and Faith. We may have a will to emancipate ourselves, but sufficient faith may be lacking. We may have a faith in our ultimate emancipation, but the will to use the necessary means may be wanting. And even if there are will and faith, we may use them with a violent attachment to the fruit of our work or with passions of hatred, blind excitement or hasty forcefulness which may produce evil reactions. For this reason it is necessary, in a work of such magnitude, to have resort to a higher Power than that of mind and body in order to overcome unprecedented obstacles. This is the need of *sādhanā*.

God is within us, an Omnipotent, Omnipresent, Omniscient Power; we and He are of one nature and, if we get into touch with Him and put ourselves in His hands, He will pour into us His own force and we shall realise that we too have our share of godhead, our portion of omnipotence, omnipresence and omniscience. The path is long, but self-surrender makes it short; the way is difficult, but perfect trust makes it easy.

Will is omnipotent, but it must be divine will, selfless, tranquil, at ease about results. 'If you had faith even as a grain of mustard-seed,' said Jesus, 'you would say to this mountain, "Come", and it

---

[1] First published in the *Standard Bearer* in 1920.

would come to you.' What was meant by the word Faith, was really Will accompanied with perfect *śraddhā*. Śraddhā does not reason, it knows; for it commands sight and sees what God wills, and it knows that what is God's will, must happen. Śraddhā, not blind but using sight spiritual, can become omniscient.

Will is also omnipresent. It can throw itself into all with whom it comes into contact and give them temporarily or permanently a portion of its power, its thought, its enthusiasms. The thought of a solitary man can become, by exercise of selfless and undoubting will, the thought of a nation. The will of a single hero can breathe courage into the hearts of a million cowards.

This is the Sadhana that we have to accomplish. This is the condition of our emancipation. We have been using an imperfect will with imperfect faith and imperfect disinterestedness. Yet the task we have before us is not less difficult than to move a mountain.

The force that can do it, exists. But it is hidden in a secret chamber within us and of that chamber God holds the key. Let us find Him and claim it.

Man and the Supermind[1]

Man is a transitional being, he is not final; for in him and high beyond him ascend the radiant degrees which climb to a divine supermanhood.

The step from man towards superman is the next approaching achievement in the earth's evolution. There lies our destiny and the liberating key to our aspiring, but troubled and limited human existence—inevitable because it is at once the intention of the inner Spirit and the logic of Nature's process.

The appearance of a human possibility in a material and animal world was the first glint of a coming divine Light,—the first far-off intimation of a godhead to be born out of Matter. The appearance of the superman in the human world will be the fulfilment of that distant shining promise.

The difference between man and superman will be the difference between mind and a consciousness as far beyond it as thinking mind is beyond the consciousness of plant and animal; the differentiating essence of man is mind, the differentiating essence of superman will be supermind or a divine gnosis.

Man is a mind imprisoned, obscured and circumscribed in a precarious and imperfect living but imperfectly conscious body. The superman will be a supramental spirit which will envelop and freely use a conscious body, plastic to spiritual forces. His physical

---

[1] Written c. 1930, published posthumously in *The Hour of God* (1959)

frame will be a firm support and an adequate radiant instrument for the spirit's divine play and work in Matter.

Mind, even free and in its own unmixed and unhampered element, is not the highest possibility of consciousness; for mind is not in possession of Truth, but only a minor vessel or an instrument and here an ignorant seeker plucking eagerly at a mass of falsehoods and half-truths for the unsatisfying pabulum of its hunger. Beyond mind is a supramental or gnostic power of consciousness that is in eternal possession of Truth; all its motion and feeling and sense and outcome are instinct and luminous with the inmost reality of things and express nothing else.

Supermind or gnosis is in its original nature at once and in the same movement an infinite wisdom and an infinite will. At its source it is the dynamic consciousness of the divine Knower and Creator.

When in the process of unfolding of an always greater force of the one Existence, some delegation of this power shall descend into our limited human nature, then and then only can man exceed himself and know divinely and divinely act and create; he will have become at last a conscious portion of the Eternal. The superman will be born, not a magnified mental being, but a supramental power descended here into a new life of the transformed terrestrial body. A gnostic supermanhood is the next distinct and triumphant victory to be won by the spirit descended into earthly nature.

The disk of a secret sun of Power and Joy and Knowledge is emerging out of the material consciousness in which our mind works as a chained slave or a baffled and impotent demiurge; supermind will be the formed body of that radiant effulgence. Superman is not man climbed to his own natural zenith, not a superior degree of human greatness, knowledge, power, intelligence, will, character, genius, dynamic force, saintliness, love, purity or perfection. Supermind is something beyond mental man and his limits, a greater consciousness than the highest consciousness proper to human nature.

Man is a being from the mental worlds whose mentality works here involved, obscure and degraded in a physical brain, shut off from its own divinest powers and impotent to change life beyond certain narrow and precarious limits. Even in the highest of his kind it is baulked of its luminous possibilities of supreme force and freedom by this dependence. Most often and in most men it is only a servitor, a purveyor of amusements, a caterer of needs and interests to the life and the body. But the superman will be a gnostic king of Nature; supermind in him even in its evolutionary beginnings will appear as a ray of the eternal omniscience and omnipotence. Sovereign and irresistible it will lay hands on the mental and physical instruments, and, standing above and yet penetrating and possessing our lower already manifested parts, it will transform mind, life and body into its own divine and luminous nature.

Man in himself is hardly better than an ambitious nothing. He is a narrowness that reaches towards ungrasped widenesses, a littleness straining towards grandeurs which are beyond him, a dwarf enamoured of the heights. His mind is a darkened ray in the splendours of the universal Mind. His life is a striving, exulting and suffering wave, an eager passion-tossed and sorrow-stricken or a blindly and dully toiling petty moment of the universal Life. His body is a labouring perishable speck in the material universe. An immortal soul is somewhere hidden within him and gives out from time to time some sparks of its presence, and an eternal spirit is above and overshadows with its wings and upholds with its power this soul continuity in his nature. But that greater spirit is obstructed from descent by the hard lid of his constructed personality and this inner radiant soul is wrapped, stifled and oppressed in dense outer coatings. In all but a few it is seldom active, in many hardly perceptible. The soul and spirit in man seem rather to exist above and behind his formed nature than to be a part of its visible reality; subliminal in his inner being or superconscient above in some unreached status, they are in his outer consciousness possibilities rather than things realised and present. The spirit is in course of birth rather than born in Matter.

This imperfect being with his hampered, confused, ill-ordered and mostly ineffective consciousness cannot be the end and highest height of the mysterious upward surge of Nature. There is something more that has yet to be brought down from above and is now seen only by broken glimpses, through sudden rifts in the giant wall of our limitations. Or else there is something yet to be evolved from below, sleeping under the veil of man's mental consciousness or half visible by flashes, as life once slept in the stone and metal, mind in the plant and reason in the cave of animal memory underlying its imperfect apparatus of emotion and sense device and instinct. Something there is in us yet unexpressed that has to be delivered by an enveloping illumination from above. A godhead is imprisoned in our depths, one in its being with a greater godhead ready to descend from superhuman summits. In that descent and awakened joining is the secret of our future.

Man's greatness is not in what he is but in what he makes possible. His glory is that he is the closed place and secret workshop of a living labour in which supermanhood is made ready by a divine Craftsman.

But he is admitted to a yet greater greatness and it is this that, unlike the lower creation, he is allowed to be partly the conscious artisan of his divine change. His free assent, his consecrated will and participation are needed that into his body may descend the glory that will replace him. His aspiration is earth's call to the supramental Creator.

If earth calls and the Supreme answers, the hour can be even now for that immense and glorious transformation.

The Path

The supramental Yoga is at once an ascent towards God and a descent of Godhead into the embodied nature.

The ascent can only be achieved by a one-centred all-gathering upward aspiration of the soul and mind and life and body; the descent can only come by a call of the whole being towards the infinite and eternal Divine. If this call and this aspiration are there, or if by any means they can be born and grow constantly and seize all the nature, then and then only a supramental uplifting and transformation becomes possible.

The call and the aspiration are only first conditions; there must be along with them and brought by their effective intensity an opening of all the being to the Divine and a total surrender.

This opening is a throwing wide of all the nature on all its levels and in all its parts to receive into itself without limits the greater divine Consciousness which is there already above and behind and englobing this mortal half-conscious existence. In the receiving there must be no inability to contain, no breaking down of anything in the system, mind or life or nerve or body under the transmuting stress. There must be an endless receptivity, an always increasing capacity to bear an ever stronger and more and more insistent action of the divine Force. Otherwise nothing great and permanent can be done; the Yoga will end in a break-down or an inert stoppage or a stultifying or a disastrous arrest in a process which must be absolute and integral if it is not [to] be a failure.

But since no human system has this endless receptivity and unfailing capacity, the supramental Yoga can succeed only if the Divine Force as it descends increases the personal power and equates the strength that receives with the Force that enters from above to work in the nature. This is only possible if there is on our part a progressive surrender of the being into the hands of the Divine; there must be a complete and never failing assent, a courageous willingness to let the Divine Power do with us whatever is needed for the work that has to be done.

Man cannot by his own effort make himself more than man; the mental being cannot by his own unaided force change himself into a supramental spirit. A descent of the Divine Nature can alone divinise the human receptacle.

For the powers of our mind, life and body are bound to their own limitations and, however high they may rise or however widely expand, they cannot rise above their natural ultimate limits or expand beyond them. But, still, mental man can open to what is beyond him and call down a supramental Light, Truth and Power to work in him and do what the mind cannot do. If mind cannot by effort become what is beyond mind, supermind can descend and transform mind into its own substance.

If the supramental Power is allowed by man's discerning assent and vigilant surrender to act according to its own profound and subtle insight and flexible potency, it will bring about slowly or swiftly a divine transformation of our present semiperfect nature.

This descent, this working is not without its possibility of calamitous fall and danger. If the human mind or the vital desire seizes hold on the descending force and tries to use it according to its own limited and erring ideas or flawed and egoistic impulses,— and this is inevitable in some degree until this lower mortal has learned something of the way of that greater immortal nature,— stumblings and deviations, hard and seemingly insuperable obstacles and wounds and suffering cannot be escaped and even death or utter downfall are not impossible. Only when the conscious integral surrender to the Divine has been learned by mind and life and body, can the way of the Yoga become easy, straight, swift and safe.

And it must be a surrender and an opening to the Divine alone and to no other. For it is possible for an obscure mind or an impure life force in us to surrender to undivine and hostile forces and even to mistake them for the Divine. There can be no more calamitous error. Therefore our surrender must be no blind and inert passivity to all influences or any influence, but sincere, conscious, vigilant, pointed to the One and the Highest alone.

Self-surrender to the divine and infinite Mother, however difficult, remains our only effective means and our sole abiding refuge. Self-surrender to her means that our nature must be an instrument in her hands, the soul a child in the arms of the Mother.

The Secret of Life—Ananda[1]

Life

The world lives in and by Ananda. From Ananda, says the Veda, we were born, by Ananda we live, to Ananda we return, and it adds that no man could even have the strength to draw in his breath and throw it out again if there were not this heaven of Bliss embracing our existence as ether embraces our bodies, nourishing us with its eternal substance and strength and supporting the life and the activity. A world which is essentially a world of bliss—this was the ancient Vedantic vision, the *dṛṣṭi* of the Vedic *draṣṭā,* which differentiates Hinduism in its early virility from the cosmic sorrow of Buddhism and the cosmic disillusionment of Mayavada. But it is possible to fall from this Bliss, not to realise it with the lower nature, in the Apara Prakriti, not to be able to grasp and possess it. Two things are necessary for the fullness of man's bliss,—the fullness of his being and the fullness of his knowledge creating by their union the fullness of his strength in all its manifestations, viryam, balam, bhrajas, tejas, ojas. For Ananda, Sat and Chit make one reality, and Chit is in its outward working pure force to which our Rishis gave the name of Tapas. To attain even here upon

---

[1] This essay and the next first appeared in *The Hour of God* (1959)

earth this fullness of bliss dependent upon fullness of existence, illumination and force, must always be humanity's drift, man's collective endeavour. To attain it within himself here and beyond, *iha ca amutra ca*, must always be the drift of the human unit, the individual's endeavour. Wherever the knowledge in him thinks it can grasp this bliss, it will fix its heaven. This is Swarga, Vaikuntha, Goloka; this is Nirvana.

The Secret of Life—Ananda

The object and condition of Life is Ananda; the means of Ananda is Tapas; the nature of Tapas is Chit; the continent and basis of Chit is Sat. It is therefore by a process of Sat developing its own Ananda through Tapas which is Chit that the Absolute appears as the extended, the eternal as the evolutionary, Brahman as the world. He who would live perfecdy must know Life, he who would know Life, must know Sacchidananda.

Pleasure is not Ananda; it is a half-successful attempt to grasp at Ananda by means which ensure a relapse into pain. Therefore it is that pleasure can never be an enduring possession. It is in its nature transient and fugitive. Pain itself is obviously not Ananda; neither is it in itself anything positive, real and necessary. It has only a negative reality. It is a recoil caused by the inability to command pleasure from certain contacts which becomes habitual in our consciousness and, long ingrained in it, deludes us with the appearance of a law. We can rise above transitory pleasure; we can get rid of the possibility of pain.

Pleasure, therefore, cannot be the end and aim of life; for the true object and condition of Life is Ananda and Ananda is something in its nature one, unconditioned and infinite. If we make pleasure the object of life, then we also make pain the condition of life. The two go together and are inseparable companions. You cannot have one for your bedfellow without making a life-companion of the other. They are husband and wife and, though perpetually quarrelling, will not hear of divorce.

But neither is pain the necessary condition of life, as the Buddhists say, nor is extinction of sensation the condition of bliss.

From: Man and Superman[1]

46

Man is a transitional being, he is not final. He is a middle term of the evolution, not its end, crown or consummating masterpiece.

47

Man is not final, he is a transitional being. Beyond him awaits formation the diviner race, the superman.

59

The evolution of the earth nature is not finished because it has manifested only three powers out of the seven-fold scale of consciousness that is involved in manifested Nature. It has brought out from its apparent inconscience only the three powers of Mind and Life and Matter.

68

Because man is a mental being, he naturally imagines that mind is the one great leader and actor and creator or the indispensable

---

[1] These are a part of the 171 notes, drafts and fragments which Sri Aurobindo wrote from 1912 to 1947. They were first published in *Essays Divine and Human* (1994).

agent in the universe. But this is an error; even for knowledge mind is not the only or the greatest possible instrument, the one aspirant and discoverer. Mind is a clumsy interlude between Nature's vast and precise subconscient action and the vaster infallible superconscient action of the Godhead.

[What follows is the continuation of aphorism 68]

There is nothing mind can do that cannot be better done in the mind's immobility and thought-free stillness.

When mind is still, then Truth gets her chance to be heard in the purity of the silence.

Truth cannot be attained by the mind's thought but only by identity and silent vision. Truth lives in the calm wordless Light of the eternal spaces; she does not intervene in the noise and cackle of logical debate.

Thought in the mind can at most be Truth's brilliant and transparent garment; it is not even her body. Look through the robe, not at it, and you may see some hint of her form. There can be a thought-body of Truth, but that is the spontaneous supramental Thought and Word that leap fully formed out of the Light, not any difficult mental counterfeit and patchwork. The supramental Thought is not a means of arriving at Truth, for Truth in the supermind is self-found or self-existent, but a way of expressing her. It is an arrow from the Light, not a bridge to reach it.

Cease inwardly from thought and word, be motionless within you, look upward into the light and outward into the vast cosmic consciousness that is around you. Be more and more one with the brightness and the vastness. Then will Truth dawn on you from above and flow in on you from all around you.

But only if the mind is no less intense in its purity than its silence. For in an impure mind the silence will soon fill with misleading lights and false voices, the echo or sublimation of

its own vain conceits and opinions or the response to its secret
pride, vanity, ambition, lust, greed or desire. The Titans and the
Demons will speak to it more readily than the divine Voices.
Silence is indispensable, but also there is needed wideness. If the
mind is not silent, it cannot receive the lights and voices of the
supernal Truth or receiving mixes with them its own nickering
tongues and blind pretentious babble. Active, arrogant, noisy,
it distorts and disfigures what it receives. If it is not wide, it
cannot house the effective power and creative force of the Truth.
Some light may play there but it becomes narrow, confined and
sterile. Or the force that is descending is cabined and thwarted
and withdraws again from this rebellious foreign plane to its vast
native heights. Or even if something comes down and remains,
it is a pearl in the mire; for no change takes place in the nature
or else there is formed only a thin intensity that points narrowly
upward to the summits but can hold little and diffuse less upon
the world around it.

75

I mean by the supermind a power, a level, an organisation of
consciousness which is not only above the human mind, but above
all that can be called mind—another higher and wider essence and
energy of consciousness altogether. Mind is that which seeks after
truth of any kind or of all kinds within its range, labours to know
it, attempts to direct and utilise it. But by supermind I mean a
divine awareness which inherently possesses truth, knows it by
its own intrinsic identity with it and puts it into action or effect
spontaneously by its own sovereign power without any need of
endeavour or labour. Mind even though it seeks after knowledge
and can sometimes grasp its figure or touch its shadow, is a product
of the cosmic Inconscient or of a Half-Conscience-Ignorance;
supermind is an eternal Truth-consciousness, a divine Knowledge

self-maintained for ever and luminous in its own right beyond all Ignorance.

79

The transition from manhood to supermanhood is, in one sense, a self-exceeding, a ceasing to be what we now are in order to become something else or more. In another sense it is a self-becoming, a flowering out of something concealed by our present state, a latent godhead that already is and always was our true being.

Supermanhood is for us a self-exceeding because man, pragmatically and to his own surface awareness, is a small, confused, limited, still ignorant formation of evolutionary Nature—if supermanhood is intended, then either he has himself to become superman or, if he cannot or will not achieve it, he must make way for some creature greater than he who will have both the will and the power.

But again supermanhood is at bottom a self-becoming because what we now call ourselves is only the surface man, a thinking and living body; but this [is] only the top of a wave, not the whole sea that secretly we are. All that makes supermanhood is there at least in material in our secret depths and on our still more occult height; what in outward fact, in appearance, in present self-awareness man is not but must become, is already there within him; he has only to find himself in order to become that greater self and nature.

The Divine Body[1]

A divine life in a divine body is the formula of the ideal that we envisage. But what will be the divine body? What will be the nature of this body, its structure, the principle of its activity, the perfection that distinguishes it from the limited and imperfect physicality within which we are now bound? What will be the conditions and operations of its life, still physical in its base upon the earth, by which it can be known as divine?

If it is to be the product of an evolution, and it is so that we must envisage it, an evolution out of our human imperfection and ignorance into a greater truth of spirit and nature, by what process or stages can it grow into manifestation or rapidly arrive? The process of the evolution upon earth has been slow and tardy— what principle must intervene if there is to be a transformation, a progressive or sudden change?

It is indeed as a result of our evolution that we arrive at the possibility of this transformation. As Nature has evolved beyond Matter and manifested Life, beyond Life and manifested Mind, so she must evolve beyond Mind and manifest a consciousness and power of our existence free from the imperfection and limitation of our mental existence, a supramental or truth-consciousness,

---

[1] This essay and the one after this, 'The Mind of Light', among the last of Sri Aurobindo's prose writings, appeared in the *Bulletin of Physical Education* in 1949-1950. They appeared in book form under the title *The Supramental Manifestation Upon Earth* (1952).

and able to develop the power and perfection of the spirit. Here a slow and tardy change need no longer be the law or manner of our evolution; it will be only so to a greater or less extent so long as a mental ignorance clings and hampers our ascent; but once we have grown into the truth-consciousness its power of spiritual truth of being will determine all. Into that truth we shall be freed and it will transform mind and life and body. Light and bliss and beauty and a perfection of the spontaneous right action of all the being are there as native powers of the supramental truth-consciousness and these will in their very nature transform mind and life and body even here upon earth into a manifestation of the truth-conscious spirit. The obscurations of earth will not prevail against the supramental truth-consciousness, for even into the earth it can bring enough of the omniscient light and omnipotent force of the spirit to conquer. All may not open to the fullness of its light and power, but whatever does open must to that extent undergo the change. That will be the principle of transformation.

It might be that a psychological change, a mastery of the nature by the soul, a transformation of the mind into a principle of light, of the life-force into power and purity would be the first approach, the first attempt to solve the problem, to escape beyond the merely human formula and establish something that could be called a divine life upon earth, a first sketch of supermanhood, of a supramental living in the circumstances of the earth-nature. But this could not be the complete and radical change needed; it would not be the total transformation, the fullness of a divine life in a divine body. There would be a body still human and indeed animal in its origin and fundamental character and this would impose its own inevitable limitations on the higher parts of the embodied being. As limitation by ignorance and error is the fundamental defect of an untransformed mind, as limitation by the imperfect impulses and strainings and wants of desire are the defects of an untransformed life-force, so also imperfection of the potentialities of the physical action, an imperfection, a limitation in the response of its half-consciousness to the demands made upon it and the grossness and stains of its original animality would be the defects of an untransformed or an imperfectly transformed body. These could not but hamper and even pull down towards themselves the action of the higher parts of the nature. A transformation of the body must be the condition for a total transformation of the nature.

It might be also that the transformation might take place by stages; there are powers of the nature still belonging to the mental region which are yet potentialities of a growing gnosis lifted beyond our human mentality and partaking of the light and power of the Divine and an ascent through these planes, a descent of them into the mental being might seem to be the natural evolutionary course. But in practice it might be found that these intermediate levels would not be sufficient for the total transformation since, being themselves illumined potentialities of mental being not yet supramental in the full sense of the word, they could bring down to the mind only a partial divinity or raise the mind towards that but not effectuate its elevation into the complete supramentality of the truth-consciousness. Still these levels might become stages of the ascent which some would reach and pause there while others went higher and could reach and live on superior strata of a semi-divine existence. It is not to be supposed that all humanity would rise in a block into the supermind; at first those only might attain to the highest or some intermediate height of the ascent whose inner evolution has fitted them for so great a change or who are raised by the direct touch of the Divine into its perfect light and power and bliss. The large mass of human beings might still remain for long content with a normal or only a partially illumined and uplifted human nature. But this would be itself a sufficiently radical change and initial transformation of earth-life; for the way would be open to all who have the will to rise, the supramental influence of the truth-consciousness would touch the earth-life and influence even its untransformed mass and a hope would be there and a promise eventually available to all which now only the few can share in or realise.

In any case these would be beginnings only and could not constitute the fullness of the divine life upon earth; it would be a new orientation of the earthly life but not the consummation of its change. For that there must be the sovereign reign of a supramental truth-consciousness to which all other forms of life would be subordinated and depend upon it as the master principle and supreme power to which they could look up as the goal, profit by its influences, be moved and upraised by something of its illumination and penetrating force. Especially, as the human body had to come into existence with its modification of the previous animal form and its erect figure of a new power of life and its expressive movements and activities serviceable and necessary to the principle of mind and the life of a mental being, so too a body must be developed with new powers, activities or degrees of a divine action expressive of a truth-conscious being and proper to a supramental consciousness and manifesting a conscious spirit. While the capacity for taking up and sublimating all the activities of the earth-life capable of being spiritualised must be there, a transcendence of the original animality and the actions incurably tainted by it or at least some saving transformation of them, some spiritualising or psychicising of the consciousness and motives animating them and the shedding of whatever could not be so transformed, even a change of what might be called its instrumental structure, its functioning and organisation, a complete and hitherto unprecedented control of these things must be the consequence or incidental to this total change. These things have been already to some extent illustrated in the lives of many who have become possessed of spiritual powers but as something exceptional and occasional, the casual or incomplete manifestation of an acquired capacity rather than the organisation of a new consciousness, a new life and a new nature. How far can such physical transformation be carried, what are the limits within which it must remain to be consistent with life upon earth and without carrying that life beyond the earthly sphere or pushing it towards the supra-terrestrial existence? The supramental consciousness is not a fixed quantity but a power which passes to higher and higher levels of possibility until it reaches supreme consummations of spiritual existence fulfilling supermind as supermind fulfils the ranges of spiritual consciousness that are pushing towards it from the human or mental level. In this progression the body also may reach a more perfect form and a higher range of its expressive powers, become a more and more perfect vessel of divinity.

The Mind of Light

A new humanity means for us the appearance, the development of a type or race of mental beings whose principle of mentality would be no longer a mind in the Ignorance seeking for knowledge but even in its knowledge bound to the Ignorance, a seeker after Light but not its natural possessor, open to the Light but not an inhabitant of the Light, not yet a perfected instrument, truth-conscious and delivered out of the Ignorance. Instead, it would be possessed already of what could be called a mind of Light, a mind capable of living in the truth, capable of being truth-conscious and manifesting in its life a direct in place of an indirect knowledge. Its mentality would be an instrument of the Light and no longer of the Ignorance. At its highest it would be capable of passing into the supermind and from the new race would be recruited the race of supramental beings who would appear as the leaders of the evolution in earth-nature. Even, the highest manifestations of a mind of Light would be an instrumentality of the supermind, a part of it or a projection from it, a stepping beyond humanity into the superhumanity of the supramental principle. Above all, its possession would enable the human being to rise beyond the normalities of his present thinking, feeling and being into those highest powers of the mind in its self-exceedings which intervene between our mentality and supermind and can be regarded as steps leading towards the greater and more luminous principle. This advance like others in the evolution might not be reached and would naturally not be reached at one bound, but from the very beginning it would be inevitable: the pressure of the supermind creating from above out of itself the mind of Light would compel this certainty of the eventual outcome. The first gleamings of the new Light would carry in themselves the seed of its highest flamings; even in the first beginnings, the certainty of their topmost powers would be there; for this is the constant story of each evolutionary emergence: the principle of its highest perfection lies concealed in the involution which precedes and necessitates the evolution of the secret principle.

For throughout the story of evolution there are two complementary aspects which constitute its action and are necessary to its totality; there is hidden in the involution of Nature the secret power and principle of being which lies concealed under the veil cast on it by material Nature and there is carried in that Nature itself the inevitable force of the principle compelling the process of emergence of its inherent powers and characters, the essential features which constitute its reality. As the evolutionary principle emerges, there are also two constant features of the process of the emergence: there are the gradations by which it climbs out of the involution and manifests more and more of its power, its possibilities, the force of the Godhead within it, and there is a constant manifestation of all types and forms of its being which are the visible, indicative and efficient embodiments of its essential nature. There appear in the evolutionary process organised forms and activities of Matter, the types of life and the living beings, the types of mind and the thinking beings, the luminosities and greatnesses of the spiritual principle and the spiritual beings whose nature, character, personality, mark the stages of the ascent towards the highest heights of the evolution and the ultimate largest manifestation of what it is in itself and must become by the force of time and the all-revealing Spirit. This is the real sense and drive of what we see as evolution: the multiplication and variation of forms is only the means of its process. Each gradation contains the possibility and the certainty of the grades beyond it: the emergence of more and more developed forms and powers points to more perfected forms and greater powers beyond them, and each emergence of consciousness and the conscious beings proper to it enables the rise to a greater consciousness beyond and the greater order of beings up to the ultimate godheads of which Nature is striving and is destined to show herself capable. Matter developed its organised forms until it became capable of embodying living organisms; then life rose from the subconscience of the plant into conscious animal formations and through them to the thinking life of man. Mind founded in life developed intellect, developed its types of knowledge and ignorance, truth and error till it reached the spiritual perception and illumination and now can see as in a glass dimly the possibility of supermind and a truth-conscious existence. In this inevitable ascent the mind of Light is a gradation, an inevitable stage. As an evolving principle it will mark a stage in the human ascent and evolve a new type of human being; this development must carry in it an ascending gradation of its own powers and types of an ascending humanity which will embody more and more the turn towards spirituality, capacity for Light, a climb towards a divinised manhood and the divine life.

In the birth of the mind of Light and its ascension into its own recognisable self and its true status and right province there must be, in the very nature of things as they are and very nature of the evolutionary process as it is at present, two stages. In the first, we can see the mind of Light gathering itself out of the Ignorance, assembling its constituent elements, building up its shapes and types, however imperfect at first, and pushing them towards perfection till it can cross the border of the Ignorance and appear in the Light, in its own Light. In the second stage we can see it developing itself in that greater natural light, taking its higher shapes and forms till it joins the supermind and lives as its subordinate portion or its delegate. In each of these stages it will define its own grades and manifest the order of its beings who will embody it and give to it a realised life. Thus there will be built up, first, even in the Ignorance itself, the possibility of a human ascent towards a divine living; then there will be, by the illumination of this mind of Light in the greater realisation of what may be called a gnostic mentality, in a transformation of the human being, even before the supermind is reached, even in the earth-consciousness and in a humanity transformed, an illumined divine life.

The Seer-Poet

The Ideal Spirit of Poetry[1]

To attempt to presage the future turn or development of mind or life in any of its fields must always be a hazardous venture. For life and mind are not like physical Nature; the processes of physical Nature run in precise mechanical grooves, but these are more mobile and freer powers. The gods of life and still more the gods of mind are so incalculably self-creative that even where we can distinguish the main lines on which the working runs or has so far run, we are still unable to foresee with any certainty what turn they will yet take or of what new thing they are in labour. It is therefore impossible to predict what the poetry of the future will actually be like. "We can see where we stand today, but we cannot tell where we shall stand a quarter of a century hence. All that one can do is to distinguish for oneself some possibilities that lie before the poetic mind of the race and to figure what it can achieve if it chooses to follow out certain great openings which the genius of recent and contemporary poets has made free to us; but what path it will actually choose to tread or what new heights attempt, waits still for its own yet unformed decision.

What would be the ideal spirit of poetry in an age of the increasingly intuitive mind: that is the question which arises from

---

[1] Chapter xxv of *The Future Poetry*, which first appeared serially in the *Arya* from December 1917 to July 1920, and was published in book form by Sri Aurobindo Ashram, Pondicherry, in 1953.

all that has gone before and to which we may attempt some kind of answer. I have spoken in the beginning of the Mantra as the highest and intensest revealing form of poetic thought and expression. What the Vedic poets meant by the Mantra was an inspired and revealed seeing and visioned thinking, attended by a realisation, to use the ponderous but necessary modern word, of some inmost truth of God and self and man and Nature and cosmos and life and thing and thought and experience and deed. It was a thinking that came on the wings of a great soul rhythm, *chandas*. For the seeing could not be separated from the hearing; it was one act. Nor could the living of the truth in oneself which we mean by realisation, be separated from either, for the presence of it in the soul and its possession of the mind must precede or accompany in the creator or human channel that expression of the inner sight and hearing which takes the shape of the luminous word. The Mantra is born through the heart and shaped or massed by the thinking mind into a chariot of that godhead of the Eternal of whom the truth seen is a face or a form. And in the mind too of the fit outward hearer who listens to the word of the poet-seer, these three must come together, if our word is a real Mantra; the sight of the inmost truth must accompany the hearing, the possession of the inmost spirit of it by the mind and its coming home to the soul must accompany or follow immediately upon the rhythmic message of the Word and the mind's sight of the Truth. That may sound a rather mystic account of the matter, but substantially there could hardly be a more complete description of the birth and effect of the inspired and revealing word, and it might be applied, though usually on a more lowered scale than was intended by the Vedic Rishis, to all the highest outbursts of a really great poetry. But poetry is the Mantra only when it is the voice of the inmost truth and is couched in the highest power of the very rhythm and speech of that truth. And the ancient poets of the Veda and Upanishads claimed to be uttering the Mantra because always it was this inmost and almost occult truth of things which they strove to see and hear and speak and because they believed themselves to be using or finding its innate soul rhythms and the sacrificial speech of it cast up by the divine Agni, the sacred Fire in the heart of man. The Mantra in other words is a direct and most heightened, an intensest and most divinely burdened rhythmic word which embodies an intuitive and revelatory inspiration and ensouls the mind with the sight and the presence of the very self, the inmost reality of things and with its truth and with the divine soul-forms of it, the Godheads which are born from the living Truth. Or, let us say, it is a supreme rhythmic language which seizes hold upon all that is finite and brings into each the light and voice of its own infinite.

This is a theory of poetry, a view of the rhythmic and creative self-expression to which we give that name, which is very different from any that we now hold, a sacred or hieratic *ars poetica* only possible in days when man believed himself to be near to the gods and felt their presence in his bosom and could think he heard some accents of their divine and eternal wisdom take form on the heights of his mind. And perhaps no thinking age has been so far removed from any such view of our life as the one through which we have recently passed and even now are not well out of its shadow, the age of materialism, the age of positive outward matter of fact and of scientific and utilitarian reason. And yet curiously enough—or naturally, since in the economy of Nature opposite creates itself out of opposite and not only like from like—it is to some far-off light at least of the view of ourselves at our greatest of which such ideas were a concretised expression that we seem to be returning. For we can mark that although in very different circumstances, in broader forms, with a more complex mind and an enormously enlarged basis of culture and civilisation, the gain and inheritance of many intermediate ages, it is still to something very like the effort which was the soul of the Vedic or at least the Vedantic mind that we almost appear to be on the point of turning back in the circle of our course. Now that we have seen minutely what is the material reality of the world in which we live and have some knowledge of the vital reality of the Force from which we spring, we are at last beginning to seek again for the spiritual reality of that which we and all things secretly are. Our minds are once more trying to envisage the self, the spirit of Man and the spirit of the universe, intellectually, no doubt, at first, but from that to the old effort at sight, at realisation within ourselves and in all is not a very far step. And with this effort there must rise too on the human mind the conception of the godheads in whom this Spirit, this marvellous Self and Reality which broods over the world, takes shape in the liberated soul and life of the human being, his godheads of Truth and Freedom and Unity, his godheads of a greater more highly visioned Will and Power, his godheads of Love and universal Delight, his godheads of universal and eternal Beauty, his godheads of a supreme Light and Harmony and Good. The new ideals of the race seem already to be affected by some first bright shadow of these things, and even though it be only a tinge, a flush colouring the duller atmosphere of our recent mentality, there is every sign that this tinge will deepen and grow, in the heavens to which we look up if not at once in the earth of our actual life.

But this new vision will not be as in the old times something hieratically remote, mystic, inward, shielded from the profane, but rather a sight which will endeavour to draw these godheads again to close and familiar intimacy with our earth and embody them not only in the heart of religion and philosophy, nor only in the higher flights of thought and art, but also, as far as may be, in the common life and action of man. For in the old days these things were Mysteries, which men left to the few, to the initiates and by so leaving them lost sight of them in the end, but the endeavour of this new mind is to reveal, to divulge and to bring near to our comprehension all mysteries—at present indeed making them too common and outward in the process and depriving them of much of their beauty and inner light and depth, but that defect will pass—and this turn towards an open realisation may well lead to an age in which man as a race will try to live in a greater Truth than has as yet governed our kind. For all that we know, we now tend to make some attempt to form clearly and live. His creation too will then be moved by another spirit and cast on other lines.

And if this takes place or even if there is some strong mental movement towards it, poetry may recover something of an old sacred prestige. There will no doubt still be plenty of poetical writing which will follow the old lines and minister to the old commoner aesthetic motives, and it is as well that it should be so, for the business of poetry is to express the soul of man to himself and to embody in the word whatever power of beauty he sees; but also there may now emerge too and take the first place souls no longer niggardly of the highest flame, the poet-seer and seer-creator, the poet who is also a Rishi, master singers of Truth, hierophants and magicians of a diviner and more universal beauty. There has no doubt always been something of that in the greatest masters of poetry in the great ages, but to fulfil such a role has not often been the one fountain idea of their function; the mind of the age has made other demands on them, needed at that time, and the highest things in this direction have been rare self-exceedings and still coloured by and toned to the half-light in which they sang. But if an age comes which is in common possession of a deeper and greater and more inspiring Truth, then its masters of the rhythmic word will at least sing on a higher common level and may rise more often into a fuller intenser light and capture more constantly the greater tones of which this harp of God, to use the Upanishad's description of man's created being, is secretly capable.

A greater era of man's living seems to be in promise, whatever nearer and earthier powers may be striving to lead him on a side path away to a less exalted ideal, and with that advent there must come a new great age of his creation different from the past epochs which he counts as his glories and superior to them in its vision and motive. But first there must intervene a poetry which will lead him towards it from the present faint beginnings. It will be aided by new views in philosophy, a changed and extended spirit in science and new revelations in the other arts, in music, painting, architecture, sculpture, as well as high new ideals in life and new powers of a reviving but no longer limited or obscurantist religious mind. A glint of this change is already visible. And in poetry there is already the commencement of such a greater leading; the conscious effort of Whitman, the tone of Carpenter, the significance of the poetry of A.E., the rapid immediate fame of Tagore are its first signs.[2] The idea of the poet who is also the Rishi has made again its appearance. Only a wider spreading of the thought and mentality in which that idea can live and the growth of an accomplished art of poetry in which it can take body, are still needed to give the force of permanence to what is now only an incipient and just emerging power. Mankind satiated with the levels is turning its face once more towards the heights, and the poetic voices that will lead us thither with song will be among the high seer voices. For the great poet interprets to man his present or reinterprets for him his past, but can also point him to his future and in all three reveal to him the face of the Eternal.

An intuitive revealing poetry of the kind which we have in view would voice a supreme harmony of five eternal powers, Truth, Beauty, Delight, Life and the Spirit. These are indeed the five greater ideal lamps or rather the five suns of poetry. And towards three of them the higher mind of the race is in many directions turning its thought and desire with a new kind and force of insistence. The

---

[2]　Walt Whitman (1819-1892) leading American poet; Edward Carpenter (1844-1929), English author and poet; A.E., the pen-name of George William Russel (1867-1935), Irish poet and mystic; and Rabindranath Tagore (1861-1941), probably India's greatest modern poet.

intellectual side of our recent progress has in fact been for a long time a constant arduous pursuit of Truth in certain of its fields; but now the limited truth of yesterday can no longer satisfy or bind us. Much has been known and discovered of a kind which had not been found or had only been glimpsed before, but the utmost of that much appears now very little compared with the infinitely more which was left aside and ignored and which now invites our search. The description which the old Vedic poet once gave of the seeking of divine Truth, applies vividly to the mind of our age, 'As it climbs from height to height, there becomes clear to its view all the much that is yet to be done.' But also it is beginning to be seen that only in some great awakening of the self and spiritual being of man is that yet unlived truth to be found and that infinite much to be achieved. It is only then that the fullness of a greater knowledge for man living on earth can unfold itself and get rid of its coverings and again on his deeper mind and soul, in the words of another Vedic poet-seer, 'New states come into birth, covering upon covering awaken to knowledge, till in the lap of the Mother one wholly sees.' This new-old light is now returning upon our minds. Men no longer so completely believe that the world is a machine and they only so much transient thinking matter, a view of existence in the midst of which however helpful it might be to a victorious concentration on physical science and social economy and material well-being, neither religion nor philosophic wisdom could renew their power in the fountains of the spirit nor art and poetry, which are also things of the soul like religion and wisdom, refresh themselves from their native sources of strength. Now we are moving back from the physical obsession to the consciousness that there is a soul and greater self within us and the universe which finds expression here in the life and the body.

But the mind of today insists too and rightly insists on life, on humanity, on the dignity of our labour and action. We have no longer any ascetic quarrel with our mother earth, but rather would drink full of her bosom of beauty and power and raise her life to a more perfect greatness. Thought now dwells much on the idea of a vast creative will of life and action as the secret of existence. That way of seeing, though it may give room for a greater power of art and poetry and philosophy and religion, for it brings in real soul-values, has by its limitation its own dangers. A spirit which is all life because it is greater than life, is rather the truth in which we shall most powerfully live. Aditi, the infinite Mother, cries in the ancient Vedic hymn to Indra the divine Power now about to be born in her womb, 'This is the path of old discovered again by which all the gods rose up into birth, even by that upward way shouldst thou be born in thy increase; but go not forth by this other to turn thy mother to her fall,' but if, refusing the upward way, the new spirit in process of birth replies like the god, 'By that way I will not go forth, for it is hard to tread, let me come out straight on the level from thy side; I have many things to do which have not yet been done; with one I must fight and with another I must question after the Truth,' then the new age may do great things, as the last also did great things, but it will miss the highest way and end like it in a catastrophe. There is no reason why we should so limit our new birth in time; for the spirit and life are not incompatible, but rather a greater power of the spirit brings a greater power of life. Poetry and art most of all our powers can help to bring this truth home to the mind of man with an illumining and catholic force, for while philosophy may lose itself in abstractions and religion turn to an intolerant otherworldliness and asceticism, poetry and art are born mediators between the immaterial and the concrete, the spirit and life. This mediation between the truth of the spirit and the truth of life will be one of the chief functions of the poetry of the future.

The two other sister lamps of God, colour suns of the Ideal, which our age has most dimmed and of whose reviving light it is most sadly in need, but still too strenuously outward and utilitarian to feel sufficiently their absence, Beauty and Delight, are also things spiritual and they bring out the very heart of sweetness and colour and flame of the other three. Truth and Life have not their perfection until they are suffused and filled with the completing power of delight and the fine power of beauty and become one at their heights with this perfecting hue and this secret essence of themselves; the spirit has no full revelation without these two satisfying presences. For the ancient Indian idea is absolutely true that delight, Ananda, is the inmost expressive and creative nature of the free self because it is the very essence of the original being of the Spirit. But beauty and delight are also the very soul and origin of art and poetry. It is the significance and spiritual function of art and poetry to liberate man into pure delight and to bring beauty into his life. Only there are grades and heights here as in everything else and the highest kinds of delight and beauty are those which are one with the highest Truth, the perfection of life and the purest and fullest joy of the self-revealing Spirit. Therefore will poetry most find itself and enter most completely into its heritage when it arrives at the richest harmony of these five things in their most splendid and ample sweetness and light and power; but that can only wholly be when it sings from the highest skies of vision and ranges through the widest widths of our being.

These powers can indeed be possessed in every scale, because on whatever grade of our ascent we stand, the Spirit, the divine Self of man is always there, can break out into a strong flame of manifestation carrying in it all its godheads in whatever form, and poetry and art are among the means by which it thus delivers itself into expression. Therefore the essence of poetry is eternally the same and its essential power and the magnitude of the genius expended may be the same whatever the frame of the sight, whether it be Homer chanting of the heroes in god-moved battle before Troy and of Odysseus wandering among the wonders of remote and magic isles with his heart always turned to his lost and far-off human hearth, Shakespeare riding in his surge of the manifold colour and music and passion of life, or Dante errant mid his terrible or beatific visions of Hell and Purgatory and Paradise, or Valmiki singing of the ideal man embodying God and egoistic giant Rakshasa embodying only fierce self-will approaching each other from their different centres of life and in their different law of being for the struggle desired by the gods, or some mystic Vamadeva or Vishwamitra voicing in strange vivid now forgotten symbols the action of the gods and the glories of the Truth, the battle and the journey to the Light, the double riches and the sacrificial climbing of the soul to Immortality. For whether it be the inspired imagination fixed on earth or the soul of life or the inspired reason or the high intuitive spiritual vision which gives the form, the genius of the great poet will seize on some truth of being, some breath of life, some power of the spirit and bring it out with a certain supreme force for his and our delight and joy in its beauty. But nevertheless the poetry which can keep the amplitude of its breadth and nearness of its touch and yet see all things from a higher height will, the rest being equal, give more and will more fully satisfy the whole of what we are and therefore the whole of what we demand from this most complete of all the arts and most subtle of all our means of aesthetic self-expression.

The poetry of the future, if it fulfils in amplitude the promise now only there in rich hint, will kindle these five lamps of our being, but raise them up more on high and light with them a broader country, many countries indeed now hidden from our view, will make them not any longer lamps in some limited temple of beauty, but suns in the heavens of our highest mind and illuminative of our widest as well as our inmost life. It will be a poetry of a new largest vision of himself and Nature and God and all things which is offering itself to man and of its possible realisation in a nobler and more divine manhood; and it will not sing of them only with the power of the imaginative intelligence, the exalted and ecstatic sense or the moved joy and passion of life, but will rise to look at them from an intenser light and embody them in a more revealing force of the word. It will be first and most a poetry of the intuitive reason, the intuitive senses, the intuitive delight-soul in us, getting from this enhanced source of inspiration a more sovereign poetic enthusiasm and ecstasy, and then, it may even be, rise towards a still greater power of revelation nearer to the direct vision and word of the Overmind from which all creative inspiration comes.

A poetry of this kind need not be at all something high and remote or beautifully and delicately intangible, or not that alone, but will make too the highest things near, close and visible, will sing greatly and beautifully of all that has been sung, all that we are from outward body to very God and Self, of the finite and the infinite, the transient and the Eternal, but with a new reconciling and fusing vision that will make them other to us than they have been even when yet the same. If it wings to the heights, it will not leave earth unseen below it, but also will not confine itself to earth, but find too other realities and their powers on man and take all the planes of existence for its empire. It will take up and transform the secrets of the older poets and find new undiscovered secrets, transfigure the old rhythms by the insistence of the voice of its deeper subtler spirit and create new characteristic harmonies, reveal other greater powers and spirits of language, proceeding from the past and present yet will not be limited by them or their rule and forms and canon, but compass its own altered perfected art of poetry. This at least is its possible ideal endeavour, and then the attempt itself would be a rejuvenating elixir and put the poetic spirit once more in the shining front of the powers and guides of the ever-progressing soul of humanity. There it will lead in the journey like the Vedic Agni, the fiery giver of the word, *yuvā baviḥ, priyo atithir amartyo mandrajihvaḥ ṛtacit, ṛtāvā*, the Youth, the Seer, the beloved and immortal Guest with his honeyed tongue of ecstasy, the Truth-conscious, the Truth-finder, born as a flame from earth and yet the heavenly messenger of the Immortals.

The Future Poetry: Conclusion[1]

The poetry of the future has to solve, if the suggestions I have made are sound, a problem new to the art of poetic speech, an utterance of the deepest soul of man and of the universal spirit in things, not only with another and a more complete vision, but in the very inmost language of the self-experience of the soul and the sight of the spiritual mind. The attempt to speak in poetry the inmost things of the spirit or to use a psychical and spiritual seeing other than that of the more outward imagination and intelligence has indeed been made before, but for the most part and except in rare moments of an unusually inspired speech it has used some kind of figure or symbol more than a direct language of inmost experience; or else, where it has used such a language, it has been within the limited province of a purely inward experience as in the lofty philosophic and spiritual poetry of the Upanishads, the expression of a peculiar psychic feeling of Nature common in far eastern poets or the poetic setting of mystic states or of an especial religious emotion and experience of which we have a few examples in Europe and many in the literature of western Asia and India. It is a different and much larger creative and interpretative movement that we now see in its first stages, an expansion of the inner way of vision to outer no less than to inner things, to all that is subjective to us and all that is objective, a seeing by a closer identity in the

---

[1] Chapter xxxii, the 'Conclusion' of *The Future Poetry*.

self of man with the self of things and life and Nature and of all
that meets him in the universe. The poet has to find the language
of these identities, and even symbol and figure, when brought in
to assist the more direct utterance, must be used in a different
fashion, less as a veil, more as a real correspondence.

The first condition of the complete emergence of this new
poetic inspiration and this vaster and deeper significance of
poetic speech must be the completion of an as yet only initial
spiritualised turn of our general human feeling and intelligence.
At present the human mind is occupied in passing the borders of
two kingdoms. It is emerging out of a period of active and mostly
materialistic intellectualism towards a primary intuitive seeking to
which the straining of the intellect after truth has been brought
in the very drive of its own impulse by a sort of slipping over
unexpected borders. There is therefore an uncertain groping in
many directions some of which are only valuable as a transitional
effort and, if they could be the end and final movement, might land
us only in a brilliant corruption and decadence. There is a vitalistic
intuitivism sometimes taking a more subjective, sometimes a more
objective form, that lingers amid dubious lights on the border
and cannot get through its own rather thick and often violent
lustres and colours to a finer and truer spiritual vision. There is
an emotional and sensational psychical intuitivism half-emerging
from and half-entangled in the vitalistic motive that has often a
strange beauty and brilliance, sometimes stained with morbid
hues, sometimes floating in a vague mist, sometimes—and this
is a common tendency—strained to an exaggeration of half-vital,
half-psychic motive. There is a purer and more delicate psychic
intuition with a spiritual issue, that which has been brought by
the Irish poets into English literature. The poetry of Whitman and
his successors has been that of life, but of life broadened, raised
and illumined by a strong intellectual intuition of the self of man
and the large soul of humanity. And at the subtlest elevation of

all that has yet been reached stands or rather wings and floats in a high intermediate region the poetry of Tagore, not in the complete spiritual light, but amid an air shot with its seekings and glimpses, a sight and cadence found in a psycho-spiritual heaven of subtle and delicate soul experience transmuting the earth tones by the touch of its radiance. The wide success and appeal of his poetry is indeed one of the most significant signs of the tendency of the mind of the age. At the same time one feels that none of these things are at all the whole of what we are seeking or the definite outcome and issue. That can only be assured when a supreme light of the spirit, a perfect joy and satisfaction of the subtlety and complexity of a finer psychic experience and a wide strength and amplitude of the life-soul sure of the earth and open to the heavens have met, found each other and fused together in the sovereign unity of some great poetic discovery and utterance.

It is possible that it may be rather in Eastern languages and by the genius of Eastern poets that there will come the first discovery of this perfection: the East has always had in its temperament a greater constant nearness to the spiritual and psychic sight and experience and it is only a more perfect turning of this sight on the whole life of man to accept and illuminate that is needed for the realisation of that for which we are still waiting. On the other hand the West has this advantage that though it is only now emerging not so much into the spiritual light as into an outer half-lit circle and though it is hampered by an excessive outward, intellectual and vital pressure, it has at present a more widely ranging thought and a more questing and active eye, and if these once take the right direction, the expression is not so much encircled by past spiritual forms and traditions. It is in any case the shock upon each other of the oriental and occidental mentalities, on the one side the large spiritual mind and inward eye turned upon self and eternal realities, on the other the free inquiry of thought and the courage of the life energy assailing the earth and its problems that is creating the future and must be the parent of the poetry of the future. The whole of life and of the world and Nature seen, fathomed, accepted, but seen in the light of man's deepest spirit, fathomed by the fathoming of the self of man and the large self of the universe, accepted in the sense of its inmost and not only its more outward truth, the discovery of the divine reality within it and of man's own divine possibilities—this is the delivering vision for which our minds are seeking and it is this vision of which the future poetry must find the inspiring aesthetic form and the revealing language.

The world is making itself anew under a great spiritual pressure, the old things are passing away and the new things ready to come into being, and it may be that some of the old nations that have been the leaders of the past and the old literatures that have been hitherto the chosen vehicles of strong poetic creation may prove incapable of holding the greater breath of the new spirit and be condemned to fall into decadence. It may be that we shall have to look for the future creation to new poetical literatures that are not yet born or are yet in their youth and first making or, though they have done something in the past, have still to reach their greatest voice and compass. A language passes through its cycle and grows aged and decays by many maladies: it stagnates perhaps by the attachment of its life to a past tradition and mould of excellence from which it cannot get away without danger to its principle of existence or a straining and breaking of its possibilities and a highly coloured decadence; or, exhausted in its creative vigour, it passes into that attractive but dangerous phase of art for art's sake which makes of poetry no longer a high and fine outpouring of the soul and the life but a hedonistic indulgence and dilettantism of the intelligence. These and other signs of age are not absent from the greater European literary tongues, and at such a stage it becomes a difficult and a critical experiment to attempt at once a transformation of spirit and of the inner cast of poetic language.

There is yet in the present ferment and travail a compelling force of new potentiality, a saving element in the power that is at the root of the call to change, the power of the spirit ever strong to transmute life and mind and make all young again, and once this magical force can be accepted in its completeness and provided there is no long-continued floundering among perverted inspirations or half motives, the old literatures may enter rejuvenated into a new creative cycle. The poetry of the English language in direct relation to which I have made these suggestions, has certain disadvantages for the task that has to be attempted but also certain signal advantages. It is a literature that has long done great things but has neither exhausted its great natural vigour nor fixed itself in any dominant tradition, but rather has constantly shown a free spirit of poetical adventure and a perfect readiness to depart from old moorings and set its sail to undiscovered countries. It has an unsurpassed power of imaginative and intuitive language and has shown it to a very high degree in the intuitive expression of the life-soul and to some degree in that of the inspired intelligence. It seems therefore a predestined instrument for the new poetic language of the intuitive spirit. The chief danger of failure arises from the external direction of the Anglo-Saxon mind. That has been a source of strength in combination with the finer Celtic imagination and has given English poetry a strong hold on life, but the hold has been also something of a chain continually drawing it back from the height and fullness of some great spiritual attempt to inferior levels. Today however the language is no longer the tongue only of the English people: the Irish mind with its Celtic originality and psychic delicacy of vision and purpose has entered into this poetic field. It is receiving too for a time an element or at least an embassy and message from the higher spiritual mind and imagination of India. The countries beyond the seas, still absorbed in their material making, have yet to achieve spiritual independence, but once that comes, the poetry of Whitman shows what large and new elements they can bring to the increase of the spiritual potentialities of the now wide-spreading language. On the whole therefore it is here among European tongues that there is the largest present chance of the revolution of the human spirit finding most easily its poetic utterance. It is also here by the union of a great vital energy and a considerable possibility of the spiritual vision that there may be most naturally a strong utterance of that which most has to be expressed, the seen and realised unity of life and the spirit.

The pouring of a new and greater self-vision of man and Nature and existence into the idea and the life is the condition of the completeness of the coming poetry. It is a large setting and movement of life opening a considerable expansion to the human soul and mind that has been in the great ages of literature the supreme creative stimulus. The discovery of a fresh intellectual or aesthetic motive of the kind that was common in the last century initiates only an ephemeral ripple on the surface and seldom creates work of the very first order. The real inspiration enters with a more complete movement, an enlarged horizon of life, a widening of the fields of the idea, a heightening of the flight of the spirit. The change that is at present coming over the mind of the race began with a wider cosmic vision, a sense of the greatness and destiny and possibilities of the individual and the race, the idea of humanity and of the unity of man with man and a closer relation too and unity of his mind with the life of Nature. It is the endeavour to make the expression of these things one with the expression of life that imparts to the poetry of Whitman so much more large and vital an air than the comparatively feeble refinement and careful art of most of the contemporary poetry of Europe—not that the art has to be omitted, but that it must be united with a more puissant sincerity of spirit and greatness of impulse and a sense of new birth and youth and the potencies of the future. The intellectual idea was yet not enough, for it had to find its own greater truth in the spiritual idea and its finer cultural field in a more delicate and complex and subtle psychic sight and experience. It is this that has been prepared by recent and contemporary poets. The expression of this profounder idea and experience is again not enough until the spiritual idea has passed into a complete spiritual realisation and not only affected individual intellect and psychic mind and imagination, but entered into the general sense and feeling of the race and taken hold upon all thought and life to reinterpret and remould them in their image. It is this spiritual realisation that the future poetry has to help forward by giving to it its eye of sight, its shape of aesthetic beauty, its revealing tongue and it is this greatening of life that it has to make its substance.

It is in effect a larger cosmic vision, a realising of the godhead in the world and in man, of his divine possibilities as well as of the greatness of the power that manifests in what he is, a spiritualised uplifting of his thought and feeling and sense and action, a more developed psychic mind and heart, a truer and a deeper insight into his nature and the meaning of the world, a calling of diviner potentialities and more spiritual values into the intention and structure of his life that is the call upon humanity, the prospect offered to it by the slowly unfolding and now more clearly disclosed Self of the universe. The nations that most include and make real these things in their life and culture are the nations of the coming dawn and the poets of whatever tongue and race who most completely see with this vision and speak with the inspiration of its utterance are those who shall be the creators of the poetry of the future.

Achievement of Indo-English Poetry[1]

1

The idea that Indians cannot succeed in English poetry is very much in the air just now but it cannot be taken as absolutely valid. Toru Dutt and Romesh[2] of the same ilk prove nothing; Toru Dutt was an accomplished verse-builder with a delicate talent and some outbreaks of genius and she wrote things that were attractive and sometimes something that had a strong energy of language and a rhythmic force. Romesh was a smart imitator of English poetry of the second or third rank. What he wrote, if written by an Englishman, might not have had even a temporary success. Sarojini[3] is different. Her work has a real beauty, but it has for the most part only one highly lyrical note and a vein of riches that has been soon exhausted. Some of her lyrical work is likely, I think, to survive among the lasting things in English literature and by these, even if they are fine rather than great, she may take her rank among the immortals. I know no other Indian poets who have published in English

---

[1] These are extracts from letters, originally written to disciples, and first published in book form as *Letters of Sri Aurobindo*, (*Third Series*), by the Sri Aurobindo Circle, Bombay, in 1947.

[2] Toru Dutt (1856-1877) and Romesh Chandra Dutt (1848-1909) were both Indian English poets. The latter was in addition a member of the ICS, a well-known author, economic historian and nationalist leader.

[3] Sarojini Naidu (1879-1949), leading Indian English poet and nationalist.

anything that is really alive and strong and original.[4] The test will be when something is done that is of real power and scope and gets its due chance. Tagore's *Gitanjali* is not in verse, but the place it has taken has some significance. For the obstacles from the other side are that the English mind is apt to look on poetry by an Indian as a curiosity, something exotic (whether it really is or not, the suggestion will be there), and to stress the distance at which the English temperament stands from the Indian temperament. But Tagore's *Gitanjali* is most un-English, yet it overcame this obstacle. For the poetry of spiritual experience, even if it has true poetic value, the difficulty might lie in the remoteness of the subject. But nowadays this difficulty is lessening with the increasing interest in the spiritual and the mystic. It is an age in which Donne, once condemned as a talented but fantastic weaver of extraordinary conceits, is being hailed as a great poet, and Blake lifted to a high eminence; even small poets with the mystic turn are being pulled out of their obscurity and held up to the light. At present many are turning to India for its sources of spirituality, but the eye has been directed only towards Yoga and philosophy, not to the poetical expression of it. When the full day comes, however, it may well be that this too will be discovered, and then an Indian who is at once a mystic and a true poet and able to write in English as if in his mother-tongue (that is essential) would have his full chance. Many barriers are breaking; moreover, both in French and English there are instances of foreigners who have taken their place as prose-writers or poets.

24. 1. 1935

---

[4] This was written some years ago (in 1935) and does not apply to more recent works in English by Indian poets. [Sri Aurobindo's note]

2

It is not true in all cases that one can't write first-class things in a learned language. Both in French and English people to whom the language was not native have done remarkable work, although that is rare. What about Jawaharlal's autobiography? Many English critics think it first-class in its own kind; of course he was educated at an English public school, but I suppose he was not born to the language. Some of Toru Dutt's poems, Sarojini's, Harin's[5] have been highly placed by good English critics, and I don't think we need be more queasy than Englishmen themselves. Of course there were special circumstances, but in your case also there are special circumstances; I don't find that you handle the English language like a foreigner. If first-class excludes everything inferior to Shakespeare and Milton, that is another matter. I think, as time goes on, people will become more and more polyglot and these mental barriers will begin to disappear.

1.10.1943

3

Many Indian write better English than many educated Englishmen.

27.2.1936

---

[5] Harindranath Chattopadhyaya (1898-1991), a poet, playwright, actor and younger brother of Sarojini Naidu.

Future of Indo-English Poetry

1

What you say may be correct (that our oriental luxury in poetry makes it unappealing to Westerners), but on the other hand it is possible that the mind of the future will be more international than it is now. In that case the expression of various temperaments in English poetry will have a chance.

If our aim is not success and personal fame but to arrive at the expression of spiritual truth and experience of all kinds in poetry, the English tongue is the most widespread and is capable of profound turns of mystic expression which make it admirably fitted for the purpose; if it could be used for the highest spiritual expression, that is worth trying.

2

As for the question itself, I put forward four reasons why the experiment could be made. (1) The expression of spirituality in the English tongue is needed and no one can give the real stuff like Easterners and especially Indians. (2) We are entering an age when the stiff barriers of insular and national mentality are breaking down (Hitler notwithstanding), the nations are being drawn into a common universality with whatever differences, and in the new age there is no reason why the English should not admit the expression of other minds than the English in their tongue. (3) For ordinary minds it may be difficult to get over the barrier of a foreign tongue but extraordinary minds, Conrad etc., can do it. (4) In this case the experiment is to see whether what extraordinary minds can do, cannot be done by Yoga.

27.2.1936

Selected Poems

Invitation[1]

With wind and the weather beating round me
    Up to the hill and the moorland I go.
Who will come with me? Who will climb with me?
    Wade through the brook and tramp through the snow?

Not in the petty circle of cities
    Cramped by your doors and your walls I dwell;
Over me God is blue in the welkin,
    Against me the wind and the storm rebel.
I sport with solitude here in my regions,
    Of misadventure have made me a friend.
Who would live largely? Who would live freely?
    Here to the wind-swept uplands ascend.

I am the lord of tempest and mountain,
    I am the Spirit of freedom and pride.
Stark must he be and a kinsman to danger
    Who shares my kingdom and walks at my side.

---

[1] Written in Alipore Jail (1908-1909). This and 'Who', 'Revelation', and 'Life and wealth' were written between (1895-1908).

Who

In the blue of the sky, in the green of the forest,
    Whose is the hand that has painted the glow?
When the winds were asleep in the womb of the ether,
    Who was it roused them and bade them to blow?

He is lost in the heart, in the cavern of Nature,
    He is found in the brain where He builds up the thought:
In the pattern and bloom of the flowers He is woven,
    In the luminous net of the stars He is caught.

In the strength of a man, in the beauty of woman,
    In the laugh of a boy, in the blush of a girl;
The hand that sent Jupiter spinning through heaven,
    Spends all its cunning to fashion a curl.

These are His works and His veils and His shadows;
    But where is He then? By what name is He know?
Is He Brahma or Vishnu? a man or a woman?
    Bodied or bodiless? twin or alone?

We have love for a boy who is dark and resplendent,
    A woman is lord of us, naked and fierce.
We have seen Him a-muse on the snow of the mountains,
    We have watched Him at work in the heart of the spheres.

We will tell the whole world of His ways and His cunning:
    He has rapture of torture and passion and pain;
He delights in our sorrow and drives us to weeping,
    Then lures with His joy and His beauty again.

All music is only the sound of His laughter,
    All beauty the smile of His passionate bliss;
Our lives are His heart-beats, our rapture the bridal
    Of Radha and Krishna, our love is their kiss.

He is strength that is loud in the blare of the trumpets,
    And He rides in the car and He strikes in the spears;
He slays without stint and is full of compassion;
    He wars for the world and its ultimate years.

In the sweep of the worlds, in the surge of the ages,
    Ineffable, mighty, majestic and pure,
Beyond the last pinnacle seized by the thinker
    He is throned in His seats that for ever endure.

The Master of man and his infinite Lover,
    He is close to our hearts, had we vision to see;
We are blind with our pride and the pomp of our passions,
    We are bound in our thoughts where we hold ourselves free.

It is He in the sun who is ageless and deathless,
    And into the midnight His shadow is thrown;
When darkness was blind and engulfed within darkness,
    He was seated within it immense and alone.

Revelation

Someone leaping from the rocks
Past me ran with wind-blown locks
Like a startled bright surmise
Visible to mortal eyes,—
Just a cheek of frightened rose
That with sudden beauty glows,

Just a footstep like the wind
And a hurried glance behind,
And then nothing,—as a thought
Escapes the mind ere it is caught.
Someone of the heavenly rout
From behind the veil ran out.

Life and Death

Life, death,—death, life; the words have led for ages
    Our thought and consciousness and firmly seemed
Two opposites; but now long-hidden pages
    Are opened, liberating truths undreamed.
Life only is, or death is life disguised,—
Life a short death until by life we are surprised.

Epiphany

Majestic, mild, immortally august,
In silence throned, to just and to unjust
One Lord of deep unutterable love,
I saw Him, Shiva, like a brooding dove
Close-winged upon her nest. The outcaste came,
The sinners gathered round that tender Flame,
The demons, by the other sterner gods
Rejected from their luminous abodes,
Gathered around the Refuge of the lost,
Soft-smiling on that wild and grisly host.
All who were refugeless, wretched, unloved,
The wicked and the good together moved
Naturally to Him, the asylum sweet,
And found their heaven at their Master's feet.
The vision changed and in His place there stood

A Terror red as lightning or as blood;
His fierce right hand a javelin advanced
And, as He shook it, earthquake reeling danced
Across the hemisphere, ruin and plague
Rained out of heaven, disasters swift and vague
Threatened, a marching multitude of ills.
His foot strode forward to oppress the hills,
And at the vision of His burning eyes
The hearts of men grew faint with dread surmise
Of sin and punishment; their cry was loud,
'O Master of the stormwind and the cloud,
Spare, Rudra, spare. Show us that other form
Auspicious, not incarnate wrath and storm.'
The God of Wrath, the God of Love are one,
Nor least He loves when most He smites. Alone
Who rises above fear and plays with grief,
Defeat and death, inherits full relief
From blindness and beholds the single Form,
Love masking Terror, Peace supporting storm.
The Friend of Man helps him with Life and Death,
Until he knows. Then freed from mortal breath
He feels the joy of the immortal play;
Grief, pain, resentment, terror pass away.
He too grows Rudra fierce, august and dire,
And Shiva, sweet fulfiller of desire.

A God's Labour

I have gathered my dreams in a silver air
    Between the gold and the blue
And wrapped them softly and left them there,
    My jewelled dreams of you.

I had hoped to build a rainbow bridge
    Marrying the soil to the sky
And sow in this dancing planet midge
    The moods of infinity.

But too bright were our heavens, too far away,
    Too frail their ethereal stuff;
Too splendid and sudden our light could not stay;
    The roots were not deep enough.

He who would bring the heavens here
    Must descend himself into clay
And the burden of earthly nature bear
    And tread the dolorous way.

Coercing my godhead I have come down
    Here on the sordid earth,
Ignorant, labouring, human grown
    Twixt the gates of death and birth.

I have been digging deep and long
    Mid a horror of filth and mire
A bed for the golden river's song,
    A home for the deathless fire.
I have laboured and suffered in matter's night
    To bring the fire to man;
But the hate of hell and human spite
    Are my meed [sic; mead] since the world began.

For man's mind is the dupe of his animal self;
    Hoping its lusts to win,
He harbours within him a grisly Elf
    Enamoured of sorrow and sin.

The grey Elf shudders from heaven's flame
    And from all things glad and pure;
Only by pleasure and passion and pain
    His drama can endure.

All around is darkness and strife;
    For the lamps that men call suns
Are but halfway gleams on this stumbling life
    Cast by the Undying Ones.

Man lights his little torches of hope
    That lead to a failing edge;
A fragment of Truth is his widest scope,
    An inn his pilgrimage.

The Truth of truths men fear and deny,
    The Light of lights they refuse;
To ignorant gods they lift their cry
    Or a demon altar choose.

All that was found must again be sought,
    Each enemy slain revives,
Each battle for ever is fought and refought
    Through vistas of fruitless lives.

My gaping wounds are a thousand and one
    And the Titan kings assail,
But I cannot rest till my task is done
    And wrought the eternal will.

How they mock and sneer, both devils and men!
    'Thy hope is Chimera's head
Painting the sky with its fiery stain;
    Thou shalt fall and thy work lie dead.

'Who art thou that babblest of heavenly ease
    And joy and golden room
To us who are waifs on inconscient seas
    And bound to life's iron doom?

'This earth is ours, a field of Night
    For our petty Flickering fires.
How shall it brook the sacred Light
    Or suffer a god's desires?'

'Come, let us slay him and end his course!
    Then shall our hearts have release
From the burden and call of his glory and force
    And the curb of his wide white peace.'

But the god is there in my mortal breast
    Who wrestles with error and fate
And tramples a road through mire and waste
    For the nameless Immaculate.

A voice cried, 'Go where none have gone!
    Dig deeper, deeper yet
Till thou reach the grim foundation stone
    And knock at the keyless gate.'

I saw that a falsehood was planted deep
    At the very root of things
Where the grey Sphinx guards God's riddle sleep
    On the Dragon's outspread wings.

I left the surface gods of mind
    And life's unsatisfied seas
And plunged through the body's alleys blind
    To the nether mysteries.

I have delved through the dumb Earth's dreadful heart
    And heard her black mass' bell.
I have seen the source whence her agonies part
    And the inner reason of hell.

Above me the dragon murmurs moan
    And the goblin voices flit;
I have pierced the Void where Thought was born,
    I have walked in the bottomless pit.

On a desperate stair my feet have trod
    Armoured with boundless peace,
Bringing the fires of the splendour of God
    Into the human abyss.

He who I am was with me still;
    All veils are breaking now.
I have heard His voice and borne His will
    On my vast untroubled brow.

The gulf twixt the depths and the heights is bridged
    And the golden waters pour
Down the sapphire mountain rainbow-ridged
    And glimmer from shore to shore.

Heaven's fire is lit in the breast of the earth
    And the undying suns here burn;
Through a wonder cleft in the bounds of birth
    The incarnate spirts yearn

Like flames to the kingdoms of Truth and Bliss:
    Down a gold-red stair-way wend
The radiant children of Paradise
    Clarioning darkness's end.

A little more and the new life's doors
    Shall be carved in silver light
With its aureate roof and mosaic floors
    In a great world bare and bright.

I shall leave my dreams in their argent air,
    For in a raiment of gold and blue
There shall move on the earth embodied and fair
    The living truth of you.

Bride of the Fire

Bride of the Fire, clasp me now close,—
    Bride of the Fire!
I have shed the bloom of the earthly rose,
    I have slain desire.

Beauty of the Light, surround my life,—
    Beauty of the Light!
I have sacrificed longing and parted from grief,
    I can bear thy delight.

Image of ecstasy, thrill and enlace,—
    Image of bliss!
I would see only thy marvellous face,
    Feel only thy kiss.

Voice of Infinity, sound in my heart,—
    Call of the One!
Stamp there thy radiance, never to part,
    O living Sun.

Written on 11 November 1935

I Have a Hundred Lives

I have a hundred lives before me yet
To grasp thee in, O spirit ethereal,
Be sure I will with heart insatiate
Pursue thee like a hunter through them all.
Thou yet shalt turn back on the eternal way
And with awakened vision watch me come
Smiling a little at errors past and lay
Thy eager hand in mine, its proper home.
Meanwhile made happy by thy happiness
I shall approach thee in things and people dear
And in thy spirit's motions half-possess
Loving what thou hast loved, shall feel thee near;
Until I lay my hands on thee indeed
Somewhere among the stars, as 'twas decreed.

Nirvana

All is abolished but the mute Alone.
    The mind from thought released, the heart from grief
    Grow inexistent now beyond belief;
There is no I, no Nature, known-unknown.
The city, a shadow picture without tone,
    Floats, quivers unreal; forms without relief
    Flow, a cinema's vacant shapes; like a reef Foundering in
        shoreless gulfs the world is done.

Only the illimitable Permanent
    Is here. A Peace stupendous, featureless, still,
        Replaces all,—what once was I, in It
A silent unnamed emptiness content
    Either to fade in the Unknowable
    Or thrill with the luminous seas of the Infinite.

Evolution

All is not finished in the unseen decree;
    A Mind beyond our mind demands our ken,
A life of unimagined harmony
    Awaits, concealed, the grasp of unborn men.

The crude beginnings of the lifeless earth,
    The mindless stirrings of the plant and tree
Prepared our thought; thought for a godlike birth
    Broadens the mould of our mortality.

A might no human will nor force can gain,
    A knowledge seated in eternity,
A bliss beyond our struggle and our pain
    Are the high pinnacles of our destiny.

O Thou who climbest to mind from the dull stone,
    Face now the miracled summits still unwon.

The Golden Light

Thy golden Light came down into my brain
    And the grey rooms of mind sun-touched became
A bright reply to Wisdom's occult plane,
    A calm illumination and a flame.

Thy golden Light came down into my throat,
    And all my speech is now a tune divine,
A paean-song of Thee my single note;
    My words are drunk with the Immortal's wine.

Thy golden Light came down into my heart
    Smiting my life with Thy eternity;
Now has it grown a temple where Thou art
    And all its passions point towards only Thee.

Thy golden Light came down into my feet;
    My earth is now Thy playfield and Thy seat.

Written on 8 August 1938; revised on 23 March 1944

Krishna

At last I find a meaning of soul's birth
    Into this universe terrible and sweet,
I who have felt the hungry heart of earth
    Aspiring beyond heaven to Krishna's feet.

I have seen the beauty of immortal eyes,
    And heard the passion of the Lover's flute,
And known a deathless ecstasy's surprise
    And sorrow in my heart for ever mute.

Nearer and nearer now the music draws,
    Life shudders with a strange felicity;
All Nature is a wide enamoured pause
    Hoping her lord to touch, to clasp, to be.

For this one moment lived the ages past;
    The world now throbs fulfilled in me at last.

Written on 15 September 1939

Advaita

I walked on the high-wayed Seat of Solomon[2]
    Where Shankaracharya's tiny temple stands
Facing Infinity from Time's edge, alone
    On the bare ridge ending earth's vain romance.

Around me was a formless solitude:
    All had become one strange Unnamable,
An unborn sole Reality world-nude,
    Topless and fathomless, for ever still.

A Silence that was Being's only word,
    The unknown beginning and the voiceless end
Abolishing all things moment-seen or heard,
    On an incommunicable summit reigned,

A lonely Calm and void unchanging Peace
    On the dumb crest of Nature's mysteries.

                Written on 19 October 1939

Divine Sense

Surely I take no more an earthly food
    But eat the fruits and plants of Paradise!
For Thou hast changed my sense's habitude
    From mortal pleasure to divine surprise.

---

[2] Or Takht-e-Suleman, a hilltop overlooking Srinagar in Kashmir, where there is
a small temple of Shankaracharya dedicated to Shiva.

Hearing and sight are now an ecstasy,
    And all the fragrances of earth disclose
A sweetness matching in intensity
    Odour of the crimson marvel of the rose.

In every contact's deep invading thrill,
    That lasts as if its source were infinite,
I feel Thy touch; Thy bliss imperishable
    Is crowded into that moment of delight.

The body burns with Thy rapture's sacred fire,
    Pure, passionate, holy, virgin of desire.

                   Written on 1 November 1939

Ascent[3]

The Silence

Into the Silence, into the Silence,
Arise, O spirit immortal,
Away from the turning Wheel, breaking the magical Circle.
Ascend, single and deathless:
Care no more for the whispers and the shoutings in the darkness,
Pass from the sphere of the grey and the little,
Leaving the cry and the struggle,
Into the Silence for ever.

Vast and immobile, formless and marvellous,
Higher than heaven, wider than the universe,
In a pure glory of being,

---

[3] Free quantitative verse with a predominant dactylic movement.

In a bright stillness of self-seeing,
Communing with a boundlessness voiceless and intimate,
Make thy knowledge too high for thought, thy joy too deep for
    emotion;
At rest in the unchanging Light, mute with the wordless self-
    vision, Spirit, pass out of thyself; Soul, escape from the clutch
    of Nature.

All thou hast seen cast from thee, O Witness.
Turn to the Alone and the Absolute, turn to the Eternal:
Be only eternity, peace and silence,
O world-transcending nameless Oneness,
Spirit immortal.

Beyond the Silence

Out from the Silence, out from the Silence,
Carrying with thee the ineffable Substance,
Carrying with thee the splendour and wideness,
Ascend, O Spirit immortal.
Assigning to Time its endless meaning,
Blissful enter into the clasp of the Timeless.
Awake in the living Eternal, taken to the bosom of love of the Infinite,
Live self-found in his endless completeness,
Drowned in his joy and his sweetness,
Thy heart close to the heart of the Godhead for ever.

Vast, God-possessing, embraced by the Wonderful,
Lifted by the All-Beautiful into his infinite beauty,
Love shall envelop thee endless and fathomless,
Joy unimaginable, ecstasy illimitable,
Knowledge omnipotent, Might omniscient,
Light without darkness, Truth that is dateless.

One with the Transcendent, calm, universal,
Single and free, yet innumerably living,
All in thyself and thyself in all dwelling,
Act in the world with thy being beyond it.
Soul, exceed life's boundaries; Spirit, surpass the universe.
Outclimbing the summits of Nature,
Transcending and uplifting the soul of the finite,
Rise with the world in thy bosom,
O Word gathered into the heart of the Ineffable.
One with the Eternal, live in his infinity,
Drowned in the Absolute, found in the Godhead,
Swan of the supreme and spaceless ether wandering winged
through the universe,
Spirit immortal.

Jivanmukta

There is a silence greater than any known
      To earth's dumb spirit, motionless in the soul
            That has become Eternity's foothold,
Touched by the infinitudes for ever.

A Splendour is here, refused to the earthward sight,
      That floods some deep flame-covered all-seeing eye;
            Revealed it wakens when God's stillness
Heavens the ocean of moveless Nature.

A Power descends no Fate can perturb or vanquish,
      Calmer than mountains, wider than marching waters,
            A single might of luminous quiet
Tirelessly bearing the worlds and ages.

A bliss surrounds with ecstasy everlasting,

An absolute high-seated immortal rapture
    Possesses, sealing love to oneness
In the grasp of the All-beautiful, All-beloved.

He who from Time's dull motion escapes and thrills
    Rapt thoughtless, wordless into the Eternal's breast,
      Unrolls the form and sign of being,
Seated above in the omniscient Silence.

Although consenting here to a mortal body,
    He is the Undying; limit and bond he knows not;
      For him the aeons are a playground,
Life and its deeds are his splendid shadow.

Only to bring God's forces to waiting Nature,
    To help with wide-winged Peace her tormented labour
      And heal with joy her ancient sorrow,
Casting down light on the inconscient darkness,

He acts and lives. Vain things are mind's smaller motives
    To one whose soul enjoys for its high possession
      Infinity and the sempiternal
          All is his guide and beloved and refuge.

                    Written on 13 April 1934

Thought the Paraclete

As some bright archangel in vision flies
Plunged in dream-caught spirit immensities,
Past the long green crests of the seas of life,
Past the orange skies of the mystic mind
Flew my thought self-lost in the vasts of God.

Sleepless wide great glimmering wings of wind
Bore the gold-red seeking of feet that trod
Space and Time's mute vanishing ends. The face
Lustred, pale-blue-lined of the hippogriff,
Eremite, sole, daring the bourneless ways,
Over world-bare summits of timeless being
Gleamed; the deep twilights of the world-abyss
Failed below. Sun-realms of supernal seeing,
Crimson-white mooned oceans of pauseless bliss
Drew its vague heart-yearning with voices sweet. Hungering,
large-souled to surprise the unconned
Secrets white-fire-veiled of the last Beyond,
Crossing power-swept silences rapture-stunned,
Climbing high far ethers eternal-sunned,
Thought the great-winged wanderer paraclete
Disappeared slow-singing a flame-word rune.
Self was left, lone, limitless, nude, immune.

Written on 31 December 1934

Rose of God

Rose of God, vermilion stain on the sapphires of heaven,
Rose of Bliss, fire-sweet, seven-tinged with the ecstasies seven!
Leap up in our heart of humanhood, O miracle, O flame,
Passion-flower of the Nameless, bud of the mystical Name.

Rose of God, great wisdom-bloom on the summits of being,
Rose of Light, immaculate core of the ultimate seeing!
Live in the mind of our earthhood; O golden Mystery, flower,
Sun on the head of the Timeless, guest of the marvellous Hour.

Rose of God, damask force of Infinity, red icon of might,
Rose of Power with thy diamond halo piercing the night!
Ablaze in the will of the mortal, design the wonder of thy plan,
Image of Immortality, outbreak of the Godhead in man.

Rose of God, smitten purple with the incarnate divine Desire,
Rose of Life, crowded with petals, colour's lyre!
Transform the body of the mortal like a sweet and magical rhyme;
Bridge our earthhood and heavenhood, make deathless the
    children of Time.

Rose of God, like a blush of rapture on Eternity's face,
Rose of Love, ruby depth of all being, fire-passion of Grace!
Arise from the heart of the yearning that sobs in Nature's abyss:
Make earth the home of the Wonderful and life beatitude's kiss.

Written on 31 December 1934

From Savitri[1]

The Vision and the Boon

Then suddenly there rose a sacred stir.
Amid the lifeless silence of the Void
In a solitude and an immensity
A sound came quivering like a loved footfall   5
Heard in the listening spaces of the soul;
A touch perturbed his fibres with delight.
An Influence had approached the mortal range,
A boundless Heart was near his longing heart,
A mystic Form enveloped his earthly shape.   10
All at her contact broke from silence' seal;
Spirit and body thrilled identified,
Linked in the grasp of an unspoken joy;
Mind, members, life were merged in ecstasy.
Intoxicated as with nectarous [sic; nectareous] rain   15
His nature's passioning stretches flowed to her,
Flashing with lightnings, mad with luminous wine.

---

[1] Savitri was first published between 1946 and 1948 in various journals of Sri
Aurobindo Ashram and in separate fascimils. The first edition of the complete
text was published in 1950-1951 by Sri Aurobindo Ashram, Pondicherry.
Canto Four of Bk III of *Savitri* brings to an end Part I of the epic, which largely
focuses on Aswapathy.

All was a limitless sea that heaved to the moon.
A divinising stream possessed his veins,
His body's cells awoke to spirit sense,   20
Each nerve became a burning thread of joy:
Tissue and flesh partook beatitude.
Alight, the dun unplumbed subconscient caves
Thrilled with the prescience of her longed-for tread
And filled with flickering crests and praying tongues.   25
Even lost in slumber, mute, inanimate
His very body answered to her power.
The One he worshipped was within him now:
Flame-pure, ethereal-tressed, a mighty Face
Appeared and lips moved by immortal words;   30
Lids, Wisdom's leaves, drooped over rapture's orbs.
A marble monument of ponderings, shone
A forehead, sight's crypt, and large like ocean's gaze
Towards Heaven, two tranquil eyes of boundless thought
Looked into man's and saw the god to come.   35
A Shape was seen on threshold Mind, a Voice
Absolute and wise in the heart's chambers spoke:
'O Son of Strength who climbst creation's peaks,
No soul is thy companion in the light;
Alone thou standest at the eternal doors.   40
What thou hast won is thine, but ask no more.
O Spirit aspiring in an ignorant frame,
O Voice arisen from the Inconscient's world,
How shalt thou speak for men whose hearts are dumb,
Make purblind earth the soul's seer-vision's home   45
Or lighten the burden of the senseless globe?
I am the Mystery beyond reach of mind,
I am the goal of the travail of the suns;
My fire and sweetness are the cause of life.
But too immense my danger and my joy.   50

Awake not the immeasurable descent,
Speak not my secret name to hostile Time;
Man is too weak to bear the Infinite's weight.
Truth born too soon might break the imperfect earth.
Leave the all-seeing Power to hew its way: 55
In thy single vast achievement reign apart
Helping the world with thy great lonely days.
I ask thee not to merge thy heart of flame
In the Immobile's wide uncaring bliss,
Turned from the fruitless motion of the years,   60
Deserting the fierce labour of the worlds,
Aloof from beings, lost in the Alone.
How shall thy mighty spirit brook repose
While Death is still unconquered on the earth
And Time a field of suffering and pain?   65
Thy soul was born to share the laden Force;
Obey thy nature and fulfil thy fate:
Accept the difficulty and godlike toil,
For the slow-paced omniscient purpose live.
The Enigma's knot is tied in human kind.   70
A lightning from the heights that think and plan,
Ploughing the air of life with vanishing trails,
Man, sole awake in an unconscious world,
Aspires in vain to change the cosmic dream.
Arrived from some half-luminous Beyond   75
He is a stranger in the mindless vasts,
A traveller in his oft-shifting home
Amid the tread of many infinities,
He has pitched a tent of life in desert Space.
Heaven's fixed regard beholds him from above,   80
In the house of Nature a perturbing guest,
A voyager twixt Thought's inconstant shores,
A hunter of unknown and beautiful Powers,

A nomad of the far mysterious Light,
In the wide ways a little spark of God.   85
Against his spirit all is in dire league,
A Titan influence stops his Godward gaze.
Around him hungers the unpitying Void,
The eternal Darkness seeks him with her hands,
Inscrutable Energies drive him and deceive,   90
Immense implacable deities oppose.
An inert Soul and a somnambulist Force
Have made a world estranged from life and thought;
The Dragon of the dark foundations keeps
Unalterable the law of Chance and Death;
On his long way through Time and Circumstance   95
The grey-hued riddling nether shadow-Sphinx,
Her dreadful paws upon the swallowing sands,
Awaits him armed with the soul-slaying word:
Across his path sits the dim camp of Night.
His day is a moment in perpetual Time;   100
He is the prey of the minutes and the hours.
Assailed on earth and unassured of heaven,
Descended here unhappy and sublime,
A link between the demigod and the beast,
He knows not his own greatness nor his aim;   105
He has forgotten why he has come and whence.
His spirit and his members are at war;
His heights break off too low to reach the skies,
His mass is buried in the animal mire.
A strange antinomy is his nature's rule   110
A riddle of opposites is made his field:
Freedom he asks but needs to live in bonds,
He has need of darkness to perceive some light
And need of grief to feel a little bliss;
He has need of death to find a greater life.   115

All sides he sees and turns to every call;
He has no certain light by which to walk;
His life is a blind-man's-buff, a hide-and-seek;
He seeks himself and from himself he runs;
Meeting himself, he thinks it other than he.   120
Always he builds, but finds no constant ground,
Always he journeys, but nowhere arrives;
He would guide the world, himself he cannot guide;
He would save his soul, his life he cannot save.
The light his soul had brought his mind has lost;   125
All he has learned is soon again in doubt;
A sun to him seems the shadow of his thoughts,
Then all is shadow again and nothing true:
Unknowing what he does or whither he tends
He fabricates signs of the Real in Ignorance.   130
He has hitched his mortal error to Truth's star.
Wisdom attracts him with her luminous masks,
But never has he seen the face behind:
A giant Ignorance surrounds his lore.
Assigned to meet the cosmic mystery   135
In the dumb figure of a material world,
His passport of entry false and his personage,
He is compelled to be what he is not;
He obeys the Inconscience he had come to rule
And sinks in Matter to fulfil his soul.   140
Awakened from her lower driven forms
The Earth-Mother gave her forces to his hands
And painfully he guards the heavy trust;
His mind is a lost torch-bearer on her roads.
Illumining breath to think and plasm to feel,   145
He labours with his slow and sceptic brain
Helped by the reason's vacillating fires,
To make his thought and will a magic door

For knowledge to enter the darkness of the world
And love to rule a realm of strife and hate.   150
A mind impotent to reconcile heaven and earth
And tied to Matter with a thousand bonds,
He lifts himself to be a conscious god.
Even when a glory of wisdom crowns his brow,
When mind and spirit shed a grandiose ray   155
To exalt this product of the sperm and gene,
This alchemist's miracle from plasm and gas,
And he who shared the animal's run and crawl
Lifts his thought-stature to the Immortal's heights,
His life still keeps the human middle way;   160
His body he resigns to death and pain,
Abandoning Matter, his too heavy charge.
A thaumaturge sceptic of miracles,
A spirit left sterile of its occult power
By an unbelieving brain and credulous heart,   165
He leaves the world to end where it began:
His work unfinished he claims a heavenly prize.
Thus has he missed creation's absolute.
Half-way he stops his star of destiny:
A vast and vain long-tried experiment,   170
An ill-served high conception doubtfully done,
The world's life falters on not seeing its goal,—
A zigzag towards unknown dangerous ground
Ever repeating its habitual walk,
Ever retreating after marches long   175
And hardiest victories without sure result,
Drawn endlessly an inconclusive game.
In an ill-fitting and voluminous robe
A radiant purpose still conceals its face,
A mighty blindness stumbles hoping on,   180
Feeding its strength on gifts of luminous Chance.

Because the human instrument has failed,
The Godhead frustrate sleeps within its seed,
A spirit entangled in the forms it made.
His failure is not failure whom God leads;   185
Through all the slow mysterious march goes on:
An immutable Power has made this mutable world;
A self-fulfilling transcendence treads man's road;
The driver of the soul upon its path,
It knows its steps, its way is inevitable,   190
And how shall the end be vain when God is guide?
However man's mind may tire or fail his flesh,
A will prevails cancelling his conscious choice:
The goal recedes, a bourneless vastness calls
Retreating into an immense Unknown;   195
There is no end to the world's stupendous march,
There is no rest for the embodied soul.
It must live on, describe all Time's huge curve.
An Influx presses from the closed Beyond
Forbidding to him rest and earthly ease,   200
Till he has found himself he cannot pause.
A Light there is that leads, a Power that aids;
Unmarked, unfelt it sees in him and acts:
Ignorant, he forms the All-Conscient in his depths,
Human, looks up to superhuman peaks: 205
A borrower of Supernature's gold,
He paves his road to Immortality.
The high gods look on man and watch and choose
Today's impossibles for the future's base.
His transience trembles with the Eternal's touch,   210
His barriers cede beneath the Infinite's tread;
The Immortals have their entries in his life:
The Ambassadors of the Unseen draw near.
A splendour sullied by the mortal air,

Love passes through his heart, a wandering guest.   215
Beauty surrounds him for a magic hour,
He has visits of a large revealing joy,
Brief widenesses release him from himself,
Enticing towards a glory ever in front
Hopes of a deathless sweetness lure and leave.   220
His mind is crossed by strange discovering fires,
Rare intimations lift his stumbling speech
To a moment's kinship with the eternal Word;
A masque of Wisdom circles through his brain
Perturbing him with glimpses half divine.   225
He lays his hands sometimes on the Unknown;
He communes sometimes with Eternity.
A strange and grandiose symbol was his birth
And immortality and spirit-room
And pure perfection and a shadowless bliss   230
Are this afflicted creature's mighty fate.
In him the Earth-Mother sees draw near the change
Foreshadowed in her dumb and fiery depths,
A godhead drawn from her transmuted limbs,
An alchemy of Heaven on Nature's base.   235
Adept of the selfborn unfailing line,
Leave not the light to die the ages bore,
Help still humanity's blind and suffering life:
Obey thy spirit's wide omnipotent urge.
A witness to God's parley with the Night,   240
It leaned compassionate from immortal calm
And housed desire, the troubled seed of things.
Assent to thy high self, create, endure.
Cease not from knowledge, let thy toil be vast.
No more can earthly limits pen thy force;   245
Equal thy work with long unending Time's.
Traveller upon the bare eternal heights,

Tread still the difficult and dateless path
Joining the cycles with its austere curve
Measured for man by the initiate Gods.   250
My light shall be in thee, my strength thy force.
Let not the impatient Titan drive thy heart,
Ask not the imperfect fruit, the partial prize.
Only one boon, to greaten thy spirit, demand;
Only one joy, to raise thy kind, desire.   255
Above blind fate and the antagonist powers
Moveless there stands a high unchanging Will;
To its omnipotence leave thy work's result.
All things shall change in God's transfiguring hour.'
August and sweet sank hushed that mighty Voice.   260
Nothing now moved in the vast brooding space:
A stillness came upon the listening world,
A mute immensity of the Eternal's peace.
But Aswapati's heart replied to her,
A cry amid the silence of the Vasts: 265
'How shall I rest content with mortal days
And the dull measure of terrestrial things,
I who have seen behind the cosmic mask
The glory and the beauty of thy face?
Hard is the doom to which thou bindst thy sons!   270
How long shall our spirits battle with the Night
And bear defeat and the brute yoke of Death,
We who are vessels of a deathless Force
And builders of the godhead of the race?
Or if it is thy work I do below   275
Amid the error and waste of human life
In the vague light of man's half-conscious mind,
Why breaks not in some distant gleam of thee?
Ever the centuries and millenniums pass.
Where in the greyness is thy coming's ray?   280

Where is the thunder of thy victory's wings?
Only we hear the feet of passing gods.
A plan in the occult eternal Mind
Mapped out to backward and prophetic sight,
The aeons ever repeat their changeless round, 285
The cycles all rebuild and ever aspire.
All we have done is ever still to do.
All breaks and all renews and is the same.
Huge revolutions of life's fruitless gyre,
The new-born ages perish like the old, 290
As if the sad Enigma kept its right
Till all is done for which this scene was made.
Too little the strength that now with us is born,
Too faint the light that steals through Nature's lids,
Too scant the joy with which she buys our pain. 295
In a brute world that knows not its own sense,
Thought-racked upon the wheel of birth we live,
The instruments of an impulse not our own
Moved to achieve with our heart's blood for price
Half-knowledge, half-creations that soon tire. 300
A foiled immortal soul in perishing limbs,
Baffled and beaten back we labour still;
Annulled, frustrated, spent, we still survive.
In anguish we labour that from us may rise
A larger-seeing man with nobler heart, 305
A golden vessel of the incarnate Truth,
The executor of the divine attempt
Equipped to wear the earthly body of God,
Communicant and prophet and lover and king.
I know that thy creation cannot fail: 310
For even through the mists of mortal thought
Infallible are thy mysterious steps,
And, though Necessity dons the garb of Chance,

Hidden in the blind shifts of Fate she keeps
The slow calm logic of Infinity's pace   315
And the inviolate sequence of its will.
All life is fixed in an ascending scale
And adamantine is the evolving Law;
In the beginning is prepared the close.
This strange irrational product of the mire,   320
This compromise between the beast and god,
Is not the crown of thy miraculous world.
I know there shall inform the inconscient cells,
At one with Nature and at height with heaven,
A spirit vast as the containing sky   325
And swept with ecstasy from invisible founts,
A god come down and greater by the fall.
A Power arose out of my slumber's cell.
Abandoning the tardy limp of the hours
And the inconstant blink of mortal sight,   330
There where the Thinker sleeps in too much light
And intolerant flames the lone all-witnessing Eye
Hearing the word of Fate from Silence' heart
In the endless moment of Eternity,
It saw from timelessness the works of Time.   335
Overpassed were the leaden formulas of the Mind,
Overpowered the obstacle of mortal Space:
The unfolding Image showed the things to come.
A giant dance of Shiva tore the past;
There was a thunder as of worlds that fall;   340
Earth was o'errun with fire and the roar of Death
Clamouring to slay a world his hunger had made;
There was a clangour of Destruction's wings:
The Titan's battle-cry was in my ears,
Alarm and rumour shook the armoured Night.   345
I saw the Omnipotent's flaming pioneers

Over the heavenly verge which turns towards life
Come crowding down the amber stairs of birth;
Forerunners of a divine multitude,
Out of the paths of the morning star they came   350
Into the little room of mortal life.
I saw them cross the twilight of an age,
The sun-eyed children of a marvellous dawn,
The great creators with wide brows of calm,
The massive barrier-breakers of the world   355
And wrestlers with destiny in her lists of will,
The labourers in the quarries of the gods,
The messengers of the Incommunicable,
The architects of immortality.
Into the fallen human sphere they came,   360
Faces that wore the Immortal's glory still,
Voices that communed still with the thoughts of God,
Bodies made beautiful by the spirit's light,
Carrying the magic word, the mystic fire,
Carrying the Dionysian cup of joy,   365
Approaching eyes of a diviner man,
Lips chanting an unknown anthem of the soul,
Feet echoing in the corridors of Time.
High priests of wisdom, sweetness, might and bliss,
Discoverers of beauty's sunlit ways   370
And swimmers of Love's laughing fiery floods
And dancers within rapture's golden doors,
Their tread one day shall change the suffering earth
And justify the light on Nature's face.
Although Fate lingers in the high Beyond   375
And the work seems vain on which our heart's force was spent,
All shall be done for which our pain was borne.
Even as of old man came behind the beast
This high divine successor surely shall come

Behind man's inefficient mortal pace,   380
Behind his vain labour, sweat and blood and tears:
He shall know what mortal mind barely durst think,
He shall do what the heart of the mortal could not dare.
Inheritor of the toil of human time,
He shall take on him the burden of the gods;   385
All heavenly light shall visit the earth's thoughts,
The might of heaven shall fortify earthly hearts;
Earth's deeds shall touch the superhuman's height,
Earth's seeing widen into the infinite.
Heavy unchanged weighs still the imperfect world;   390
The splendid youth of Time has passed and failed;
Heavy and long are the years our labour counts
And still the seals are firm upon man's soul
And weary is the ancient Mother's heart.
O Truth defended in thy secret sun,   395
Voice of her mighty musings in shut heavens
On things withdrawn within her luminous depths,
O Wisdom-Splendour, Mother of the universe,
Creatrix, the Eternal's artist Bride,
Linger not long with thy transmuting hand   400
Pressed vainly on one golden bar of Time,
As if Time dare not open its heart to God.
O radiant fountain of the world's delight
World-free and unattainable above,
O Bliss who ever dwellst deep-hid within   405
While men seek thee outside and never find,
Mystery and Muse with hieratic tongue,
Incarnate the white passion of thy force,
Mission to earth some living form of thee.
One moment fill with thy eternity,   410
Let thy infinity in one body live,
All-Knowledge wrap one mind in seas of light,

All-Love throb single in one human heart.
Immortal, treading the earth with mortal feet
All heaven's beauty crowd in earthly limbs!   415
Omnipotence, girdle with the power of God
Movements and moments of a mortal will,
Pack with the eternal might one human hour
And with one gesture change all future time.
Let a great word be spoken from the heights   420
And one great act unlock the doors of Fate.'
His prayer sank down in the resisting Night
Oppressed by the thousand forces that deny,
As if too weak to climb to the Supreme.
But there arose a wide consenting Voice;   425
The spirit of beauty was revealed in sound:
Light floated round the marvellous Vision's brow
And on her lips the Immortal's joy took shape.
'O strong forerunner, I have heard thy cry.
One shall descend and break the iron Law,   430
Change Nature's doom by the lone spirit's power.
A limitless Mind that can contain the world,
A sweet and violent heart of ardent calms
Moved by the passions of the gods shall come.
All mights and greatnesses shall join in her;   435
Beauty shall walk celestial on the earth,
Delight shall sleep in the cloud-net of her hair,
And in her body as on his homing tree
Immortal Love shall beat his glorious wings.
A music of griefless things shall weave her charm;   440
The harps of the Perfect shall attune her voice,
The streams of Heaven shall murmur in her laugh,
Her lips shall be the honeycombs of God,
Her limbs his golden jars of ecstasy,
Her breasts the rapture-flowers of Paradise.   445

She shall bear Wisdom in her voiceless bosom,
Strength shall be with her like a conqueror's sword
And from her eyes the Eternal's bliss shall gaze.
A seed shall be sown in Death's tremendous hour,
A branch of heaven transplant to human soil;   450
Nature shall overleap her mortal step;
Fate shall be changed by an unchanging will.'
As a flame disappears in endless Light
Immortally extinguished in its source,
Vanished the splendour and was stilled the word.   455
An echo of delight that once was close,
The harmony journeyed towards some distant hush,
A music failing in the ear of trance,
A cadence called by distant cadences,
A voice that trembled into strains withdrawn.   460
Her form retreated from the longing earth
Forsaking nearness to the abandoned sense,
Ascending to her unattainable home.
Lone, brilliant, vacant lay the inner fields;
All was unfilled inordinate spirit space,   465
Indifferent, waste, a desert of bright peace.
Then a line moved on the far edge of calm:
The warm-lipped sentient soft terrestrial wave,
A quick and many-murmured moan and laugh,
Came gliding in upon white feet of sound.   470
Unlocked was the deep glory of Silence' heart;
The absolute unmoving stillnesses
Surrendered to the breath of mortal air,
Dissolving boundlessly the heavens of trance
Collapsed to waking mind. Eternity   475
Cast down its incommunicable lids
Over its solitudes remote from ken
Behind the voiceless mystery of sleep.

The grandiose respite failed, the wide release.
Across the light of fast-receding planes   480
That fled from him as from a falling star,
Compelled to fill its human house in Time
His soul drew back into the speed and noise
Of the vast business of created things.
A chariot of the marvels of the heavens   485
Broad-based to bear the gods on fiery wheels,
Flaming he swept through the spiritual gates.
The mortal stir received him in its midst.
Once more he moved amid material scenes,
Lifted by intimations from the heights   490
And in the pauses of the building brain
Touched by the thoughts that skim the fathomless surge
Of Nature and wing back to hidden shores.
The eternal seeker in the aeonic field
Besieged by the intolerant press of hours   495
Again was strong for great swift-footed deeds.
Awake beneath the ignorant vault of Night,
He saw the unnumbered people of the stars
And heard the questioning of the unsatisfied flood
And toiled with the form-maker, measuring Mind.   500
A wanderer from the occult invisible suns
Accomplishing the fate of transient things,
A god in the figure of the arisen beast,
He raised his brow of conquest to the heavens
Establishing the empire of the soul   505
On Matter and its bounded universe
As on a solid rock in infinite seas.
The Lord of Life resumed his mighty rounds
In the scant field of the ambiguous globe.

Pioneers of the Future

The Mother[1]

1

There are two powers that alone can effect in their conjunction the great and difficult thing which is the aim of our endeavour, a fixed and unfailing aspiration that calls from below and a supreme Grace from above that answers.

But the supreme Grace will act only in the conditions of the Light and the Truth; it will not act in conditions laid upon it by the Falsehood and the Ignorance. For if it were to yield to the demands of the Falsehood, it would defeat its own purpose.

These are the conditions of the Light and Truth, the sole conditions under which the highest Force will descend; and it is only the very highest supramental Force descending from above and opening from below that can victoriously handle the physical Nature and annihilate its difficulties . . . There must be a total and sincere surrender; there must be an exclusive self-opening to the divine Power; there must be a constant and integral choice of the Truth that is descending, a constant and integral rejection of the falsehood of the mental, vital and physical Powers and Appearances that still rule the earth-Nature.

The surrender must be total and seize all the parts of the being. It is not enough that the psychic should respond and the higher

---

[1] First published in 1928 in Calcutta by the Arya Sahitya Bhawan. Parts of this small book were originally written as letters to disciples.

mental accept or even the inner vital submit and the inner physical consciousness feel the influence. There must be in no part of the being, even the most external, anything that makes a reserve, anything that hides behind doubts, confusions and subterfuges, anything that revolts or refuses.

If part of the being surrenders, but another part reserves itself, follows its own way or makes its own conditions, then each time that that happens, you are yourself pushing the divine Grace away from you.

If behind your devotion and surrender you make a cover for your desires, egoistic demands and vital insistences, if you put these things in place of the true aspiration or mix them with it and try to impose them on the Divine Shakti, then it is idle to invoke the divine Grace to transform you.

If you open yourself on one side or in one part to the Truth and on another side are constantly opening the gates to hostile forces, it is vain to expect that the divine Grace will abide with you. You must keep the temple clean if you wish to instal there the living Presence.

If each time the Power intervenes and brings in the Truth, you turn your back on it and call in again the falsehood that has been expelled, it is not the divine Grace that you must blame for failing you, but the falsity of your own will and the imperfection of your own surrender.

If you call for the Truth and yet something in you chooses what is false, ignorant and undivine or even simply is unwilling to reject it altogether, then always you will be open to attack and the Grace will recede from you. Detect first what is false or obscure in you and persistently reject it, then alone can you rightly call for the divine Power to transform you.

Do not imagine that truth and falsehood, light and darkness, surrender and selfishness can be allowed to dwell together in the house consecrated to the Divine. The transformation must be integral, and integral therefore the rejection of all that withstands it.

Reject the false notion that the divine Power will do and is bound to do everything for you at your demand and even though you do not satisfy the conditions laid down by the Supreme. Make your surrender true and complete, then only will all else be done for you.

Reject too the false and indolent expectation that the divine Power will do even the surrender for you. The Supreme demands your surrender to her, but does not impose it: you are free at every moment, till the irrevocable transformation comes, to deny and to reject the Divine or to recall your self-giving, if you are willing to suffer the spiritual consequence. Your surrender must be self-made and free; it must be the surrender of a living being, not of an inert automaton or mechanical tool.

An inert passivity is constantly confused with the real surrender, but out of an inert passivity nothing true and powerful can come. It is the inert passivity of physical Nature that leaves it at the mercy of every obscure or undivine influence. A glad and strong and helpful submission is demanded to the working of the Divine Force, the obedience of the illumined disciple of the Truth, of the inner Warrior who fights against obscurity and falsehood, of the faithful servant of the Divine.

This is the true attitude and only those who can take and keep it, preserve a faith unshaken by disappointments and difficulties and shall pass through the ordeal to the supreme victory and the great transmutation.

2

In all that is done in the universe, the Divine through his Shakti is behind all action but he is veiled by his Yoga Maya and works through the ego of the Jiva in the lower nature.

In Yoga also it is the Divine who is the Sadhaka and the Sadhana; it is his Shakti with her light, power, knowledge, consciousness, Ananda, acting upon the Adhara and, when it is opened to her, pouring into it with these divine forces that makes the Sadhana possible. But so long as the lower nature is active the personal effort of the Sadhaka remains necessary.

The personal effort required is a triple labour of aspiration, rejection and surrender—

an aspiration vigilant, constant, unceasing— the mind's will, the heart's seeking, the assent of the vital being, the will to open and make plastic the physical consciousness and nature;

rejection of the movements of the lower nature—rejection of the mind's ideas, opinions, preferences, habits, constructions, so that the true knowledge may find free room in a silent mind—rejection of the vital nature's desires, demands, cravings, sensations, passions, selfishness, pride, arrogance, lust, greed, jealousy, envy, hostility to the Truth, so that the true power and joy may pour from above into a calm, large, strong and consecrated vital being—rejection of the physical nature's stupidity, doubt, disbelief, obscurity, obstinacy, pettiness, laziness, unwillingness to change, Tamas, so that the true stability of Light, Power, Ananda may establish itself in a body growing always more divine;

surrender of oneself and all one is and has and every plane of the consciousness and every movement to the Divine and the Shakti.

In proportion as the surrender and self-consecration progress the Sadhaka becomes conscious of the Divine Shakti doing the Sadhana, pouring into him more and more of herself, founding in him the freedom and perfection of the Divine Nature. The more this conscious process replaces his own effort, the more rapid and true becomes his progress. But it cannot completely replace the necessity of personal effort until the surrender and consecration are pure and complete from top to bottom.

Note that a tamasic surrender refusing to fulfil the conditions and calling on God to do everything and save one all the trouble and struggle is a deception and does not lead to freedom and perfection.

3

To walk through life armoured against all fear, peril and disaster, only two things are needed, two that go always together—the Grace of the Divine Mother and on your side an inner state made up of faith, sincerity and surrender. Let your faith be pure, candid and perfect. An egoistic faith in the mental and vital being tainted by ambition, pride, vanity, mental arrogance, vital self-will, personal demand, desire for the petty satisfactions of the lower nature is a low and smoke-obscured flame that cannot burn upwards to heaven. Regard your life as given you only for the divine work and to help in the divine manifestation. Desire nothing but the purity, force, light, wideness, calm, Ananda of the divine consciousness and its insistence to transform and perfect your mind, life and body. Ask for nothing but the divine, spiritual and supramental Truth, its realisation on earth and in you and in all who are called and chosen and the conditions needed for its creation and its victory over all opposing forces.

Let your sincerity and surrender be genuine and entire. When you give yourself, give completely, without demand, without condition, without reservation so that all in you shall belong to the Divine Mother and nothing be left to the ego or given to any other power.

The more complete your faith, sincerity and surrender, the more will grace and protection be with you. And when the grace and protection of the Divine Mother are with you, what is there that can touch you or whom need you fear? A little of it even will carry you through all difficulties, obstacles and dangers; surrounded by its full presence you can go securely on your way because it is hers, careless of all menace, unaffected by any hostility however powerful, whether from this world or from worlds invisible. Its touch can turn difficulties into opportunities, failure into success and weakness into unfaltering strength. For the grace of the Divine Mother is the sanction of the Supreme and now or tomorrow its effect is sure, a thing decreed, inevitable and irresistible.

4

Money is the visible sign of a universal force, and this force in its manifestation on earth works on the vital and physical planes and is indispensable to the fullness of the outer life. In its origin and its true action it belongs to the Divine. But like other powers of the Divine it is delegated here and in the ignorance of the lower Nature can be usurped for the uses of the ego or held by Asuric influences and perverted to their purpose. This is indeed one of the three forces—power, wealth, sex—that have the strongest attraction for the human ego and the Asura and are most generally misheld and misused by those who retain them. The seekers or keepers of wealth are more often possessed rather than its possessors; few escape entirely a certain distorting influence stamped on it by its long seizure and perversion by the Asura. For this reason most spiritual disciplines insist on a complete self-control, detachment and renunciation of all bondage to wealth and of all personal and egoistic desire for its possession. Some even put a ban on money and riches and proclaim poverty and bareness of life as the only spiritual condition. But this is an error; it leaves the power in the hands of the hostile forces. To reconquer it for the Divine to whom it belongs and use it divinely for the divine life is the supramental way for the Sadhaka.

You must neither turn with an ascetic shrinking from the money power, the means it gives and the objects it brings, nor cherish a rajasic attachment to them or a spirit of enslaving self-indulgence in their gratifications. Regard wealth simply as a power to be won back for the Mother and placed at her service.

All wealth belongs to the Divine and those who hold it are trustees, not possessors. It is with them today, tomorrow it may be elsewhere. All depends on the way they discharge their trust while it is with them, in what spirit, with what consciousness in their use of it, to what purpose.

In your personal use of money look on all you have or get or bring as the Mother's. Make no demand but accept what you receive from her and use it for the purposes for which it is given to you. Be entirely selfless, entirely scrupulous, exact, careful in detail, a good trustee; always consider that it is her possessions and not your own that you are handling. On the other hand, what you receive for her, lay religiously before her; turn nothing to your own or anybody else's purpose.

Do not look up to men because of their riches or allow yourself to be impressed by the show, the power or the influence. When you ask for the Mother, you must feel that it is she who is demanding through you a very little of what belongs to her and the man from whom you ask will be judged by his response.

If you are free from the money-taint but without any ascetic withdrawal, you will have a greater power to command the money for the divine work. Equality of mind, absence of demand and the full dedication of all you possess and receive and all your power of acquisition to the Divine Shakti and her work are the signs of this freedom. Any perturbation of mind with regard to money and its use, any claim, any grudging is a sure index of some imperfection or bondage.

The ideal Sadhaka in this kind is one who if required to live poorly can so live and no sense of want will affect him or interfere with the full inner play of the divine consciousness, and if he is required to live richly, can so live and never for a moment fall into desire or attachment to his wealth or to the things that he uses or servitude to self-indulgence or a weak bondage to the habits that the possession of riches creates. The divine Will is all for him and the divine Ananda.

In the supramental creation the money-force has to be restored to the Divine Power and used for a true and beautiful and harmonious equipment and ordering of a new divinised vital and physical existence in whatever way the Divine Mother herself decides in her creative vision. But first it must be conquered back for her and those will be strongest for the conquest who are in this part of their nature strong and large and free from ego and surrendered without any claim or withholding or hesitation, pure and powerful channels for the Supreme Puissance.

5

If you want to be a true doer of divine works, your first aim must be to be totally free from all desire and self-regarding ego. All your life must be an offering and a sacrifice to the Supreme; your only object in action shall be to serve, to receive, to fulfil, to become a manifesting instrument of the Divine Shakti in her works. You must grow in the divine consciousness till there is no difference between your will and hers, no motive except her impulsion in you, no action that is not her conscious action in you and through you.

Until you are capable of this complete dynamic identification, you have to regard yourself as a soul and body created for her service, one who does all for her sake. Even if the idea of the separate worker is strong in you and you feel that it is you who do the act, yet it must be done for her. All stress of egoistic choice, all hankering after personal profit, all stipulation of self-regarding desire must be extirpated from the nature. There must be no demand for fruit and no seeking for reward; the only fruit for you is the pleasure of the Divine Mother and the fulfilment of her work, your only reward a constant progression in divine consciousness and calm and strength and bliss. The joy of service and the joy of inner growth through works is the sufficient recompense of the selfless worker.

But a time will come when you will feel more and more that you are the instrument and not the worker. For first by the force of your devotion your contact with the Divine Mother will become so intimate that at all times you will have only to concentrate and to put everything into her hands to have her present guidance, her direct command or impulse, the sure indication of the thing to be done and the way to do it and the result. And afterwards you will realise that the divine Shakti not only inspires and guides, but initiates and carries out your works; all your movements are originated by her, all your powers are hers, mind, life and body are conscious and joyful instruments of her action, means for her play, moulds for her manifestation in the physical universe. There can be no more happy condition than this union and dependence; for this step carries you back beyond the border-line from the life of stress and suffering in the ignorance into the truth of your spiritual being, into its deep peace and its intense Ananda.

While this transformation is being done it is more than ever necessary to keep yourself free from all taint of the perversions of the ego. Let no demand or insistence creep in to stain the purity or the self-giving and the sacrifice. There must be no attachment to the work or the result, no laying down of conditions, no claim to possess the Power that should possess you, no pride of the instrument, no vanity or arrogance. Nothing in the mind or in the vital or physical parts should be suffered to distort to its own use or seize for its own personal and separate satisfaction the greatness of the forces that are acting through you. Let your faith, your sincerity, your purity of aspiration be absolute and pervasive of all the planes and layers of the being; then every disturbing element and distorting influence will progressively fall away from your nature.

The last stage of this perfection will come when you are completely identified with the Divine Mother and feel yourself to be no longer another and separate being, instrument, servant or worker but truly a child and eternal portion of her consciousness and force. Always she will be in you and you in her; it will be your constant, simple and natural experience that all your thought and seeing and action, your very breathing or moving come from her and are hers. You will know and see and feel that you are a person and power formed by her out of herself, put out from her for the play and yet always safe in her, being of her being, consciousness of her consciousness, force of her force, Ananda of her Ananda. When this condition is entire and her supramental energies can freely move you, then you will be perfect in divine works; knowledge, will, action will become sure, simple, luminous, spontaneous, flawless, an outflow from the Supreme, a divine movement of the Eternal.

6

The four Powers of the Mother are four of her outstanding Personalities, portions and embodiments of her divinity through whom she acts on her creatures, orders and harmonises her creations in the worlds and directs the working out of her thousand forces. For the Mother is one but she comes before us with differing aspects; many are her powers and personalities, many her emanations and Vibhutis that do her work in the universe. The One whom we adore as the Mother is the divine Conscious Force that dominates all existence, one and yet so many-sided that to follow her movement is impossible even for the quickest mind and for the freest and most vast intelligence. The Mother is the consciousness and force of the Supreme and far above all she creates. But something of her ways can be seen and felt through her embodiments and the more seizable because more defined and limited temperament and action of the goddess forms in whom she consents to be manifest to her creatures.

There are three ways of being of the Mother of which you can become aware when you enter into touch of oneness with the Conscious Force that upholds us and the universe. Transcendent, the original supreme Shakti, she stands above the worlds and links the creation to the ever unmanifest mystery of the Supreme. Universal, the cosmic Mahashakti, she creates all these beings and contains and enters, supports and conducts all these million processes and forces. Individual, she embodies the power of these two vaster ways of her existence, makes them living and near to us and mediates between the human personality and the divine Nature.

The one original transcendent Shakti, the Mother stands above all the worlds and bears in her eternal consciousness the Supreme Divine. Alone, she harbours the absolute Power and the ineffable Presence; containing or calling the Truths that have to be manifested, she brings them down from the Mystery in which they were hidden into the light of her infinite consciousness and gives them a form of force in her omnipotent power and her boundless life and a body in the universe. The Supreme is manifest in her for ever as the everlasting Sachchidananda, manifested through her in the worlds as the one and dual consciousness of Ishwara-Shakti and the dual principle of Purusha-Prakriti, embodied by her in the Worlds and the Planes and the Gods and their Energies and figured because of her as all that is in the known worlds and in unknown others. All is her play with the Supreme; all is her manifestation of the mysteries of the Eternal, the miracles of the Infinite. All is she, for all are parcel and portion of the divine Conscious-Force. Nothing can be here or elsewhere but what she decides and the Supreme sanctions; nothing can take shape except what she moved by the Supreme perceives and forms after casting it into seed in her creating Ananda.

The Mahashakti, the universal Mother, works out whatever is transmitted by her transcendent consciousness from the Supreme and enters into the worlds that she has made; her presence fills and supports them with the divine spirit and the divine all-sustaining force and delight without which they could not exist. That which we call Nature or Prakriti is only her most outward executive aspect; she marshals and arranges the harmony of her forces and processes, impels the operations of Nature and moves among them secret or manifest in all that can be seen or experienced or put into motion of life. Each of the worlds is nothing but one play of the Mahashakti of that system of worlds or universe, who is there as the cosmic Soul and Personality of the transcendent Mother. Each is something that she has seen in her vision, gathered into her heart of beauty and power and created in her Ananda.

But there are many planes of her creation, many steps of the Divine Shakti. At the summit of this manifestation of which we are a part there are worlds of infinite existence, consciousness, force and bliss over which the Mother stands as the unveiled eternal Power. All beings there live and move in an ineffable completeness and unalterable oneness, because she carries them safe in her arms for ever. Nearer to us are the worlds of a perfect supramental creation in which the Mother is the supramental Mahashakti, a Power of divine omniscient Will and omnipotent Knowledge always apparent in its unfailing works and spontaneously perfect in every process. There all movements are the steps of the Truth;

there all beings are souls and powers and bodies of the divine Light; there all experiences are seas and floods and waves of an intense and absolute Ananda. But here where we dwell are the worlds of the Ignorance, worlds of mind and life and body separated in consciousness from their source, of which this earth is a significant centre and its evolution a crucial process. This too with all its obscurity and struggle and imperfection is upheld by the Universal Mother; this too is impelled and guided to its secret aim by the Mahashakti.

The Mother as the Mahashakti of this triple world of the Ignorance stands in an intermediate plane between the supramental Light, the Truth life, the Truth creation which has to be brought down here and this mounting and descending hierarchy of planes of consciousness that like a double ladder lapse into the nescience of Matter and climb back again through the flowering of life and soul and mind into the infinity of the Spirit. Determining all that shall be in this universe and in the terrestrial evolution by what she sees and feels and pours from her, she stands there above the Gods and all her Powers and Personalities are put out in front of her for the action and she sends down emanations of them into these lower worlds to intervene, to govern, to bathe and conquer, to lead and turn their cycles, to direct the total and the individual lines of their forces. These Emanations are the many divine forms and personalities in which men have worshipped her under different names throughout the ages. But also she prepares and shapes through these Powers and their emanations the minds and bodies of her Vibhutis, even as she prepares and shapes minds and bodies for the Vibhutis of the Ishwara, that she may manifest in the physical world and in the disguise of the human consciousness some ray of her power and quality and presence. All the scenes of the earthplay have been like a drama arranged and planned and staged by her with the cosmic Gods for her assistants and herself as a veiled actor.

The Mother not only governs all from above but she descends into this lesser triple universe. Impersonally, all things here, even the movements of the Ignorance, are herself in veiled power and her creations in diminished substance, her Nature-body and Nature-force, and they exist because, moved by the mysterious fiat of the Supreme to work out something that was there in the possibilities of the Infinite, she has consented to the great sacrifice and has put on like a mask the soul and forms of the Ignorance. But personally too she has stooped to descend here into the Darkness that she may lead it to the Light, into the Falsehood and Error that she may convert it to the Truth, into this Death that she may turn it to godlike Life, into this world-pain and its obstinate sorrow and suffering that she may end it in the transforming ecstasy of her sublime Ananda. In her deep and great love for her children she has consented to put on herself the cloak of this obscurity, condescended to bear the attacks and torturing influences of the powers of the Darkness and the Falsehood, borne to pass through the portals of the birth that is a death, taken upon herself the pangs and sorrows and sufferings of the creation, since it seemed that thus alone could it be lifted to the Light and Joy and Truth and eternal Life. This is the great sacrifice called sometimes the sacrifice of the Purusha, but much more deeply the holocaust of Prakriti, the sacrifice of the Divine Mother.

Four great Aspects of the Mother, four of her leading Powers and Personalities have stood in front in her guidance of this Universe and in her dealings with the terrestrial play. One is her personality of calm wideness and comprehending wisdom and tranquil benignity and inexhaustible compassion and sovereign and surpassing majesty and all-ruling greatness. Another embodies her power of splendid strength and irresistible passion, her warrior mood, her overwhelming will, her impetuous swiftness and world-shaking force. A third is vivid and sweet and wonderful with her deep secret of beauty and harmony and fine rhythm, her intricate and subtle opulence, her compelling attraction and captivating grace. The fourth is equipped with her close and profound capacity of intimate knowledge and careful flawless work and quiet and exact perfection in all things. Wisdom, Strength, Harmony, Perfection are their several attributes and it is these powers that they bring with them into the world, manifest in a human disguise in their Vibhutis and shall found in the divine degree of their ascension in those who can open their earthly nature to the direct and living influence of the Mother. To the four we give the four great names, Maheshwari, Mahakali, Mahalakshmi, Mahasaraswati.

Imperial MAHESHWARI is seated in the wideness above the thinking mind and will and sublimates and greatens them into wisdom and largeness or floods with a splendour beyond them. For she is the mighty and wise One who opens us to the supramental infinities and the cosmic vastness, to the grandeur of the supreme Light, to a treasure-house of miraculous knowledge, to the measureless movement of the Mother's eternal forces. Tranquil is she and wonderful, great and calm for ever. Nothing can move her because all wisdom is in her; nothing is hidden from her that she chooses to know; she comprehends all things and all beings and their nature and what moves them and the law of the world and its times and how all was and is and must be. A strength is in her that meets everything and masters and none can prevail in the end against her vast intangible wisdom and high tranquil power. Equal, patient and unalterable in her will she deals with men according to their nature and with things and happenings according to their Force and the truth that is in them. Partiality she has none, but she follows the decrees of the Supreme and some she raises up and some she casts down or puts away from her into the darkness. To the wise she gives a greater and more luminous wisdom; those that have vision she admits to her counsels; on the hostile she imposes the consequence of their hostility; the ignorant and foolish she leads according to their blindness. In each man she answers and handles the different elements of his nature according to their need and their urge and the return they call for, puts on them the required pressure or leaves them to their cherished liberty to prosper in the ways of the Ignorance or to perish. For she is above all, bound by nothing, attached to nothing in the universe. Yet has she more than any other the heart of the universal Mother. For her compassion is endless and inexhaustible; all are to her eyes her children and portions of the One, even the Asura and Rakshasa and Pishacha and those that are revolted and hostile. Even her rejections are only a postponement, even her punishments are a grace. But her compassion does not blind her wisdom or turn her action from the course decreed; for the Truth of things is her one concern, knowledge her centre of power and to build our soul and our nature into the divine Truth her mission and her labour.

MAHAKALI is of another nature. Not wideness but height, not wisdom but force and strength are her peculiar power. There is in her an overwhelming intensity, a mighty passion of force to achieve, a divine violence rushing to shatter every limit and obstacle. All her divinity leaps out in a splendour of tempestuous action; she is there for swiftness, for the immediately effective process, the rapid and direct stroke, the frontal assault that carries everything before it. Terrible is her face to the Asura, dangerous and ruthless her mood against the haters of the Divine; for she is the Warrior of the Worlds who never shrinks from the battle. Intolerant of imperfection, she deals roughly with all in man that is unwilling and she is severe to all that is obstinately ignorant and obscure; her wrath is immediate and dire against treachery and falsehood and malignity, ill-will is smitten at once by her scourge. Indifference, negligence and sloth in the divine work she cannot bear and she smites awake at once with sharp pain, if need be, the untimely slumberer and the loiterer. The impulses that are swift and straight and frank, the movements that are unreserved and absolute, the aspiration that mounts in flame are the motion of

Mahakali. Her spirit is tameless, her vision and will are high and far-reaching like the flight of an eagle, her feet are rapid on the upward way and her hands are outstretched to strike and to succour. For she too is the Mother and her love is as intense as her wrath and she has a deep and passionate kindness. When she is allowed to intervene in her strength, then in one moment are broken like things without consistence the obstacles that immobilise or the enemies that assail the seeker. If her anger is dreadful to the hostile and the vehemence of her pressure painful to the weak and timid, she is loved and worshipped by the great, the strong and the noble; for they feel that her blows beat what is rebellious in their material into strength and perfect truth, hammer straight what is wry and perverse and expel what is impure or defective. But for her what is done in a day might have taken centuries; without her Ananda might be wide and grave or soft and sweet and beautiful but would lose the flaming joy of its most absolute intensities. To knowledge she gives a conquering might, brings to beauty and harmony a high and mounting movement and imparts to the slow and difficult labour after perfection an impetus that multiplies the power and shortens the long way. Nothing can satisfy her that falls short of the supreme ecstasies, the highest heights, the noblest aims, the largest vistas. Therefore with her is the victorious force of the Divine and it is by grace of her fire and passion and speed if the great achievement can be done now rather than hereafter.

Wisdom and Force are not the only manifestations of the supreme Mother; there is a subtler mystery of her nature and without it Wisdom and Force would be incomplete things and without it perfection would not be perfect. Above them is the miracle of eternal beauty, an unseizable secret of divine harmonies, the compelling magic of an irresistible universal charm and attraction that draws and holds things and forces and beings together and obliges them to meet and unite that a hidden Ananda may play from behind the veil and make of them its rhythms and its figures. This is the power of MAHALAKSHMI and there is no aspect of the Divine Shakti more attractive to the heart of embodied beings. Maheshwari can appear too calm and great and distant for the littleness of earthly nature to approach or contain her, Mahakali too swift and formidable for its weakness to bear; but all turn with joy and longing to Mahalakshmi. For she throws the spell of the intoxicating sweetness of the Divine: to be close to her is a profound happiness and to feel her within the heart is to make existence a rapture and a marvel; grace and charm and tenderness flow out from her like light from the sun and wherever she fixes her wonderful gaze or lets fall the loveliness of her smile, the soul is seized and made captive and plunged into the depths of an unfathomable bliss. Magnetic is the touch of her hands and their occult and delicate influence refines mind and life and body and where she presses her feet course miraculous streams of an entrancing Ananda.

And yet it is not easy to meet the demand of this enchanting Power or to keep her presence. Harmony and beauty of the mind and soul, harmony and beauty of the thoughts and feelings, harmony and beauty in every outward act and movement, harmony and beauty of the life and surroundings, this is the demand of Mahalakshmi. Where there is affinity to the rhythms of the secret world-bliss and response to the call of the All-Beautiful and concord and unity and the glad flow of many lives turned towards the Divine, in that atmosphere she consents to abide. But all that is ugly and mean and base, all that is poor and sordid and squalid, all that is brutal and coarse repels her advent. Where love and beauty are not or are reluctant to be born, she does not come; where they are mixed and disfigured with baser things, she turns soon to depart or cares little to pour her riches. If she finds herself in men's hearts surrounded with selfishness and hatred and jealousy and malignance and envy and strife, if treachery and greed and ingratitude are mixed in the sacred chalice, if grossness of passion and unrefined desire degrade devotion, in such hearts the gracious and beautiful Goddess will not linger. A divine disgust seizes upon her and she withdraws, for she is not one who insists or strives; or, veiling her face, she waits for this bitter and poisonous devil's stuff to be rejected and disappear before she will found anew her happy influence. Ascetic bareness and harshness are not pleasing to her nor the suppression of the heart's deeper emotions and the rigid repression of the soul's and the life's parts of beauty. For it is through love and beauty that she lays on men the yoke of the Divine. Life is turned in her supreme creations into a rich work of celestial art and all existence into a poem of sacred delight; the world's riches are brought together and concerted for a supreme order and even the simplest and commonest things are made wonderful by her intuition of unity and the breath of her spirit. Admitted to the heart she lifts wisdom to pinnacles of wonder and reveals to it the mystic secrets of the ecstasy that surpasses all knowledge, meets devotion with the passionate attraction of the Divine, teaches to strength and force the rhythm that keeps the might of their acts harmonious and in measure and casts on perfection the charm that makes it endure for ever.

MAHASARASWATI is the Mother's Power of Work and her spirit of perfection and order. The youngest of the Four, she is the most skilful in executive faculty and the nearest to physical Nature. Maheshwari lays down the large lines of the world-forces, Mahakali drives their energy and impetus, Mahalakshmi discovers their rhythms and measures, but Mahasaraswati presides over their detail of organisation and execution, relation of parts and effective combination of forces and unfailing exactitude of result and fulfilment. The science and craft and technique of things are Mahasaraswati's province. Always she holds in her nature and can give to those whom she has chosen the intimate and precise knowledge, the subtlety and patience, the accuracy of intuitive mind and conscious hand and discerning eye of the perfect worker. This

Power is the strong, the tireless, the careful and efficient builder, organiser, administrator, technician, artisan and classifier of the worlds. When she takes up the transformation and new-building of the nature, her action is laborious and minute and often seems to our impatience slow and interminable, but it is persistent, integral and flawless. For the will in her works is scrupulous, unsleeping, indefatigable; leaning over us she notes and touches every little detail, finds out every minute defect, gap, twist or incompleteness, considers and weighs accurately all that has been done and all that remains still to be done hereafter. Nothing is too small or apparently trivial for her attention; nothing however impalpable or disguised or latent can escape her. Moulding and remoulding she labours each part till it has attained its true form, is put in its exact place in the whole and fulfils its precise purpose. In her constant and diligent arrangement and rearrangement of things her eye is on all needs at once and the way to meet them and her intuition knows what is to be chosen and what rejected and successfully determines the right instrument, the right time, the right conditions and the right process. Carelessness and negligence and indolence she abhors; all scamped and hasty and shuffling work, all clumsiness and *à peu près* and misfire, all false adaptation and misuse of instruments and faculties and leaving of things undone or half-done is offensive and foreign to her temper. When her work is finished, nothing has been forgotten, no part has been misplaced or omitted or left in a faulty condition; all is solid, accurate, complete, admirable. Nothing short of a perfect perfection satisfies her and she is ready to face an eternity of toil if that is needed for the fullness of her creation. Therefore of all the Mother's powers she is the most long-suffering with man and his thousand imperfections. Kind, smiling, close and helpful, not easily turned away or discouraged, insistent even after repeated failure, her hand sustains our every step on condition that we are single in our will and straightforward and sincere; for a double mind she will not tolerate and her revealing irony is merciless to drama and histrionics and self-deceit and pretence. A mother to our wants, a friend in our difficulties, a persistent and tranquil counsellor and mentor, chasing away with her radiant smile the clouds of gloom and fretfulness and depression, reminding always of the ever-present help, pointing to the eternal sunshine, she is firm, quiet and persevering in the deep and continuous urge that drives us towards the integrality of the higher nature. All the work of the other Powers leans on her for its completeness; for she assures the material foundation, elaborates the stuff of detail and erects and rivets the armour of the structure.

There are other great Personalities of the Divine Mother, but they were more difficult to bring down and have not stood out in front with so much prominence in the evolution of the earth-spirit. There are among them Presences indispensable for the supramental realisation—most of all one who is her Personality of that mysterious and powerful ecstasy and Ananda which flows from a supreme divine Love, the Ananda that alone can heal the gulf between the highest heights of the supramental spirit and the lowest abysses of Matter, the Ananda that holds the key of a wonderful divinest Life and even now supports from its secrecies the work of all the other Powers of the universe. But human nature bounded, egoistic and obscure is inapt to receive these great Presences or to support their mighty action. Only when the Four have founded their harmony and freedom of movement in the transformed mind and life and body, can those other rarer Powers manifest in the earth movement and the supramental action become possible. For when her Personalities are all gathered in her and manifested and their separate working has been turned into a harmonious unity and they rise in her to their supramental godheads, then is the Mother revealed as the supramental Mahashakti and brings pouring down her luminous transcendences from their ineffable ether. Then can human nature change into dynamic divine nature because all the elemental lines of the supramental Truth-consciousness and Truth-force are strung together and the harp of life is fitted for the rhythms of the Eternal.

If you desire this transformation, put yourself in the hands of the Mother and her Powers without cavil or resistance and let her do unhindered her work within you. Three things you must have, consciousness, plasticity, unreserved surrender. For you must be conscious in your mind and soul and heart and life and the very cells of your body, aware of the Mother and her Powers and their working; for although she can and does work in you even in your obscurity and your unconscious parts and moments, it is not the same thing as when you are in an awakened and living communion with her. All your nature must be plastic to her touch—not questioning as the self-sufficient ignorant mind questions and doubts and disputes and is the enemy of its enlightenment and change; not insisting on its own movements as the vital in man insists and persistently opposes its refractory desires and ill-will to every divine influence; not obstructing and entrenched in incapacity, inertia and tamas as man's physical consciousness obstructs and clinging to its pleasure in smallness and darkness cries out against each touch that disturbs its soulless routine or its dull sloth or its torpid slumber. The unreserved surrender of your inner and outer being will bring this plasticity into all the parts of your nature; consciousness will awaken everywhere in you by constant openness to the Wisdom and Light, the Force, the Harmony and Beauty, the Perfection that come flowing down from above. Even the body will awake and unite at last its consciousness subliminal no longer to the supramental superconscious Force, feel all her powers permeating from above and below and around it and thrill to a supreme Love and Ananda.

But be on your guard and do not try to understand and judge the Divine Mother by your little earthly mind that loves to subject even the things that are beyond it to its own norms and standards, its narrow reasonings and erring impressions, its bottomless aggressive ignorance and its petty self-confident knowledge. The human mind shut in the prison of its half-lit obscurity cannot follow the many-sided freedom of the steps of the Divine Shakti. The rapidity and complexity of her vision and action outrun its stumbling comprehension; the measures of her movement are not its measures. Bewildered by the swift alteration of her many different personalities, her making of rhythms and her breaking of rhythms, her accelerations of speed and her retardations, her varied ways of dealing with the problem of one and of another, her taking up and dropping now of this line and now of that one and her gathering of them together, it will not recognise the way of the Supreme Power when it is circling and sweeping upwards through the maze of the Ignorance to a supernal Light. Open rather your soul to her and be content to feel her with the psychic nature and see her with the psychic vision that alone make a straight response to the Truth. Then the Mother herself will enlighten by their psychic elements your mind and heart and life and physical consciousness and reveal to them too her ways and her nature.

Avoid also the error of the ignorant mind's demand on the Divine Power to act always according to our crude surface notions of omniscience and omnipotence. For our mind clamours to be impressed at every turn by miraculous power and easy success and dazzling splendour; otherwise it cannot believe that here is the Divine. The Mother is dealing with the Ignorance in the fields of the Ignorance; she has descended there and is not all above. Partly she veils and partly she unveils her knowledge and her power, often holds them back from her instruments and personalities and follows that she may transform them the way of the seeking mind, the way of the aspiring psychic, the way of the battling vital, the way of the imprisoned and suffering physical nature. There are conditions that have been laid down by a Supreme Will, there are many tangled knots that have to be loosened and cannot be cut abruptly asunder. The Asura and Rakshasa hold this evolving earthly nature and have to be met and conquered on their own terms in their own long-conquered fief and province; the human in us has to be led and prepared to transcend its limits and is too weak and obscure to be lifted up suddenly to a form far beyond it. The Divine Consciousness and Force are there and do at each moment the thing that is needed in the conditions of the labour, take always the step that is decreed and shape in the midst of imperfection the perfection that is to come. But only when the supermind has descended in you can she deal directly as the supramental Shakti with supramental natures. If you follow your mind, it will not recognise the Mother even when she is manifest before you. Follow your soul and not your mind, your soul that answers to the Truth, not your mind that leaps at appearances; trust the Divine Power and she will free the godlike elements in you and shape all into an expression of Divine Nature.

The supramental change is a thing decreed and inevitable in the evolution of the earth-consciousness; for its upward ascent is not ended and mind is not its last summit. But that the change may arrive, take form and endure, there is needed the call from below with a will to recognise and not deny the Light when it comes, and there is needed the sanction of the Supreme from above. The power that mediates between the sanction and the call is the presence and power of the Divine Mother. The Mother's power and not any human endeavour and tapasya can alone rend the lid and tear the covering and shape the vessel and bring down into this world of obscurity and falsehood and death and suffering Truth and Light and Life divine and the immortal's Ananda.

Sri Aurobindo's Teaching and Method of Sadhana[1]

The teaching of Sri Aurobindo starts from that of the ancient sages of India that behind the appearances of the universe there is the Reality of a Being and Consciousness, a Self of all things, one and eternal. All beings are united in that One Self and Spirit but divided by a certain separativity of consciousness, an ignorance of their true Self and Reality in the mind, life and body. It is possible by a certain psychological discipline to remove this veil of separative consciousness and become aware of the true Self, the Divinity within us and all.

Sri Aurobindo's teaching states that this One Being and Consciousness is involved here in Matter. Evolution is the method by which it liberates itself; consciousness appears in what seems to be inconscient, and once having appeared is self-impelled to grow higher and higher and at the same time to enlarge and develop towards a greater and greater perfection. Life is the first step of this release of consciousness, mind is the second; but the evolution does not finish with mind, it awaits a release into something greater, a consciousness which is spiritual and supramental. The next step of the evolution must be towards the development of Supermind

---

[1] This essay in the third person was written in August 1934 and first published in *Sri Aurobindo on Himself and the Mother,* by Sri Aurobindo International University Centre, Pondicherry, in 1953.

and Spirit as the dominant power in the conscious being. For only then will the involved Divinity in things release itself entirely and it become possible for life to manifest perfection.

But while the former steps in evolution were taken by Nature without a conscious will in the plant and animal life, in man Nature becomes able to evolve by a conscious will in the instrument. It is not, however, by the mental will in man that this can be wholly done, for the mind goes only to a certain point and after that can only move in a circle. A conversion has to be made, a turning of the consciousness by which mind has to change into the higher principle. This method is to be found through the ancient psychological discipline and practice of Yoga. In the past, it has been attempted by a drawing away from the world and a disappearance into the height of the Self or Spirit. Sri Aurobindo teaches that a descent of the higher principle is possible which will not merely release the spiritual Self out of the world, but release it in the world, replace the mind's ignorance or its very limited knowledge by a supramental Truth-Consciousness which will be a sufficient instrument of the inner Self and make it possible for the human being to find himself dynamically as well as inwardly and grow out of his still-animal humanity into a diviner race. The psychological discipline of Yoga can be used to that end by opening all the parts of the being to a conversion or transformation through the descent and working of the higher still concealed supramental principle.

This, however, cannot be done at once or in a short time or by any rapid or miraculous transformation. Many steps have to be taken by the seeker before the supramental descent is possible. Man lives mostly in his surface mind, life and body, but there is an inner being within him with greater possibilities to which he has to awake—for it is only a very restricted influence from it that he receives now and that pushes him to a constant pursuit of a greater beauty, harmony, power and knowledge. The first process of Yoga is therefore to open the ranges of this inner being and to live from there outward, governing his outward life by an inner light and force. In doing so he discovers in himself his true soul which is not this outer mixture of mental, vital and physical elements but something of the Reality behind them, a spark from the one Divine Fire. He has to learn to live in his soul and purify and orientate by its drive towards the Truth the rest of the nature. There can follow afterwards an opening upward and descent of a higher principle of the Being. But even then it is not at once the full supramental Light and Force. For there are several ranges of consciousness between the ordinary human mind and the supramental Truth-Consciousness. These intervening ranges have to be opened up and their power brought down into the mind, life and body. Only afterwards can the full power of the Truth-Consciousness work in the nature. The process of this self-discipline or Sadhana is therefore long and difficult, but even a little of it is so much gained because it makes the ultimate release and perfection more possible.

There are many things belonging to older systems that are necessary on the way—an opening of the mind to a greater wideness and to the sense of the Self and the Infinite, an emergence into what has been called the cosmic consciousness, mastery over the desires and passions; an outward asceticism is not essential, but the conquest of desire and attachment and a control over the body and its needs, greeds and instincts are indispensable. There is a combination of the principles of the old systems, the way of knowledge through the mind's discernment between Reality and the appearance, the heart's way of devotion, love and surrender and the way of works turning the will away from motives of self-interest to the Truth and the service of a greater Reality than the ego. For the whole being has to be trained so that it can respond and be transformed when it is possible for that greater Light and Force to work in the nature.

In this discipline, the inspiration of the Master, and in the difficult stages his control and his presence are indispensable—for it would be impossible otherwise to go through it without much stumbling and error which would prevent all chance of success. The Master is one who has risen to a higher consciousness and being and he is often regarded as its manifestation or representative. He not only helps by his teaching and still more by his influence and example but by a power to communicate his own experience to others.

This is Sri Aurobindo's teaching and method of practice. It is not his object to develop any one religion or to amalgamate the older religions or to found any new religion—for any of these things would lead away from his central purpose. The one aim of his Yoga is an inner self-development by which each one who follows it can in time discover the One Self in all and evolve a higher consciousness than the mental, a spiritual and supramental consciousness which will transform and divinise human nature.

The Fifteenth of August 1947[1]

August 15th is the birthday of free India. It marks for her the end of an old era, the beginning of a new age. But it has a significance not only for us, but for Asia and the whole world; for it signifies the entry into the comity of nations of a new power with untold potentialities which has a great part to play in determining the political, social, cultural and spiritual future of humanity. To me personally it must naturally be gratifying that this date which was notable only for me because it was my own birthday celebrated annually by those who have accepted my gospel of life, should have acquired this vast significance. As a mystic, I take this identification, not as a coincidence or fortuitous accident, but as a sanction and seal of the Divine Power which guides my steps on the work with which I began life. Indeed almost all the world movements which I hoped to see fulfilled in my lifetime, though at that time they looked like impossible dreams, I can observe on this day either approaching fruition or initiated and on the way to their achievement.

I have been asked for a message on this great occasion, but I am perhaps hardly in a position to give one. All I can do is to make a personal declaration of the aims and ideals conceived in my childhood and youth and now watched in their beginning of fulfilment, because they are relevant to the freedom of India,

---

[1] Broadcast on *All India Radio*, Tiruchirappalli, on 14 August 1947.

since they are a part of what I believe to be India's future work, something in which she cannot but take a leading position. For I have always held and said that India was arising, not to serve her own material interests only, to achieve expansion, greatness, power and prosperity—though these too she must not neglect—and certainly not like others to acquire domination of other peoples, but to live also for God and the world as a helper and leader of the whole human race. Those aims and ideals were in their natural order these: a revolution which would achieve India's freedom and her unity; the resurgence and liberation of Asia and her return to the great role which she had played in the progress of human civilisation; the rise of a new, a greater, brighter and nobler life for mankind which for its entire realisation would rest outwardly on an international unification of the separate existence of the peoples, preserving and securing their national life but drawing them together into an overriding and consummating oneness; the gift by India of her spiritual knowledge and her means for the spiritualisation of life to the whole race; finally, a new step in the evolution which, by uplifting the consciousness to a higher level, would begin the solution of the many problems of existence which have perplexed and vexed humanity, since men began to think and to dream of individual perfection and a perfect society.

India is free but she has not achieved unity, only a fissured and broken freedom. At one time it almost seemed as if she might relapse into the chaos of separate States which preceded the British conquest. Fortunately there has now developed a strong possibility that this disastrous relapse will be avoided. The wisely drastic policy of the Constituent Assembly makes it possible that the problem of the depressed classes will be solved without schism or fissure. But the old communal division into Hindu and Muslim seems to have hardened into the figure of a permanent political division of the country. It is to be hoped that the Congress and the nation will not accept the settled fact as for ever settled or as anything more than a temporary expedient. For if it lasts, India may be seriously weakened, even crippled: civil strife may remain always possible, possible even a new invasion and foreign conquest. The partition of the country must go—it is to be hoped by a slackening of tension, by a progressive understanding of the need of peace and concord, by the constant necessity of common and concerted action, even of an instrument of union for that purpose. In this way unity may come about under whatever form—the exact form may have a pragmatic but not a fundamental importance. But by whatever means, the division must and will go. For without it the destiny of India might be seriously impaired and even frustrated. But that must not be.

Asia has arisen and large parts of it have been liberated or are at this moment being liberated; its other still-subject parts are moving through whatever struggles towards freedom. Only a little has to be done and that will be done today or tomorrow. There India has her part to play and has begun to play it with an energy and ability which already indicate the measure of her possibilities and the place she can take in the council of the nations.

The unification of mankind is under way, though only in an imperfect initiative, organised but struggling against tremendous difficulties. But the momentum is there and, if the experience of history can be taken as a guide, it must inevitably increase until it conquers. Here too India has begun to play a prominent part and, if she can develop that larger statesmanship which is not limited by the present facts and immediate possibilities but looks into the future and brings it nearer, her presence may make all the difference between a slow and timid and a bold and swift development. A catastrophe may intervene and interrupt or destroy what is being done, but even then the final result is sure. For in any case the unification is a necessity in the course of Nature, an inevitable movement and its achievement can be safely foretold. Its necessity for the nations also is clear, for without it the freedom of the small peoples can never be safe hereafter and even large and powerful nations cannot really be secure. India, if she remains divided, will not herself be sure of her safety. It is therefore to the interest of all that union should take place. Only human imbecility and stupid selfishness could prevent it. Against that, it has been said, even the gods strive in vain; but it cannot stand for ever against the necessity of Nature and the Divine Will. Nationalism will then have fulfilled itself; an international spirit and outlook must grow up and international forms and institutions; even it may be such developments as dual or multilateral citizenship and a voluntary fusion of cultures may appear in the process of the change and the spirit of nationalism losing its militancy may find these things perfectly compatible with the integrity of its own outlook. A new spirit of oneness will take hold of the human race.

The spiritual gift of India to the world has already begun. India's spirituality is entering Europe and America in an ever increasing measure. That movement will grow; amid the disasters of the time more and more eyes are turning towards her with hope and there is even an increasing resort not only to her teachings, but to her psychic and spiritual practice.

The rest is still a personal hope and an idea and ideal which has begun to take hold both in India and in the West on forward-looking minds. The difficulties in the way are more formidable than in any other field of endeavour, but difficulties were made to be overcome and if the Supreme Will is there, they will be overcome. Here too, if this evolution is to take place, since it must come through a growth of the spirit and the inner consciousness, the initiative can come from India and although the scope must be universal, the central movement may be hers.

Such is the content which I put into this date of India's liberation; whether or how far or how soon this connection will be fulfilled, depends upon this new and free India.

A Message to America[1]

I have been asked to send on this occasion of the fifteenth August a message to the West, but what I have to say might be delivered equally as a message to the East. It has been customary to dwell on the division and difference between these two sections of the human family and even oppose them to each other; but, for myself I would rather be disposed to dwell on oneness and unity than on division and difference. East and West have the same human nature, a common human destiny, the same aspiration after a greater perfection, the same seeking after something higher than itself, something towards which inwardly and even outwardly we move. There has been a tendency in some minds to dwell on the spirituality or mysticism of the East and the materialism of the West; but the West has had no less than the East its spiritual seekings and, though not in such profusion, its saints and sages and mystics, the East has had its materialistic tendencies, its material splendours, its similar or identical dealings with life and Matter and the world in which we live. East and West have always met and mixed more or less closely, they have powerfully influenced each other and at the present day are under an increasing compulsion of Nature and Fate to do so more than ever before.

---

[1] Given in response to a request for a message on the occasion of Sri Aurobindo's birth anniversary celebrations in New York on 15 August 1949, this essay was written on 11 August 1949.

There is a common hope, a common destiny, both spiritual and material, for which both are needed as co-workers. It is no longer towards division and difference that we should turn our minds, but on unity, union, even oneness necessary for the pursuit and realisation of a common ideal, the destined goal, the fulfilment towards which Nature in her beginning obscurely set out and must in an increasing light of knowledge replacing her first ignorance constantly persevere.

But what shall be that ideal and that goal? That depends on our conception of the realities of life and the supreme Reality.

Here we have to take into account that there has been, not any absolute difference but an increasing divergence between the tendencies of the East and the West. The highest truth is truth of the Spirit; a Spirit supreme above the world and yet immanent in the world and in all that exists, sustaining and leading all towards whatever is the aim and goal and the fulfilment of Nature since her obscure inconscient beginnings through the growth of consciousness is the one aspect of existence which gives a clue to the secret of our being and a meaning to the world. The East has always and increasingly put the highest emphasis on the supreme truth of the Spirit; it has, even in its extreme philosophies, put the world away as an illusion and regarded the Spirit as the sole reality. The West has concentrated more and more increasingly on the world, on the dealings of mind and life with our material existence, on our mastery over it, on the perfection of mind and life and some fulfilment of the human being here: latterly this has gone so far as the denial of the Spirit and even the enthronement of Matter as the sole reality. Spiritual perfection as the sole ideal on one side, on the other, the perfectibility of the race, the perfect society, a perfect development of the human mind and life and man's material existence have become the largest dream of the future. Yet both are truths and can be regarded as part of the intention of the Spirit in world-nature; they are not incompatible with each other; rather their divergence has to be healed and both have to be included and reconciled in our view of the future.

The Science of the West has discovered evolution as the secret of life and its process in this material world; but it has laid more stress on the growth of form and species than on the growth of consciousness: even, consciousness has been regarded as an incident and not the whole secret of the meaning of the evolution. An evolution has been admitted by certain minds in the East, certain philosophies and Scriptures, but there its sense has been the growth of the soul through developing or successive forms and many lives of the individual to its own highest reality. For if there is a conscious being in the form, that being can hardly be a temporary phenomenon of consciousness; it must be a soul fulfilling itself and this fulfilment can only take place if there is a return of the soul to earth in many successive lives, in many successive bodies.

The process of evolution has been the development from and in inconscient Matter of a subconscient and then a conscious Life, of conscious mind first in animal life and then fully in conscious and thinking man, the highest present achievement of evolutionary Nature. The achievement of mental being is at present her highest and tends to be regarded as her final work; but it is possible to conceive a still further step of the evolution: Nature may have in view beyond the imperfect mind of man a consciousness that passes out of the mind's ignorance and possesses truth as its inherent right and nature. There is a Truth-Consciousness as it is called in the Veda, a Supermind, as I have termed it, possessing Knowledge, not having to seek after it and constantly miss it. In one of the Upanishads a being of knowledge is stated to be the next step above the mental being; into that the soul has to rise and through it to attain the perfect bliss of spiritual existence. If that could be achieved as the next evolutionary step of Nature here, then she would be fulfilled and we could conceive of the perfection of life even here, its attainment of a full spiritual living even in this body or it may be in a perfected body. We could even speak of a divine life on earth; our human dream of perfectibility would be accomplished and at the same time the aspiration to a heaven on earth common to several religions and spiritual seers and thinkers.

The ascent of the human soul to the supreme Spirit is that soul's highest aim and necessity, for that is the supreme reality; but there can be too the descent of the Spirit and its powers into the world and that would justify the existence of the material world also, give a meaning, a divine purpose to the creation and solve its riddle. East and West could be reconciled in the pursuit of the highest and largest ideal, Spirit embrace Matter and Matter find its own true reality and the hidden Reality in all things in the Spirit.

Thoughts and Aphorisms

From *The Goal*

When we have passed beyond knowings, then we shall have Knowledge. Reason was the helper; Reason is the bar.

When we have passed beyond willings, then we shall have Power. Effort was the helper; Effort is the bar.

When we have passed beyond enjoyings, then we shall have Bliss. Desire was the helper; Desire is the bar.

* * *

When we have passed beyond individualising, then we shall be real Persons. Ego was the helper; Ego is the bar.

* * *

When we have passed beyond humanity, then we shall be the Man. The Animal was the helper; the Animal is the bar.

What I cannot do now is the sign of what I shall do hereafter. The sense of impossibility is the beginning of all possibilities. Because this temporal universe was a paradox and an impossibility, therefore the Eternal created it out of His being.

To rotate on its own axis is not the one movement for the human soul. There is also its wheeling round the Sun of an inexhaustible illumination.

Not to go on for ever repeating what man has already done is our work, but to arrive at new realisations and undreamed-of masteries. Time and soul and world are given us for our field, vision and hope and creative imagination stand for our prompters, will and thought and labour are our all-effective instruments.

From *Man, the Purusha*

God cannot cease from leaning down towards Nature, nor man from aspiring towards the Godhead. It is the eternal relation of the finite to the infinite. When they seem to turn from each other, it is to recoil for a more intimate meeting.

God and Nature are like a boy and girl at play and in love. They hide and run from each other when glimpsed so that they may be sought after and chased and captured.

The animal is Man disguised in a hairy skin and upon four legs; the worm is Man writhing and crawling towards the evolution of his Manhood. Even crude forms of Matter are Man in his inchoate body. All things are Man, the Purusha.

From *The End*

The meeting of man and God must always mean a penetration and entry of the divine into the human and a self-immergence of man in the Divinity.

Delight is the secret. Learn of pure delight and thou shalt learn of God.

From *Thoughts and Glimpses*

Providence is not only that which saves me from the shipwreck in which everybody else has foundered. Providence is also that which while all others are saved snatches away my last plank of safety and drowns me in the solitary ocean.

The delight of victory is sometimes less than the attraction of struggle and suffering; nevertheless the laurel and not the cross should be the aim of the conquering human soul.

Help men, but do not pauperise them of their energy; lead and instruct men, but see that their initiative and originality remain intact; take others into thyself, but give them in return the full godhead of their nature. He who can do this is the leader and the *guru*.

* * *

The world knows three kinds of revolution. The material has strong results, the moral and intellectual are infinitely larger in their scope and richer in their fruits, but the spiritual are the great sowings.

Each religion has helped mankind. Paganism increased in man the light of beauty, the largeness and height of his life, his aim at a many-sided perfection; Christianity gave him some vision of divine love and charity; Buddhism has shown him a noble way to be wiser, gentler, purer, Judaism and Islam how to be religiously faithful in action and zealously devoted to God; Hinduism has opened to him the largest and profoundest spiritual possibilities. A great thing would be done if all these God-visions could embrace and cast themselves into each other; but intellectual dogma and cult egoism stand in the way.

From *Jnana*[1]

2. Inspiration is a slender river of brightness leaping from a vast and eternal knowledge, it exceeds reason more perfectly than reason exceeds the knowledge of the senses.

---

[1] 'The Goal,' 'Man, the Purusha', 'The End' and 'Thoughts and Glimpses', were written in or around 1913 and first published in the Arya in May 1915 and May 1916. 'Jnana,' 'Karma', and 'Bhakti,' were written in or around 1913 and first published in Thoughts and Aphorisms (1958).

7. What men call knowledge, is the reasoned acceptance of false appearances. Wisdom looks behind the veil and sees.

9. Either do not give the name of knowledge to your beliefs only and of error, ignorance or charlatanism to the beliefs of others, or do not rail at the dogmas of the sects and their intolerance.

10. What the soul sees and has experienced, that it knows; the rest is appearance, prejudice and opinion.

19. Chance is not in this universe; the idea of illusion is itself an illusion. There was never illusion yet in the human mind that was not the concealing [shape] and disfigurement of a truth.

37. The Atheist is God playing at hide and seek with Himself; but is the Theist any other? Well, perhaps; for he has seen the shadow of God and clutched at it.

40. Sometimes one is led to think that only those things really matter which have never happened; for beside them most historic achievements seem almost pale and ineffective.

50. To feel and love the God of beauty and good in the ugly and the evil, and still yearn in utter love to heal it of its ugliness and its evil, this is real virtue and morality.

53. This is a miracle that men can love God, yet fail to love humanity. With whom are they in love then?

65. Because God is invincibly great, He can afford to be weak; because He is immutably pure, He can indulge with impunity in sin; He knows eternally all delight, therefore He tastes also the delight of pain; He is inalienably wise, therefore He has not debarred Himself from folly.

66. Sin is that which was once in its place, persisting now it is out of place; there is no other sinfulness.

67. There is no sin in man, but a great deal of disease, ignorance and misapplication.

75. Systematise we must, but even in making and holding the system, we should always keep firm hold on this truth that all systems are in their nature transitory and incomplete.

78. When knowledge is fresh in us, then it is invincible; when it is old, it loses its virtue. This is because God moves always forward.

79. God is infinite Possibility. Therefore Truth is never at rest; therefore, also, Error is justified of her children.

86. Great saints have performed miracles; greater saints have railed at them; the greatest have both railed at them and performed them.

96. Experience in thy soul the truth of the Scripture; afterwards, if thou wilt, reason and state thy experience intellectually and even then distrust thy statement; but distrust never thy experience.

102. To the senses it is always true that the sun moves round the earth; this is false to the reason. To the reason it is always true that the earth moves round the sun; this is false to the supreme vision. Neither earth moves nor sun; there is only a change in the relation of sun-consciousness and earth-consciousness.

103. Vivekananda, exalting Sannyasa, has said that in all Indian history there is only one Janaka. Not so, for Janaka is not the name of a single individual, but a dynasty of self-ruling kings and the triumph-cry of an ideal.

From *Karma*

208. He who acquires for himself alone, acquires ill though he may call it heaven and virtue.

219. Love God in thy opponent, even while thou strikest him; so shall neither have hell for his portion.

221. The saint and the angel are not the only divinities; admire also the Titan and the giant.

224. Sacrifice, sacrifice, sacrifice always, but for the sake of God and humanity, not for the sake of sacrifice.

226. Very usually, altruism is only the sublimest form of selfishness.

228. Respect human life as long as you can; but respect more the life of humanity.

235. Our country is God the Mother; speak not evil of her unless thou canst do it with love and tenderness.

264. If thy aim be great and thy means small, still act; for by action alone these can increase to thee.

266. There are three forms in which the command may come, the will and faith in thy nature, thy ideal on which heart and brain are agreed and the voice of Himself or His angels.

271. He who would win high spiritual degrees, must pass endless tests and examinations. But most are anxious only to bribe the examiner.

299. Turn all things to honey; this is the law of divine living.

300. Private dispute should always be avoided; but shrink not from the public battle; yet even there appreciate the strength of thy adversary.

301. When thou hearest an opinion that displeases thee, study and find out the truth in it.

309. There are two who are unfit for greatness and freedom, the man who has never been a slave to another and the nation that has never been under the yoke of foreigners.

366. Act according to the Shastra rather than thy self-will and desire; so shalt thou grow stronger to control the ravener in thee; but act according to God rather than the Shastra; so shalt thou reach to His highest which is far above rule and limit.

369. What is the use of only knowing? I say to thee, Act and be, for therefore God sent thee into this human body.

370. What is the use of only being? I say to thee, Become, for therefore wast thou established as a man in this world of matter.

377. Mankind has used two powerful weapons to destroy its own powers and enjoyment, wrong indulgence and wrong abstinence.

404. Distrust of the curative power within us was our physical fall from Paradise. Medical Science and a bad heredity are the

two angels of God who stand at the gates to forbid our return and reentry.

From *Bhakti*

410. Others boast of their love for God. My boast is that I did not love God; it was He who loved me and sought me out and forced me to belong to Him.

412. To commit adultery with God is the perfect experience for which the world was created.

414. The Jew invented the God-fearing man; India the God-knower and God-lover.

418. If you cannot make God love you, make Him fight you. If He will not give you the embrace of the lover, compel Him to give you the embrace of the wrestler.

420. Most of all things on earth I hated pain till God hurt and tortured me; then it was revealed to me that pain is only a perverse and recalcitrant shape of excessive delight.

424. The next greatest rapture to the love of God, is the love of God in men; there, too, one has the joy of multiplicity.

428. What is the use of admiring Nature or worshipping her as a Power, a Presence and a goddess? What is the use, either, of appreciating her aesthetically or artistically? The secret is to enjoy her with the soul as one enjoys a woman with the body.

437. When I saw others than Krishna and myself in the world, I kept secret God's doings with me; but since I began to see Him and myself everywhere, I have become shameless and garrulous.

447. Life, Life, Life, I hear the passions cry; God, God, God, is the soul's answer. Unless thou seest and lovest Life as God only, then is Life itself a sealed joy to thee.

448. 'He loves her', the senses say; but the soul says 'God God God'. That is the all-embracing formula of existence.

454. In those whom God loves, have delight; on those whom He pretends not to love, take pity.

462. At first whenever I fell back into sin, I used to weep and rage against myself and against God for having suffered it. Afterwards it was as much as I could dare to ask, 'Why hast thou rolled me again in the mud, O my playfellow?' Then even that came to my mind to seem too bold and presumptuous; I could only get up in silence, look at him out of the corner of my eyes—and clean myself.

482. My lover took away my robe of sin and I let it fall, rejoicing; then he plucked at my robe of virtue, but I was ashamed and alarmed and prevented him. It was not till he wrested it from me by force that I saw how my soul had been hidden from me.

484. Love of God, charity towards men is the first step towards perfect wisdom.

512. To be master of the world would indeed be supreme felicity, if one were universally loved; but for that one would have to be at the same time the slave of all humanity.

515. He who has done even a little good to human beings, though he be the worst of sinners, is accepted by God in the ranks of His lovers and servants. He shall look upon the face of the Eternal.

529. Indiscriminate compassion is the noblest gift of temperament, not to do even the least hurt to one living thing is the highest of all human virtues; but God practises neither. Is man therefore nobler and better than the All-loving?

539. God's negations are as useful to us as His affirmations. It is He who as the Atheist denies His own existence for the better perfecting of human knowledge. It is not enough to see God in Christ and Ramakrishna and hear His words, we must see Him and hear Him also in Huxley and Haeckel.

Sources of the Selections[1]

Towards Swaraj and the Regeneration of India

The Doctrine of Passive Resistance—Conclusions and, The Morality of Boycott, and Asiatic Democracy: *SABCL* 1; Uttarpara Speech, The Ideal of the Karmayogin, and The Hindu Sabha: *CWSA* 8; *CWSA* 20; Message for National Education Week: *SABCL* 27; Indian Culture and External Influence: *CWSA* 20.

On the Vedas, Upanishads, and the Gita

The Problem and Its Solution, A Retrospect of Vedic Theory, and Selected Hymns: The Colloquy of Indra and Agastya, Rig-Veda: *CWSA* 15; The Discovery of the Absolute Brahman: *SABCL* 12; Our Demand and Need from the Gita and The Core of the Teaching: *CWSA* 12.

From *The Life Divine* CWSA 21 and 22.

A New Global Agenda

The Turn towards Unity: Its Necessity and Dangers, The Inadequacy of the State Idea, *The Ideal of Human Unity*: Summary

---

[1] While all these texts are now available in the *CWSA* edition, I have retained the source citations as per the 2nd edition when its publication was still in progress.

and Conclusions, The Cycle of Society, and *CWSA* 25; The Human Mind: *SABCL* 17.

Integral Yoga and its Sadhana

SABCL 3; The Yoga and Its Objects: *CWSA* 13; The Object of Our Yoga: *CWSA* 12; The Integral Knowledge and the Aim of Life; Four Theories of Existence: *SABCL* 20; Life and Yoga, Synthesis: *SABCL* 21; From Letters on Yoga: *SABCL* 22 and 24.

The Supramental Transformation

Certitudes, The Superman, [The Experiment of Human Life], The Hour of God, *CWSA* 12; The Real Difficulty: *SABCL* 17; Man and the Supermind, The Path, [Life], [The Secret of Life—Ananda], From Man and Superman, The Divine Body: *CWSA* 12; The Mind of Light: *CWSA* 13

The Seer Poet

The Ideal Spirit of Poetry, The Future Poetry: Conclusion: *CWSA* 26; Achievement of Indo-English Poetry: *SABCL* 9; Invitation, Who, Revelation, Life and Death, Epiphany, A God's Labour, Bride of Fire, I Have a Hundred Lives, Nirvana, Evolution, The Golden Light, Krishna, Advaita, Divine Sense, Ascent, Jivanmukta, Thought the Paraclete, Rose of God: *SABCL* 5; From *Savitri* Book III, Canto 4: The Vision and the Boon: *CWSA* 33.

Pioneers of the Future

The Mother: *SABCL* 25; Sri Aurobindo's Teaching and Method of Sadhana, The Fifteenth of August 1947, A Message for America: *SABCL* 26.

Thoughts and Aphorisms

From The Goal, Man, The Purusha, The End, and Thoughts and Glimpses: *CWSA* 13; from Jnana, Karma and Bhakti: *CWSA* 12.

Glossary

Sanskrit and Indian words, as they appear in Sri Aurobindo's works in this anthology, are included here, except those explained by Sri Aurobindo in the text itself.

Abkari: Excise on liquor and spirits

adesh, adesh: voice, impulsion, command

adhara: vehicle, vessel, support

adhyāropa, adhhyaropa: imposition

ahaṅkāra, ahankara: ego-sense, ego-idea, the notion of the divisive and separative 'I'.

ānanda, ananda: bliss, beatitude, ecstasy, delight

ānandamaya, anandamaya: filled with bliss, joy, delight

anantaguna, anantaguna: having infinite qualities

artha: 1. one of the four cardinal values or purusharthas; refers to material, economic necessities; 2. object, thing; 3. meaning, significance of a word.

āsana, asana: fixed posture (in Hatha Yoga); a place and a fixed position, like a seat.

Asuras: in the Vedas, used to refer to the Devas; later, to the dark Titans; the strong and mighty ones

ātman, atman: Self; Spirit; our original and essential nature; our Self in its true and highest sense as the Supreme.

ātmasamarpaṇa, atmasamarpana: self-surrender

ātmasatkaraṇa, atmasatkarana: an assimilation; making something
    one's own by converting it into a part of our self-being.

avatar, avatar: Incarnation; descent into form

Avidya: Ignorance; nescience

Avrtti: repetition

balam: strength

Bhakta: devotee, lover of the Divine

bhoga, bhoga: enjoyment, possession

bhedabheda: difference-sameness

Brahman: the Eternal, the Absolute, all-pervading Spirit

Brahmin: properly Brahmana, a member of the highest of the four
    orders of society; a learned and pious person

brahmacarin: a student; one who practises brahmacharya or sexual
    abstinence

Brahmaloka: the world of Brahman; the highest state of pure
    existence

brahmatejas, brahmatejas: the power and glory of Brahman;
spiritual power and illumination

buddhi, buddhi: intelligence, understanding, intellect

chandas: rhythm, refers to the Vedas

chaturvarṇa, chaturvarna: the fourfold division of society into
    brahmanas, kshatriyas, vaishyas and sudras.

chhotalok: In Bengali, a pejorative for the lower orders of society

cinmaya, chinmaya: made up of consciousness; the transcendental

cinmaya deha, chinmaya deha: spiritualized body

citta, chita: mind-stuff, consciousness

citta-suddhi, chita suddhi: purification of the the chitta

deśa, desa: place, country.

dharma, dharma: that which upholds; law, cosmic order; the
    social, moral, and personal code of conduct; religious practice

dhyana: meditation, contemplation; higher concentration.

draṣṭā, drasta: the seen; also the seer.

dhṛti, dhriti: steadfastness, persistence of will

dṛṣṭi, drsti: seeing, sight, vision

dvandva, dvandva: pair of opposites

guṇa, gunas: quality, character, property; the three gunas or modes of nature, sattva, rajas and tamas; vowel modification in Sanskrit grammar.

guru, guru: teacher, spiritual preceptor

hājat, hajat: In Hindustani, lock-up or jail

haṭha yoga, hatha yoga: A system of *yoga* which aims at perfecting the body through *asanas* (yogic postures) and *pranayama* (breath control)

jaganmithyā, jaganmithya: the world is an illusion

Jagatguru: the World-Teacher

jāgrat, jagrat: the awake; the waking state

jala: water, one of the five elements

jiva: living being

jnata: the knower

jyoti, jyoti: light, flame of truth

jyotirmaya deha: radiant or luminous body

Kaliyuga: the age of Kali, the iron age

karana: cause

karmayogin, karmayogin: the one who follows the path of karmayoga or desireless action.

kartā, karta: the doer of works

kartavyam: that which should be done

kartavyam karma, kartavyam karma: the thing to be done, the work we have to do.

kriyā, kriya: effective practice

kundalani: the coiled serpent of spiritual energy within each of us

līlā, lila: the cosmic play

līlā maya, lilamaya: playful

manas, manas: mind-stuff, as distinct from the intellect

maṅgala, mangala: good fortune

Māyā, Maya: in the Veda, it signified comprehensive and creative knowledge but later, the illusion of the phenomenal world

mithyā, mithya: a lie

mokṣa, moksha: release, liberation

mumukusutva, mumukusutva: passion for release, desire for liberation

mukti: liberation, freedom

nadi-suddhi: purification of nerves

nirvāṇa, Nirvana: extinction of ego, desire, mentality

nityamukta, nityamukta: perpetually in a state of liberation ojas: essential energy

pāpa, papa: sin, demerit

prakāśa, prakasa: light; radiance; enlightenment

Prakriti: 'working out,' Nature, or Nature-Force

prāṇāyāma, pranayama: the science of respiration; regulation of life force and vital energy by means of prescribed exercises

pratishtha: support, foundation

praviśya, pravisya: having entered

puṇya, punya: merit, virtue, good

puruṣa, Purusha: Person, Conscious Being; the lord and witness of creation

Puruṣottama, Purusottama: The Supreme Being

rāgadveṣa, ragadvesa: like and dislike, attraction and repulsion

Rajayoga: a system of Yoga outlined in Patanjali's Yoga Sutras *rajas*, rajas: one of the three gunas; the quality of action, desire, passion

Rakshasa: ogre; a power of darkness

retas: semen

sabda: sound, vibration, word

śabda-brahman, sabdabrahman: the Word; the oral expression of God

śabdabrahmātivartate, sabdabrahmativartate: passes beyond the sachchidananda the Ultimate Reality which is constituted by the trinity of Existence, Consciousness and Bliss

sādhaka, sadhaka: the practitioner of any system of spiritual discipline; one who seeks siddhi or perfection through such practice.

sādhanā, sadhana: the practice by which perfection (siddhi) may be attained; any spiritual discipline or exercise

sādharmyamukti, sadharmyamukti: liberation by assumption of Divine Nature

sālokyamukti, salokyamukti: liberation by existence in a Divine world

śama, sama: divine quiet, peace, rest

Samadhi: Yogic trance; the transcendental state

samrāṭ, samrat: ruler or emperor

saṁhati, samhati: cohesion

saṁskāra, samskara: cyclic movement; the world; the ordinary life of ignorance

samyama, samyama: self-control; concentration; containment

sanātana dharama, sanatana dharama: the eternal way; India's spirtual and religious tradition

Samhita: 'Conjunction'; The text of the Vedas

saṅkalpa, sankalpa: resolution

sānta, santa: finite

śantam alakṣanam, santam alaksanam: calm, featureless

sarvadharmān, sarvadharman: all *dharmas*

sarvakarmāṇi, sarvakarmini: works of all kinds

satsaṅga, satsanga: association with the good; good company

sattva: one of the three gunas, the quality of calm, poise, and light

satyayuga, satyayuga: the Age of Truth, the Golden Age

sayujyamukti: liberation by absorption into the Divine

shakti: Energy, Force, Strengh, the Power of the Lord

śastra, Shastra: any systematic teaching or science; the texts in which such knowledge is expounded

siddhi, siddhi: perfection, fulfilment, accomplishment of the objectives of yoga; extraordinary or occult power.

śiva, siva: the good, the blessed, the auspicious; the Lord of tapas; one of the Hindu trinity.

so'ham: He am I

śraddha, sraddha: faith, belief

śrijut srijut: Or Sriyukta, An honorific title like 'Mr', literally means with Sri or Lakshmi

śruti, sruti: hearing; revealed Scriptures

śubha, subha: light, enjoyment, bliss; the auspicious

śūnyam, sunyam: the void, the Nothing which contains the All.

suṣupta, susupti: deep, dreamless sleep

svabhāva, svabhava: own being; nature, self-principle

svadharma: own law of action; true rule and way of being

svapna: the dream-state

svarāṭ, svarat: self-ruler

swadeshi: indigenous, produced in one's own country

Swaraj: self-rule, independence

tamas, tamas: one of the three gunas, ignorance, inertia, darkness

tapas, tapas: heat; askesis, austerity, energism

tapasya: effort, austerity, ascetic force

tattwa: 'thatness'; a fundamental cosmic principle

tejas: light of energy; force

triguṇātīta, trigunatita: beyond the three gunas

vairāgya, vairagya: distaste; disgust with the world; cessation of desire and attachment

varṇa, varna: colour, quality, termperament; used for case or class

varṇasaṇkara, varnasankara: confusion and mixing of the above types

vibhūti, Vibhuti: Divine power; a power of God in human forms

vichara: thought; intellectual reflection

vidyut: lightening, electricity

vijñaña, vijnana: higher mind; the divine intelligence; unifying knowledge

viryam: dynamic force, heroism

viveka: discrimination, discernment

yoga: joining, union of the soul with the Divine; the system which leads to such a goal

yajamāna, yajamana: the giver of the sacrifice, the doer of action

yajña, yajna: sacrifice, ritual conscecration

yugadharma: the best or ideal *dharma* of the age

yuktivāda, yuktivada: line of argument

Bibliography

I: Sri Aurobindo's Works

The Sri Aurobindo Birth Centenary Library (SABCL) was published by the Sri Aurobindo Ashram, Pondicherry, in thirty volumes in 1972 to commemorate the 100th anniversary of his birth. A new edition of Sri Aurobindo's works, *The Collected Works of Sri Aurobindo (CWSA)*, in 37 Volumes, also published by the Sri Aurobindo Ashram, Pondicherry, began appearing from 1997. Except vol. 37, consisting of the index, glossary, editorial notes, supplementary texts, all other volumes have been published and are available at https://www.sriaurobindoashram.org/sriaurobindo/writings.php.

II: Biographies

Das, Manoj. *Sri Aurobindo: Life and Times of the Mahayogi.* Pondicherry: Sri Aurobindo International Centre of Education, 2020.

Heehs, Peter. *The Lives of Sri Aurobindo.* New York: Columbia University Press, 2008.

Iyengar, K.R. Srinivasa. *Sri Aurobindo: A Biography and a History.* 4th ed. Pondicherry: Sri Aurobindo Ashram, 1985.

Purani, A.B. *The Life of Sri Aurobindo.* 4th ed. Pondicherry: Sri Aurobindo Asharam, 1978.

IV: Other Relevant Works

Chattopadhyaya, D.P. *History, Society and Polity: Integral Sociology of Sri Aurobindo.* New Delhi: Macmillan, 1976.

Chaudhuri, Haridas and Frederic Spielgelberg, eds. *The Integral Philosophy of Sri Aurobindo.* London: George Allen and Unwin, 1960.

Chakermane, Gautam and Devdip Ganguli eds. *Reading Sri Aurobindo.* New Delhi: Penguin, 2022.

Gandhi, Kishor. *Social Philosophy of Sri Aurobindo.* Pondicherry: Sri Aurobindo Society, 1965.

Iyengar, K.R. Srinivasa, ed. *Sri Aurobindo: A Centenary Tribute.* Pondicherry: Sri Aurobindo Ashram Press, 1974.

Joshi, Kireet. *Sri Aurobindo and the Mother.* New Delhi: The Mother's Institute of Research and Motilal Banarsidass, 1989.

McDermott, Robert A., ed. *Six Pillars: Introductions to the Major Works of Sri Aurobindo.* Chambersburg, PA: Wilson Books, 1974.

Mother, The. *Collected Works.* 17 vols. Pondicherry: Sri Aurobindo Ashram, 1979-1987.

Maitra, S.K. *An Introduction to the Philosophy of Sri Aurobindo.* Calcutta: The Culture Publishers, 1941.

Mohanty, J.N. *Essays on Indian Philosophy, Traditional and Modern.* Delhi: Oxford University Press, 1986.

Nandakumar, Prema. *A Study of Savitri.* 1962; Pondicherry: All India Books, 1985.

Nirodbaran. *Talks with Sri Aurobindo.* 2nd ed. Pondicherry: Sri Aurobindo Ashram, 1986.

------. *Correspondence with Sri Aurobindo.* 2nd Complete ed. Pondicherry: Sri Aurobindo Ashram, 1995.

Pandit, M.P. *Dictionary of Sri Aurobindo's Yoga.* Pondicherry: Dipti Publications, 1973.

------. *Sri Aurobindo.* Delhi: Munshiram Manoharlal, 1998.

Purani, A.B. *Evening Talks, First and Second Series.* 3rd ed. Pondicherry: Sri Aurobindo Ashram, 1982.

Richard, Paul. *The Dawn over Asia.* Madras: Ganesh & Co., 1920.

Roy, Dilip Kumar. *Sri Aurobindo Came to Me.* 1952; Pondicherry: All India Books, 1984.

Satprem. *Sri Aurobindo and the Adventure of Consciousness.* Tr. by Luc Venet. New York: Institute for Evolutionary Research, 1984.

------. *Mother's Agenda,* 13 vols. New York: Institute for Evolutionary Research, 1979-1983. English translation of *L'Agenda de Mère.* 13 vols. Paris: Institut de Recherches Evolutives, 1978-1981.

Sethna, K.D. (or Amal Kiran). *The Poetic Genius of Sri Aurobindo.* 2nd ed. Pondicherry: Sri Aurobindo Ashram, 1974.

Singh, Karan. *Prophet of Indian Nationalism.* 3rd ed. Bombay: Bharatiya Vidya Bhavan, 1991.

Singh, Pariksith. *Sri Aurobindo and The Literary Renaissance of India.* Noida: Kali, 2022.

Van Vrekhem, Georges. *Beyond Man.* Delhi: Harper Collins, 1997.

Verma, V.P. *The Political Philosophy of Sri Aurobindo.* 2nd ed. Delhi: Motilal Banarsidas, 1976.

V: Journals

The Advent, Bulletin of Sri Aurobindo International Centre of Education, Mother India, and *Sri Aurobindo: Archives and Research,* all published by the Sri Aurobindo Ashram, Pondicherry.